T0369053

THE FIRE WITHIN
An Autobiography

By Peter R. Vallas

Order this book online at www.trafford.com
or email orders@trafford.com

Most Trafford titles are also available at major online book retailers.

© Copyright 2009 Peter R. Vallas.
All rights reserved. No part of this publication may be reproduced, stored in a retrieval system, or
transmitted, in any form or by any means, electronic, mechanical, photocopying, recording, or
otherwise, without the written prior permission of the author.

Note for Librarians: A cataloguing record for this book is available from Library
and Archives Canada at www.collectionscanada.ca/amicus/index-e.html

Printed in Victoria, BC, Canada.

ISBN: 978-1-4269-1-6960 (SC)

ISBN: 978-1-4269-1845-2 (DJ)

Library of Congress Control Number: 2009935540

*Our mission is to efficiently provide the world's finest, most comprehensive book publishing
service, enabling every author to experience success. To find out how to publish your book, your
way, and have it available worldwide, visit us online at www.trafford.com*

Trafford rev. 9/25/2009

 www.trafford.com

North America & international
toll-free: 1 888 232 4444 (USA & Canada)
phone: 250 383 6864 ♦ fax: 812 355 4082

Dedications:

TO THE MEMORY OF PARENTS, SOPHIA AND PETER VALLAS

To all the people who had faith in me and kept me striving ahead to be successful, to my wife, Eleni and my son, Peter who made it possible to be where I am today; to all the firefighters who made the great sacrifice to save others.

ABSTRACT

One can only imagine the emotion and strong feelings involved in writing about their life. All my life I kept journals of almost every move. I never thought I would ever be where I am today.

As of this writing I spent 48 years involved in the fire service from fire firefighter to lieutenant to captain and then to fire marshal. I have been credited with saving 42 lives in my career, and have been decorated by two presidents, Ronald Reagan and Jimmy Carter. I also had the honor of receiving the American character award in Washington, D.C. on September 14, 1982. The award was given to me in the Senate Caucus room by the president and pro tempore Strom Thurmond and Dr. Norman Vincent Peale and Rand Araskog, chairman, president, and chief executive officer of ITT.

This is the story of my life and how anyone can make it in this wonderful country, the U.S.A. I never gave up and followed my dreams to the end. It is the story of the most intimate nature and how it all came about. I always wanted to be a professional artist and I became one. I wanted to be a writer and published several books: My Own Reflections, My Own Reflections II, Recipes and Remembrances. I also wanted to be a movie actor and was in the movie "Exit". I became a member of the screen actor's guild and I am working on a movie of my own.

This book takes you on my journey through life and is an inspiration to all to be successful.

ACKNOWLEDGMENTS

Many people helped me to write this book and I thank them for all their contributions:

Velissairo Kabarakis
Michael Matticola
Doris Grillo
Karen Larvin
Peter S. Vallas
Eleni Vallas
Victoria Kramer
Statue of Liberty
Ellis Island Foundation
Linda D'Jimas
Thanasi D'Jimas
Consulate of Greece
Editor: anonymous
Photographer and cover by: Emily Jerome

Contents

•

CHAPTER–ONE
The Family

Chapter–One The Family

The Early Days...The Beginning Year 1948

It was a cool spring night in May 1948 and my mother took me to New York City to see a movie "The Last of the Mohicans". I was eight years old and my cousin Doris was babysitting for my sister Linda who was two years old. My father was at work in his restaurant at Journal Square in Jersey City, NJ. Half way through the movie mom wanted to leave because the movie was full of murder, blood, and guts. We took the subway also known in New York City as the "tubes" then back to NJ. As we were walking down Pavonia Avenue past my grandmother's house my mother said, "Why are all the lights on in our house?" We lived on the fourth floor of the apartment at, 135 Garrison Avenue, Jersey City, NJ. She said something was wrong, and she had, had a premonition in the movie theater. When we climbed the four flights of the stairs to our apartment, mom walked in with me tracking behind and saw dad sitting on the kitchen chair with his entire head and arms in white bandages. Mom screamed, emotional as she always was, then started to cry. I remember I was very frightened and went to my bedroom. I remember Cousin Doris saying, "Sophia calm down!" Dad told mom he went to light the pilot on the gas burner to put the heat on the furnace and it exploded burning his hair, face, and arms. He went to Dr. Jacob Rosenberg, our family doctor and he covered dad with Vaseline and wrapped him in gauze bandages. (Today this is not the way we treat burns). Slowly I crawled down the hallway and peaked around the kitchen to see dad. Dad was trying to light a cigarette through this hole in the bandage where his mouth was. There was a small hole for his nose and two for his eyes. He put his arm around me and said he was all right and not to be afraid. I went to bed that night and kept thinking about what happened. This incident was when I first became interested in fire.

My Father and His Family

My father came to the United States of America from Greece in 1919 with my Uncle George. Dad had spent a year in Italy and learned Italian until he could come to the U.S. The problem was with his papers. When dad arrived in Italy with Uncle George he could not board the boat to the U.S. He wound up spending a year in Italy until his papers were correct and worked in an Italian restaurant until he was able to come to the U.S. Dad came on the Martha Washington from Italy paying $25.00 for a spot in the Steerage, which took 14 days. It was during the time of the Worldwide Pandemic Spanish Flu. On arrival at Ellis Island his name was Pantelis Condizzi. After he arrived he began to use the last name of Vallas and Pantelis meant Peter.

His older brother George Velissairo took him to Youngstown, Ohio and got him a job in a steel mill. Dad was 16 years old then. He got a room at the YMCA for $3.00 a week. One day Uncle George left to go to Springfield, Mass to work in a restaurant. After six months dad got hit in the eye with a small piece of steel shaving and had to be treated at the hospital. When he went back to work two days later his boss told him he didn't need him anymore. He called his brother George in Massachusetts and was told to meet him in NY. Dad took a bus to NYC. He didn't hear from his brother so he walked around Manhattan looking for a job. He got a job at the Waldorf Astoria as a waiter and worked there for several years. He met other Greeks and made a few friends. His family in Greece was poor and he would send money to them when he could. Dad also said to make extra money, he would fight at the Golden Gloves in Manhattan. He said he never won a fight, but would get paid $25.00 for each fight anyway. About this time he heard from his brother George who now moved to Tarpon Springs, Florida where he was diving for sponges.

My grandmother in Greece "Angeliki" had 14 children. She had been divorced and that is why dad's name was Condizzi. I will later explain this when I get to the time when I went for my Greek citizenship. Dad's older brother George Velissairo was about nine years his senior. Dad was born October 1, 1907. The family moved to Athens from the Island of Kalimnos when dad was two years old and they lived in the Plaka just beneath the Acropolis. They went to church at the 700 year old St. Catherine's in the Plaka. Dad was also baptized there. Athens was a large city as compared to the Island of Kalimnos where dad was born. This was an island located off the coast of Turkey between Rhodes, Kos and Teros. I never knew my family in Greece except my Uncle George who we would visit in Springfield, Mass. The many stories dad told me about the family were very sad.

When I was about five or six years old, I saw dad many times carrying trunks every few months down the stairs full of medicine and clothes to send to his family in Athens. He would take them to the Hoboken, NJ shipyard and send them to Greece. He would always get letters from his sister Marika. During the war, 1940 to 1949, three brothers were killed by the Germans when Germany occupied Greece. One brother was killed in northern Greece when he tried to keep the German soldiers from taking his family's food and blankets from his home. He was shot in front of his family. Another brother, Father Spiro was caught hiding some Jews in the basement of his church and they were all shot; machine gunned to death. The last brother to die was Nikos who was in the underground. He was in the village of Lia in 1947 and was shot outside of St. Demetrios' church by the communist guerillas. Interestingly enough, it was not far from Eleni Gatzoyianuis house near the Chapel of St. Nicholas where she was executed on August 28, 1948 and greeted by the same German guerillas. Eleni Gatzoyianuis tried to get her children out of Lia, which she

3

did, but was tortured and executed. Her son Nicholas Cage later on in 1983 wrote the book "Eleni" which is a wonderful story about his mother.

My Mother and Her Family

Now on my mother's side it was totally different. My Grandmother Sophie's father was born in Germany in 1849. His name was Frederick Roes. His wife Katie was born in New York in 1855. My grandmother Sophie was born in 1881. My mother Sophia was born July 23, 1911. Around the years 1919 to 1923 they moved to Massachusetts for a short time then returned to Jersey City, NJ. My Aunt Mary, my mother's sister, had married a Dutchman by the name of Kenneth DeMooy. He was a pilot and a captain for the Pennsylvania Railroad tug boats. My Aunt Mary had a big job with the H.C. Reese Co., which supplied all the cruise ships. They both did very well for those times. Uncle Kenneth was from Rotterdam, Holland. They bought the house on 829 Pavonia Avenue in which all the brothers and sisters lived along with Grandma Sophie and Grandpa George. I loved their house and was very close to my Aunt Mary. I used to sleep over many times from 1944 to 1945 during World War II. It was an old three story house with two attic rooms with a steep staircase almost like a ladder. The second floor had one large bedroom (Aunt Mary and Uncle Ken's), a small office for Uncle Ken, two other bedrooms, with one of the bedrooms for my grandparents, Sophie and George. There was one bathroom in the house which everyone had to use. This was quite a challenge with eleven kids, grandparents, and Aunt Mary and Uncle Ken. The first floor had a large living room with a fireplace and a large dining room with a fireplace. The kitchen was small and had a large walk-in pantry. The basement had a stove where grandma used to do all her baking. In the rear of the basement were two large coal bins to hold the coal for the boiler. There was also a large yard, which Aunt Mary always planted flowers and tended to her peach tree. During the summer I used to play in the yard and under a water spray. I always wondered as I grew up why Aunt Mary and grandma liked me to stay over and as I got older I found out why. Grandpa George worked in a Rubber Factory in Jersey City for a time and lost his job over his drinking. He had many other jobs and when he came home from work he would stop at the Tube Bar in Journal Square for shots and beers. In those days women were not allowed in bars. When he came home he was always loud and nasty to everyone. When I was there he was a bit more careful. When he died I remember in those days the Jersey City Medical Center would send a policeman to the residence to notify them that the person was on the "danger list". When this happened I was seven years old and he died several days later of sclerosis of the liver. Personally, I think everyone was relieved because I can't remember anyone crying for Grandpa Francis. The other problem was Uncle Kenneth. He was an alcoholic too and he would stop at the

Tube Bar just like Grandpa Francis. When he didn't come home for dinner grandma and Aunt Mary would send me to the bar to get him. Again when I was around, he didn't yell and scream as much. One son as I recall, Alfred Francis, died of sclerosis of the liver at age 41 in 1945.

My Childhood Years

One Christmas we took the tubes to Macy's in NY. I was about four years old then. Dad also came and I ended up getting lost and after about an hour I went to a man at the elevator who was in some kind of uniform. He then took me to an office where mom and dad were. After mom yelled at me and dragged me out, we went home. A few years later I remember dad telling the story to his friends. He said mom was very upset when she couldn't find me. She yelled at dad to go look for me so he did, but he then lost mom when he went to another floor. He then went to the security office and saw a man walking with me toward the same place. When they went in dad said, mom looked at the man and asked, "Could you help me? I lost my Peter." The man replied, "Lady, I didn't know you had one." Everyone laughed including dad, but mom didn't get it. Anyway, soon after, I was brought in and I got spanked by mom.

CHAPTER–TWO
The Restaurants

Chapter-Two The Restaurants

As mentioned earlier dad had gotten a job as a waiter at the Waldorf Astoria and was living at the YMCA. This was during the 1920s era. At this time in 1925, Uncle George contacted dad and told him he was going to move to Springfield, Massachusetts which he did and got married to Aspicia. He then worked in a restaurant there. Every year we would travel to Springfield, Mass to visit him. Uncle George never had children.

One day when dad was carrying a tray of food to a table, someone bumped into him and the tray of food fell to the floor. The dining room captain told dad he had to pay for the food. Dad quit on the spot, then moved to Jersey City to the YMCA on Bergen Avenue. He had saved a few thousand dollars which, was a lot at that time. He had met several Greeks in church and became friendly with them. One was Andrew Xentelis and the other, Mike Sotiris. Dad wanted to own his own restaurant so he became a partner with Andrew and Mike and they opened the New Journal Restaurant in Journal Square, Jersey City, NJ. This was around the years 1934 to 1937 and dad was about 27 years old. One of his regular customers William Becker invited dad to his wedding. He was marrying my mother's sister Catherine. This was when he met the Francis Clan, Grandma Sophie, Grandpa George, my mother Sophia, and Aunts; Mary, Viola, Helen, Ann, Lillian, Edna, and Uncles; George, Warren, Walter, and Alfred. Dad began to date mom and they were married in the St. Mary's Church in Jersey City on July 16, 1933. Dad was successful and always brought the Francis family shoes, food, and other items particularly during the war years.

Around 1937 dad bought a cocktail lounge and restaurant in Paterson, NJ. It was then when he met my godfather to be. He drove a bread truck for Holsom Bread and delivered bread to the New Journal Restaurant. They became good friends. I was born on December 5, 1940 and George Stathakis and his wife Hazel became my godparents.

During the war I remember the blackouts which I was terrified of. Since then, I could never sleep without a light on to this day. On Saturdays, dad would take me for a haircut to Mike the barber next to dad's restaurant. Then I would hang out there until dad took me home. In 1947 the partners at the New Journal Restaurant's . lease was soon to expire and if they wanted they could buy the building. Andrew and Mike didn't want to, so they split up. Andrew and Mike opened a diner in Union City. Dad sold his lounge in Paterson and leased the Park Restaurant on Hudson Boulevard in Jersey City. He took a partner, George Athanas, who was another friend of dad's. These friends all went to St. Demetrios' Church on Montgomery Street for years.

Every Sunday dad took all of us to church and I had to wear a shirt and tie. I was also an altar boy at that time. George was working nights and dad, days. George was a heavy drinker and drank on the job all night. Eventually he would divorce his wife Catherine. My father and mother were good surrogate parents for their son Tommy. The restaurant failed and they had to close it at a loss. Dad was very upset because he had lost a lot of money in the stock market and now the restaurant. Things were tough, but dad went out and bought an old bus which was connected to a lunch wagon. I will never forget it. It had a floor shift, no heat and an open side door with a long handle you had to pull to open or close the door. He got permission from the boss of Tidewater Trucking in South Kearny, NJ to park the bus there. His name was Red and he liked my dad. The rent was $50.00 a month. My godfather George had borrowed $5,000.00 from dad and he opened a restaurant called Al's Diner in Jersey City. Dad stopped in with me one day. It was a cold day with light snow. I would always go to the bus on Saturdays to help dad. I don't know how dad did it for two years. He was so sick with pleurisy. Dr. Rosenberg told him to stay home but he wouldn't listen. One day one of his customers, Angelo Mesina, who owned the Esso Station next to dad's bus, told dad he could put a small luncheonette in the station. The station was actually a truck stop; so dad took the offer. He got rid of the bus and opened Linda's Luncheonette. This was about 1950. I would also go there on Saturdays to help him.

CHAPTER–THREE
My Childhood Years

Chapter–Three - My Childhood Years

During the time my Aunt Lil and Uncle Bernie were living in East Keansburg there was terrible flooding. The house was ruined and my cousin Lorraine came to live with us. I was about eight years old then. My cousin Barbara went to stay with my Aunt Ann and Uncle Mike. Our apartment was not large so things were tough. Lorraine went to public school number 23 where I was going. Some of the things we did were funny but not always good. Linda was only two years old; she slept in one bed and I slept in another. Lorraine slept on a cot between the two of us. Lorraine and I were always fighting about who would eat off the Blue Plate mom had. Then she would forget her sneakers for school. She would yell from the sidewalk, "Aunt Sophie!" until mom opened the window and threw them down to her. This was almost a daily occurrence. We were not allowed to wear sneakers to school in the winter because mom said we would catch cold through our feet. In this period of time we still had the rag man with his horse and drawn wagon. The milkman would deliver our milk from Borden's Co. We also had the vegetable and fruit man who would go down the block yelling, "Two pounds of tomatoes for 20 cents" and so on. Mom would open the window and tell him what she wanted and he would bring it up. I still remember when I was about seven years old when the ice man would carry up a block of ice every three days and put it in the ice box. One day the rag man was outside with his horse and wagon and when he went into our building to pick up a pile of rags, I started to fool with the horse. All of a sudden the horse began to walk away and continued on down the block. When the rag man came out he ran after the horse and wagon. One of the neighbors had seen me and told my mother. Well, what are a few more scratches on my arms trying not to get hit in the face? One Saturday dad gave Lorraine and Barbara and me, 75 cents to go to the movies. We were going to the Stanley Theater and stopped at the candy store at Journal Square. We didn't have money for candy so I would slide candy bars down and Lorraine and Barbara would put them into their open pocketbooks. We only did this once because we were afraid of getting caught. On Sundays dad gave us church envelopes and we would open them and take the money for soda and candy. All three of us were devils. This was also about the time when mom became Greek Orthodox and dad and mom got re-married in St Demetrios' Church. This was on October 13, 1951. Lorraine stayed with us for one year and then Aunt Lil and Uncle Bernie got a house in Port Monmouth, NJ.

In December 1948 mom took me to Rockefeller Center to ice skate. While skating I found a black wallet. I took it to mom and we both went to the office to turn it in. As we walked in, there was a woman standing there with the manager. I gave him the wallet and he said, "Son, you have done a fine thing turning over the wallet." He then gave the wallet to the woman standing there. She was smiling at me and gave me a big kiss. It was Sonya Henie, the famous ice skater. We then received two free passes for the future. That week mom was angry with me for cursing and she screamed and said I was causing her to get sick. She lay on the kitchen floor pretending that she passed out. I took a pot and filled it with water then poured it over her face. She chased me to the bathroom. I locked the door and remained there until dad came home. I heard her telling dad what happened and when he came to the door of the bathroom, I opened it. I could see a smirk on his face. He asked, "Why did you pour water on your mother's face?" I said, "Dad, I saw Groucho Marx pour water on his brothers' faces when they were knocked out so I did the same thing for mom and she woke up. Dad couldn't stop laughing.

Back to the Diner

In 1953 dad was approached by Red at Tidewater who first let him park the bus on his property. He told dad he was very impressed with his determination to be successful and that he worked harder than anyone he knew. He said that if dad wanted, he would lease him a piece of property next to the Esso station so he could build a small diner. Dad had a year to go on his lease with Angelo. We later found out that Angelo had told Red one day, "When the Greek's lease expires next year, I am going to double his rent and he won't be able to do anything about it." So Red knew this and wanted to help dad. Dad didn't have much money and things were rough, but he still sent mom, Linda, and I to the farm every year for the summer.

With a little help from my Aunt Mary, dad built what became, "Pete's Diner"; a small building with 15 counter stools and 10 stools on the side counters. All through high school I worked after school peeling potatoes and onions, washing dishes, etc. I also learned how to cook which later in life gave me the opportunity to publish "Recipes & Remembrances: The Vallas Family Cookbook".

Growing Up

I came home from school one day, some time in December about the 2nd or 3rd, 1949 and it was snowing. I was in the third grade then and walked to public school #23; three blocks from my home. In those days, there was no bussing and we went to school with "colored people" as they used to say. I played with them and never remember having a problem, even through high school. It was very cold that day as I walked up Pavonia Avenue stopping at Snyder's Candy Store as I did every day to buy my egg cream or Pepsi, and a piece of one cent candy. I used to love this one candy, which was on a strip of white paper. There were little dots of chocolate on it and I would bite each dot off. Dad always stopped in to get his New York Journal American, Daily News, and Jersey Journal. One thing about dad was that he always read his newspapers everyday. During these years, with dad working mostly nights

I saw very little of him, except when he was off. It was about 1944 when dad would take us up to the Catskill Mountains for the summer. This was to continue after Linda was born and until I was about 14 when I became interested in girls. We would then go to Manasquan, N.J., for the month of August.

The Catskills

We would stay at a boarding house in Halcott Center, NY. Every year after school closed for the summer dad would drive up Route 9W to Kingston, NY then up Route 28 to Fleischmann's to Halcott Center, about six miles north. Population then was about 200. The local general store was also the post office. The boarding house was one mile from the store which I would walk to almost everyday. The house was on a farm owned by Ida Gorden who we always called "grandma". It was a two-story farm house with 12 rooms on the second floor and two bathrooms. The first floor had five more bedrooms, a large dining room and the kitchen was very large with a large wood burning stove and oven. Every morning Laura Wildman, who was Grandma Gorden's daughter, would ring a bell to wake everyone up for breakfast. Everyone would come down and sit at the two large tables. Everything was served country family style. Lunch was at noon and the bell would ring as it did for dinner at 5:30pm. The food was wonderful. Laura would place large bowls of fresh vegetables from the garden that they had on the two tables. Grandma Gorden baked her own bread, made her own butter, and had her own chickens, which every Sunday was the meal. It was a large farm in the hills covering about 500 plus acres. The help included Percy, grandma's brother, and Simon who was called "Simy", both alcoholics, who did the haying, planting, and took care of the forty cows and two horses. I always spent the days on the hay wagon helping out.

Every morning I would get up at 5am to help round up the cows and herd them into the stalls to feed and milk. Just the smell of the barn and hay was so countrified that I loved it. About 6:30am we let the cows out to graze and I would help shovel the manure with the manure wagon. When the wagon was full, we would hook up the horses and spread the manure over the fields for fertilizer. There were apple trees, raspberry patches, blackberry patches, and of course fresh milk and cream. Grandma Gorden made the best pies I ever had. I spent many an hour picking berries and vegetables from the garden. The country was just beautiful. I loved walking along the streams picking watercress and mint. As I became 9 years old, I began fishing for rainbow trout. Grandma Gorden had the same people every summer. It was a combination of Greeks and Jews. The women would spend the whole summer and the men would come up on the weekends. Dad had a 1945 Plymouth and the trip from New Jersey in those days took about five hours. On weekends the men would play poker and pinnacle for hours during the afternoons. At night, after dinner, some of us would go to a big hotel such as the Grand Hotel, The Acropolis, or the Sunset Springs Hotel in Haines Falls, NY.

One summer in 1951, I built a tree house all by myself. I loved being in the woods alone and would sit on the stone walls watching the woodchucks, chipmunks, birds, and crows. This was America and I felt so free and peaceful. The morning sunrise and the rooster's "cock-a-doodle-do" were just wonderful. Then at night when the sun went down it would get cool at about 60 degrees. The only sound would be the noise of the water over the rocks. Mom would always make me go to bed at 7pm. She was the tough one. If I spilled my drink or did something at the table she would hit me across the face with her hand. A few times when I said a bad word she would grab me with her nails and beat me. I remember several times my arms were bleeding from her nails. She always yelled at me and would say, "You're going to make me die." She lived to be 93 years of age. Maybe we should all be that lucky to live as long as she did.

I loved it when dad came. On Saturday mornings I would go about a mile down the road, climb up on the stone wall where the intersection was to turn up to Halcott Center and wait for him. He would pick me up and as he approached the farm, he would always blow the horn and everyone knew Pete was home.

Then there was Jimmy Demetrakis whose father was in the restaurant business and would drive up with dad. Sometimes Jimmy would stay a few weeks with his sister Harriet. Jimmy was two years older than me. We had a lot of fun together. Dad had bought me a BB gun one year and Jimmy and I would go shooting. One weekend dad's former partner Mike Sotiris was there and yelled at Jimmy and me for making noise while they were playing cards on the porch. Later I shot a BB at his car and hit the windshield. The next day Jimmy told dad and I said it was an accident. Of course, mom beat me and sent me to my room. In those days you rented the room and everyone stayed in the same room.

The Puppy Love Years

One of the last years I was on the farm, I was getting interested in girls. I was 14 then and one girl Sylvia Sussman, whose father was a jeweler in NYC stayed for a week. We would go for walks in the woods and I showed her my tree house. After a few days we got along great and one afternoon I took her through the woods to the pine forest. We went under the trees and sat down on the pine needles. The smell of the evergreens and pine cones were wonderful. What a fragrance; a little bit of Christmas and country was in the air. A slight breeze was blowing and we had the cacophony of the sounds of birds and rabbits running about. We would sit still and watch the rabbits running through the trees. Sylvia said, "Peter you are such a nice guy. I wish you lived in NY near us." I liked her too because she was my type; thin, small breasts like lemons, and nice legs. She was wearing a short skirt and a whole top sweater. I told her maybe I could take the Tubes someday and meet her. We held hands and after a few nervous minutes I decided to kiss her. She liked it and we continued for about five minutes until we sort of fell over on the ground with our arms around each other. I touched her breast and she did not resist. We obviously became excited. When I ran my hand up her skirt she began to stop me, but I started to rub her and she said no more. This was my first experience with sex with a girl and I think her first experience, too. We returned to the farm and we did the same thing the next couple of days until she left. I never saw Sylvia again.

Year 1953 - Military School

The summer of 1953 was a time when dad and mom sent me to Oakland Military Academy. My godfather sent his son Jon also. We arrived just after school closed for the summer. Dad dropped me off. We were assigned a bed in a large room just like a barracks. There were about 50 kids there. The bugle blew at 7am. We got dressed and breakfast was at 7:30am. Then there were calisthenics and running. There were classes which we marched to. After lunch there was swimming, biking, and once in a while horseback riding. I hated the whole routine so I called mom and she said I had to stay. I told her I would run away, so that Saturday, dad picked me up because mom was up at the farm and we drove to Grandma Gorden's. That is when dad told me he received a letter that his mother had passed away.

It was now getting to the time when dad was going to take us back home. He arrived the first weekend in September of 1953 and that next day I saw clouds of smoke coming from the town area. I asked dad to take me there because I heard sirens in the distance. Back then each house or property had a plaque on the front gate or pole with a number. This was for the Volunteer Fire Dept. so when you called in a fire, they would look up the number and go to that farm. My mother yelled because I insisted on going to see what was burning. She said, "You are crazy; what's wrong with you?" I was very angry. Finally dad took me and we got close to the fire, which was in a large hotel about six miles away. Dad pulled over and I ran two blocks to the fire. It was entirely in flames and men were pulling hoses. I saw one fireman, as they were called back in those days, trying to get the kinks out of the hose. I began to do the same thing until I got chased away. I stayed about an hour then I found dad who was waiting for me and watching the fire. When we got back to the farm my mother kept saying I needed a psychiatrist. Two days later we left for home.

CHAPTER–FOUR
Learning Experiences

Chapter–Four – Learning Experiences

The year was 1950 and I was back to school. My routine was playing ball after school then going down the block to the fire house on Garrison and Sip Avenue. I would go there everyday and sometimes go to the store for them up the block. Everyone got to know me and soon they were showing me the trucks and equipment. This was Engine 15 and Truck 9 and the deputy chief was also there. I became obsessed with the fire department and would go after school everyday. When mom would ask where I was, I told her I was playing ball in the school yard. Every time I heard the fire trucks passing our house, I would watch them go by. There was a hook and ladder with the tiller which was painted white on Truck 9. Engine 15 was also white at that time. If I saw smoke I would go to the basement and get my bike and go to the fire. Mom didn't know because I would say I am going out to ride my bike.

It was Christmas 1952 at about 2am and snowing lightly, when I suddenly heard sirens and went to the window of my bedroom. My sister Linda was now seven years old. We both slept in the same room. When I looked out I saw the apartment a half block away with flames and smoke emanating from the 3rd floor. I quickly got dressed and ran to the kitchen door. Linda had heard me get up and she yelled, "Mommy! Peter is going out." Mom yelled, "Get back here now!" I kept going down the apartment stairs and ran to the fire. A second alarm had been sounded because of the large fire. After about an hour with the whole neighborhood watching from their windows and some at the scene I saw the fireman carrying out two bodies and laid them on the street. Today this would not be an acceptable practice until an investigation was conducted. I thought to myself, I hope it wasn't the kids who lived there that I knew and went to my school. When I went home my mother smacked me in the head and said I couldn't go out all week after school. Dad was leaving for work at 4:30am and he said, "Sof, leave him alone." It turned out the next day that there were visitors from Massachusetts for the holidays. The boys, who I knew, got out safely. Since that fire, I kept thinking, "What causes these terrible fires?" I went to the fire station the next day and spoke to Captain Finn. He told me they think it was from a short in the lights on the Christmas tree.

Year 1953 - The Jersey Shore

In 1953 dad started to take us to the farm in the Catskills from the end of June until the end of July. Then we would take a room at a bungalow owned by Gus Vallas, "not a relative" and spent the month of August at the beach. We stayed in the same room with a small kitchen. Actually it was closer for dad to spend weekends with us. I was in my glory meeting girls on the beach, and at night on the boardwalk. Even though I had to be home by 9pm, it was great. Gus Vallas owned a small deli on the beach and I worked four hours a day at the deli to make spending money. Sometimes on Sundays we went to the Greek Church in Asbury Park. My parents would always make me wear a tie and jacket. I met several girls that summer and one of them was Donna who met me every night at the boardwalk's arcade. We danced quite a bit; actually she taught me. This was the time the Everly Brothers record "Dream" came out. One night Donna had a party at her house on Main Street and there were about 20 kids there. We danced to the songs of the early fifties and yes there was beer and wine. Her parents were away for the weekend at a wedding. Nobody was old enough to drive so most of them got drunk. I was afraid to drink too much so I only had two beers. Donna and I went to her bedroom and kissed and fooled around on her bed. Feeling and kissing was about all we did back then.

I met a girl by the name of Letty whose father owned a fishing boat. She took me out on it one day and I threw up the entire day. After that her father didn't want Letty and I see each other anymore. I think he wanted a fisherman. I always got motion sickness even in dad's car or on a bus. I had to carry an empty Maxwell House coffee can to use to if I got sick. Sometimes in October around Halloween I would take the bus from Jersey City to my Aunt Lil's and Uncle Bernie's in Keansburg, NJ. My cousins Lorraine, Barbara, and Bernice would always get in trouble when I was there. Lorraine and Barbara were several years older than me. We had so much fun then. The best was when the sirens went off for the fire department in East Keansburg and I would take my bike to find the fire. I watched many fires there and would ride over to their fire station and hang out. We didn't have TV then and at night we would listen to the "Shadow", a scary program and we would all jump at the sounds and screams. We also listened to "Man against Crime" with Ralph Belamy. Most of the time, mom and dad would pick me up at Aunt Lil's on Sunday. If not, I would take the bus back. Again I had to have my coffee can ready no matter what. I only wish they had two pound cans then, because I always filled the one pound can up. There were good memories in those days. I just loved my Uncle Bernie. He was always teasing me, but I was also always getting into some kind of trouble. They had a collie named Dutchess. One time I took Dutchess for a long walk for over an hour. Uncle Bernie came home and didn't see his dog. He went crazy looking all over. I never told anyone I was taking Dutchess. All of a sudden Uncle Bernie pulled up in his Hudson and screamed at me. After a wild ride back to the house I went to Aunt Lil. She calmed Uncle Bernie down. Another time he bought Bernice, my younger cousin a new bike for Christmas. I took Bernice on the handle bars and went down to Fish House Road near the water. I started to peddle fast to go up the bridge and when we went down the other side I lost control and we crashed. Bernice was bleeding from the side of her leg from a bad abrasion. The handle bars were bent and the fender came off. I was all right. I walked the bike to the First Aid Squad and of course everyone knew Uncle Bernie. They called him and he came to pick us up.

When I saw the look on his face I ran away. I ran all the way back to the house and told Aunt Lil what happened. She felt bad and told me as long as Bernice was okay we could always get the bike fixed.

Summer 1953

One summer mom and dad were taking Linda and me to Atlantic City. In 1953 there was no Garden State Parkway, so we had to drive on the old roads. The road to the Jersey Shore was very dangerous. There were three lanes. The middle lane was for passing so there were many head on collisions then. Traffic was always bad. The first aid squads would always be on the side of the highways and put out a sheet on the ground and people would throw money onto it. We stopped at Aunt Lil's for a couple of hours and Uncle Bernie said to my father, "Pete, there is a farm not far from here and I know the owner and he told me to come and pick anything I want because he sold the property." Dad and I went and filled the trunk of his 1950 Chrysler to the hilt with red and green peppers for the diner. When we got back, mom was angry because he put the suitcases on the back seat to make room for the peppers. We left Aunt Lil's and headed for Atlantic City. It was starting to get dark and somewhere near Tom's River dad got a flat. Mom was furious because we had to unload all the peppers by hand. They weren't in boxes and we had to place them behind the car so dad could get the spare and jack out. Dad moved the car about eight feet forward so he could work. Believe me, dad was no mechanic. He could not get the jack to work so we had to walk about a half mile to a home and the people we found called us a tow truck. We walked back to the car where mom and Linda were waiting. After an hour we saw a tow truck approaching from the rear and guess what? Yes, the tow truck ran over the peppers. Dad was more upset about the peppers than the car. The man changed the tire and after dad paid him, he left. The best of this story was when dad and I began to salvage the peppers that weren't crushed and mom flipped her lid. She made him leave all the peppers and get on the road. I don't think they spoke a word until dad got to Atlantic City and got lost trying to find the hotel. After mom, yelling at him to turn here and there she would say, "You know Pete there is something wrong with you. Get your head examined." Mom always said this to me, too many times as I was growing up. She was really funny when she got angry. Mom never learned to drive "thank God", but she always used her right foot for a brake. This brings to mind one time dad was driving to Keyport, N.J. to a restaurant, the Keyport Inn, which we always went to for seafood. He had to make a quick defensive move and mom put her imaginary brake on and broke her high heel. Linda and I were laughing hysterically in the back seat. The best was dad trying to find a shoemaker in Keyport. He would drive around block by block. Mom was yelling again, "Why don't you ask someone?" Dad would say "Sof" please be quiet and I will find one. He stopped at a hardware store and asked the proprietor if there was a shoe repair shop. He was told the local shoemaker died last week and the nearest one was in Hazlet. Dad bought a jar of contact cement and I thought mom would go crazy. He glued the heel on and after getting some on his fingers he touched the steering wheel and now as mom was yelling again he went back in the store for some cleaner. Well, we were on the way again to the restaurant. When we finished eating on the way out mom's heel fell off again and of course she yelled at dad again as she hopped to the car. We arrived home at 135 Garrison Avenue and climbed up the four flights of stairs to our apartment. When dad turned the key to open the top lock, mom said, "Hurry Pete I have to go". When mom had to go to the bathroom she couldn't hold it long. Even when she laughed hard she would cross her legs and walk funny to get to the bathroom. Anyway dad turned the door knob and it didn't open. Mom started to yell at him then she crossed her legs. Dad tried the top lock again and the door still didn't open. Mom was now screaming at him. Apparently one of the locks was not locked so when dad tried to open the door, he locked one lock and opened the other. After he kept trying a large puddle was forming beneath mom. Linda and I were laughing so hard we both had to go. Finally the door opened and we all ran to the bathroom. Mom was still angry and yelling at dad as she cleaned the floor in the hall.

After school I continued to go to the fire house everyday. There was a big fire on Grand Street downtown and Deputy Chief Michael Burke pulled out of the station with his chauffer and went to the fire. I listened at the station to the radio activity. About one half hour after a second alarm was sounded, someone called over the radio that a fireman fell into a scuttle hole in the roof and was trapped in the void at the bottom. Later we found out it was Chief Burke. He died at the Jersey City Medical Center. I was pretty shook up. Two days later I went downtown to the funeral home. He was laid out in his full dress uniform. I would never forget this in the years to come.

There was a friend of mine, Jack Ellison, who lived a few blocks away on Van Rypen Avenue. He was overweight and a couple of years older than me. He had quit school when he was sixteen, had no parents, and lived with his two aunts. He also hung out at the fire station. I learned a lot in the next two years about the fire department before I graduated in 1955 and entered high school. When there was a fire close by Jackie and I would help drain hoses and roll them up. Most of the deputy chiefs and battalion chiefs knew me as well as the firemen. They liked me and I was allowed in the fire station whenever I could get there. I even helped wash and wax the trucks, eat lunch and watch TV. Mom thought I was nuts, but I did it anyway. My usual routine during the week was, after school, I would go to grandma's house and go to the store for her. Aunt Mary had let me use one of her rooms on the top floor for an art studio. I always did a lot of oil paintings and was pretty good. After an hour or so I would then go to the firehouse. At 5pm I had to be home otherwise mom would punish me. Dinner at five was a must. Mom always made dinner according to the days. For example, Monday was meat loaf, Tuesday was steak, Wednesday was ham, Thursday was spaghetti, and Friday was fish. Saturday dad would take us to dinner at the Oyster Bay Restaurant, and Sunday we usually went to Aunt Ann's house or Aunt Catherine's house for dinner. My cousin Doris and her husband Willie lived with Aunt Catherine and we always had a good time with them. Willie used to make his own wine and I loved helping him crush the grapes and, then after they fermented in a few weeks, we would take the wine and drain it into two 50 gallon barrels. He also had a press which we would put the stems in and press the remaining skins. He would make Grappa from this. He would always start making the wine around September of every year. He would call me and then we would go to Hoboken Rail Yards to buy the grapes. He would buy cases of Alaganti, Zinvandel, and Granada grapes for the red wines and white muscatel for the white. Usually by Christmas the wines were ready to drink. Of course, Willie would let me taste some because if mom saw me drinking she would kill me.

New Year's Eve was the best. We always went to Aunt Catherine's. I took the bus to her house. In those days the bus and trains were the way we got around. Most families did not have cars then. That year, 1953, I went to Aunt Catherine's and what a party we had. Willie played the clarinet, Cousin Billie played the drums, and I strummed a guitar. We all sang the old songs which I still do today. Aunt Catherine and Uncle Paul were great cooks and they always let me have a glass of wine or two. At Aunt Mary's house I was not allowed. So every year I went to Aunt Catherine's for New Years.

Year 1954

It was 1954 and I was really into music. This was the beginning of Rock'n Roll and I listened to Bing Crosby, Dean Martin, and Frank Sinatra. For a young guy like me this was rare but I loved to sing their songs. I was still in grammar school and had one more year to go. One of my teachers Mrs. Moskowitz was always annoyed with me because I bit my nails. She gave me a failing grade and I asked why. My mother was angry with me and was going to punish me when she found out about my failing grade. She took me to school and spoke to the teacher. The teacher said she was failing me because I bit my nails. She told my mother to take me to the doctor. Mom took me to Dr. Rosenberg and told him the story. I will never forget what she said to Dr. Rosenberg, she said, "Peter always bites his nails". Dr. Rosenberg said, "Well, I bite my nails, too." Well, she then went to the principal Mr. Carr and all was resolved. I still bite my nails to this day.

This brings to mind a funny story which dad always told at a party. I was about five years old and dad and mom took me to see Santa at Macy's in NY. We would take the tubes to NY and always returned with those beautiful red gift boxes with the white Christmas ties on them. While shopping I got lost and I guess I kept getting off on different floors. I wasn't scared at all. Another time in Macy's I tried to ride on the escalator rail and fell. About 10 people fell on me because of that. My mother "cleaned" Macy's floor with me that particular day. Getting back to 1954 I played with the school basketball team; my last two years until graduation. I was good and the last year we won the championship. Unfortunately, dad never came to any games. He was always working. I certainly didn't want mom to come because she would worry about me getting hurt. Uncle Walter used to take me to the ball games at Yankee Stadium to see Joe DiMaggio, Mickie Mantel, Phil Resuto, etc. Things were so different then. There was little crime, and everyone could ride the subways and walk on the streets at night. These were the good old days.

Christmas was my favorite time of the year. I always wanted to decorate on December 1st. Mom always insisted on an artificial tree because she didn't like pine needles falling on the floor. Finally dad said we would get a real tree. It was snowing the day we went to the lot on Tonelle Avenue not far from our apartment. It was cold and at the lot where every year they sold Christmas trees, the 50 gallon drums had a fire in it to keep the workers warm. As we neared the lot, there was a smell the burning pine. It was beautiful as we walked between the rows of trees. We picked a small tree and paid the man $3.00. He gave us each a cup of eggnog and we carried the tree home. Mom was ready with the vacuum and we put the tree in the stand. It made the house smell wonderful. Mom was making Greek cookies called "Kouburakia". Dad and I, with Linda getting in the way, put the lights on the tree, then the bulbs, and then the red bows. We let Linda put the candy canes and tinsel on the tree. Next we set up the set of Lionel trains around the tree. The last two weeks of December with Linda's birthday on the 21st was always the best. We would visit everyone and leave presents under their trees for Christmas day. Christmas day was always spent at Aunt Mary's. She always invited her friends from church and altogether there were about 20 people. Dad would always carve the turkey and the feast began. After we had dinner we would open presents. The next week there was no school so I went to the diner, a couple of days, to help dad then back to the fire house each day.

Back to school after New Year's I was heading toward graduation in June; I met a girl named Janet Stemple. She was very pretty. This was my first puppy love. She lived in the Marion Gardens Project; a low income area. I would walk to her block on Dales Avenue every day and we would see each other. She had a few sisters older than she and they always watched us. We couldn't seem to get away from them. One day after school we were walking behind one of the buildings and there was a large discarded cardboard box, probably from a refrigerator. We went inside and after a few minutes we kissed. This was great and I was very excited in more ways than one. I don't think I need to go any further. When mom found out she wouldn't let me go down there anymore. She said I should meet girls at the church. I had been going to Greek school about a year now but didn't learn much because I was always fooling around in class. I finally stopped going because things were going on in school for graduation and I didn't want to miss anything. We just received our autograph books and after school we had our friends sign it. Spring came and I was excited because of graduation. Dad asked me if I would work for Theodore the Florist the day before Easter and Easter Sunday delivering flowers. Theodore Antos was one of dad's Greek friends from the church. I took the job and I had to deliver them by bus. Sometimes I had two or three plants and made several stops then returned to the flower shop on Journal Square and got more. This was a great job because I made about $50.00 for the two days in tips plus what Theodore gave me. Finally graduation came and mom and dad had a party for me at my Aunt Mary's and grandma's house, all family of course, because mom didn't want me going to any other party so she planned this party for me with family only. It was very nice and I made plenty of money. My family and I spent the summer for one month at the farm and the best was August in Manasquan, NJ. That is the summer I will never forget. It was this summer when dad and his partner John Sophanis decided to split weekends off so they could have a Saturday and Sunday together with their families. Dad was the big money partner. John had an interest in the diner, which was named Pete's Diner.

This summer dad came to the shore on Friday and went back on Monday morning about 3am to beat the traffic. The first weekend dad came down we rented a small 12 foot boat with a motor on it and went fishing. We were in Barnegat Bay for two hours and we caught several flounders. We put them on a string and hung them over the rear of the boat into the water. I had a crab net and we caught about a dozen crabs, which we had in a pail on the boat. We decided to leave and I started the motor on the outboard, pulled the anchor, and headed back to the boat house. I said to dad, "Let's go out in the ocean through the Manasquan inlet." Dad said okay so out we went to the inlet and south along the coast. On the way back I stopped, but the anchor wouldn't touch the bottom so dad and I drifted and tried to fish. That's when I noticed the flounders were gone. A large fish must have eaten them. A wind came up and dad and I began to feel sick. I started the boat and we went back with just the crabs. When we told mom, she said her usual, "There's something wrong with you both; you need your heads examined." As soon as we brought the crabs in she chased us out. We were renting two rooms from Gus and Helen at their bungalow. They were friends of mom and dad's. I worked part-time in Gus's bakery on the beach. Gus cooked the crabs and told me they were great.

CHAPTER–FIVE
My Lifeguard Experience

Chapter–Five - My Lifeguard Experience

This was the summer I tried out for a lifeguard position at the "Little Beach" which was on the river. I was too young for the ocean. I got the job and worked the rest of the summer there. They had another older lifeguard work with me. We had about 12 pulls, as they would say, and saved four kids that summer. It was the first time I had to do artificial respiration and it was on someone 16 years old...a girl, thank God. It was fun and I will never forget that summer and it came to an end very quickly. I had quite a few girlfriends, actually a total of three. One of them I had just met one week before the lifeguard's ball. Her name was Jean and our first date was on the boardwalk where I bought her a hamburger and soda. When it got dark we went on the beach. I was 15 years old now and wanted more than a kiss. Well, I got more than a kiss. We laid on each other and felt each other...clothes on of course, but had to break it up when the beach patrol came by. I asked her to the lifeguard's ball and she said, yes. Mom and dad had to take me and pick me up. I had a big fight over it because it was at the Sea Girt Inn, a couple of miles away from where we were. I told them dad could drive Jean and me to the ball but we would get a ride back with someone or take a taxi. Dad said okay but mom was not happy about it. Again dad needed his head examined. I didn't have a suit so I asked dad to take me to the store in town. I had money but dad got a kick out of me and paid the $35.00 for a suit, a white shirt, and a real thin tie which was the style then. I had shoes already that I polished for the party.

The night of the ball, dad picked up Jean and dropped us off. What mom and dad didn't know was that most of the lifeguards from Asbury Park and Manasquan were older than I was. They were within the range of 18 and 25. In NJ the age to drink was 21. The ball was great. Those who sneaked in the booze had it in pint bottles. Jean and I walked around, danced to the fifties music and ate at the buffet. Afterwards we really wanted to go somewhere so I called a taxi about 9:30pm. I had to be home by 10:30pm so we went to the Manasquan boardwalk and walked around. We couldn't go on the beach because of the way we were dressed so I came up with a bright idea and said let's go to the lifeguard station at the little beach since I had a key. Off we went and made sure no one saw us even though it was dark. We went in and I spread a blanket on the floor. We started to make out and we both got naked. I tried to really have sex with her but she wouldn't. It didn't take but a few minutes and I was done if you know what I mean. It still was wonderful. We got dressed and I walked her home. When I got in mom was waiting. I was one hour late. She smelled my breath and was satisfied I was not drinking so I went to bed. That next week I was to start Dickenson High School.

High School Years

I was a bit nervous the first day. I had a shirt and tie on which mom insisted I wear but in those days "dungarees" as they were called were not allowed. My home room class had about 30 kids. My graduation class, four years later was 600. It was hard to find all my old friends because some went to other schools. For example, some girls went to St. Dominick's Academy, Snyder High, Ferris High, and St Al's Academy. The guys went to the same or St. Peter's Prep. So I had to meet many new friends. Donald Caruso lived in the same building as my Aunt Ann on Van Wagnan Avenue. My father's partner John Sofianos lived there also along with my Aunt

Viola. Everyone was in walking distance from my house. Donald Caruso was my closest friend and we spent a lot of time together. He lived in the same apartment building. Don and I hung out and played handball across the street at PS 23 where we graduated from. There were no busses in those days; everyone walked to school.

I found my home room 217 and everyone sat down. We received our schedules for the next six months. The first few days were a little difficult but soon we figured out where to go. Dickenson High was a large school with two gyms. The old gym and the new gym were built on a hill overlooking downtown Jersey City and New York skyline. Donald and I walked the mile to school and back everyday. We couldn't wait until we could get our licenses to drive and then get a car. As a freshman I was picked on a lot, even punched, and had my books knocked on the floor. I stayed away from those guys as much as I could.

A couple of months later in the school cafeteria this guy knocked my tray on the floor. He was a senior and a real bully. His name was Donald Boscoit. I went back on line and got another tray with three orders of mashed potatoes. I then walked past where he was sitting and dropped it on his head. Everyone was laughing, but he started to beat me up until a teacher came over and broke it up. We had to go to the advisor's office. I told my story and was put on detention one week along with him. After detention every day when I started to walk home he would kick me or push me, then go to his car laughing with his friends. His car was a 1950 Chevy and it had a large dent in the trunk. It also had a Dickenson High sticker on the rear window. Several weeks later I was in North Bergen, N.J. at a shopping area. I had taken a bus there to buy some stamps for my stamp collection. There was a large parking lot in the rear of the store and I spotted the guy's car. Actually I saw him and a girl walking away. They went into the movie theater so I went back to the car and when no one was around I flattened all four tires. I took the stems out with the cap. I was very delighted because I got even and he would never know who did it. I ran into him a few more times and he still pushed me and knocked my books out of my hand. I was sixteen and he was graduating that January, thank God.

It was just before the senior prom when I went to the library to do some research.

I sat down and noticed some books and notebooks on the table. No one was around so I picked them up and was going to give them to the librarian and I noticed a yearbook on the bottom. Guess what? Yes, it was Donald Boscoit's books. I walked out and straight to the back of the school where the hill was. I threw everything over the hill to the bottom in the trees. I was sure he was not happy to lose his work and especially his yearbook which by then everyone must have signed. One day Donald Caruso met me and said we should go to lunch around the corner from the school at this deli that made the best tuna sandwiches on Italian bread. After that it became our daily hang out for tuna and Pepsi. Walking the mile and a half to school one day in February it was 20 degrees, windy, and snowing heavily. Every few blocks I would dash into a store front to rest. It was brutal. I did have bus coupons at a discount but I always felt sick riding on a bus so I walked. I started to meet girls in school and would walk home with them after school. Sometimes we would stop for a Pepsi or an egg cream. Pepsi was big then and with its red and blue labels made in the glass bottle itself. Egg cream was made with chocolate syrup, a drop of milk, and the rest seltzer. Fountains were all over then and everyone hung out at one or another. As a matter of fact, they all had juke boxes which made it better. Rock'n roll, Alan Freid radio was also a big hit. I started buying 45 records about that time I had a little Victrola (RCA), but the sound was bad and it only played one at a time.

Summer 1955

Just before the summer of 1955 there was a band made up of six boys at school and they played and sang the song "Sincerely". It was great. Spring arrived and love was in the air. We went to the farm for a few weeks in July but I wanted to go to the Jersey Shore. At the end of the month we came home, but I stayed in Jersey City. I was hanging out with Donald and other guys next to the Dairy Queen which just opened. It was next to my Aunt Ann's and Donald's house. This was also two blocks from my house. Sometime after the 4th of July, 1955, I took the bus to Aunt Lil's in Port Monmouth, on Collins Avenue. The last time I was there I met a girl named Barbara who lived on Collins Avenue also and I went to her party. I liked her and we kissed that night. Now I called her and told her I was coming down this weekend and maybe we could get together. She said she had a boyfriend but would see me on Sunday. I met her Sunday morning at 10am at the Dixie Lee Bakery. We walked around for about an hour then we got behind a building near the boardwalk in Keansburg. We were kissing and then I felt her breast. We were getting hot but it was too open to do anything. I knew Uncle Bernie was working as a special cop that day so I went to look for him. I found him on the beach and asked if I could have the keys to his car so I could put a package in it. He gave a funny look and said if I lose the keys he would kill me. I went to his car which was parked in a parking lot behind a bar. Barbara and I got in the back and we made love but no intercourse, only a finger job. It was great then I brought Uncle Bernie's keys back.

Late August there was a block party and Van Wagnan Avenue was closed off for the day. There were ice cream trucks, hot dog and hamburger wagons, and a small stage and music. It was that day I met Irene Rimer. Donald and I were talking to a bunch of girls and Irene was with a guy Charlie Hanson. After our introduction Charlie had an ice cream cone and pushed it in Irene's face. He thought it was funny but I didn't. Donald and I walked away and I said to Donald, "Is that her boyfriend?" Donald told me not really, he was a friend of one of Irene's girlfriends. I told him I kind of liked her so set it up so I could meet her again.

1956 Sixteen Years Old

Several weeks later Donald and I were going to the Dickenson High football game, so we asked Irene and her girlfriend to go. Irene said she would bring lunch to the game. When it came time to eat lunch, I cracked up when Donald opened his sandwich. One thing he hated was a meat sandwich without mustard. He had a ham sandwich with mayonnaise, squeezing out. He never said a word then he looked at me and we both started laughing uncontrollably. The girls wanted to know what was funny but we never told them. I was beginning to see Irene more frequently. Dad and mom had planned to move to a larger apartment in North Bergen, N.J. in a two family house. They would rent from Betty and Dino Korinis. Betty was the daughter of Andy Xenitellis who had been in business with dad and Mike Sotiris one time. They were friends for years also. I was happy because I would have my own room and Linda would too. Just before we moved I was at the fire house and one of the men said a plane crashed into an apartment house in North Bergen and the buildings were on fire. He said it was on either 76th Street or 74th Street. I left the fire house and took the bus to North Bergen. I immediately went to the house at 432 76th Street where we were moving to. It was not affected so I ran down the block when I saw the smoke and fire engines. I watched and helped pull the hose with one of the Fairview volunteer fire department engineers who was there on mutual aid. A woman had jumped from her 4th floor apartment during the fire. I walked around the alley and saw the body just before they covered it. That was the first body I saw out of hundreds I would see in my career. I stayed at the scene for about two hours then took the bus back to Jersey City. We moved some time in March and mom was busy decorating and painting. I had to take the bus from North Bergen to Jersey City to school everyday. The Boulevard Bus went about seven miles and stopped at almost every block. It took about an hour to get to school. After a week or two I started leaving about 5am then when I got to Jersey City, I walked about ten long blocks to Irene's house. I would have coffee then we would walk the mile to school. After about a month of that I decided to change schools mid term. I enrolled in Memorial High School in West New York, N.J. closer than Dickenson. After a month in Memorial I hated it. I left school and planned to go back to Dickenson in the fall. I ended up losing six months because of it.

CHAPTER–SIX
Teenage Troubles

Chapter–Six – Teenage Troubles

Mom was visiting grandma Francis every day for years in the nursing home. She took a bus there, stayed an hour and then went home. I would hang out this summer on Van Wagnon Avenue with Donald and other friends. My Aunt Viola, who was divorced, would let Donald and I go up to her apartment and we would drink beer. She was a "piss" and we always laughed. If we wanted beer, she would always get it for us. I really didn't like the school much because these were the blackboard jungle days and you had to belong to a gang if you wanted to stay healthy. I got involved with the "Drifters" in West New York, N.J. I was a bit frightened, but I joined anyway. I had to go through an initiation first. I didn't know what to expect, and one night we all met at North Hudson Park. There were about 12 of us including four girls. They had black jackets on with "Drifters" written on the back. One of the girls, Sue was also being initiated. The head of the gang was a guy named Billy. He told me I had to pick one of the eight guys and fight him. This was something I didn't expect. I looked at everyone and decided on the smallest one. They all laughed at my pick which I figured, "wrong choice" he must be the toughest. After getting my ass kicked many times in Dickenson High, one of my Greek friends, James Demetrakis told me one time it was all psychological. If you act tough and attack first and fast you will have the advantage. Well, it worked. I walked down the line and when I got to this guy, by the way his name was Greg, I said, "So you're the little bastard whose ass I am going to kick." I punched him so fast in the face; I knocked him down and kept punching him. They stopped me after pulling me off of him. His mouth was bleeding and obviously he was "pissed". Billy said, "Enough I don't want you to kill him". I passed that part of my initiation. Sue was next and she had to pick someone. I'll say one thing, she could sure pull hair, and she kept up a good fight but she was beaten and had a bloody nose. They passed her also. I think the fighting part was to see if you had the guts to stand up to anyone. We were taken from the park and walked to a house on 79ᵗʰ Street. It was a two story house and we went to the basement by a side door. There was a couch, two chairs and an oriental rug on the floor. Sue and I were given a small glass of whiskey and told to down it in one shot. We did and then with everyone watching they told Sue she had to undress me. I was now shaking and I am sure she was too. She said to Billy, "Do I have to?" and everyone laughed. The answer was yes, and I stood there in fear. Sue began to undress me down to my shorts. She looked at everyone and one of the girls said do it or leave now. Then they told me I had to undress Sue. She got very nervous and I thought she was going to cry. They kept telling her it was all part of the game and they all did it at initiation time. Well, I started and off came her blouse and pants. Then I took her bra off. She had a great breast like two large apples. She covered them with her hands. Then I took off her panties. Well there we were naked as a jay bird. Billy said everyone would leave the room and we had to make love to each other and they wouldn't be there. They left the room and we looked at each other and she said, "I can't do it." I never did it and I am scared. I told her to lie down on the couch and we could make believe. I got on top of her and of course I was aroused. She told me don't do it.

I pretended to and I came to a climax. All of a sudden they all came out and clapped. Billy came over and saw my sperm on her leg. He then said we could get dressed. We were told we were now members. Everyone left and we walked away on Bergen Avenue. Two days later I saw Sue and we talked. She was embarrassed but we liked each other. After that we went to a couple of meetings.

There was going to be a fight that Saturday night with the Falcons in Union City at some park. I met Sue about 7pm and one block before the park we had police cars with lights and sirens pulling into the area. We hid in the doorway of a drug store and saw an ambulance drive in also. Both of us took our jackets off and walked back to a bus stop. We were lucky that a bus came along right away and we got on to go back to North Bergen. We both decided that night we would quit the club. The next day we found out that Billy was stabbed in his arm. The cops arrested three people from the Falcons for possession of weapons. I was lucky because I never went back to Memorial High. One other time during the summer, I decided to start my own club, "The Cycles" with my friend, Donald Caruso and a couple of others, including Sue. It was now September and I was back in Dickenson High. I used to hide my motorcycle boots and jacket in the basement of our house so dad and mom wouldn't see them. I had started to smoke then, but they didn't know it.

One night I was in Fitchin's Ice Cream Parlor with two guys and a few girls who looked like whores. Betty Korinis passed the window and saw me inside smoking. She went home and told my mom and dad. I was standing in the store with my back to the door. I never saw dad come in. All I know is he smacked me across the face knocking the cigarette out of my mouth then he threw me on the floor, ripped off my jacket and took off my boots. He was yelling and saying, "You don't belong with these hoodlums." He made me walk home in my socks and when I got upstairs to our apartment he whacked me a few times more. Of course, mom was yelling also. I was also yelling back and said to mom to stop being a bitch. Dad heard that and for the first time in my life he came in my room and punched me several times. He also smashed all of my model airplanes; about 15 of them, tossed my phonograph on the floor and more or less trashed my room. I was crying and closed the door to my room. I had a large duffle bag in my closet which I packed with my things. As I left the house I told mom I was running away. I started to walk down Bergenline Avenue and a few blocks away a police car was slowly following me. They stopped me and asked what I had in the bag. I said I was going to do laundry. They then put me in the police car and took me to headquarters. When I got there I was put in a small cell. A few minutes later a police officer came in and asked me questions and I told him I ran away. He said he was going to call my parents. What I didn't know was dad had called the police because our neighbor was a police officer, John Batey, and he told him what had happened. So they set it up to put me in a cell. John Batey was on the desk that night, but I didn't see him when I came in. Finally the officer came back and said dad told him to send me to the Juvenile Home. I started crying and said please let me speak to him. Little did I know dad was already outside and they must have had a good laugh. Then dad came in and I swore I would never do that again and we went home. I went to my room and I was not allowed out at night for weeks. Someone had put my jacket and boots in the doorway to the house and mom promptly threw them in the garbage. After a few weeks things got better.

Back at school things were better also. Unfortunately, I lost six months and my friends would be graduating ahead of me. I got on the baseball team as manager and that kept me busy. I couldn't wait to get my learner's permit so I could drive when I became 17 years old. I was seeing Irene and everyday after school I took the bus to Pete's Diner and worked until 8pm. I took the bus home or got a ride with the Hudson County Police. They were friends of dad's and he always gave them free coffee and food. I knew how to drive because dad would let me drive when I was on the farm. I got my driving permit and drove with dad. Mom would not go in the car if I was driving. When I wasn't at the diner I would still go to the fire station. I continued to go to the large fires and help. One Chief Gibney was a pain. If he saw me helping he would chase me away. One day he was at Engine 15 and I was there. He saw me and said, "I don't want you hanging around here." The Captain, Mike Finn, told him all the good I do for them and he just went up to his office. Soon after that I saw him another time working at Engine 15. I went up to his office and I said, "Hi Chief, I'm going to the store for the guys do you need anything?" He looked at me and said, "Sit down, son. Do you want to be a fireman?" I told him yes. He started to tell me a story about his joining the Fire Department. I smelled liquor on his breath just like my Uncle Kenneth when he was drinking. He kept talking for about fifteen minutes and asked me what store I was going to and I said Feldman's Deli. It was the best Jewish deli around. He wanted a pastrami sandwich on rye which I brought back and he loved it. Well I made a friend and we got along fine after that.

One afternoon Donald Caruso said there was going to be a big fight at Marion Gardens on Dales Avenue between two gangs at 7pm tonight. Irene lived there so I said let's get the guys together and we will park at Irene's and watch. I borrowed dad's Chrysler and picked up Donald and three others. It was about 6:30pm and we drove down Dales Avenue. All of a sudden police cars came from every direction and stopped me. They made us get out of the car and put us in two police cars. They searched dad's car and found a small Billy club dad kept in the glove compartment in case he was robbed. They also took from the truck empty soda bottles which dad forgot to throw away from our trip to Massachusetts. They took two screwdrivers also. Then they told me to drive to the police station on Montgomery Street. They followed me there and I parked out front. Then, they put all five of us around a large table and took each of our phone numbers and names. This one detective came in; a big guy and said we are all going to jail because we had weapons and were going to a fight. I told him it was my dad's car and there were no weapons and we were going to my girlfriend's house. He didn't believe me. He left the room and one by one he questioned each of us by bringing us to a cell in the back. We were all scared, of course, and after the questioning we were back at the table again. They informed us that our parents were all called and they were coming to the station. As we sat down I said to the guys, "Too bad we don't have a deck of cards. We could have a game of poker." Everyone started to laugh because when I said it that same detective was behind me. He punched me in the side of my head and his ring cut me. More of a scratch, but I had a bump. Each parent came and everyone was released to them and we had to come back in two days at 10am to meet before the judge. Dad was the last to come because he had to take a bus from North Bergen to Jersey City. I was the one in trouble. On a table in another room were the screwdrivers, bottles and Billy club along with my four hub caps from my car which were in dad's trunk. I also didn't have dad's registration. He forgot to give it to me. Dad walked in about 10:30pm and there was a captain behind the desk. He saw dad and said, "Hi Pete how are you?" He always stopped at dad's diner to eat. Dad told him he was called about me. The captain came in the room with dad and the detective said I was being charged with having a weapon, stolen hub caps, and a stolen car. Dad looked at me then told the captain and the detective it was his car. He forgot to give me the registration; the Billy club was his and began to tell them the story about the bottles. Three of them left the room and a few minutes later dad and I carried the bottles, screwdrivers, hub caps, and Billy club to the car and we left. I told dad the truth and he believed me. When I got home it was a different story. Mom was wild and said, "You are disgracing me. What is the family going to think?" I'm putting you away because there is something wrong with you. Dad went to bed. Two days later we were all at the station with our parents. Mom had to take me because dad worked. Three of the parents told mom their sons were not allowed to hang out with me any longer. The captain was present and explained to the juvenile judge the story. The judge gave us all a lecture about fighting and let us all go home. At the end mom told the judge and captain that her Peter was wonderful and was never in trouble. Mom said there was no reason for him getting hit in the head by the detective. In these days they got away with that.

Winter 1957

Finally December 5 came and I was 17. I asked Uncle Warren to take me for the driver's test at Roosevelt Stadium. When the motor vehicle inspector got in the car, which was dad's 1953 Chrysler he said, "Okay, start the car and drive out of the parking lot." Guess what? The car didn't start. I pushed the starter button again and it still wouldn't start. The tester said to come back in two weeks when you learn how to start the car. I was "pissed!" Uncle Warren got in and after several tries the car started. I called the guy back and he was nasty. He said come back in two weeks. Two weeks later I went back and passed the test. Dad would let me take his car once in a while at night. I would drive to Irene's then home by 9pm. I started to look for a car but I didn't have any money. I saw a 1948 Chevy for $90.00. I borrowed the money from my Aunt Mary. One night after I had the car for two weeks, Irene and I, and our friends, Anglina and Dennis were in my car and we went to West Side Park and stopped. We were making out about an hour and decided to leave. When I started the car it went forward and jumped the island in front of the car. I had forgotten to put the clutch in. All four tires were in the air and my muffler was crushed. Some guys came to help and pushed me off. What a noise it made all the way home. When I pulled into my house, mom and dad heard the noise. They came out and mom said, "Pete, why did you let him buy such an old car?" A couple of days later I bought a 1954 Plymouth Belvedere, which was very nice, and also automatic.

Summer 1957

Summer of 1957 was coming to a close and I was getting ready for school. Dad and mom took me to Schlesinger's for new clothes. Sid Schlesinger, who knew dad for years, was always very accommodating. Dad bought his suits and shirts, etc. there for years. Sid had been dressing me since I was four years old. Now at 17 years old I was pretty picky about my choice of jackets, etc. I was very much into Rock'n Roll and would sing all the songs at parties and even on street corners in Jersey City with Donald and other friends. This day I bought a nice looking gray sports jacket, slacks, and several new shirts. I was being fitted when Sid showed me a pink jacket with a gray velvet collar. I went nuts! I wanted it and I did buy it. Mom again came out with her usual remark, "You need your head examined." When I went back to school that fall, all the girls loved it. Irene and I had gone on American Bandstand a couple of times and I wore it

then. My report cards were not all that good. I would pass everything but I didn't study much because I was working at the diner until 8:30 or 9pm. I would stop at the fire house for a while then go home. One night there was a two bagger (two alarm fires) on Newark Avenue and I went there for two hours. That night mom was at the door yelling I should be in bed then she smelled the smoke on me. She made me take my clothes off in the hall. It was October and I had just bought a fire helmet, boots, and rubber coat. In those days we used the Carnes NY helmet, a rubber coat and regular fire boots. I knew as soon as I was 18 years old I would be able to be an auxiliary fireman at Engine 15 and Truck 9. Auxiliary firemen would sign in and ride the truck to the scene but weren't allowed in the fire buildings. The first time I rode a fire truck was towards the end of October where there was a large meadow fire in Secaucus, N.J. I was passing by and saw the large clouds of smoke so I drove to the fire. I took out my gear and went to the fire ground. No one questioned me and one officer yelled to me and two other firemen to get on the engine we were going to the other side of the fire. I jumped on the tail (in those days we did not have cabs, we rode on the back tail hanging on to the rail. After working the fire for about an hour we went back to where we came from. The chief saw me and asked who I was. I said auxiliary fireman, Jersey City. He said thanks for helping. I left and went to the diner. I loved the fall and Irene and I went up to the Catskills several times to see Grandma Gorden and of course, the foliage. Thanksgiving came and we had dinner at my house with Uncle Walter, Aunt Dolores, their kids, Aunt Lil, Uncle Bernie, and Irene.

CHAPTER–SEVEN
The Navy

Chapter–Seven - The Navy

I had been thinking about the Navy. Lately things were kicking up in Vietnam and Cambodia. Uncle Walter was in the Navy during World War II and I always had an interest in the Navy rather than the Army or the Air Force. That week before my 18th birthday I went to the navy recruiter. After spending an hour there he gave me a bunch of booklets to take and read. I had one booklet that spoke about the Navy Reserve. It explained that you spend time once a month at the reserve center, two weeks a year on active duty, then after graduation from high school two years of active duty and another year of reserve. I thought this was great. After school the next day I went down to Essex Street in Jersey City to the reserve center. I was taken on a tour and had a great time. I then decided to join. I had to have dad's signature since I was not 18 years of age. I filled out all the necessary papers and made arrangements for the physical. When I went home I told mom and dad. Yes, you guessed it. Mom said I was crazy and needed my head examined. Dad just said, "Are you sure you want to do this?" I said yes while mom was still yelling. Maybe I should explain about mom. She was a good person always doing things for people, always had company and was a great cook. She was from the old school for example I had to have a spoon of cod liver oil every morning with my oatmeal. I always had to wear a hat in the winter so I didn't catch cold. That as well as sneakers. I was not allowed to wear them to school. I remember one time when I was about nine or ten years old I was in the bath tub and she came in. For some reason I had an erection and she said, "Don't you touch yourself or you will go blind." I laugh about those things to this day. Anyway, back to the Navy. I passed the physical and on May 16, 1958 I was sworn in with dad at my side. I didn't want mom to come because she would want to tell the commander all about her "Peter". Within a few weeks I was measured for all my uniforms and had gotten all my shots. Once a month from then on I went to drill and it was great. I wanted to be a fireman and corpsman so that was what I would study along with the usual training.

Summer 1958

Summer of 1958 I worked at the diner and dad was outside smoking in the phone booth. When he came out he said his brother George died and we were going to the funeral on Saturday. On July 1st I had my final U.S. Navy Drill and went to active duty for fourteen days at the Great Lakes Naval Training Center in Chicago, Ill. My first flight was on a TWA constellation. I was very spirited. I landed at O'Hare field and then took a train to Waukegan, IL to the base. After check in I was assigned to my barracks called Camp Dewey. My company commander was called Demko. We would march every morning on the grinder as well as calisthenics then go to class all day. I loved the damage control training and medical classes. Everything was very military like. One thing I didn't like was the bathrooms. There were 25 toilets on one side and 25 toilets on the other side all facing each other making the usual noises, etc. Another funny thing was the sinks. They were long troughs which water ran through. About 10 men each would stand there brushing their teeth and spitting into the troth. I was always the first one but the others had to watch everyone else's spit go by. My first weekend leave was Saturday and Sunday. I took the train to Chicago on Saturday morning with the other guys. We walked around and stopped at several bars. About 6pm we were all a little drunk and we stopped at a tattoo parlor. The two guys with me decided to get a tattoo so in we went. I didn't want one so I watched. Both had an anchor on their forearm with their name above. A few more sailors came in at that time and they all started to tease me and call me chicken. I finally gave in and had the same thing on my forearm only below the anchor I had "Irene" put there. After I left I knew I would have to hide it from mom and dad. The three of us then went to another bar. The object was for all of us to get laid. I met one girl and we started to talk. I was half drunk then and she said she wanted $20.00 to go to bed with me. I agreed and we left the bar and walked about two blocks to a small hotel. She took me up to a room and we went in. She seemed nice enough and we talked a little. Then she took off her blouse and bra. She walked around the room and poured two glasses of whisky. She gave me one and she drank from hers and we toasted. She started to take my uniform off after lying me down on the bed. That's all I remembered. I woke up at 4am with the worst headache I have ever had. She was gone of course, and so was my last $50.00 or so dollars I had. She did leave me $2.00 on the dresser. I got up, threw up, washed my face and left. I remembered the three guys were going to stay at the Savoy Hotel that Saturday night so I went there, and located our room. I banged on the door because I had no key. The other guys opened the door and I told them what happened. They wanted to sleep another hour or so, so I lay on a small couch in the room. I still remember the smell of mildew and that damp musty odor. I went in the bathroom and it was dirty. The grout in the ½ inch floor tile was black and the edges of the tub were green with fungus. I went down to the front of the hotel after I cleaned up a little and oh….I forgot about the toilet paper…you pulled on the paper and got a single 4 inch sheet. You needed about 20 sheets to wipe yourself. Anyway, I went down and they didn't even have a cup of coffee. I went next door to a small restaurant and had a 15 cent muffin and 10 cent coffee. When the guys came down later we had more coffee, then walked around State Street. I wasn't feeling good so I headed for the train station at 10am. The other guys gave me $5.00 so that I could get back to the base. On the way to the station I saw smoke coming from the basement of a store which was below an apartment house. I ran to the corner and pulled the alarm box then returned and started to bang in all the doors on all two floors. When the firemen arrived I told them it was I who pulled the box. They had already found the fire in some trash which was burning below a grate on the sidewalk. The captain thanked me and I headed back to the base. When I got off the train I walked to the base entrance which was guarded by the marines. I showed my ID and he said, roll up your sleeves. When I did he saw the bandage and said did you get a tattoo? I said yes, and he said wait here. He went in his booth with my ID and came out and returned the ID along with a yellow slip. He said I had to go to the Captain Mast on Monday because I destroyed government property by getting this tattoo. When I got to my barracks I found out I wasn't the only one. I was scared shit as they say and couldn't sleep all night. After role call I showed the slip to my commanding officer Demko who sent me to the captain's office. There were six other guys and we were all sitting on a long bench after handing our slips to the woman sitting at the desk. One by one we were called in to the captain. I saluted and said Peter Vallas 494-38-05 reporting as ordered sir. He said sit down. As I sat down I noticed his name was Pappas. He asked me questions about my family and of course, I told him about dad and the diner. Actually we had a great conversation. Then he said I would have to clean the bathrooms at the barracks for two mornings. That is 50 toilets. I saluted and left. After I cleaned them on Tuesday I lined up on the grinder for morning assignments. My company commander Demko called me front center. He handed me a slip to report to Lt. J.G. Pappas. I left wondering what I did now. I walked into the office which had about eight men waiting. The desk officer recognized me and I was called in next. I saluted at Pappas and sat down. He could see I was nervous and said I wonder if you could do me a favor. I said yes what is it? He was having some guests on Friday evening and wanted me to make Greek appetizers if I could. In our conversation two days before I had told him I could cook. I said yes and he took me to the officer's galley and introduced me to the head cook who was a Chief Petty Officer. He told him to get anything I wanted and gave me free range of the galley. I was relieved of all other duties. I had to prepare for twelve people. It was to be a cocktail party at his quarters. A frantic call to mom was made on the base phone and I got all the recipes I needed. Then I gave a list to a seaman who drove to Chicago to get the supplies. I looked up a Greek Mediterranean Store in the phone book and they got the order ready to be picked up. Lt. Pappas gave me a credit card number, government classified to use. When the order arrived I was surprised everything was there. With some help in the galley I made two trays of spinach pie "SPANAKOPETA", 100 stuffed grapevine leaves "DOLMADES", and a tray of cheese pie "TIROPETES", 50 Greek meatballs "Keftedes", 2 pounds of cucumber spread "SATZIKI", and two pounds of feta cheese. I worked all day and everything was great. Lt. Pappas stopped in and was impressed. I told him he should have ordered retsina wine and he said good idea Peter and sent someone to Chicago to get six bottles of retsina wines from Greece. The next day I went to Lt. Pappas' quarters and set up two tables in an "L" shape He had supplied all the dishes, Silverware, trays, etc. I set up the tables and planned to be back at 6pm because the guests were coming at 7pm. I was enjoying all this and hoped his party would be great. Well, as it goes, the party was great and I met all the big shots. I didn't have to clean up because he had two other sailors do it. He also gave me a weekend pass and I was happy. Saturday morning I had just enough money to take the train to Chicago and back. I walked around State Street and noticed a restaurant on the side street so I went in to get a coffee. It was a Greek place so I spoke with the boss and he was very nice. I was drinking my coffee and he asked if I wanted anything to eat and I knew I didn't have money so I said no. He looked at me and said, your father is in the same business and you are Greek and serving the country so please have breakfast on me. I had a feta omelet and toast and I thanked him very much. I returned to the base and went to bed. Sunday I spent hanging around and got ready for graduation. The next few days we practiced marching and got ready for the formal exercise. Graduation day went well and we returned to the barracks to pack. I had my ticket for the train and flight which was government issued. Next morning I left after all the good byes. That afternoon mom, dad, Linda and Irene met me when I arrived. Well, now that I was back home I got back into my routine at the diner. I spent the summer working at the diner, seeing Irene and visiting Uncle Walter and Aunt Dolores. I also used to take Aunt Mary grocery shopping. None of my aunts ever drove a car, so I would take them to the stores. I even worked as a helper when any of the Acme Market truck drivers needed me. They all ate at the diner and if they were short on weekends I would drive with them and unload the orders at the stores. Walter Keller and Jack Webb were two of the drivers who I worked for. They all knew dad for years. The other trucking companies that were customers for years were St. Johnsbury, Roadway, Coastal, and many others from there.

When I was not working for the trucking company I was working with dad at the diner. Dad's diner in South Kearny was across from Western Electric and we had many customers. One night we both left the diner together to go home. I was following dad on Tonelle Avenue when he stopped short. I didn't see him stop and I ran into him. The old Chrysler had no damage but the front of my 1954 Plymouth was crushed. There was a Hudson County cop in his car right there and he came over and saw dad. He said to my father, "Don't worry Pete I will take care of this guy." Dad said that guy is my son. Well, the cop laughed and said this is a first for me. They towed the car and I drove home with dad. We told mom what happened and she said you shouldn't have a car anyway. I had to wait three weeks to get my car back so it was back on the busses.

Fall 1958 Senior Year High School

Fall of 1958 school began and I was working on the cover of a book for my art class. I always loved painting oils in particular. My studio was at Aunt Mary's house in the room at the top. I did many paintings and sold them at art shows. I was getting involved in many projects this year at school. Irene never liked school and when she became 16 she quit. Life was not easy for her. Her father was in the Army and died in September, 1942. He fell off a train when he was returning from leave with a bunch of buddies. Irene's mom Kay told me they said they were all drinking on the train when this happened. Kay never worked but received a check from the government. They lived in a project called the Marion Gardens. It was a low end apartment complex. They rented one room to a woman called Edie. Her cousin, Arthur lived there too. At age sixteen he was an alcoholic and never worked. Kay's sister, Helen lived there also and sometimes, Cousin Bobby Ebersole. Everyone drank and there were many fights. I kept Irene out of the house most of the time, because she had to put up with a lot. I think everyone lived off Kay's checks. Between the cigarettes and booze there wasn't much left for other things.

A strange thing happened to me during this period of time. A friend of dad's told dad a guy by the name of Ted Gaynor owned a drugstore and he needed a part-time person for three days a week from 4pm to 7pm and maybe on Sundays also. So between the diner and the drugstore, I worked both jobs. There was one kid working there I didn't like. He was always hanging around the register and never liked stocking shelves. One morning I went in before opening and Irene and I were going to a wedding so I wanted a new $20.00 bill. I opened my register and found two new twenties so I took them out and put my two old ones in. The store was getting ready to open and Mr. Gaynor kept the door locked. He called us to his counter. He said over the past two weeks he was missing $150.00 dollars. He asked the guys to empty our pockets and the girls, two employees to empty their pocket books. He went from one to the other checking twenty dollar bills. When he came to me he checked the twenties and said my two twenties were the ones missing from the register. I told him the truth and he said the register was missing $40.00. He called the police and they arrested me, handcuffed me and took me to the police station. Dad was called and during that time the police questioned me and I told them what I did. No one believed me. Dad bailed me out for $50.00 and I went home. We called Lou Sorrentino; Aunt Dolores's bother who was an attorney. We met with him and he said he would look into it. A few days later dad said Mr. Gaynor would drop the charges if I admitted it and paid him $500.00. Lou said it would be the best thing to do. We paid the money after I admitted it and the charges were dropped. This is not right and I was very upset about it. I did pay dad back the $500.00 over time. Mom of course, said you should stick to working for your father. Irene's other cousin Dolores was married to Lou Hazel who was from Czechoslovakia. He had a small restaurant on Bergen Avenue. Dad met Lou several times and if a trucker came by the diner selling meats or on one occasion meat slicers, dad called Lou and if Lou wanted anything he would buy things for him, too. I was at work to help dad that week everyday. His partner John Sophanis went to Pittsburg for a week's vacation to visit a relative. John was so cheap he rode there with one of the truck drivers. John had the same furniture since he came to America in 1912. He and his wife Irene had a boy named Steve who got sick about three years ago with tuberculosis. John and Irene took care of him but stayed away from the doctor. Steve died at 17 years of age.

I was now 18 years old and was running as Chief of the Jersey City Civil Defense Corp which responded to all the large fires. One of the men at the Gong Club, an organization made up of retired firemen, went to all two alarm fires and up to serve refreshments to the firemen, would call me whenever they were called out. My love for the fire department continued on and I had to wait until I finished with the Navy active duty to pursue a career as a fireman.

Winter 1958

December 5 was my birthday and mom was having a party for me at the house. Some of her Greek ladies and dad's friends were expected. That day I left the diner at 5:30pm and was going to pick up Irene. I was driving down Dales Avenue and something happened to the gas pedal and I lost control and hit a car pretty hard. I was thrown on the floor and my back hit the heater. The ambulance came and someone recognized me and ran to Irene's house to get her. I arrived at the Jersey City Medical Center and after x-rays; the doctor said I was okay except for the muscles in my back that were badly bruised. Someone had called dad and he came to the hospital. Mom stayed home with the company. I was released after I was put in a back brace and dad took me home. Everyone was waiting and I opened my gifts. The next morning I could not move. Mom called Dr. Rosenberg's son who was a back specialist. He immediately had me admitted to the Long Island College Hospital in Brooklyn. After a week of physical therapy and a brace I went home.

Halloween 1958

It was around Halloween on a Friday and I had just come home from the diner about 9:30pm. Betty Korinis was in the kitchen talking to mom. Dad was asleep and so was my sister, Linda who was now 12 years old. I went to my room but overheard mom telling Betty when she was in the Shop Rite food market today, she was pushing her carriage and the clerk stopped her and said, "Excuse me ma'am but are you going to buy all those oranges?" Mom looked at the carriage and everyone laughed because she was pushing a cart half full of oranges that the produce man was putting on the display. She had not looked and was pushing his cart. I got the bright idea to fool mom. That Sunday mom was having Uncle Walter and Aunt Dolores for dinner and I was going to be there with Irene, too. So Saturday about 10am I called mom from

the diner and I disguised my voice and said, "Is this Mrs. Sophia Vallas?" She said yes it is. I proceeded to tell her she was caught on tape at the Shop Rite yesterday and filmed by Candid Camera. I said we would like to have permission to air it on TV tomorrow at 8pm. Mom got all excited and said yes. When I came home that afternoon mom had already called half the family and she told me about the call. I could hardly keep my composure. What I didn't realize was she would call half the world up including all her Greek friends. Now I started to feel bad. I drove down to Irene's and she said I should tell her the truth. When I went home that night I stopped at Aunt Mary's and called mom. I said I was from Candid camera and the film strip wasn't going to be shown. Mom was disappointed but a lot of laughs came out of it. Several weeks later I told her the truth.

Christmas 1958

Christmas was two weeks later and I was doing my Christmas shopping at Journal Square. I heard the fire truck and saw lots of smoke coming from Newark Avenue. I went to my car and drove to the area where a large tenement was burning. I parked and put my gear on and worked the fire for about an hour. When I went back to my car I found the shopping bag with the presents gone. I forgot to lock the back door. Cars in those days had individual locks and I left one open. When I went home I got the usual, "you smell of smoke, get those clothes off." I decided to have Christmas dinner at Kay's house, Irene's mother's house. They had moved to Clinton Avenue in Jersey City; a better area, and with Edie and Bobby. Helen and Arthur were still with them, too. It was a basement apartment but it was better than before. When I arrived about 12 noon, Arthur and Bobby said they were taking me to our local bar for a Christmas drink. I went with them even though I wasn't old enough to drink. All I remember was they kept buying me shots and beer. I also remember crawling on the floor of the bar. They picked me up and walked me back to Irene's. They stood me against the door, knocked on the door and they both left. Kay opened the door and I fell in. I was drunk and Irene was so angry with them. She gave me food and I was dizzy. She put me on the couch and after an hour I was so sick. I kept throwing up. Finally Irene had to call my mother and told her I would stay there that night because I was sick. The next day I was a mess. I finally went home and it took two days before I returned to normal. Mom wasn't happy because she knew I must have been drunk, and after her lecture I went to bed. Dad never said much; he was such an easy going guy. New Year's

Eve I went to Aunt Catherine's house. I loved being there on New Years. My Uncle Paul always smoked and gave me a drink of wine. My Cousin Doris' husband Willie was a great guy; we always had a lot of fun. Willie would make homemade wine every year and I always helped him. Behind Aunt Catherine's house was a large shed where we made the wine. Willie and Doris lived above Aunt Catherine's who owned the house.

January 1959

January was a cold month and I was in my last year of high school. This was the best time because I was a senior now and I couldn't wait to graduation in June. I spent a lot of time at the fire house and I was hoping to take the test after graduation even though I was going away for my two year's active duty. The good part was once I got on the list they had to keep me until I returned home because I was in the service. Since Irene had quit school we spent a lot of time together and we were getting ready for the senior prom. I had made reservations at the Hawaiian Room in New York City. At least in New York we could drink. I was working on the yearbook which I was the "class clown". I was known for all my jokes and tricks. One time when we returned after summer vacation, I went to my new home room class and when the teacher passed around the sign in sheet, I added the name Dick Hurtz to the list. When she got the sheet back she called everyone's name, and we stood up one at a time. When she got to Dick Hurtz she didn't see anyone stand so she said, "Who's Dick Hurtz?" and everyone started to laugh. She was a bit embarrassed. I had passes for every excuse you could think of. I never really was a great student. I always worked after school and got home after 8pm most of the time, so I had little time to study. Well, prom time came and the Hawaiian Room was also great.

I had been thinking of a new car since the accident and for some time and had wanted a 1957 Chevy. I finally bought 1956 Mercury. It was a hot car and the best deal I could make. It was a two door with a hard green top. I loved it and so did everyone else. The 50s were wonderful; the music was great with Elvis, the Five Satins, the Platters, etc. I still had to have dad sign and always paid him for the insurance and half the car payments every week. He would still put the money rolled in a rubber band in his pocket. I had been smoking a little then, Winston's 25 cents a pack and funny, gas was about 25 cents a gallon. As I am writing this book gas is now $2.55 a gallon and rising (2006). I was still having problems with my back and I kept wearing the brace. While on my next drill I made arrangements to go on active duty after the summer. I wanted July and August off to prepare. I was at Mount Carmel Church one evening at the canteen with Irene and I met one of her girlfriends who lived on Corbin Avenue. Her name was Susie. We talked a little and she said she would like to meet sometime alone. She was very pretty and had a great body. She gave me her number which I quickly put in my pocket. The next day I called her and we set a date after school to meet which was a drive-up, called the Flaming Hamburger with service at the car window. We had shakes and a hamburger and she said she always liked me but because I was going steady with Irene she didn't try to get close to me. Now because I was graduating she just wanted me to know. Before I took her home we stopped at West Side Park and one thing led to another and we were kissing and did quite a bit of petting. I took her home and after a few days decided I really was in love with Irene so I called her and said I didn't want to get involved. She said she understood and that was that.

Summer 1959 - High School Graduation

Graduation was June 24, 1959 and mom arranged for a party at the house. I really didn't' want a party I wanted to go to other parties which I was invited to, but I was not really a drinker and there was always accidents on graduation nights so I didn't feel bad. At the party I had told everyone I was taking the summer off then going away in the Navy. After opening gifts my last gift was from mom and dad. Dad handled me a brown paper bag and said, because you met your responsibilities and worked hard this is your reward. I opened the bag and in it was all the rubber banded money I gave dad over the years for my car and insurance. Just think every week when I gave him the money he just put it in this bag. There was a total of $4,075.00 after spending one hour to count it. I just couldn't believe what he did. July and August I worked at the diner and took a few trips to the mountains with Irene. I received my orders from the Navy around August 15th. I was to report to the Headquarters of the Commandant Third Naval District, 90 Church Street, New York City, NY. After my physical in NYC at Naval Headquarters on September 30th, 1959, I reported to the Navy in uniform with all my gear. The night before mom had company and everyone said good bye. When I arrived in NYC I was in the medical unit and they were examining me. When they checked my back they were concerned. They contacted Dr. Rosenberg and about four hours later a Navy specialist came in with x-rays that Dr. Rosenberg provided. He must have sent them over right away. After another two hours they cancelled my active duty status and sent me home. I was embarrassed to go home but I had no choice. Several weeks later I was notified that I was to continue as a reservist to help train others going on to active duty. When I received notice I went to the next reserve meeting and spoke to C. Locher, SMC, VSNR-R. I did not want to be discharged so he said I could serve my four years in the reserve. With that over I bought a new 1960 Chevy, candy apple red, two-door. It was beautiful. Now I had to begin to check when I could take the fire department test. After a few weeks I checked with Dr. Rosenberg and he said maybe in a year I could pass the physical. I was disappointed so I decided I would get a job.

CHAPTER–EIGHT
Central Technical Institute

Chapter–Eight – Central Technical Institute

Fall 1959

I found out about Central Technical Institute in Hartford, CT. They had an airline training division. I called and they sent someone to the house to explain everything. Mom and dad were there. Dad was going to pay for it since I didn't want to go to college. The program sounded great. It was a four month course and they would place me with an airline at graduation. I could be a station agent in departments such as ticket or reservations, cargo or many other positions offered. The best part of a job like this was the free travel. I signed up and dad and mom drove to Hartford, CT. I rented a room in a house which was a three-story house owned by Ms. Daniels. She lived there also. It was a nice room but the bathroom was in the hall used by three of us who had a room on the top floor. No girls were allowed in the house and no animals. Everyone who rented a room was either a college student, airline student, or going to some other school. On the first floor there was a large living room with a fireplace. Everything was very Early American and cozy. I planned to move in on October 1, 1959. I could go home on weekends if I didn't have to study for a test. The drive was about three hours. The day arrived and I drove to Hartford and checked in. After I unpacked I took a walk down the block where there was a small luncheonette and store. This is where I would have breakfast and dinner. When I came back to the house I met a guy by the name of Joe Bustin from Pawtucket, R.I. He was going to the University of Hartford and we became best friends. My school was in downtown Hartford about one mile from the house. I took the bus back and forth every day because it was easier than to try and park. The first week was busy meeting other students which was mostly girls. I loved it and felt very comfortable. During the first week I went to the Fire Headquarters and was taken on a tour. This was a great fire department. They were one of the first cities which controlled the traffic lights so the fire department could respond without stopping. The captain was a great guy and we spent about an hour together. I should mention that during the next few months I went to several fires when I saw them. At night Joe and I would be together and would eat mom's Greek cookies which I had a good supply of. When I would go home for the weekend mom would always give me more. It was cold in October and my room was next to the fire escape which went from the third floor to the ground. It was more like a staircase going down to each level. I would store soda, milk, cheese, etc. because we didn't have a refrigerator. I had a small coffee pot in the room also. The fall was beautiful and I became friendly with a couple of the girls in class. One in particular was Ellen from Oswego, NY. Everyone lived in the same general area as I did. Most of these homes were rented to students. Ellen and I shared study information and once in a while went to the movies. There was a lot of studying and memorizing the city airport codes such as EWR for Newark Airport, etc. Actually I liked the school and the studying.

November came and I knew we had three days for Thanksgiving so I didn't go home until then. I was still the class clown and Joe and I had many laughs. I think I drove Ms. Daniels a bit crazy. I called mom twice a week and she wanted to know why I didn't come home every weekend. I told her I had to study a lot. I did the same with Irene also. It wasn't an easy course. We had meteorology, ticketing, reservations, how to load the planes, weights, mail, freight, and safety. The girls who were going to be stewardesses had some different courses. The only problem I had was I would run out of money each week. I had to ask mom to send me a check for $20.00 once in a while. One weekend Joe had gone home and I took Ellen on Saturday morning for a drive to New Hampshire. It was a beautiful day and the foliage was so outstanding. The colors of the trees and the falling leaves were a sight to see. We stopped at a small restaurant near a farm to get lunch. It was cold and there was a slight breeze. The place was an old wooden building, from the early 1900s. There was even a hitching post outside with an old wood plank walkway. Inside it was warm and cozy and we stayed near the fireplace. We ordered hot chocolate and a sandwich and soup. The waitress was the daughter of the owner and was very pleasant. We talked a lot since it wasn't a very busy place. We both had a cigarette and when I paid the bill she said if we wanted we could go up the dirt road next to the restaurant about a mile and see the countryside and their farm. We thanked her and did just that. As we drove up the road there were several cows and horses roaming on the hillside. As we turned around a curve, there was the old farmhouse and a large barn nearby. We went over a small wooden bridge over a creek and continued past the house. On one side a small cornfield behind it was appropriate for this time of year. We stopped near the barn and walked near the creek. The scenery in the background and the sounds of the water trickling around the rocks was like a beautiful painting. It made me realize how beautiful America is. Ellen and I sat on a log and held hands for a while observing the beautiful scene. We began to get cold so we got up and she kissed me and said thanks for such a beautiful day. We left the farm and drove about an hour more. We stopped at an antique barn and I bought an old milk bottle. I collected bottles and this one was only 50 cents. On the way back we stopped at the same restaurant for hot chocolate again and thanked the waitress for letting us see the farm. When we arrived back in Hartford early evening I dropped her off at her dormitory. We began to kiss and soon the windows were all fogged up. This also became one of the best petting sessions I had to date. Ellen finally went in and I returned to my room. I drove home for Thanksgiving weekend and Irene and I had dinner at mom's. Uncle Walter, Aunt Dolores were there also. Dinner was great as usual and I had plenty of leftovers to take back to school.

The next day I drove back and Joe arrived also. We spoke about our holiday and he spoke about his girlfriend Marcia. I told Joe I was probably going to get engaged when I finished school and got a job. I still wanted the fire department but I was concerned about my back being discovered and then I would be turned down. This week was again very busy at school. I had two tests and I did study hard. I would be up at 4am making coffee, and of course had my cookies while I studied. I always all my life got up early usually about 5am. In two weeks I would become 20 years old. Joe and two other guys and I decided to do something this coming weekend so Joe and the other guys and I decided to go to Albany, NY to Green Street. There was a place called the Jazz Corner of the World. Saturday afternoon we left and drove to Albany. It was very cold that day but we had a good trip. We arrived about 3:30pm and went to the bar on Green Street. A Jazz band was playing and we all ordered drinks. I saw something I had never seen before. All of the liquor bottles were in a rack upside down. The bartender held the glass under it, pushed up and the exact amount of liquor came out. There was a great Jazz band playing with four black men and one white man. They were fantastic. The crowd was mixed; some white, some black and everyone was having a great time. I didn't drink much because I had to drive back. We planned to leave about 8pm to return but that didn't happen. We were all talking to different people.

One of the black girls told us when we go outside later there is a brick apartment house across the street. If you whistle you will see a couple of shades go up and a girl would be in the window waving. If you wanted her you could go in the building and she would come down and get you. The cost was $20.00. We all started to laugh but she wasn't kidding. Finally after 10pm we decided to leave. When outside one of the guys whistled and sure enough shades went up. We waved at all of them then went to the car. On the trip back everyone was falling asleep and I was having trouble keeping my eyes open, so I yelled for everyone to start singing. We opened the windows every few minutes to let the cold in so we wouldn't fall asleep. We sang all the way back to Connecticut arriving at 2am. There were some snow flurries which slowed us down some. I was in bed by 2:30am and it was a good thing we didn't have to go to school that day. I awoke at 9am anyway and made coffee and had my Greek cookies. I went downstairs and sat in the living room by the fire to study. Ms. Daniels came over and said you and Joe got in late this morning. She always knew everything. I think she sat up every night. I met Joe later and we went to the luncheonette that afternoon. I met Ellen and another girl who was going to become a nun last year then she quit. Men weren't allowed in their dorm either so we always had to meet outside or in a restaurant.

That night Joe, a few others, and I were in the living room talking and in came this puny looking guy about 90 pounds and looked like an absent minded professor. He lived in the room next to me and whenever I saw him he would just nod. I thought he was a little weird. He came over to Ms. Daniels and said something to her then went back upstairs. Ms. Daniels came over to Joe and I and said Ben had complained he heard you come in at 2:39 am when you opened the door to your room. All the doors squeaked in that house so it was no wonder Ms. Daniels knew what time we came in. The next day at school Ellen and her girlfriend told me I was invited to a party next Friday night at another girl's house. I decided to go so I figured I would go home Saturday morning. Well, that didn't happen. Joe was going home Saturday also. I went to the party and met Carol from Vermont. I did see her in school a few times but we never spoke to one another. We hit it off and she was beautiful; blonde hair down to her shoulders, blue eyes, and a great figure. Ellen was not there because she had to go back to Oswego because her mother was ill. Carol lived in the dorm also. After a few beers I asked Carol if she wanted to take a drive and she said she would love to. The party was a bit of a bore anyway. There were a couple of guys that were getting drunk and loud. One guy was I believe from South Carolina. His name was Dell Shafer and another guy was Brad something. We both left around 11:30pm and drove around town and parked. We began to make out and to my surprise I had no trouble petting and even opened her pants. I told her we could go to my room but I had to take her up the fire escape. She said ok so I went in the house up to my room, and opened the door very quietly. Then I went in the hall and opened the fire escape door where she was waiting. I had showed her where to go and she was there. I sneaked her in my room quietly and we sat on the bed. We began to kiss then we undressed and got under the covers. She said she was still a virgin so we had great oral sex and then we did it again. After two hours I had to slip out with her down the fire stairs and drove her to the dorm. I went back and went to bed. I got up at 9:30am and drove home to N.J. I spent the weekend home, saw Irene for a few hours on Sunday, then drove back. The trip back was long because it was snowing and the Merritt Parkway was very slippery. Next week I would go home because it was my birthday. I saw Ellen in school and she gave me the cold shoulder. I guess she found out I was with Carol. You know how girls talk so she must have heard something. Dell saw me that day and asked me why I left the party last week. He wanted to introduce me to a girl named Carol from Vermont who expressed an interest in me. I didn't tell him I left with her. He said there was going to be a Christmas party in two weeks at the school. Just before Christmas vacation. This week I had a lot of studying so I didn't go out much. I saw Joe every day when he came from school and we ate together. I left for home and got in at 9pm. The next day mom had family and friends over for my birthday. Mom loved to entertain and I got a kick out of my sister, Linda, following her around the kitchen. She was now 14 and I said to mom, "Teach her everything so she can cook and bake just like you". It was a nice evening and after everyone left I had a long talk with dad about the future. The next day I packed all my goodies and went back to school.

The next two weeks would be rough. I had three exams to look forward to. I saw Joe and we talked about the girls and I told him I was still thinking of getting engaged to Irene.

That week in school I saw Carol and she said she and two other girls were planning to go to NYC next weekend by bus and stay overnight. I offered to drive them down on Saturday morning and drop them off at Times Square. Then on Sunday morning they would take a bus from NY to North Bergen to my house. They loved the idea, so I called mom and asked if I could have them for early afternoon dinner at our house. Mom said it was okay. Saturday I dropped them off at Times Square, and went home. I told them which bus to take from the Port Authority terminal to North Bergen and I would meet them. Sunday, Carol called when they got to the bus stop and I went to pick them up. They had a great time in NYC. Mom and dad put out the super meal as usual and the girls couldn't get over it. We all left with baklava and Greek cookies about 5pm to go back. The next day I saw Ellen and she wanted to get together and she asked me if I was going to the party Friday. It was going to be from 3pm to 6pm at the school. I said yes but I was leaving the same night to go home for the holiday. She met me after school at the pizza place down the block and we had early dinner. She said she had a six pack of Schafer Beer in her trunk so we got in her car and drove to park uptown. I drank two beers and she drank three. We kissed and made out for about an hour then left. I got home and studied about two hours over coffee and cookies then fell asleep.

Friday morning came and I took my laundry and things to the car so I could leave right from the school. After 2:30 pm the party started and I saw Carol. She invited me to Vermont but I couldn't go. I told her I would see her after Christmas. I ran into Dell and he asked if I wanted to share an apartment with him and another guy named Bill. He said we could have our own rooms and girls and booze. It sounded great so I told him I would think about it. There was plenty of food, soda, punch, eggnog but no booze. Dell had hidden a bottle of rum and was spiking all the drinks. I had to drive so I refused the drinks. All of a sudden there was a fight between Dell and someone else and a glass door got broken. I don't like trouble so I left the party at 5pm and met Carol downstairs and we went to her car. We made out until both of us were satisfied and we left to go to our respective homes. On the way home on the Merritt Parkway I started to fall asleep. I opened the window but after I closed it I guess I fell asleep. All I remember was a noise and looked out and saw that I was heading for the ditch on my right. I hit the brakes and skidded into the grass in a 45 degree angle. I saw another car pull over which was the one I side swiped. I got out and climbed the embankment and we both spoke. I told him I must have fallen asleep. The damage didn't look like much; just a double scrape on both our cars. Just then a State Trooper pulled over and put his lights on (one red light on top, not like today). He walked over and I told him it was my fault. He smelled my breath and said well you are not drunk at least. He checked our licenses and I told the driver I would call him at home tomorrow. He was a nice guy; a student also. We exchanged information and the trooper let him go. He then called a tow truck to pull me up the incline. I was freezing so we sat in his car to wait. I expected a ticket and asked him how much would the fine be. He said because you were honest and didn't blame the other guy; he was not going to give me a ticket. After I got pulled out I gave the driver the only $15.00 I had. He wanted $20.00 but I told him I would send it to him. He refused at first and was going to keep my car until the trooper told him, "This guy is honest and will send it otherwise call him if I don't." I finally got home and didn't say anything that night. The next morning dad was home and I told him the story. Mom's remark was the usual, "You see Pete he shouldn't have a car." Dad called the other fellow's house and spoke to his father. They agreed to see what his damage was and dad said I would send a check. He called back and he said it would cost $250.00. Dad said the check is on the way. My damage turned out to be a little less. We never had to tell the insurance company but I had to pay it all. I also sent the truck driver his $5.00. Would you believe I got a Christmas card from both of them? Because Christmas was near and there were sales I decided to look for an engagement ring. I went to a jewelry store around the corner on Bergenline Avenue because Dino knew the owner. I found one with a nice diamond and put a deposit on it. I gave him her size which I knew because I had given her a friendship ring before. I split the Christmas holidays going to everyone's house each night. New Year's Eve Irene and I went to Aunt Catherine's early then to her house. The next day it was back to school in the afternoon. Monday I saw Dell and saw the apartment that evening. I liked it and it would cost the same as Ms. Daniel's. When I told her she called mom and that Saturday without telling me dad, mom, and Irene showed up at Ms. Daniels. I was pissed and after a long conversation I gave in and I stayed, mainly because dad said I would have to pay everything if I left.

We all went to the diner including Joe. Then they went home. Actually I had saved about $3,000.00 and still could have done it but I decided not to. This trip I took $200.00 in cash with me. We didn't have ATMs then, so we would have to cash a check instead. It was a very hard week at school and I only had a month and a half left to graduation. Carol didn't come back from Vermont until Tuesday. You could miss only three days during the class. I never missed one day. I passed my two tests that week and my grades were in the 90s. I felt pretty good because I never had a test score lower than 90. In January, those who would graduate their advisor would start contacting the airlines. This school did the placement in each person's area. Mine would be Newark, La Guardia, or Idlewild, now known as Kennedy Airport. I was quite excited about this. I was hoping for TWA. Carol came back Wednesday and I met her after school. We drove to the Pizza Place and talked until we had to leave. We had pizza and soda that cost $2.50. Can you imagine? She thought I was taking the apartment and was disappointed when she found out I wasn't. I figured it out; she thought she could stay with me in my room and she could get out of the dorm. She had a great body and face so I certainly wouldn't have minded, but then again I still liked being alone. She said she wasn't driving home this coming weekend so I said we would get together. Thursday I had another test and a 4pm interview with my advisor. I went back to my room and I saw Joe. I told him we should go out tonight and get a bottle of scotch. I drove to a liquor store and wasn't asked for ID so I bought three bottles; one scotch, one vodka, and one rye. Joe and I went back to the house and we brought some ice and snacks. Well, Joe got drunk and I was trying to get him to his room but he was loud and laughing. I was silly also and he went down the stairs singing. Guess who came out in the hall? It was Ms. Daniels who was mad, but I could see she was getting a kick out of Joe. I put him to bed and the next day we got our scolding.

Lunchtime I saw Carol and she said let's go to Rutland, VT and stay over Saturday night then come back Sunday. We would split the cost. I said, "Great idea". That night after school she said she made a reservation at the small lodge she knew about. We left at 6am Saturday morning for Rutland. We stopped for coffee and had a beautiful drive arriving at about 10am. We checked in as Mr. and Mrs. Vallas with no problem. It was a great place. We had lunch and walked around. Neither of us wanted to ski so we went on a two hour hike in the woods next to the slopes. It was so beautiful. We rented snow shoes and that in itself was an experience. We walked through the pine trees and forest following the tree markers so we wouldn't get lost. We came back to the lodge about 3pm and changed. We then went to the main lodge and sat by the fireplace. It was warm and there were only a few people around. We drank two drinks each. Then it started to get crowded and loud. I never liked crowds so we decided to eat dinner. We ate dinner about 6:30pm and after we had some brandy at the lounge. We went back to the room and I don't have to tell you that we made love and fell asleep. At 5am I couldn't help it and I rolled her over and we went at it again. We fell asleep again awaking at 9:00am. After breakfast we checked out and drove back to school. It was a night to remember! On the way back she told me she was getting engaged in June to a real nice guy and this was her last fling. I told her the same. What I didn't tell her was I never had a fling. The next week I studied hard because it involved memorizing data and I was nervous about the next test. Joe was also studying and I really liked him. He had a typical Massachusetts accent but lived in Rhode Island. He was also a sincere, honest good guy.

The weekend was coming up and I was going home because I wanted to pick up the ring. I drove home Saturday morning and I picked up the ring. I brought it home and then mom told me we had an invitation to my Cousin Donald's wedding on Valentine's Day. Irene and I were invited so I thought what a good time to get engaged. So I called Donald and told him and everything was set. When I went back to school I found out Carol got the job with Eastern Airlines and had left that week. I never saw her again. I had four weeks to go and I decided to see Ellen again. She was a typical upstate NY girl. I liked her but she was a bit stiff. Joe and I were really getting into our future and one day I saw Ellen after school. I said pretty soon we will graduate and then off to another adventure. She said let's keep in touch and I said, "I don't think so. I am getting engaged in February and my future is spoken for". She said she understood and that was that. The last week of January 1960 I was studying hard and looking forward to graduation. I saw fire trucks going toward my area so I followed behind them. I saw the sky lit up and lots of smoke. It was a large house on the next street from mine. I was chased away by a cop. I watched for an hour then went home. Joe and I walked around the corner to get something to eat, then to the room to study. Friday morning at school I saw Ellen and we decided to get together that night for a movie. After school I went home and changed. I ran into the puny guy next door to me and he finally said hello. He was leaving with a suitcase so I asked him if it was for good. He said no, he was going to NYC for an assignment at some insurance company for special training for two weeks. Well he won't be listening for noise so my mind was already thinking about who would come up the fire stairs next? I met Ellen later and we went to a movie. I asked her to come back to my room for a drink but she said no. I dropped her off then went home. Saturday morning I went for breakfast and met this girl Ann who I had seen several times but we never spoke. She was sitting on the stool next to me. She told me she was from Mobile, Alabama and was in Hartford for three months training with Prudential Insurance Company. I loved her accent and she was very pretty. She was a little taller than me with dark black hair over her shoulders, very slim, small breasts, and a beautiful ass. I never saw her legs but I bet they were beautiful also. We talked for quite a while but we had to leave to make room for others. She lived in another house on the block where the fire was. She was three years older than me as was Carol. I decided to ask her out that night and she accepted. I picked her up and we drove to a place for dinner that she liked. It was a one story restaurant with two fireplaces, very cozy and definitely New England style. I was hoping it was not expensive because it had tablecloths and flowers on the tables. We sat down and the waitress came over who she knew. She ordered a martini and I ordered a scotch. We had a lot of laughs and when we finished eating the bill was only $16.00. We went and sat by the fireplace and ordered a couple of brandies. After an hour we saw that it was snowing hard so we left. I drove her to her house and to my surprise she invited me in. She had her own apartment at the rear of the house over a garage. Inside it was warm and cozy. There was a large oriental rug on the wall and living room floor. There was a couch, sofa chair, TV, and a cocktail table (all early American style). There was also a small kitchen, and a bedroom which I didn't see yet. She said she didn't have Scotch only Jack Daniels which was okay with me. She opened a bottle of wine and we sat on the couch talking. She then asked if I liked to hear some music. I said sure and she put on two 33 records; both were French. We danced a little and got closer to each other.

Then we noticed the snow was coming down hard. We both had a cigarette on the back porch watching the snow fall. We came back inside, hung up our coats and had a couple more drinks and more dancing. This time I began to kiss her and we sat down and continued to kiss. Finally I continued to explore her body and finally opened her pants. It was at this point she took my hand and led me to her bedroom. There was a large wool blanket on the bed made with autumn colors. You could tell it must have been homemade. Around the room on a rocking chair were several stuffed dogs and one large white stuffed cat. We began to kiss and get undressed. Finally naked I saw those beautiful legs. We made love and both fell asleep. About 5am I cuddled up with her and we made love again. I had to pull out both times because I didn't have any rubbers with me. She said next time I should bring them. I said to myself, next time I guess we will do it again. That morning it was still snowing and I had to shovel the car in her driveway so I could drive around the corner. Ms. Daniels saw me come in and said you didn't come home last night. I told her I stayed at a friend's because I had a little too much to drink. She looked me in the eye and said, "Was she nice?" I started to laugh and she said, "Your mother should know you came in this time."

I saw Joe and again we went to breakfast. You couldn't drive so we walked to the restaurant. I spent the rest of the day studying and went back to the restaurant for dinner. Monday, in school, I met Ellen again and she said maybe we could get together again. I told her I was too busy with studying and had to pass. Each night I went back to my house hoping Ann would leave me a message. I didn't have her number and at this time there were no cell phones so we had to depend on public phones. Three nights passed and I didn't hear from her. Thursday when I came home there was a message to call Ann and she left her number with Ms. Daniels. We could make local calls from the phone in the living room but she would shut the phone off at 9pm. I called her and we talked. She invited me over the next night which was Friday. After school Friday I went to a drugstore to buy rubbers. I hated this because in those days you had to ask for them and there was always a girl at the counter. My luck the owner's wife was there and I didn't ask her. I went to another drugstore downtown and there was an older man so I asked for two rubbers. He said what kind and I said it didn't matter. Then he said we have a three pack for 79 cents. I said yes and that was the end of that. I went home, took a shower and I also took a bottle of wine I had to bring to her. I got there at 6:15pm and she looked great. We had a drink and she said she cooked dinner for me. On went the French music and so be it the evening was great. I used all three rubbers and in the morning I didn't leave until 10am when I took her for breakfast. That morning everyone was there, Ellen, Dell, and a few other girls from the school. When we left I could just imagine the gossip the next day.

CHAPTER-NINE
The Job Placement

Chapter–Nine – The Job Placement

Winter 1960

Monday I was called in to the advisor's office to discuss several choices for a placement. He said I had an opportunity to go to Braniff Airways, Allegany Airlines or American in Idlewild. He said Braniff was an up and coming airline out of Dallas Love Field. I decided on Braniff and filled out their application which he would send in with a copy of my diploma. I knew that I would graduate. The rest of the week was busy and finally we were into the last week.

Graduation was on February 5th so we had a week and a half to prepare. I heard from my advisor that I had an interview on February 20th in Dallas at the main office at Braniff. He said the tickets were in the mail to my house in North Bergen. I was so excited. I called Ann and told her so we decided to celebrate by going out to dinner at the same restaurant we went to a few weeks ago. It was great and we returned to her place and I spent the night. I did buy three more rubbers that week so I was okay. The next morning I went to my room early, took a shower and went to school. Ms. Daniels gave me a funny look but said nothing. Everyone was getting excited and we had only a few days left. Most of the time, everyone was filling out applications for job placements. One more day to graduation so that night I called Ann and left a message. Joe and I had a couple of drinks in my room and we agreed to stay in touch which we did to this day. Joe went to bed and I went to the living room. I was just about to go to bed when Ann called at 8pm. Ms. Daniels gave me the phone and Ann said she just got into Prudential. She had an evening meeting with the adjusters. She wanted to see me before I left for good so I said I would see her tomorrow night after graduation. The next day I was called into the office. My advisor said he had a letter for me from Braniff. I opened it and the airline tickets and a letter with instructions letting me know how to get to the proper office at Love Field. I was jumping for joy. The afternoon was a 3pm graduation and everyone received their diplomas. I went back to my room and packed. I said good bye to everyone and said I was leaving in the morning. At about 6pm I loaded the car then cleaned my room. I went out never to return again. I drove around the block to Ann's and she brought in dinner after her work and we spent our last night together. Saturday morning I left early for home. I stopped at the house and unpacked. Then I went to Irene's. That night Irene and I went to dinner at the Canton Tea Garden at Journal Square. Irene had gotten a job at a bank in downtown Jersey City as a page. There she met a girlfriend, Rosemary Gargulo. Irene had banker's hours and in those days, I would pick her up after work to take her home. I was back to work at the diner whenever dad needed me. Finally February 20th arrived and I had an early morning flight on Braniff's new Electra. What a plane, four engine turbo prop. In the rear of the plane was a lounge and the seating was beautiful. The stewardesses knew I was what they call a non-rev. I spoke to them about my interview and they told me if they weren't interested I wouldn't be on the plane. We landed at Dallas Love Field and I went into the terminal. I noticed a large mosaic map of the U.S. on the floor. I followed my directions to the office and checked in. I sat down and the secretary gave me a cup of coffee. I was fifteen minutes early. I was always early even to this day. I was called in right on time and met with the interviewer who was a female. We spent about thirty minutes and got along well. I was told to come back at 1pm after lunch. I walked around the airport and stopped for a sandwich. At one o'clock I was sitting in the office when she called me in. With her was a man who she introduced me to by the name of Mr. Carl Boyle. He was the new station manager at Newark Airport. It just so happened he was in Dallas for a meeting so the woman interviewer (I can't remember her name) told him I was applying for a position so he said he would stop in to meet me. We spoke for about ten minutes and he shook my hand and said, "Congratulations Mr. Vallas, you are hired as a station agent in Newark." He left and the woman gave me papers to fill out for hospitalization and employment agreements, etc. I was to report for work in one week then I was sent to another office where I ordered my uniforms. They would be sent to Newark next week by Comat which was company material. When I boarded my return flight to Newark, I saw Mr. Boyle in first class and said hello and he smiled. When I got back to Newark Airport I stopped at Braniff ticket counter and spoke to one of the agents. He took me in the back and I met several of the cargo guys and other agents. One guy named Bob took me on a Tug (the small vehicles which pull the baggage carts) and showed me around. He showed me where to park at the Air Freight Building then called for a ride to the main terminal. When I got home I told dad and mom everything. I think they were just as excited as I was. That week I went to Jersey City to the fire department. I wanted to take the test and found out I had to live in Jersey City if I passed. The next test would be in six months. I was still determined to get on a fire department someday. I went to NYC also. In those days you had to be 21 years old to apply. I was waiting for a call from Braniff to tell me what shift I was on. I picked Irene up from work and we went to her house for dinner. When I got home that night mom told me Braniff called and left me the telephone number of operations. I called in and they told me I would work 7am to 3pm, Monday through Friday then the following week I would work midnights.

Spring 1960

The good thing was my cousin Donald Francis and Phyllis were getting married that Saturday and I planned to get engaged at the wedding because it was Valentine's Day, February 14, 1960. Saturday arrived and I picked Irene up and we went to the church in Little Ferry. It was at the reception I gave Irene the ring and made the announcement. Everyone really knew because I am

sure mom mentioned it and in my family within minutes everyone was on the phone. I went to work at 7am and all the introductions were made. The first day I spent with the supervisor Ken. He showed me around then explained I would work midnights loading and unloading planes. Everything was done by seniority and I was on the bottom. My uniforms were there and I had changed and was assigned a locker. Everyone was very nice but I started to listen to the gossip from some of the guys. I found out that some of these guys had been working the ramp for three years and still hadn't moved up to the ticket counter or operations. After this first week on days I started the midnight shift and we had two flights that night. In between flights, I was told by my shift supervisor that on the midnight shift the three ramp cargo men had to wash and wax the office floors. I began thinking I went to school for this? The other nights were spent scraping paint from the carts and painting them. I didn't want my family to know because they all thought I had a great job. The benefits were great because you could travel free as a non-rev. Your immediate family could also travel free, but my heart was still with the fire department. After a few weeks I learned the ropes and was convinced it would take me at least five years to advance to the ticket counter which was the first move up. I thought what a waste of money to go to school to wax floors and paint carts. I was working for dad part-time and starting to save money. I was only making $150.00 a week then about $8,000 a year with some overtime. We had set the date for April 16, 1961. When I told mom she said dad and she would pay for the wedding because Irene's mom didn't have any money. I knew mom wanted a big wedding so she could invite all her Greek friends as well as our large family. Irene's family was small. She had an Uncle George and Aunt Julia in Perth Amboy; a few cousins and I believe two other aunts. I liked all of them. The family on her father's side was Polish and George was a very creditable builder in South Jersey. He also held a position in the Builder's Association.

I was kept busy working between the diner and the airport and trying to save some money. On my time off I would go to the fire house and still go to big fires where ever they were. I made a lot of friends in the fire station by now, including other fire departments. More and more I wanted to be a fireman. I was already tired of waxing floors, painting carts, and felt like a janitor. I did service planes but Braniff didn't have but two flights each shift. I signed up for a non-rev trip for mom, dad, and Linda to go to Colorado Springs for a vacation. They had to pay for their own expenses but the flight was for free. I guess staying with Braniff just for the benefits would be wise at this time. I also applied for a station agent's position to TWA, Capitol Airlines, Northwest, and Allegany. Braniff had some bad luck with the Electra. One exploded in midair killing all who were aboard and so did another airline. Jets, mainly the 707, was just beginning to be used. Air Force One landed at Newark Airport and I met President Eisenhower just before he got into his limo because I had to bring a couple of carts to the ramp. It was now May and the trip for mom, dad, and Linda was set. I was working the ramp that day when they left. They flew to Dallas then on a Braniff Convair to Colorado Springs. They had a great week and I met them when they returned and they greeted me with a cowboy hat. Irene and I were always visiting on weekends at Uncle Walter's and Aunt Lil's. My shift kept changing from 4pm to 12pm then to midnights, 12am to 8am. I hated midnights because we had to wash and wax floors in the offices. When a flight came in we would unload the bags, cargo, and mail. Then we would pick up the same and load another plane. Another job was to stand behind each engine as it started with a large fire extinguisher. Once the props were turning we went to the next engine. During the cold winter it was brutal. There was word that Newark Airport would soon be receiving the new 707 and DC8 jets. Howard Hughes who owned TWA was buying some of the jets and Braniff had several on order.

Spring finally arrived and there were much better working conditions. Irene was still working at the bank and was close to her girlfriend Rosemarie. I still worked for dad and still hung out at the firehouse. One weekend in July, dad, mom, Linda, Irene, Donald, and Phyllis went to Wildwood, NJ. That Saturday we all went to the beach to swim. Mom never learned how to swim but she would go in up to her waist. Dad and Phyllis were out quite far for some time and there was a strong under toe that day. Linda and I were wading at the water's edge when I saw Phyllis struggling. Dad swam to her and they both were in trouble. I dove in and swam out and grabbed Phyllis. I yelled to dad to swim to the side then go in to shore. Once I got a hold on Phyllis I kept her head above water and what seemed like forever and I finally pulled her in. All this time the life guard never saw a thing until I was almost in, then the lifeguards ran to us. I told them to watch dad who was almost in. All three of us were exhausted. This was the second time I saved someone. The first time I saved someone was in Manasquan, NJ one summer when I was a life guard.

The next few weeks I was busy working at the diner and Braniff. I also had kept up on dates for the fire department tests. Irene and I took day trips on weekends visiting relatives. During the week we would see each other at night a couple of hours to park and pet. We never had sex because Irene was still very naïve. We went to her Aunt and Uncle's house so I could meet them and I liked them very much. They were going to buy Irene's mother a dress for our upcoming wedding. Irene and I went to a place on Route 17 in Hasbrouck Heights called the Fiesta to see about the reception. It was a typical wedding catering place but we liked it. When I brought my mother to see it she said it was cheap and she didn't like it. Well, she was paying for the wedding so, that was it. Mom always wanted the best. She was spoiled by my father. Fall came and she made contact with the George Stratis Orchestra for the reception. She had gone to the Military Park Hotel in Newark, NJ and put a deposit on the Grand Ballroom for April 16, 1961. Irene and I went to see it and it was great. We needed a large place because the orchestra had nine people and mom was inviting about 250 people. Mom said I would have to pay for the flowers, and I agreed.

CHAPTER–TEN
Year 1960
The Pre-Wedding Arrangements

Chapter–Ten - Year 1960 - The Pre-Wedding Arrangements

One Saturday night Irene, her girlfriend Angelina, her boyfriend, who I knew, Dennis O'Donnell; and I went to Westside Park to park. We were necking and petting and the windows would be all steamed up. When it came time to leave because I had to be home by 10pm, I started the car off, but I didn't have my foot on the clutch. It was in first gear and the car went forward over the island and there I was with all four wheels off the ground and the muffler crushed. A bunch of guys helped us push the car off, but the noise without the muffler was tremendous. When I got back to North Bergen and pulled into the driveway everyone heard me. Mom and dad came out, Betty and Dino, and the people next door. Mom started yelling at dad that he needed his head examined for letting me buy a car like that. Little did they know what had happened? That week dad and I went to Belleville, NJ to a car dealer Uncle Mike used. We bought a 1954 Plymouth Belvedere. Dad financed it and I would pay him back with the money I made at the diner. The car was nice but it wasn't a "cool" car as they would say.

I was now going to dad's diner everyday after school to work. Dad used to take the numbers then for a guy named, Scoopie. The cops used to play the numbers and horses, too. Dad had nothing to worry about. One day I saw a Greek horse that was running at Belleview. I gave dad $10.00 and told him to put it on number nine. Dad said I was crazy that it was a long shot 30 to 1. I insisted so he did. He didn't like me to gamble but once in a while I did. I did play the numbers everyday. The next day when I got to work after school, John Sophanis, dad's partner, had a big smile on his face and Genie the waitress, too. When I saw dad he put his cigarette down and even the customers were laughing. I said, "What is so funny?" Dad said you hit the jackpot; the horse came in first 30 to 1. I won $1,300.00. The horse was the Golden Greek. Every Friday I gave dad the money for my car insurance. It was $70.00 a month then, and also half of the car payment. He paid half and I paid half. I was still chasing fires but now I could drive to the scene of the big ones. I had a lot of friends in the fire department in Jersey City. I went to the American Red Cross and got my first aid card. I made a large first aid kit for my car. After, I went for my instructor's card which I received after many weeks of training I was now stopping at accidents and giving first aid. Everyone thought I was crazy. Mom was my biggest critic. On weekends Irene and I would drive to Uncle Walter's house, sometimes to Aunt Lil's or to my cousin Lorraine and Barbara's down the Jersey Shore. I did work at the diner on some Saturdays when dad needed me. Usually Friday nights I closed the diner at 8pm and cleaned up. It would take about an hour. I would get paid by dad on Fridays just before he left at 5 or 5:30pm to go home. Then I would give dad $15.00 and he always put a rubber band on it and put it in his pocket. This was to pay for the insurance and part of the car payment.

We were approaching Thanksgiving, November 18, 1960 and I drove mom to the nursing home to see grandma and when we went in to go upstairs they told us she had just died. Mom went crazy and I had a hard time with her. I felt bad but she was an old lady who had 14 children…what could I say? Mom started screaming and crying jumping up and down totally out of control. I couldn't believe it. Grandma had 14 children, lived a good life, and she was, I think, 80 or something. We are all going to die when we get old was my thought. I used the phone in the lobby and called dad then Aunt Mary. I took mom to Aunt Mary's and by then everyone was coming to Aunt Mary's house. I left after dad came to go to Irene's. After the plans were made for the funeral, I went every night "three nights". Mom was still screaming and making a scene. All the other brothers and sisters were talking with people and laughing. This was my first family death and I thought it strange. After the funeral I drove back to the house and dad and mom came back also. Betty and Dino came up and we all had something to eat. Mom said, "I don't know what I am going to do now." Mom is dead. That was when I made my usual big mouth mistake. I said, "Mom, you went to the nursing home everyday almost for six years." You just won't have to do that anymore. I got the five fingers in my face again. My Uncle Walter and Aunt Dolores came in and thought that was funny. Uncle Walter told mom, "Sophie, now you won't have to go to the nursing home anymore." I jumped in and said to mom, "Why don't you hit Uncle Walter?" Dad almost died laughing and had to leave the room. Anyway the next couple of weeks, mom was on the phone talking with the Greek ladies and the family.

I had Thanksgiving dinner at Irene's and then I went home. I had to be at work at midnight. I started my Christmas shopping and went to Bergenline Avenue in West New York. It was very cold that Saturday and I had to keep a scarf across my face, because the wind was 10-15 knots. I stopped in a Woolworth's 5&10 and had some hot chocolate. When I left I had to walk a few blocks to my car in this 25 degree temperature. It was great to get in the car but it took a long time to get the heat up to par and I had to scrape the windows. I couldn't wait to get home. Mom was cooking because she was having company for dinner. I put my packages in the closet and drove to Irene's. That night we went to Aunt Ann's house to visit. Uncle Mike hurt his back again which happened quite often. We had dinner there and Aunt Ann made sauce, meatballs and macaroni. She always opened the door to everyone. I got home and mom was cleaning up. She said I hope you didn't tell anyone, Walter and Dolores were here. This was typical of the Francis family. They always did this so as not to tell each other who was coming. I thought it was crazy but they all did it. Christmas was spent at Uncle Walter's and Irene's. We split our day to be with everyone. New Year's Eve we went to Aunt Catherine's as usual. On New Year's Day we had dinner at mom's. I made my mind up to leave Braniff so I began to look at other jobs. Irene and I ordered the favors for the tables which was a small dish with each person's name on it to be used as a seating place card, and our name and date on it also. Irene also spoke to our priest at St. Demetrios' church and she became Greek Orthodox. Mom went with Irene for the wedding gown and worked on the invitations when they came back. Poor dad was looking at the bills and he said they had to borrow on his life insurance policy. I paid for the invitations, and Irene's wedding dress. It was quite a busy month.

One morning when I was off I remember it was snowing and very cold. It was about 6am and I walked through the North Hudson Park a few blocks from my house. I needed some time to think and this was a perfect time; very peaceful with no one around. The snow was hitting my face and I walked through the trees and it was so beautiful. The street lights were glowing and I could see how fast the snow was falling. After about an hour I started to return and I noticed that my tracks had been covered by the snow. Shortly I heard the snow plow coming through the park. I got to the end of the park and decided to walk to the Fairview Diner. Fairview was the beginning of Bergen County. I started to speak with the owner who was Greek of course, and he told me there was a Greek Church in Fairview. I told him I was getting married in April and was looking for a place to live. He said I should look in Cliffside Park because a friend of his just bought some garden apartments on Oakdean Place. I wrote down the name and I walked back to my house. It was still snowing hard so I decided to stay home. I picked up a newspaper on the way to look in the real estate section. When I got home I started to brush the snow off my car and shovel around my car only to have it plowed in again. The problem with the snow storms were

after I got my car out, and then returned home someone else would be in my spot where I had shoveled. I used to put a garbage can in the spot but someone would always remove it. I mentioned to mom about Cliffside Park and she said I should go and check it out. Finally the snow stopped and I went to the diner. I had one more day off before I had to go back to work at the airport. I told Irene about the new apartments and we decided to look the next day. I picked Irene up and we drove to Cliffside Park and saw a sign in front of the building at 201 Oakdean Place. It was a lovely red brick two story apartment complex. There was a phone number on the sign so we drove to the Fairview Diner and called the number. A woman answered and it was the wife of the owner who lived on the premises. She told us to come right over and so we did. She was young, about 30, and she took us to the first floor apartment. It was beautiful, two bedrooms, living room, 2 baths, and a kitchen which had a beautiful mural painting on the wall. It was $165.00 a month which was $65.00 more than we really could afford and we still had to buy furniture. In those days I was making about $155.00 a week and about $50.00 with dad. Well, we liked it so much we took it. We told mom and she was happy. This turned out to be a very busy month.

The first week of February, I left the diner to go for an interview at Lite O'Lear Company in Jersey City. Just after I parked my car I saw smoke coming from a house next to where I was going. I ran to the house and saw a woman coming out. She was very upset. She screamed at me that she couldn't find her son. I ran in and saw the fire was in the kitchen and flames were rolling over the ceiling. I quickly closed the door then looked for the kid. I found him in the rear patio area. I grabbed him and went out the back just as the fire department arrived. He was nine years old. I smelled like smoke when I went for the interview so I explained the situation to the woman who interviewed me. Incidentally, I didn't get the job. I was back on midnights that week so it was time to get furniture. Mom took us to Stone Furniture downtown Jersey City because she dealt with them many years and he would finance everything off the floor so we could move in right away before the wedding. Mom gave Irene a shower at the Oyster Bay Restaurant and we did great. We got everything, linens, towels, dishes, silverware, glasses, appliances, etc. We had to use two cars to take everything to our new apartment. That weekend we went to Uncle Walter and Aunt Dolores' for diner. He loaded me up with liquor, canned goods and many other things. He worked for First National Stores and always gave me things. I discussed my leaving Braniff with Uncle Walter and he said if I was not happy I should leave. The next week I gave two week's notice. Uncle Walter said he would see if he could get me a job with one of the food brokers. I told mom and she said I needed my head examined after she spent all that money to send me to school. When I went to work that night my boss called me in and I had to fill out some papers. I asked him why they hired me as a station agent and I was waxing floors and painting. He said most of the ramp people were hired off the street but when the airline school called they would hire someone from there. Now I realized everything was bull-shit. I could have just been hired if I had walked in without any schooling. I didn't bother to tell mom because she wouldn't believe me anyway. I called Uncle Walter and he told me I should call Mr. Joe Ferolie from Gash & Ferolie Food Brokers in NYC. I called and had an interview the first week of March which was in two days. I went there March 3. It was a three story brownstone building. That's when I met Steve Santa Maria who would be my boss in NJ. Everything went well and I would get a company car and expense account. The next few weeks I would meet Steve at his house in West New York, NJ, about 15 minutes from my house, and ride with him on the route I was going to get. My job was to go to the supermarkets and check on all the products they handled such as Progresso Foods, Swannie tissue, Louis Sherry Jellies, etc. It was great and thanks to Uncle Walter, who was the buyer for the First National Stores that Steve called on. The first few weeks I met many of the store managers for Shop Rite, Food Town, Grand Union, Acme, First National and a few others.

Year 1961 Wedding Preparations

I mentioned to Steve that I was getting married April 16 and was planning to go on my honeymoon to Florida for a week and would like to have off without pay of course. He said I could take that week off. The third week of March the furniture was being delivered so mom went there with me so I could show her where everything should go. Irene had given notice at the bank because it was too far to travel from Cliffside Park by bus because she didn't drive. I also sold my Chevy to Genny at the diner and I bought a 1956 Olds for cash. This way I wouldn't have car payments. Mom and I also went to the florist which was a relative of my godfather's. We ordered the flowers for each table, the church, and other pieces for the wedding party and ushers. By the end of March everything was done and set. Irene had picked up her dress and now I was checking the return invitations. I had made reservations to fly on TWA to Miami and drive to the Castaways Hotel on Collins Avenue. We had to leave for the airport right after the wedding to catch a 2:30am flight. Jackie Ellison said he would take us.

The last week of March on March 29, 1961, I came home to my house and before I could get in the front door, Betty Korinis stopped me and said, "Go to the diner right away, your father is waiting for you". Uncle Bernie was killed by a train that morning. I was devastated because he was such a good guy. I got to the diner and mom, dad, and I went to Aunt Lil's house on Collins Avenue in Port Monmouth, NJ. Everyone was there and I remember Aunt Lil and Bernice sitting on the bed crying. This was my first death experience and I was truly upset. Aunt Dolores's brother Lou Sorrentino was there because he was an attorney. Uncle Bernie worked for Middletown Township and that morning he was in a Township dump truck sitting in the middle when the driver drove over the railroad tracks and the truck was hit by a train. Uncle Bernie and another man were killed. The driver survived, however, injured for life. The funeral was so sad that Irene and I were sick. I cried and cried at the funeral home then drove to the cemetery, Shoreland Memorial Gardens, on Route 35 in Keyport. Uncle Bernie died two weeks before my wedding.

I was at our new apartment on April Fools day to bring more things such as cleaning supplies, canned goods, spices, etc. This way when we returned from Florida we could go right to the apartment. We even brought most of our clothes with us to the new apartment as well. When I was ready to leave I heard sirens and a few minutes later I saw a fire truck go by. I decided to find the fire house which I did on Anderson Avenue. I went in and introduced myself. They told me they had a part paid department and the rest was volunteer. Well, I don't have to say anymore, I was ready to join when I got back from Florida with hopes of becoming a paid fireman in the future. Now I was really excited but I kept my mouth shut. If I heard I needed my head examined once more from my mother I probably would leave. The day before the wedding Joe Bustin and his girlfriend Marcia arrived from Cranston, R.I. and stayed with us. Irene and I packed everything for the trip because we would be leaving right after the reception. That night I

didn't see Irene and we stayed home. I never had a bachelor night because I really didn't have many friends. I preferred it that way. The next morning we all had breakfast and I made final arrangements. It was not a good weather day and rain was in the forecast. Finally we went to the church and it was raining hard. The church was packed and the flowers were on the end of each pew. The flower girl and ring bearer were Irene's cousin's children. The ceremony was Greek Orthodox and went over well. It was pouring rain when we left to go to the Military Park Hotel in Newark. We had a large suite to use so we could change after the reception. The photographer took a few pictures before the reception. There were no videos in those days and most photos were black and white. Some people were using the 8mm movie cameras but until this day I had never seen any taken at the wedding. Irene looked great and the music was the best. We danced Greek folk songs as well as American. One funny thing was when Irene threw the flowers my cousin Bernice jumped up and her gown dropped exposing her breasts. After all the festivities we collected the envelopes and some gifts and went to the suite. Mom and dad came up and we opened all the envelopes. I gave mom the money for the flowers which was $560.00. I took a thousand dollars in cash with me for the trip. We didn't have credit cards then so it was cash or travelers checks.

April 16, 1961 - The Honeymoon

My friend, Jack Ellison drove us to the airport and we checked in. The flight to Florida was the first time on a 707 TWA jet. It was great. When we arrived in Miami we got our rental car and drove to the beach and then north on Collins Avenue. Our check in time at the Castaways Hotel was noon so we had a few hours to tour the famous Miami Beach. I was wearing a mint green jacket and it was warm. It was beautiful and everything looked so clean. We drove up and down the strip and couldn't get over how beautiful it was. We finally checked in and had lunch. This definitely was a honeymoon place. The hotel took our pictures for their photo album which was kept for years for people to see. We finally went to the room and I don't have to tell you what we did there. We were lying in bed and all of a sudden I heard what I thought was a knock on the door. Then I heard it again and I thought I hope to hell it's not mom. I got up and then I heard the noise again and realized it was the diving board. We were near the pool and every time someone jumped off it made this noise. Well we both laughed and decided to go to the pool. That's where we met a lovely couple from Staten Island, Santa and Barry O'Neil. We hit it off right away and after a few drinks we all went back to our rooms for more fun. Later we met them in the lobby and we went across the street to the restaurant. We had a good time but we went to bed early because we were so tired. The next day at the pool we all got together and we met another couple from Elizabeth, N.J. That night we all went to dinner at another hotel where we were given Union and Confederate hats. Even though we weren't 21 years old we had no trouble getting served. The next day I noticed the gas tank on my car was full and the car was washed. I couldn't believe it; the rental car company did this for all their customers. Again we had fun at the pool and that night Irene and I drove to Fort Lauderdale for dinner at the Mai Kai, a Polynesian Restaurant with music and a show. It was great also. When we got back to Miami Beach we stopped at the bar and went to bed. The next day I called Johnny Caldes, one of my mother's Greek friend's sons. He lived in Fort Lauderdale with his wife, Anna. I was the ring bearer at his wedding years before. They invited us to their house that night and we accepted. We had a nice time and then returned to the Castaways Hotel. The next few nights we spent with Santa and Barry and we all exchanged addresses and phone numbers. The week went so fast I couldn't believe it, but I also couldn't wait to get home to our new apartment. As I was driving to the airport on Sunday, I thought to myself I am going to live in Florida someday.

Irene had a good time but she was always a bit on the quiet side. We arrived home and mom and dad met us at the airport and took us to our apartment in Cliffside Park, NJ. The next day I had to work and we were tired. Irene had to look for a job so we would have to figure out how we could do this since I still was using my own car. April 21, I received my discharge from the Navy. The next day I met Steve and we worked until 6pm. I got home at 6:30pm and Irene made dinner, our first. Steve told me that day I would be getting my company car that week, which was a Chevy station wagon. On Wednesday Steve picked up the car. I filled it with samples of our products which we would exchange for the supermarket's damaged goods or dented cans. Irene had been looking at ads and had an interview with Green Associates, a real estate firm as a secretary. I took her the next morning before I left to go to my first stop. She got the job and I was happy. My hours were pretty much my own so I would drive her to work at 8am then go on my way. I would also pick her up if I got back early otherwise she took the bus. Her office was on the same street where we lived, only about one mile north, in Fort Lee. I came home early one afternoon and went to the fire station.

CHAPTER–ELEVEN
Special Police Officer

Chapter–Eleven – Special Police Officer

I met the chief, Mr. Mc Grath and spent about an hour with him and he showed me around town and stopped at Station 2 on Palisades Avenue. I met the police chief McEnvoy and he said if you are interested he needed another special police officer to work at Palisades Amusement Park. I told him I would think about it because I wanted to be on the fire department. He then said I could be on both. It was a great meeting and I went home and told Irene about it. Now I was on a roll to get on the fire department. The next day I came home early, but I would be at my first stop at 7am when the stores opened instead of 9am. At 3pm I went to the fire house and filled out the papers and that Thursday I was sworn in. I got my badge and everyday after work I went to the fire house to train. In those days they didn't even have Scott air packs. We used the old Navy MSA masks, which were just a filter type mask. During the night that week the sirens went off and I went to my first fire. I got to the station and rode on the back tailboard of the American La France pumper. We arrived at a structure fire and heavy black smoke was emanating from the basement. I stepped off the engine and pulled a 2 ½ inch line to the hydrant. After I connected it I stood by to turn it on when told to. I got the word and turned on the water hydrant. Then I went and put on an MSA. I couldn't avoid going into the fire. That is when I first met Captain Johnny Nagle. He was a paid captain and he saw me do the hook up so he came over and said, "O.K. kid, follow me we are going down into the basement." We followed a couple of men going down with the line and he said, "You're not a fireman until you eat smoke." Well down we went and the smoke was thick and I could feel lots of heat. I saw a glow a distance away and as soon as the line was advanced and opened, the fire was knocked down and there was more smoke. I began to choke a little which meant it was time to get out. Captain Nagle kept holding me back by pushing me to the side. After a few more minutes the smoke started to thin out because the side windows of the basement were broken out and the basement was vented. I helped with the mop up and overhaul then went outside. Captain Nagle came over to me and said, "Good job kid, you're going to be fine." After dragging the hoses and rolling them up we went back to the station, cleaned up and went home. I was thrilled finally doing what I always wanted.

CHAPTER–TWELVE
The Police Department

Chapter–Twelve – The Police Department

The next day I went to the Police Department after work and spoke to Captain Gerity. I filled out all the paperwork and was finger printed. Irene and I went to visit her mother that Saturday and her cousin Arthur was there also. He lived with Kay (Irene's mother) but he never worked. He was also an alcoholic. He told us he was given a little dog which was a Chihuahua but Kay didn't want it in the house. It was beautiful and I said we would take it home. It was already housebroken and we loved it. We named him Chico. Over the next few weeks he adjusted to us wonderfully.

One afternoon while I was at the fire house I was taught how to answer the switchboard. When the hot line rang you plugged the wire into the hole and took the call. Those were the days with the old telephone systems with wires. Fire calls came into our number or to the police department. If a fire came in whoever was at the desk would push the button to set off the siren at both stations to alert the volunteers. Actually at headquarters there would be a paid captain and two paid firemen on duty. One would drive the hook and ladder and one the engine and sometimes we had someone to drive the rescue truck. We also had an old Cadillac ambulance. When needed, we had to call for a police officer to come to the station. Then a fireman and police officer went to the call. These were the old days. The second week in June I answered several fire calls, all small, but my big interest was in how these fires started. Then I got a call from the Police Department to come in and after work that day I went to headquarters. I was told I was accepted and was given badge 683. I was also issued a 38 caliber revolver and told where to go for my uniform and leather. I was now a special officer and would be paid for my time. I told them I would be available nights and weekends. I still did my job at Gash & Ferolie's everyday, but I wanted to get home early so I could go to the fire house. The rest of June I got my uniforms and went to the police pistol range to practice with my weapon. Can you imagine getting appointed a special officer and being given a gun without any training? While I was shooting there was a motorcycle accident on the street and I ran to assist. The victim had a compound fracture of the leg and I had to stop the bleeding, and keep him from going into shock. I later found out I saved his life. I did ride a few weeks in a patrol car with a trained officer and learned how to write tickets, etc. I had my own ticket book also. By the end of June I was assigned to work three nights a week from 7pm to 1am at Palisades Amusement Park including Saturdays and Sundays. Palisades Amusement Park was half in Fort Lee, N.J. and half in Cliffside Park, NJ. It was a very famous place, I think the largest in the country, and was owned by Irving Rosenthal and his wife Gladys Shelly. The amusement park had a large roller coaster, stands, rides, bars, restaurants, and a full stage for shows. Rosenthal had the most modern rides and he traveled to Germany and went all over Europe to buy new rides.

The park was very large and was situated on the Cliffs overlooking the Hudson River, adjacent to the George Washington Bridge. As a matter of fact, it wasn't far from the "Rivera" where Frank Sinatra would sing. That was a mob affiliated place but had great entertainers like Sammy Davis, Jr., Dino, etc. The park also had the largest saltwater pool with waves in the country. The first night I worked, my partner was Joe Burrell. He was at one time a famous boxer but was now retired. The first week I worked he showed me all the problem places. He showed me the bath houses where sex was rampid, the trouble bars, the trouble employers, and all the quick ways to cut through the park if an emergency call was announced. When we heard over the loud speaker system, "Gladys Shelly", we went to whatever location they said. It meant all officers from Fort Lee and Cliffside Park were to go to that location. Usually it was a fight, stabbing or assault. I was making good part-time money and I became a good police officer. I was trying to save money to buy a house one day so this was great. I also ate there for free any place I wanted. I also was able to get many free tickets for my friends. I still did my job with the fire department and Gash & Ferolie, but I could see that one day I would be a fireman.

July 4th the park was full the entire weekend. There were fireworks, stage shows, and special entertainment such as groups from the 50s. I was assigned to escort some of them and that alone was a thrill. My best time was when I was assigned to Elvis Presley. I never left his side the three hours he was there. There were other performers, Frankie Lyman, and Sal Mineo. I can't remember all of them but this job was exciting. The last week in July there was a big fight at the bar area and this was the first time I used my club. One guy threw a chair at me and I hit him in the face with my club. I handcuffed him to the table and went on helping the other officers. We arrested 14 people that night. Several were taken to Englewood Hospital for treatment. The weekends were always crazy at the park. I was working hard during the day with Ferolie, and working the police job at night.

CHAPTER–THIRTEEN
The Fire Department

Chapter–Thirteen – The Fire Department

At the end of July1961, I was asked to work as a paid fireman when I could to fill in for vacationers. So I had to juggle my time around all jobs but I was making money to save for a house. Irene and I didn't go out much because I was working all the time, but we did have company occasionally. We kept in contact with Barry Santa and went to Staten Island to visit them. I became close to Lt. Arthur Glesmire on the fire department. He was the inspector for the department. I started to learn about investigations and fire codes. I went with him several times to learn as much as I could. I slept at the station when I filled in for someone. It was an old building and there were rats in the basement which was our day room. The switchboard was also located there. If a fire call came in when the sirens were blown, one of the volunteers who lived next door would come over and take the switchboard over, and then the firefighter on duty could leave and take the rescue truck. I found out during the summer that to get on the fire department permanently it was a political appointment. I had a couple of friends in the fire department who were volunteers like Bob Bajer, and Charlie Silverman. We sort of hung together. We all belonged to Engine Company 2 on Palisades Avenue. Another fireman was Philly Ferrara; a short guy who also wanted to get on permanently. We would all go across the street after our meetings or a fire to a bar there for beer. I was always served because we were all fireman and no one ever asked me for my ID. August was a wild month at the park. In total I made about 14 arrests.

One night Captain Joe Borrell and I were on patrol on August 11, 1961, and we received a call to the Penny Arcade. When we arrived Joe was in front of me. Joe was a retired captain working at the park and was up in years. This guy Mario Lopez punched Joe in the face breaking his glasses. I then punched Lopez and took him down. In the process several friends of Lopez jumped me. I fought them off then took my night stick and they weren't too happy to be on the receiving end of that. Help came and all were arrested.

I was doing a good job with Ferolie and I had no complaints. Steve Santa Maria insisted I go on a hunting trip for quail in November with a couple of guys including his father. I decided to go. I had never done this before, and he was going to loan me a shotgun. The next time I went to the Police Pistol range I practiced with a department shotgun. I really didn't like hunting but the boss asked so I went. September came and we had a briefing at the Police Department because Labor Day weekend was always busy at the park. The park would close for the season then. Extra officers were added and were all over the place. That Friday night there was a big fight at the Casino Bar which we broke up but sent three to the hospital. They were also arrested. On Saturday and Sunday I had to work from 7am until midnight when the park closed. Saturday I had two purse snatchings, one pick pocket, and two assaults. I also had to escort one of the employer's of the office who picked up money bags. I had to walk with him around the park with my gun out then return to the office. There were three or four perhaps a day and a different officer was used each time.

It was about 9:30pm Saturday, September 3rd. I was checking around the bath houses when I heard crying. I investigated and found a girl about 17years old completely naked. She said two boys stripped her then assaulted her. They took her clothes and pocketbook. I went to the front of the pool and got her a large towel. We walked through the rest of the bath house and she saw the two guys leaving the park by the rear bus area. We didn't have portable radios then so I put her in a change booth with one of the girls and had them call a Gladys Shelly to the bus lot. I ran out and saw them get on the bus for New York. I got on the bus and told the driver to get off. When other officers arrived we went on the bus to get them. One guy ran to the back and opened the emergency door and jumped out but we had the bus surrounded and we got them both. I had to go to headquarters in Fort Lee to make the arrest and the girl was taken to the hospital to be examined. I didn't get back to the park until 12:30 then I went into Hiram's Hot Dog Place on Palisades Avenue across from the park to get a hot dog and a beer. They had the best hot dogs, deep fried with large French fries. I saw two of my other officers eating so I walked over to them to sit down when we heard a scream and saw some guy punching his girlfriend. We all jumped up, handcuffed him then called for a car and went back to the Police Station again. I finally got home at 2am.

Sunday was a better day; just a few calls but it was very hot so we had quite a few people passing out. After the park closed at midnight we all had a party at the bar and picked up our checks. End of season; say no more. The next week Willie DiBona, my Cousin Doris's husband called me and asked if I would help him make his yearly wine. Every year Willie would make two or three barrels of red wine. The next Saturday, Irene and I went to their house on Nelson Avenue in Jersey City. My Aunt Catherine lived below them. Willie and I went to the Hoboken train yards and we bought many cases of Zinvandel, Alaganti, and Granada grapes. When we got back to the house we put them in the shed in the backyard. We spent the day crushing the mixture of grapes through the grinder into the barrels. Now the grapes fermented for a few weeks. Every couple of days Willie would push the grapes from the top down into the juice then cover the barrels with cheese cloth to prevent splattering from the fermentation. We had dinner and returned home. Our upstairs neighbor was a couple, Mr. and Mrs. Seaforth who had a daughter who was dating our Mayor Jimmy Madden. I met the mayor and he was a great guy. He was an attorney and as I would learn years later, he became a judge in Bergen County. I told Mr. Seaforth that when the wine was finished I would give him a bottle. Now that the Palisades Amusement Park was closed for the season, I was spending more time working at the fire department. One night there was a fire call at about 1am at Palisades Amusement

Park. The park was closed for the season, but security discovered smoke coming from the fun house. When we arrived there was heavy black smoke coming from the west side. We dropped a line from the hydrant to the rear of the fun house. Captain Nagle called for assistance from the Fort Lee F.D. Another fireman; I don't remember who, and I broke down a rear door. Just then the Chief arrived on the scene and he came over to me. I was on the nozzle waiting for water. He said, "Put the nozzle down and let's go in and see what we have." Both of us went in about 25 feet and could see the entire roof area and about 50 feet further everything was burning. He told me when we advance in hit those areas with a heavy stream of water mainly from the roof area and beyond. As we turned to exit we heard a large cracking and parts of the roof began to fall. We both ran and dove out the rear door just in time. I met other guys and we now had water. After about an hour we had control of the fire and moved in to begin mop up operations. I asked the chief later over coffee at the rescue station if I could assist in the investigation with Lt. Glesmere and he said sure. I stayed throughout the day and I learned plenty about fire patterns, depth of char, and how the fire started. It was in the ceiling area where the deepest burn though occurred. The falling joists which were on the ground revealed a blow through on a BX cable which was secured to the joist. Part of the BX cable had a 1 inch hole in it and that joist had burned almost completely through. The copper wires just inside the cable were all melted and shorted. This was my first inspection and investigation. From then on I went to many other investigations with Lt. Glesmire.

Two weeks later I was elected Lt. of Engine 1. I was so excited and happy. I still worked with Ferolie and would leave very early in the morning to be at my first stop at 7am when the store employees would be in. I did this so I would be home early and go to the fire headquarters. Sometimes I had to meet Steve at his garage to turn in damaged goods and get more replacement goods. One early morning a fire at a house occurred at 5:30am and I was tied up until 9am. When I got to my first stop it was 10:30am and of all times Steve Santa Maria was there. He said he was waiting for me to discuss putting up an Italian Festival display for Progresso foods. I told him why I was late and he was annoyed. He didn't care much about the fire department and made a remark that I should not do it if it interferred with the job. I was annoyed because I always did my job. The last week of October I went to mail a letter across the street from my apartment and as I opened the mail box I saw Chico running towards me. I didn't know he came out the door when I did and I yelled for him to stop but he came into the roadway and was hit by a car. I told Irene and then we buried him in the lot behind our apartment. That weekend I had invited Steve and his cousin Joe Santa Maria for dinner at our house. I made chicken, vegetables, and appetizers. Irene really wasn't a good cook because her mom, Kay cooked very easy and plain things, such as cut up hot dogs and lima beans in tomato sauce. The dinner went well and they had a good time.

The next weekend was the hunting trip so we talked about that and I really wasn't looking forward to that. Steve said I could go home early on Friday because we were leaving about 5am that next morning. I had a busy week working and one day at the firehouse one of the guys gave me a hunting jacket to borrow. I had bought a red hat and I had boots and dungarees which are now called jeans. We left on time Saturday at 5:30am. Steve, Joe, his father and another cousin (I don't remember his name) came with us. We drove up to the mountains in New York State. When we arrived Steve gave me a license to put on my back. We went into the woods and I was instructed to be with Joe. We would split up and head north in pairs so no one should be ahead of each other. Steve was with his father and we set out about 25 yards from each other. I actually was enjoying the woods and fields looking at the small animals. We were hunting for quails and rabbits. We all got together for lunch about 12 noon and had salami, bread, cheese, and wine. We all left again but I was cold. The wind picked up and it started to get cloudy and cooler, almost like it was going to snow. I heard several shots in the distance but it wasn't from any of us. About an hour later I heard a shotgun go off then I heard Steve in the distance screaming. "Pop got shot. Nobody shoot." I got up and ran to where I heard Steve yelling. Pop was on the ground and his face was bleeding. I told Steve to take off his undershirt and started ripping strips. I checked Pop out and he had about 100 pellets on his chest, arms, face, but nothing below his belt. He was talking and I felt he was not in any immediate danger but did need to get to the hospital. Most of the pellets were in about ¼ inch. Except for two near his eyes, the bleeding, and his age 83 I told everyone, after I get him bandaged with the strips of the T-shirt, to get him to the car. Steve was very upset so I calmed everyone down and we half carried him and walked him about ½ a mile to the car. We headed to the nearest town and asked for the location of the nearest hospital. It was about 20 meters away so we headed there. At the hospital he was admitted. After we were assured he would be okay. Steve said he would stay and Joe should drive us back to N.J. When I got home I was full of blood and Irene couldn't believe it. That was the last time I ever went hunting. What had happened was the same thing that happened to V.P. Dick Chaney recently. We didn't notify the Press either. The hospital had to notify the Police and they made a report. The following week I stopped at Willie's and he gave me a dozen bottles of wine from the barrel. I got home and put the wine in a cool place. The next night I gave a bottle to Mr. Seaforth upstairs for his Thanksgiving.

Next Thursday was Thanksgiving and we were going to Uncle Walter's. The weekend came and Irene and I went to the Jersey Shore to see Aunt Lil and Bernice. When Irene and I got home Sunday evening I just got in the door and Mr. Seaforth knocked on my door. He handed me a bag and in it was the broken wine bottle. He said he put it on his piano and while they were out that day it exploded all over his white living room rug and piano. I went up and couldn't believe the stains. His apartment was always very warm and the wine must have fermented more and blew up. I felt terrible and apologized. He said that he would call his insurance company in the morning. The next day an adjuster came to the house and they sent a cleaning service which spent the whole day getting out the stains, etc. That night when I got home there was a note to call the adjuster. I did and explained the whole story. They couldn't clean the rug, but the piano, walls and one curtain was cleaned. The insurance company said he could get a new rug. His deductible was $100.00. I offered to give him half since I told him he should put the wine in a cool place. He would not take it so Irene and I bought him a gift. The next two weeks I was working with Steve at setting up a Progresso Festival display at Acme Markets.

December 1961

December 5th arrived and I was now 21 years old. Irene and I went to Mom's house and we had dinner. Now I could also take the fire department test in the larger cities. I didn't tell mom I still wanted to go to the fire department. I told her I made Lt. and she said the usual. "You're crazy." We went shopping for Christmas gifts; our first Christmas and we bought ornaments, a tree, and trimmings. We decorated the house because I always liked everything done early. We did a lot of entertaining that month with friends, family, guys from the fire department, and police department. It was great. I cooked, baked, and now I could buy my own liquor. New Year's Eve we invited some of our friends including Rosemary and her husband Leo.

January, 1962

January was a bad month for weather. It was very cold, snowy and we had quite a few fires. I kept learning about investigating fires. We had several Mutual Aid calls, one in Union City at a lumber yard fire on Hudson Blvd, and another in Ridgefield Park at a house. I also worked as a patrolman on and off since the park closed making extra money. Irene and I were also thinking of moving to a larger apartment when our lease was up in April. We wanted to get a cheaper place because they were going to raise the rent $30.00 more a month. We had a couple of bad snow days and so I went to the fire house. I took mom food shopping at the Shop Rite after a bad storm. Dad was stuck at the diner. Irene still worked for Mr. Green who was also in politics in Bergen County. Things were going well but I wasn't able to save a lot of money. I still helped my dad when I could, but not often. My desire was to buy a house and have some children in the future. The weather got better in February however it was still cold. One weekend Irene and I went to visit Santa and Barry in New Dorp, Staten Island. Barry took me to his local hang out which was a bar. He introduced me to a couple of his friends and we had a beer. One of the guys came over and said there were some gang members there and they wanted us to join them in a fight. I said to Barry, "I am leaving; I don't need to get into trouble". We both got out just when the chairs began to fly. We ran towards the car and I ran into a lot next to the bar and fell. Barry helped me up and I was full of blood. I looked, and my right hand was cut open 1 inch. I put my handkerchief over it and we got in Barry's car and he sped to the hospital. On the way a police car pulled him over and the cop looked in and saw all the blood. He gave us an escort the rest of the way. When I got out we got in the emergency room and I passed out hitting my head on the floor. I remember them stitching me up but I had to be admitted because of a possible concussion due to the head injury and loss of blood. Barry went home and got my wife and came back. I remembered speaking to her for a minute then I must have fallen asleep. Irene had to stay overnight at Barry's and came back in the morning. I was awake and waited until 10am when the doctor came in. He said I could go home at 11am. Just then Irene, Barry, and Santa came in just in time for me to get dressed. My hand was all bandaged and I was ready to go. They took me back to Barry's house and had lunch. After lunch I drove home to Cliffside Park. I was really upset over this since it was my right hand. I went to work the next day and Steve popped up at one of my stores. I just told him I cut myself on a piece of glass. I was still able to work so I continued on my route. Two days later I was at a meeting at the fire house and we went across the street to the bar. We all had a couple of beers and as I got off the bar stool I fell and hit my hand on the floor. All my stitches opened up. I got in my car and drove home. There was a doctor's office in my apartment so I went to him. He was in his office; I was lucky but it sure hurt when he re-stitched my hand. It meant another week only this time I was careful. After 8 days he removed the stitches. That night we answered a mutual aid call to Palisades Park, N.J. on a large house fire. I got home about 3am, took a shower and stayed up and went to work to a store in Union, N.J. I called the office in New York and I had a message from Steve to meet him at the Grand Union in Paterson, N.J. Remember there were no cell phones in those days so we called in once a day. I met Steve and he wanted to set up another Progresso Festival at this store in three weeks so I took care of the ordering and made the arrangements with the manager. Steve seemed a little annoyed that I was already at a store at 9am in Union because he called my house at 8am and I was gone. Irene didn't realize it but she was getting ready to go to work and told Steve I was at a fire all night and left early since I was up. Steve didn't like the idea that I was on the fire department but he also knew, "I think", that I would never give it up. He had no complaints about me because I got along with everyone and the store managers liked me. As a matter of fact, one of our products, Lewis Sherry Jelly never sold much before I took the route and now I had sold more than any other route. Steve stayed with me all day until 6pm I think just for spite. I had a fire department sticker on the car and he told me to take it off because it was a company car. I now knew he didn't like firemen. I had sold my 57 Chevy to Ginny at the diner in March of last year and

I had a 53 Olds which I also sold a few weeks ago. Since Irene didn't drive I was okay with the company car which was a Chevy Station wagon. Valentine's Day was in a few days and I was at one of my stores in Nyack, NY and someone backed into the car. It was only a small dent but I had decided to make a report to Steve. That is when he said, "Are you sure you didn't do this going to a fire?" I said if you look it is at the rear of the car. He said I was meaning to tell you I don't want you to use the car going to fires. I didn't say much but I decided to buy another car. I didn't want to because I was saving money but I could see that things were not as nice as I thought regarding Steve and me. I started to look while I was working but didn't like much of what I saw and what I did like was too expensive. I spoke with Irene and we decided to look for another place. My salary was about $140.00 a week and until the amusement park opened again in April I only made a few extra dollars from the fire department. One of the firemen told me about a second floor apartment in a two family house a couple of blocks away. It was at 101 Crescent Avenue. We went to look at it. The owner lived on the first floor. He was a middle aged Italian with two daughters about 9 years old. It was quite large, two bedrooms, baths, living room and a large kitchen. We gave him a deposit and said we would move in on March 15th. I signed a one year lease at $135.00 a month less than I was paying. I then let my landlord know I would be leaving so they could rent the apartment. That week I saw an ad for a new Chevy II. I went to look at it at a dealer in Fort Lee. I liked it and so did Irene. It was a white convertible and the payments were $62.00 a month. Irene made about $70.00 a week so we thought we could handle it especially since the park would be opening soon. The new landlord Mr. Iacovelli said we could come in two weeks before if we wanted to paint, which we did. We started painting and Rosemary also came one day and helped. That night we ordered Pizza and went back to our house. We started to pack things and bring them over to the new apartment. Actually things went well because all we had left was the furniture. I got a truck and a couple of firemen, Charlie Silverman and Bob Bajer, and we moved in. The park had its meetings with the cops from Fort Lee and us, and we got our schedules. I was now working three nights a week at the park and Saturday and Sunday all day from 11am to 11pm. Now I could save for a house. May was also a busy month especially with Mother's Day weekend. There were many drunks, fights, and a couple of assaults. They came by the bus loads from the Bronx, Queens, Brooklyn, Jersey City, Newark and many other cities. Most of these were organizations, and clubs. That Saturday night was the first time I pulled my gun. I was around the back of the bath houses and saw some guy holding a knife to a girl about 16 years old. He had tried to take her pocketbook. I yelled for him to let her go when he turned to run. He had no way out but to pass me so I pulled my gun. He kept coming so I pointed my gun at him and was about to fire when he dropped the knife. I made him lie down on the ground and handcuffed him. I walked him up to the gate and called a car to take him to headquarters. A really funny thing happened on June 2. We were answering a call about a fight at one of the amusement rides and one man tried to run away and he punched me in the shoulder and got away. I arrested the other guy identified as Gerard Goodwin of Valley Stream, Long Island. That week when I went to court, Goodwin was there and I saw the guy that punched me who was with Gerard. How stupid is that? I immediately arrested him and he was tried right way. He told the judge he was a Valley Stream auxiliary policeman and he just brushed into me while he was running away. He was found guilty and fined.

During the day on July 11, 1962, I was driving down 17th Street in Newark, NJ on the way to a Food Town Market when I saw smoke coming from a three story building. I pulled the car on to the sidewalk and there was a black woman screaming that her two boys were in there. I ran in and as I was going up the stairs I could see flames going up the walls. I looked around, yelled, and heard one of the boys crying. I ran down the hallway and found them hiding in a closet. I grabbed them and wrapped them in my suit jacket and ran for the stairs. The flames were now coming up the sides and rear stairs. I went to the porch, and then I got to the bottom sidewalk. I had taken a lot of smoke and was coughing quite a bit. I don't remember what happened next. I woke up at Martland Medical Center where I was treated for smoke inhalation. After a few hours the Newark Police drove me back to my car. I was dirty and smelled of smoke. When I got home I told Irene about it and she didn't seem that impressed. Mom thought I was crazy as usual. The next day the newspapers and radio were full of the story. When I saw Steve that next morning he was not happy. He said I should mind my own business because I was working and I had a company car. I finally told him that I would continue to be a fireman on my off time and if I had to save someone again while I was working I would.

Three days later Steve told me to meet him at the garage. I arrived at 8am and he said he wasn't happy with my work and he let me go. He drove me home and I think I was more upset because of Uncle Walter getting me the job. So I got fired for saving two boys lives. I told Irene when I picked her up and she wasn't too happy. I did get more hours working at the park and I worked as a paid fireman to fill in for vacations so for the next few months I was okay. Again many fights and arrests occurred during the month of July. One night after work all of us would to Hiram's for hot dogs and another night to Callahan's. They always gave us half price. One day when I was off the whistles went off and as I drove to my station I noticed heavy black smoke coming from the south which looked like Edgewater. When I got to the station I learned it was a mutual aid to Weehawken. The whole waterfront was burning. We waited until we had at least four men then headed down the long hill along the Palisades. I was riding tail which I usually did. When we got halfway down the hill the engine stopped and we were told to drop a double lay, which was 2 – 2 ½ lines to the bottom of the hill then hook up to our engine. Fort Lee, who would be behind us, would hook up on top of the hill and connect to our two lines. Then they would supply our Engine Company and we would stretch more lines to a Deluge set up. A deluge was a large fixed nozzle on a stand which would provide a heavy stream to the fire area. Flames were all over many buildings, docks, and warehouses, and the wind was blowing about at 20 mph. We, along with Edgewater F.D., and Fort Lee F.D., tried to hold it but it was too much. Weehawken F.D. was at the front end and they declared a General Alarm which brought all East Bergen Communities but it would be too late to control so for four hours we forgot the fire until there was nothing else to burn. The first week of August I was taking Irene to work in the morning and a car stopped short in front of me. I hit the brakes but Irene's head went into the windshield and it broke. Her hair was tangled into the glass. The police car came and they saw it was me and called for the ambulance. Irene had a small cut and a large bump. After she was checked out she returned to work. I spoke to Mr. Green a few minutes and he told me if I wanted to be a Sheriff's Department Officer he could arrange it. I told him yes and two days later I went to the Bergen County Sheriffs office and filled out papers and was fingerprinted. Those days everything was political. I didn't hear anything for several weeks then I was called for an interview. I was told I got the job and would start in the middle of September. That was great because the park would be closed then.

It was August 5th and I was on patrol near the Casino Bar when I heard they found Marilyn Monroe dead. Everyone was talking about it. The next week I had a call to the "Whip Ride" about an assault. When I got there first, a 14 year old boy was on the ground bleeding very badly from the head. Everyone was screaming that the ride operator hit him with a crowbar. I told someone to put a shirt over his head and apply pressure while I went after the guy. He was still next to the ride when I confronted him. He raised the bar and I told him to stop. I couldn't take my gun out because there were people all around, so I yelled to him that the cop behind him is going to shoot and as he turned to look I tackled him and just then help arrived. I handcuffed him and we took him away. Most of these ride operators drank and were pretty nasty guys. Every year we would arrest a few of them sometimes despite Irving Rosenthal's objections. When I got home that night there was a letter from the N.J. Fireman's Mutual Benevolent Association. The letter was notifying me I was to receive an award on September 17th at the Deauville Hotel in Atlantic City with 4,800 firemen from the state in attendance I was to receive the award from Mayor Hugh Addonizio and Governor Hughes. There were calls from the newspapers and many other people. I was quite excited and so was the fire department. I am sure Steve Santa Maria saw it in the newspapers, and basically that is why he let me go. I made my reservations in Atlantic City and couldn't wait. The end of August was very busy at the park. One Sunday afternoon a woman came to me with a wallet. She said she found it on the ride "The Whip". I looked inside it and it had an ID and $76.00.

I brought it to the office and when I got there a young man and his wife came in looking for it. After checking the ID, I gave him the wallet. He wanted to give me $20.00 but I refused because the woman who found it was gone and it should have gone to her. We were now getting close to the end of the season and we were plenty busy. I worked two days at the F.D. and the rest of the week at the park. Labor Day weekend was the end and then I needed a job. I also needed a little rest. I had one week until I started at the Sheriffs department.

The first week I would be on days for the training then it would be midnights to 8am. I stopped at the Acme Market on Anderson Avenue where I knew the manager from servicing his store for Ferolie. I told him the story and asked if I could work part time. He said yes and I could even put in my own schedule. He said whenever I punch in, stock wherever it was needed. He knew I was a fireman and police officer and he liked me. I filled out the application and got my time card that same week. Walter Derig, who owned a bar on Palisades Avenue asked me if I would bartend two nights a week. I told him I would but there would be no steady times because of my other jobs. He said it was okay because it was just so he could get off a few hours so it was set. I now had five jobs.

September 17th, Irene and I went to Atlantic City and I received my award. It was quite the experience. The next day the newspapers had it all. I was now the celebrity in Cliffside Park and I was to start at the Sheriff's Department the next day. I reported for duty at 7am and met the Warden Captain Larson. I found out I had to work in the jail first so I was put on floor 3 with another deputy to train. All week I was booking in prisoners, taking photos, fingerprinting, and searching cells for contraband. Quite an experience; I was learning a lot. That weekend I worked Saturday at Acme and Sunday at the bar. We had two fires at night both minor. Irene worked Monday so I went to the fire house. Lunchtime Philly Ferrara and Chimanski and I went to our local bar for lunch. Then I went to pick Irene up from work then we went home. I had to go to work at midnight so after we ate I went to bed. Midnight wasn't bad but the nutty prisoners always acted up. We each had a floor and just outside the cellblock we had a small desk and phone. The jail was built in a circle and we had a stairway from the first floor to the top. At the top floor was a large open area which housed about 30 prisoners all up for a year sentence. They were called trustees. They had jobs in the kitchen, cleaning, and doing laundry. These guys would make pocketbooks out of cigarette packs then sell them to the guards for $7.50. I even bought one made out of Winston's. I smoked Winston's at that time so I had to have one. They all slept on cots, which was nicer than what other prisoners had. In the morning I would unlock one cell block at a time and take six guys to the shower. I would watch each guy then put him in another area with a razor to shave. The jail had no air-conditioning and it smelled. If a guard had trouble with a prisoner or there was a fight he would lean out over the circle area and yell on "3" or on "4" whatever floor it was. All of us would secure our block and run up or down to help. If we had a real bad guy we would take him to the green room. This was a room with nothing in it except a hole in the floor for a bathroom. If he hit a guard sometimes they would stick a hose in a hole in the door and keep spraying him. You couldn't do that today. I was saving money now with all these jobs but still wanted an appointment for the Fire Department. There were no openings yet so I knew I had to wait. It was October 1st about 7:30pm and I had gone to the store on Palisades Avenue. On the way back I was passing Lafayette Avenue when a friend of mine saw me and waved me down. At the same time another patrolman Joseph Piccininni came out of a doctor's office and my friend said he saw two guys break into Palisades Park and they were running with two large skulls. Joe and I captured them and a police car came with Patrolman Irwin Ornstein and John Terrano. They had received a call also from the former Mayor Gerald Calabrese. I arrested both boys and they were taken to Juvenile Detention. I went to work at midnight as usual and everything was quiet. The next morning I stopped at the fire house for coffee and the chief called me in. He said he was at a meeting with Mayor Madden and the council and they were going to give me the Cliffside Park Award for Valor. I hadn't heard this yet so I said nothing until the following day when I received the letter from the city notifying me I was to be presented the Valor award on November 7th at City Hall. One afternoon I was working at the Acme when I heard sirens and saw a Fort Lee fire truck go by. I called our headquarters and found out there was a mutual aid call to Union City on Hudson Blvd. at the lumberyard. I left the store and drove to the fire and met up with my engine company. This was a large fire taking in two blocks and the radiant heat was affecting the apartment houses across the street. We set up water screens in front of the building and we saved them. The fire went on for four hours and then we were released. I went to a pay phone and called Irene to say I was on my way home. It was 6:30pm and I had to go to work at midnight. It was 11:15pm and I was on Route 46 in Little Ferry when a white Cadillac flew by me about 70mph. I took off after him, flashed my lights, and he pulled over. The driver got out and he had a beard. He started to make jokes but I gave him a ticket for speeding. The next day I was told he was Buddy Hackett. That was not the name on his license.

I proceeded to go to work. After the cell block check I slept in my chair for about two hours then made my three o'clock check, and went down to the kitchen for coffee. They were already preparing for breakfast, and I was hungry so I had oatmeal and toast. We could always eat when we wanted which was good. The food was pretty good for a jail. November 7th Irene and I went to the borough hall and I received the Mayor and Council Valor Award. Mayor James Madden said, "It is altogether fitting that the people of his own community express their appreciation to Mr. Vallas for his heroic action. The Public Safety Chairman, William Linton said it was an honor to present the award to a resident of the community who through his "excellent and heroic" actions brought honor to Cliffside Park. Hello Steve Santa Maria, thank you for firing me

for this action. The weather began to get cold. We had a few fires in oil burners and I was working more at the Acme Market. I left the bar because Walter was having a problem and wanted me to work more. I couldn't do anymore than two nights so I quit. Irene and I began to look at houses a little bit in our area. They were all older.

I was off that Saturday before Thanksgiving and we drove to Tice's Farm in Woodcliff Lake, NJ to shop. They had everything from cider, pies, vegetables, and jellies. It was always a fun trip with the fall chill and beautiful trees changing colors. We stopped at Uncle Walter's then went home. December 5th arrived and now I was 22 years old. When I went to work that night I was assigned to floor 4. On this floor I had a guy who killed his wife. He came home and found her in bed with someone else and shot them both. He was from Cliffside Park. I spoke to him that morning before I got off because he was crying. I felt sorry for him but he was still a murderer. During the rest of the month I was taking prisoners to the visitor's room when I had to work days for a week. There was this black man who had to serve a year and a day because he couldn't pay his child support and punched his wife in an argument. I liked the guy because he was always talking about his kids and she would never bring them to see him. I spoke to him quite a bit over the year and I guess it was good therapy for him. I did this for others also. On Christmas Eve I worked and in my lunch bag I brought Christmas candy for many of the prisoners I liked. Christmas Day Irene and I went to mom's house for dinner. New Year's Eve we had a small party at our house with Leo and Rosemarie. She had gotten married and was living in Elizabeth, NJ.

CHAPTER–FOURTEEN
January And February 1963
OUR NEW HOME

Chapter–Fourteen - January And February 1963 – Our New Home

January and February were very busy months and also very cold months. I was putting in all the time I could at Acme to make extra money. At that time I was getting $1.25 an hour. Cigarettes were 25 cents a pack. February I saw an ad about new homes by Levitt & Sons in Matawan, NJ. Irene and I drove down to look at the models on Route 34. We saw a cape cod we liked very much with two bedrooms and a bath on the second floor and two bedrooms and bath on the first floor. There was a large kitchen and dining room and a large living room. The house had a garage and laundry room as well. The price was $15,500.00 on a large corner lot. We would have to put $500.00 down and finance the rest with the Dime Savings Bank of Brooklyn. I had $700.00 in savings so I knew we could get the down payment. I left a $200.00 check as a deposit and we went home. The next week we went back with mom and dad to show them the model. They liked it too. The house came with a washer and dryer and dishwasher, and garbage disposal. Of course, we could upgrade but we were satisfied with everything. I gave the $300.00 more for the down payment. We filled out all the papers and picked out the colors. Mom and dad said as a gift they would carpet the entire house for us. We were so excited. The completed date was to be sometime in August. The floors came with vinyl tile so we would wait until the house was built before ordering the rugs.

In March I was giving a class in First Aid to the residents in Cliffside Park at the high school. Irene wanted to know what I would do about the job. I said she would have to quit her job and after we moved in she could find another. I told her she should learn how to drive. I would play it by ear and see what jobs were in the area for me. All the fire departments were volunteers and yes I planned to join when I moved there. I was saving every penny now because we would need lots of things such as a lawn mower, garden tools, lamps, some furniture, etc. I sold my stamp collection, train sets, and quite a few paintings I had. I was a good artist and had sold paintings before. I made a few hundred dollars with all that. I didn't say much to anyone in Cliffside Park because the house had not gone through yet. I had said in my application that I had $500.00 in a savings account, but I gave that as the down payment. The bank called me that week. It was around Greek Easter in April, 1963 and the banker said my bank account only had $200.00 in it. I told her I had cash at home and the girl who I spoke with was very nice. She said it was a requirement to have an equal amount of money to what the down payment was in savings. She said get the money in the bank and then call her and she would do the checking again. I spoke to my Aunt Mary and she gave me $500.00 to put in the bank and I said I would give it back as soon as the mortgage was approved. Within two weeks the mortgage was approved. I withdrew the money and gave it back to Aunt Mary.

It was now May, and one weekend Irene and I had gone to a house party at one of the policeman's house. We all had a bit too much to drink and when Irene and I got home I wanted to have sex. I remember she had on a yellow dress and she looked quite sexy. Irene never was aggressive and I always had to make the first move. This time I was very excited and put her on the bed, took her panties off and made love. This was the first time I didn't use a condom. Well soon after Irene became pregnant. I didn't think she was too happy, but I was.

The amusement park had opened again and I worked as much as I could. We were making plans and Rosemary came over and she was talking with Irene about Leo. Something was wrong but I didn't know exactly what. We both went to Matawan to see how things were going and it looked good. The roads were not in yet and hundreds of homes were under construction. We walked from a dirt road to see the cement foundation and walls going up. I was hoping everything would be done by August.

Working at the amusement park was very helpful. I kept trying to save money. Irene told Mr. Green we were leaving sometime in September so he could look for someone. July and August 1963, I worked from 11am to 10pm at the park then 12pm to 8am at the jail. I would sleep from about 9am until 2pm. I did have days off so it wasn't too bad. It was August 1st when I was told the house was ready for inspection. I went down and, except for a few miner corrections, it was ready. I would close on the house September 1, 1963 or earlier. I called mom and made arrangements for us to go to Sears to pick out the rug color then make an appointment for the man to meet me at the house to measure. We went to Sears and picked out a tangerine carpet and at the same time we looked at drapes and curtains. That weekend Sears came and measured everything. While I was at the house I went to the office and I was friendly with the guy who sold us the house and he let us close on the house that day. I got the keys and we went back and did the check list. He said they would finish the landscaping and grass seed when we moved in so we could water the seed every day. So as of August 10th we owned our house.

I decided to leave the Sheriffs Office so I gave two week's notice. I also received a letter of recommendation from Cliffside Park's mayor, fire department, police department, and Sheriffs Office. Warden Larsen said I could go to the Monmouth Country Jail in Freehold to let them know and he would make a call for me. We called a mover to move us on September 15th. My landlord was very good about everything letting us leave although he kept my deposit. I spent two weeks saying good bye to everyone and we finally moved to Matawan, 10 Norwood Lane. Levitt & Sons had built hundreds of houses there in different sections and was called Strathmore. After we set the furniture and unpacked, which took a few days, we had to shop for many things. I called the office and they sent the landscaper who then seeded the entire lawn and yard. He also put in some trees and bushes. I had to buy hoses and sprinklers, a shovel, hoe, etc. and we watered the lawn everyday.

One afternoon I heard sirens and saw plenty of smoke across town in Cliffwood Beach. I drove over to the Oak Shades Fire House but everyone was gone. I hung around for about an hour until the trucks came back. I introduced myself to the chief who was Louis Auriemma. He showed me around and said Matawan Township was expanding so much my service would be greatly appreciated especially since I had a lot of experience. They had a nice building which housed three engines. They didn't have a ladder truck because there were no tall buildings in the Township. They also had a second floor meeting room, and behind the engine room was a large party hall with a stage. It also had a bar. They made money by renting out the hall for different events such as weddings, parties, etc. This was a large fire department covering many square miles. The township was split between Oak Shades F.D. and Cliffwood Beach F.D. with two chiefs. Cliffwood Beach fire trucks were white and ours were red. That Thursday I was sworn in. I installed my blue light on my car which was the 1956 Olds-red in color. I didn't owe anything on it so that was good. Chief Auriemma worked as a driver for Poole Trucking. There really weren't any good jobs around this area. The police department wasn't hiring as I inquired earlier. Irene had gotten a job at Sears in Middletown and she also got her driver's license.

I took a job with Fuller Brush Company and after training for one week I was given my route which was all of Monmouth County. I liked working my own schedule since it was like owning your own business. It was a very interesting job and I called on many of the horse farms. I mostly dealt with women who were home during the day although I received orders in the mail and on telephone also. The products were shipped to my home and I would deliver them.

There was one woman whose husband worked in France and was never home. She was about 35 years old and she liked me. Every time I called on her she always offered me a drink or coffee and I always said no. I was happily married and didn't want to fool around. Just before I eventually left Fuller Brush I was only making about $75.00 to $100.00 a week then, I stopped at her house to deliver a crumb roller. She knew I was coming that day and when I went in the house she had on a sheer white nightgown that you could see through. I thought I would die. She kept talking and I could smell booze on her breath. She offered me a martini and I said no. She kept getting close to me and I couldn't help getting excited. I was waiting for her to pay me and she walked past her glass door and I could see everything. When she came over she said, "Peter here is the money and keep the change." Then she put her arms around me and squeezed me close. She then kissed me still holding me close. I told her this was not a good idea and I had to leave, which I did.

CHAPTER–FIFTEEN
New Employment

Chapter–Fifteen – New Employment

That week I decided to get another job. I answered an ad in the Red Bank Register for a collection manager position at Bell Finance Company in Red Bank, NJ. I called and made an appointment for the next day at 8am. I showed up and my interview was with Mr. Ralph Belknap, President. He was very interested in me because of my police background, but I could tell he was a tough boss. He introduced me to his son-in-law Howie Cohen who was the manager of all his six offices. After two hours, I was hired and could start as soon as possible. It was a good job and he said I did have the opportunity to become a manager if I worked out. The job as a collection manager was a start. I would receive hospitalization which I needed and two weeks vacation, two personal days and five sick days. When I went home I told Irene. She was happy and I started on Monday. I called Fuller Brush and told them I would continue working on a part-time basis until they found a new person. This was okay with them. That weekend I went to Sears and bought shirts and ties for the job. The Olds was starting to give me trouble but one of the firemen, Tom Falco had a brother who owned a Sunoco Station on the highway so I took it to him to fix what he could. He told me if I as going to use it for work I should look for a new car. I thought about it because Bell Finance would pay for gas and mileage. I took the car to the Keyport Rambler and gave him my car as a down payment and bought a small Rambler American; brand new. Payments would be $69.00 a month. My first week was training on collecting overdue accounts by telephone. They were impressed with my ability to get them to pay. The second week I was collecting P&L accounts. These were the hard ones because people skipped out, moved, or changed jobs and were difficult to locate. I was very successful and things were looking good. I went on the road tracking down people and collecting money. I was dong real well. It was a 9am to 5pm job, but I would go in at 8am. Howie was my main boss. Irene was still working and we were okay. They said the baby was going to be born at the end of January. In those days we didn't know what we were going to have. I took a job at the fire house cleaning up after parties and weddings, and once a week I would clean the bar and meeting room. That was $30.00 a party and $20.00 for the other events.

The grass was coming in beautifully so I went to Grants and bought a lawnmower. Mom and dad bought Aunt Mary down one Sunday and we made dinner. Aunt Mary went with me to the local nursery and bought us 12 yew bushes for the front of the house. I took them home and planted them. I was doing well at Bell Finance and liked the job. My house to Red Bank was only about a half hour. I had gotten friendly with the fire chief, Lou, and his wife Carol. They were great people and so were their friends Dick and Carol. I had them over to the house and we had been to their house. Lou was remodeling his house and I would help him occasionally. I would learn a lot from Lou in the next few years. November arrived and I had beautiful grass which was now getting its winter look. My landscaping was great and I loved taking care of it. I just had a concrete patio put in and now I wanted to put in a white picket fence. I called a fence company but it was very expensive. Richie Lewicki, a fireman said I should do it myself. I wanted to do it before my baby was born but that didn't happen.

The fire department had just issued us an Electron radio for the house. When a fire call came in it would broadcast it after a tone. The sirens would still blow in case we were outside. November 22, 1963 I was in my office in Red Bank just getting ready to go on the road when Mrs. Morgan; Mr. Bellnap's secretary came in and said President Kennedy had been shot in Dallas. I left the office and was driving down Highway 35 in Shrewsbury when I saw a policeman lowering the flag in front of the police station. I pulled over and put the radio on. I couldn't believe what I was hearing. I was so upset I was crying. I saw many cars pulling over. The whole community was in shock. Even though I was a Republican he was my president, not like today where people hate George W. Bush and have no respect for the president. I drove to a shopping center a few miles away and stopped to get a coffee. When I walked in there were people crying. I got my coffee and went into Grants Department Store and I couldn't believe the scene. I started to fill up again so I left and drove back to the office. I just couldn't work. I tried to do some phone work but the whole office was in distress. When I went home, I was glued to the TV all night. Except for a house fire I couldn't sleep. On the day of the president's funeral, the boss gave everyone the day off. Many companies gave their employees off. I spent the whole day in our TV room. I spoke to dad at the diner and he said they were packed. All the truck drivers were in and dad had put a radio on for all to hear the news.

Thanksgiving was at my house this year and we all had a good time. I was at the fire house one night and Jimmy Vena and his brother Bob said let's all go to Kalerts. This was a bar on Route 35 which had a big plane on its roof. Everyone knew the Vena's and we were all drinking beer. The place was great and had music. Country music was big in South Jersey. It ended up that at least once a week we went there at night for a couple of hours. Irene and I were getting ready for our first Christmas in the new house. I bought lights for outside, and other exterior decorations. I just loved the house and I thought I had the perfect life. I was hoping for a boy, and Irene was getting really big and people would say that means a boy. Irene had a baby shower and we were given many gifts. We set up the baby's room upstairs crib and all. We decorated the house and it was beautiful. Lou and Carol were big on Christmas too and they did a great job of decorating their house also. Bell Finance had a Christmas Party at the Molly Pitcher Hotel in Red Bank. Everyone got a bonus. We had a lot of company; my family, Irene's mother and cousin, friends, etc. It was just a great holiday. New Year's Eve we went to Uncle Walters's house. After midnight, we left and used the Garden State Parkway to go home. As we approached Nutley, there was a bad car accident just in front of us. The car hit the side of the overpass, turned over, and caught on fire. I pulled over and ran to the car. There was a girl on the passenger side and a boy driving. Both were hurt badly. I smashed the window and pulled the girl out first. The fire was all over because the gas tank had ruptured. I passed the girl out. A state trooper had arrived and he helped me out. That was two more lives saved. I didn't realize it then but my raincoat was burned and I didn't' know it.

I had the clean up detail New Year's Day but it was extra money. The third week of January, 1964 Irene started having pains at about midnight. I called for our first aid squad because it was snowing very heavily. We got to the Riverview Hospital in Red Bank, but after being checked out, it was a false alarm, so they took us back home.

CHAPTER–SIXTEEN

February 3, 1964 It's A Boy!

Chapter–Sixteen – February 3, 1964 It's A Boy!

On February 3, 1964, Irene woke me up and she was standing there with her water running down her legs. I got her in the car and took her to the hospital. After she was admitted I went to my Cousin Barbara's house in Belford to wait. In the late afternoon Lorraine called Barbara's house and said Donna had a very high fever. I took my car over to Lorraine's and drove them to the hospital. As I was walking through the emergency room the head nurse called out to me and

said," Congratulations, you just had a 10 pound baby boy!" Everyone knew me because of the fire department. I couldn't believe this. Lorraine stayed with Donna and I went up to maternity. I saw Irene who was doing fine. The nurse took me to see our boy who we already named Peter Steven. Steven was Irene's father's name. I looked through the glass and saw the name tag "Vallas". He was the largest boy born there to date and he looked a little Chinese. After seeing Irene again I went down to emergency and they had treated Donna so I drove them home. I drove home to start the phone calls to the family. I picked Irene and Petee up a few days later and it was bitter cold. We were both excited and couldn't wait for people to see him, but we waited a couple of weeks first so we could train ourselves with the baby. He didn't cry much at night but there were days when he did. Everything was great and I was very happy; I had my family. Everything was going great and Irene was doing great as a mother.

One night in the second week of February we had a big fire on Route 34 in Holmdel at a paint factory. It was freezing and we had to use our suction because there was no water supply. We chopped a large hole in the ice at the pond to get water. The Paint Factory was on a hill and we kept sliding and falling. It took 4 ½ hours to finally get all the flames out. I went to work that morning quite tired but managed to get through the day. March arrived and I went looking for a fence. I went to a lumber yard on Route 35 in Middletown and purchased the fence. I had a large pie shaped piece of property and the section came in 6 foot pieces all wood with pickets unpainted including two gates. I didn't realize then I had to paint two coats on it which would take forever. They delivered the fence and posts a week later and I put them in the yard. I bought a post-hole digger and started to put the fence in. Richie Lewicki advised me what to do and with some help from the firemen. I had it finished within three weeks. Now it was time to paint. What a pain this was. It took me four weeks to put two coats of white paint on it. When it was done it looked great. Petee was doing fine and I got the brainstorm to turn the garage into a playroom. I guess because I was helping Lou with his remodeling I got the bug. I started the job and Lou came over to show me what to do. I made the plan, and then waited until I had some extra money to buy the 2 x 4's, etc. They were starting the Monmouth County Fire College classes in April and I signed up. Mr. Belknap was putting a new office on Route 35 in Middletown and everyone was wondering who was going to be the manager. The Eatontown manager, Mr. Bassinger wanted the promotion so I thought he was going to get it. On March 17th, St. Patrick's Day, Mr. Belknap called me into his office and said because I was doing a great job I was being promoted to manager of the new Middletown office. He said Howie Cohen would work with me for a month so I could learn how to make loans, how to post payments, interest rates, credit reports, and how to run the office. I couldn't wait to go home to tell Irene my pay increased by $40.00 a week. The next week I graduated Fire College, which was on weekends and nights because all volunteers had to work.

Monday morning I was in my new office. In my section was a girl named Lisa. She came from the Red Bank office so I knew her. She was a pretty 19 year old girl and was with Bell Finance Company for one year. My new business cards had my picture on them as all managers did. All of April I worked with Howie and within two weeks he started to leave me alone and come in a couple of hours a day to check up on me. Mr. Belknap stopped by twice to see me. I would open the office at 9am and close at 5pm but most of the time I was in the office at 7:30 or 8am and sometimes left at 5:30 or 6pm. Every month we had a 7am breakfast meeting which all managers had to attend. The first meeting I saw Mr. Bassinger gave me a dirty look, I guess he was angry that I got Middletown. After the meeting Bassinger said to me, "Thanks for taking my job away." I said, "If you were a better man than me, then you would have gotten the position". We never got along after that and, as a matter of fact, he quit six months later. I found out later he was with Bell Finance three years but was lazy, and he had a college degree in business and I had no college at all. One morning I went next door to the "2 Guys from Harrison" to buy some towels and a coffee machine for the office. I was at the door at 9am but the door was locked. I stood there and a few minutes later a short heavy woman with a bunch of keys opened the door. She said she was sorry she was late but the store manager had a meeting. Since I was next door I introduced myself and she said she was Helen Higgins, security supervisor. We became friendly and spoke almost every day. She said she lived with her sister who also worked for 2 Guys. I was getting better and better at my job and of course some of the other mangers were jealous because I got a brand new office. I was also at the top of the list for making new loans. Mr. Belknap called me into his office one day and wanted me to join the Kiwanis Club in Middletown so I could be a part of the community affairs and also promote business. They had a lunch meeting once a month which was great. It went on my expense account. I also made loans to almost all the firemen. You could only go up to $500.00 loans then with a payment of $26.77 each month.

My sister Linda was graduating high school in June and I was planning on going. I made arrangements for Howie Cohen to cover for me while I was away. We went to Linda's graduation at the North Bergen High School then mom's house after the ceremony, and then Irene and I went home. We had beautiful flowers blooming in front of our house and I started a small vegetable garden in the backyard. I finally finished with the last orders for Fuller Brush Company and cleaned out the garage. I still wanted to make a playroom but didn't want to start until I had the money. Irene and I would visit a lot with Barbara and Ted, and Lorraine and Danny. We all lived within a few miles of each other. We also went to square dances once in a while.

We had been planning the baptism for Petee and we had it at the Greek Orthodox Church. Petee was baptized Greek Orthodox because Irene and I were both Greek Orthodox. Jonathan Stathakis was the godfather. There was no godmother because John was not married.

CHAPTER–SEVENTEEN
The Baby Boy

Chapter–Seventeen – The Baby Boy

June 1964 – My Blue Revolving Light

We rarely used a babysitter. Irene had made friends with a girl she met at the doctor's office and would stop at her house once in a while. My Rambler was getting on my nerves because it was very small. I went to the Chevy dealer in Red Bank while I was at work one day and I traded it in for a new yellow Chevy Malibu. It was beautiful and had a lot of room. On the way home I was stopped at a light and Cousin Bernice was next to me and waved. When I got home I installed my blue revolving light on the windshield. Petee was growing fast for a five month old. He was a good baby.

July 1964 – The Annual Fire Department Fair

At the fire department we were preparing for the annual F.D. Fair. It was held in a large lot a few acres near Route 34 in Strathmore. It ran for one week, Monday through Sunday. They always made good money and since we were volunteers, we needed it. Every night after work I would work on of the stands. There were rides, foods stands, and all sorts of games. Then on the weekend we were jammed and we also had entertainment Saturday and Sunday. We were all tired at the end of the week. Our fire commissioner was a guy by the name of Frank Divino. He owned the local bowling alley. He was a nice guy and was also a volunteer fireman. I had just gotten on the bowling team for the F.D. and Frank was going to build a new large bowling alley on Route 34 in Strathmore.

I went to a wet-down in Marlboro on Saturday. I had never been to one before. About eight of us took our Engine to the Fire House in Marlboro and so did many other towns. A wet-down was to celebrate the delivery of a new fire truck. There was plenty of beer and food and then all the trucks would spray water on its new truck as well as water fights with each other. Things got pretty wild then and everyone would get drunk. We would also purchase a glass beer mug that was printed with a picture of a fire truck with the date and name of the department.

August 1964 – My Job at Bell Finance

I was doing very well at Bell Finance and enjoyed my job. I also got involved with the Kawanis and some of their projects. I was appointed Scoutmaster of Troop 237 by James Nottings of the Monmouth Council of Boy Scouts.I was a very busy man, even though I was working two jobs, I somehow managed to do it all. Irene was with Petee and I looked forward to playing with him in his crib with his little toys. Lou, my fire chief had brought his cousin into the Fire Department. His name was

Butch. He seemed like a nice guy, young and good looking. He was always around and stayed at Lou's house. His mother had passed away and I felt sorry for him. I had invited him over to my house for dinner a few times. Irene's girlfriend Rosemary came down for an overnight stay. She was having trouble with her husband, Leo. I didn't know what the problem was but I knew she was pregnant. I did overhear her say once she had the baby she would take him for everything.

Butch had come over a few times and he liked Rosemary. I knew he saw her a few times after that, where I don't know. I had liked Leo and could not imagine him being a problem in any way. Something was going on but I didn't know what. I heard from mom and she said Uncle Walter gave my sister, Linda a job as a secretary in his office, and she bought a new Camaro. I was happy for her and wished I could see her more often.

September 1964 – Many Fires

We were having quite a few fires lately. The weather had been dry and we had many brush fires. We also had several mutual aid calls. The weekends were always busy for me. Sometimes I would go to the office for a couple of hours then I would cut the grass and plant bushes. We always liked to have company on Sunday's. I loved the fall season when it got cooler and the leaves started to change colors. Even the air smelled better.

October 1964 – Halloween

The pumpkins were out along the roads at the nurseries and it was beautiful. I placed two large pumpkins outside our front door and put some corn husks on the fence posts. We had a beautiful Indian summer that weekend and on Sunday I barbequed chicken, and ribs. Doris and Willie came down to visit.

November and December 1964 – The Holidays

Thanksgiving, Irene and I went to Irene's mothers so she could see the baby. Along came another birthday and I was 24 years old. Getting ready for Christmas was always a great time. I always put the tree up and decorated the first week of December. I loved Christmas time. I did all the shopping early and Irene shopped for the baby. We also had gotten a small terrier and it liked Petee. This was Petee's first Christmas and he played with his toys and it was a great event. We later drove to mom's for dinner. We went to the fire house for New Year's Eve so we took Petee to Kay's house in Jersey City. She said she would baby sit for us. The New Year's Eve party was great. When Irene and I got home she called her mother. Kay was drunk and we heard Petee crying.

January and February 1965 – Taking Care of Petee

We both left immediately for Jersey City and picked Petee up and brought him home. New Year's Day I had to clean up after the party which was a big job, but I was getting paid for it so I didn't mind. Petee's first birthday arrived and that night we had a little cake and had Lou and Carol come over. It was a week day so we didn't have a party. Irene was acting a little strange on and off but I was very busy working and brushed it off.

I invited Jack Ellison and his wife to come for a weekend. He had gotten married to someone he met in Albuquerque, New Mexico. We had a nice weekend and she seemed very nice. For the rest of February I was still very busy with Bell Finance and I also worked a couple of Saturdays for dad. It was only about a half hour drive to the diner in South Kearny. I always made out well working for dad.

March and April 1965 – Brush Fires

March turned out to be a very dry month. The Kawanis Club had a St. Patrick's Day dinner and cocktails. Irene didn't go to that and I stayed only about an hour because Petee had a bad cold and I wanted to be home in case we had to take him to the doctor's. The Saturday after St. Patrick's Day we had a mutual aid fire in Hazlet on Route 34; a large two story wooden business building and the winds were so bad, we had trouble containing it. After a couple of hours we left.

April was still dry and the winds were bad. We had dozens of brush fires; a couple of bad ones on the Garden State Parkway where it had to be shut down. On Saturday and Sunday I had fire college and completed that course. The second week of April I was promoted to second Lieutenant. The next day was Sunday and there was a large fire in New Brunswick, NJ about 20 miles away on Route 18. I was on the tail of the pumper all the way bouncing up and down. I could see the smoke for miles. This fire was moving fast and already burned about a dozen houses. We drove through some thick smoke down a street and our assignment was to try and save whatever we could. We were gone a whole day and we went home very tired. Eventually, the next week it began to rain and things quieted down.

May 1965 - Gardening

Spring was here and gardening was once again becoming necessary. I loved working in the yard and garden. Petee was now walking and we played in the yard. He was a good kid and liked to run all over the place.

June 1965 – My Family's Trip to Greece

The first week of June I spoke to mom and she said dad was so excited because

Linda, dad, and she were going to Greece for two weeks and would be attending my cousin Velessairios' wedding to Katie. This would be the first time dad returned to Greece to see his sisters; the only two left. Everyone else had died. Irene, Petee, and I went to Idlewild Airport in NY to see them off. Uncle Walter, Aunt Dolores, and Aunt Mary came, too and we all ate dinner at the airport. We got home and dropped Aunt Mary off in Jersey City then Irene, Petee, and I went home to Matawan.

I came home from work one day and Irene was on the patio with Petee with the neighbor's boy and his mother. The two boys were playing and having fun. After they went home I was getting ready to sit down to eat and there was a knock on the door. When I opened the door this tall man said he was a neighbor who lived a few houses away. He said his son was over to my house with his wife earlier and my son stole his airplane. I couldn't believe what he said and told him I would look out back and sure enough it was in the grass. I gave it to him and said I thought he had some nerve to accuse a two and a half year old boy of stealing. He answered, "You had the plane didn't you?" I told him don't ever come near my house again because you have no brains. Did I get that from mom? The next week we drove to Idlewild to pick up mom, dad, and Linda; they had a wonderful time. Mom said they were all at the airport with flowers and dad was crying. That was the last time he would see his sisters, and his nephew Odessa, who a couple of years later had a massive heart attack at a soccer game, and died.

July 1965 – The Annual Fireman's Fair

After the 4th of July holiday, we had the annual fireman's fair. I then started to build the new rooms in the garage. Lou helped me frame it out. By the end of July I was getting ready to put in the BX cable. Each week I would buy the boxes and wire, etc. until I had it all, then I would start.

August 1965 – The Firehouse

I was getting busy in August helping dad a couple of Saturdays, and working at the fire house. We were also getting ready to go to the Fireman's Convention in Atlantic City. Irene called me at work one day and said Petee got hit in the head with a swing at her girlfriend's house. I took off and met her at the doctor's office. Poor Petee was screaming and Irene was crying. I had to hold Petee down while the doctor stitched him on the bridge of his forehead. When I got home, Petee was calmed down and Butch was at the house. I noticed lately when I was working Butch was always around. I was contacted by the Republican Club and asked if I would run for office as councilman. I was surprised but, why not? It would be an experience. Plenty of meetings went on and the announcement of the candidates would be on October 26, 1965. There were many articles and meetings until the election. Mr. Belknap was happy because my name was in the papers all the time mentioning I was manager of Bell Finance Company. Frank Divino had since opened the new bowling alley on Route 34 in Strathmore. It was great and we held many meetings there.

September through December 1965 – Election Results

Well, election night came and even Irene came to the bowling alley to await the results. Finally we found out all the Republicans lost. I felt bad but I must say I learned a lot about politics. I also knew I would never run for an office again. Aunt Mary had been diagnosed with breast cancer, and they started something new, "Chemotherapy". Irene and I went to visit her and it was around my birthday. While she was in the hospital, she went into a coma.

On December 8th, I went to the hospital with mom. Aunt Helen was there which was unusual. Aunt Helen very seldom bothered with Aunt Mary and always talked about her and her waspy friends. Uncle Walter came and we told Aunt Helen she could leave. She left to go home and I walked into the room and was holding Aunt Mary's hand when she died. Mom went down to tell Aunt Helen before she got on the bus. Aunt Helen looked away from her and crossed the street. Something was funny because when we left to drive home Uncle Walter saw her at the bus stop and told her to get in the car, but she turned away. We went back to Uncle Walter's and there was a big discussion. Aunt Mary told mom and Uncle Walter that her safe deposit key was in the drawer next to her bed in the hospital and when she died she said to take it. Uncle Walter was the executor of the will and mom was to get the house. Everything was laid out. Uncle Ken was an alcoholic and he was known to like to touch all the women. Uncle Walter called for a meeting at Aunt Mary's house after the funeral and Aunt Helen and Aunt Catherine were upstairs with Uncle Ken. When they came down Uncle Walter wanted to get the key to the safe deposit box and go to the bank to get the will. Aunt Helen said she didn't have it. Uncle Walter said he wants nothing to do with this anymore and left. That was a bad move because in the days to come someone got into the safe deposit and took the will. Aunt Helen who Aunt Mary couldn't stand for years had somehow through politics and the bank managers got into the box. Aunt Helen took over Uncle Kenneth's role and after that who knows. Helen got everything and Uncle Ken died soon after in Helen's control. Aunt Helen told Uncle George that Uncle Kenneth left everything to Aunt Catherine and her. After that the family had no contact with Helen anymore. The price she paid for her deeds were the loss of her three children and then she died suddenly sometime later. Aunt Catherine was also shunned for several years until I saw my cousins, Doris and Willie a few years later.

January 1966 – The Fires on New Year's Eve

On New Year's Eve Irene and I went to the fire house. I believe it was after midnight when the horns went off for a mutual aid call to Matawan Borough for a supermarket fire. The Bell's Foodtown was fully involved. Everyone sobered up pretty fast and we stretched 2,000 feet of hose to pump water from Lake Lefferts and 4,000 feet from Matawan Lake. Matawan Wines and Liquors was next door but somehow we saved it except for some smoke damage. What a night that was, I will never forget it.

New Year's Day I had to clean up the party mess. Irene was still acting strange and never showed any affection to me. If I didn't make a move in bed we probably never would have sex. Ever since Petee was born she was acting funny. I wasn't perfect because I worked so much but I tried to make everything right. I finally lost my temper one night and punched the wall. Petee was 2 years old now and I was doing okay. Finances were a little tight but still I felt something wasn't right. Rosemary was divorcing Leo and Irene and she were on the phone many times.

February 1966 – Mom and Dad's First Home

Petee was now two years old and getting into everything. I also noticed a big difference in Irene. It was almost as if she didn't want to bother with me.

I gave a fire prevention class for kids at the local school and received a nice letter from them. Mom and dad finally bought a house in Washington Township, NJ. The house was just built and it was beautiful. It was a two story with four bedrooms, a two-car garage, and a large lot with a stream running behind it. Dad was very excited with their first home and so was mom. They offered Irene and me to move in with them and down the road they would give us the house. Irene wouldn't hear of it but again I think there was another reason why but I wasn't sure.

March 1966 – My Job at the Airport

I had gotten a call from Allegany Airlines and they offered me a station agent's job. The salary would be more than what I was making now. I was making $4,800.00 a year now and I would go to $5,500.00 plus overtime. I was working on Saturday's at the diner and if I took the job at the airport I could work more for dad. The money from dad was always cash. I went for an interview to see that the job was going to be what I wanted. It was better than I thought so I gave notice to Bell Finance and they were disappointed but I gave them two week's notice. I got measured for uniforms when I accepted the job. I started on the 4pm to 12midnight shift and I didn't mind it because I was home with Petee and Irene during the day. She was still acting strange and I was thinking about moving to Bergen County. I had said I wanted to sell the house and move to Bergen County. We called the realtor and put our house on the market. I was doing great on the new job and working extra at the diner so the money was better. I was getting ready to get more materials to finish the extra room for Petee.

April 1966 – Marital Problems

Irene and I had a bad argument one day and I lost my temper. I ended up screaming at her. All was forgiven and I knew something was up. She was on the phone a lot with Rosemary and if I walked near her she would whisper and acted suspicious. I was doing a lot of work around the house because the weather was great. We had our normal number of brush fires so I was busy with that also.

May 1966 – Moving from Our First Home

One weekend when I was off we went to visit mom and dad and we all went shopping. Mom and dad bought Irene several dresses. When we came home that day I barbequed some steaks in the backyard on the patio. I changed shifts to days and I was able to work on Saturday at the diner. It was the last week in May and I had started to do the electrical wiring. Lou came over and showed me what to do. I bought the rest of what I needed and little by little I was making progress. I received a call from the real estate agent and they had a buyer who I showed the house to. They were setting up the paperwork.

June 1966 – Marital Problems Continue

I was back on the 4pm to 12am shift for two weeks to cover for someone in operations. I was home during the day again which I liked. It was around the middle of June and I was off that Saturday and Sunday. When I got home Friday I got a call from dad and he asked me if I could open the diner with him at 3am because John was sick. I told him, yes then told Irene I would get up at 2am to go to the diner. I went to bed after dinner and got up at 2am. I drove up the Garden State Parkway and something was bothering me. I kept thinking that something was going on at home that I didn't know about. When I got to the diner dad had pulled up and when I saw the lights on I said, "Why are the lights on dad?" He said he didn't know. The door was open to the kitchen and John was there. He said he felt better and decided to come in. I told dad I wanted to go home that I didn't feel well myself. Since John came in dad said okay and gave me $10.00. The phone was ringing outside the public phone booth. We didn't have a phone in the diner. Calls were 10 cents then. When I answered it was one of the firemen who said please don't ever tell anyone I called you. He said Butch was at my house as we spoke. I hung up and took off. I drove home in thirty minutes and as I turned into Norwood Lane, I saw the lights on in the house in the kitchen and in the upstairs bedroom. There was Butch's car in my driveway. I went to the front door and put the key in and the chain was on the door. I yanked the door so hard that the chain broke. Butch was in the kitchen and Irene came down after about two minutes. She certainly heard the door chain break. I said to Butch, "What are you doing here at 4:15am?" He said he saw the lights on in the kitchen and thought something was wrong. I asked, "What were you doing on my street; was there a fire?" He said he was just driving around. Then he said I have to go and he left. I yelled at Irene and asked what he was doing here? She said she called him because she thought Petee was sick. I immediately went up to Petee's room and he was sound asleep. I went in our bedroom and the whole bed was messed up with pillows on the floor. Irene would never have a bed like that particularly my side of the bed. I went nuts and started to cry. She insisted nothing was going on but obviously I knew different. The next few hours I asked her why she was doing this and she said I never help her clean or do laundry. She said it was tough taking care of Petee. I told her I was working my ass off so Petee and she could have a new home and everything the best. After an hour of my crying and talking I said I would forgive her and we would work things out.

During work that day I called Lou Sorrentino and hired him to represent me if I got a divorce but mainly to handle the closing of the house. I went to work at the airport the next day and when I got home that night Irene was gone. I called her mother in Jersey City and she was there at her mom's apartment on Clinton Avenue. I begged her to come home so I went to get Petee and her. I didn't' go to work the next day. I was so upset. I didn't' know what to do. I started to vacuum the rugs and asked what I could do. She didn't say much at all; she made a phone call and I didn't know to whom. Later on I went to the store to get milk for Petee and I called her mother. Kay told me she didn't know what was wrong with Irene and she told her she should be home with her husband. When I went to work the next day I told my friend John Pierson about what happened. I had no one to talk to and I certainly wouldn't tell mom and dad. When I got home at about 5:30pm I stopped and bought flowers then when I went in she wasn't home. I checked around and saw Petee's things were gone and some of her things. I called my friend who called me at the diner and he said Butch picked her up and took her to her mother's. I called her mother and she wouldn't speak to me. I cried all night and walked around the house in a daze. I couldn't go to work the next day again. I told Lou and Carol what happened and of course the whole town knew that day. Personally I think they all knew about it before me.

One night about a week later, I got a call from Elaine Ferguson, a friend of Lou and Carol's and she said she wanted to come over with Pinkey, Lou's cousin. They both came over to cheer me up. They also knew what was going on and everyone was angry with Butch. We all had a drink and I put some music on. I danced with both of them and they left. I spoke with Pinkey the next day and asked her to come over that night to talk. She came over and talked for a long time. We also danced and I kissed her and was glad she was there for me. After she left I continued to drink then I decided to kill myself.

I went upstairs to look for my gun and it was gone. Irene must have taken it. I went to go back downstairs and I fell head first to the first floor. I couldn't move my neck or back. I crawled to the kitchen and somehow I pushed the phone of the hook. I called the operator and she sent the first aid and police. Lou was notified also because he was the fire chief and I was a lieutenant. They broke the door in and used a backboard and collar support then transported me to the Riverview hospital. I was admitted and Lou called my mother.

July 1966 – My Hospital Stay

The next day I was in traction and I called mom. I told her not to come down. I would tell her everything later. That night some of the firemen came to visit and so did Elaine and Pinkey. I just wanted to see my son. Pinkey was great and she was the last person with me before my fall. The next day I couldn't believe it Butch appeared with Petee. Irene was not there. He didn't say much but I was glad to see Petee.

It was after the 4th of July and one of my supporters picked me up and drove me to the house. When we got there my car was in the driveway where I left it. I noticed it was open and I looked in and saw a picture of my mother taped on the steering wheel and someone had poured oil all over my clothes in the back seat. When my friend saw this she cried. When I went in the house the furniture was gone. A neighbor came over and said Irene and another girl moved everything out. Guess who that was? None other than Rosemary. The only thing left was the spare room couch and a chair. I cried and so did she. She could not believe Butch caused all this. I received a call from Lou Sorrentino from the closing and he said Irene wanted more money. I said to foreclose on the house. I won't give her anything. About a half hour later she accepted and we closed. I was able to pay off my car and still had $800.00 left.

I made a drink and we both got a little tipsy. She started to kiss me and before I know it we were making love on the couch. Believe me that surprise was a big help. Neither of us knew that would happen. Later that night after she left I went to sleep on the couch.

July 1966 – My Return to the Catskills with My Family

The next morning I called mom and she said dad and she were leaving with Linda to go to Sunset Springs in the Catskills for a long weekend. She said I should go there and stay with them. I left that morning and drove to Sunset Springs arriving about 11am. I found mom, dad, and Linda and I told them what was going on. Dad was upset and said I should move back home because I was going to sell the house. That night I felt better and we all went to the dance which they had. A Greek band was playing and I met the wife of the bouzouki player. She spoke very little English and during a break her husband was having a bad argument with her outside and he made her cry. When he went back to play I spoke to her and we took a walk. She said she wanted to go back to Greece because he was always seeing American girls. It was a cool night where just a jacket was needed, so we went into the game room downstairs. We started to kiss and pet but this wasn't practical because we were standing up. I took her out to my car in the parking lot which was very dark. We made love and it was great. We got back just in time for the next break. I went to the table where everyone was sitting and had a drink.

The next day we all left to go home and I never saw her again. After work at the airport John Pierson said to look for an apartment in Bayonne. That afternoon I put a $50.00 down payment to rent an $85.00 a month apartment, a one bedroom on the fourth floor. The next day off I painted everything and moved in whatever I took from the house. I had to buy a couple of twin beds because John Pierson was going to move in and be my roommate. There was one window with an A/C unit in the bedroom. At least we could sleep. John and I worked different shifts so it wasn't too bad. I would work for dad when he needed me but I was getting bored during the days I was off. I remembered Helen Higgins from "2 Guys from Harrison" in Middletown and she had said she was going to be the security supervisor at the Union City store. I drove up to the store one day and spoke to her about working part-time. She said she would hire me anytime. I filled out the paperwork and told her I would let her know when.

August 1966 – The Separation

I had been giving Irene money every couple of weeks. We were not divorced yet and the lawyers were friends of each other as I found out later. Lou Sorrentino had told me he wanted $1,000.00 for the divorce so I paid him with the money from the sale of the house. I was very busy so I didn't really date anyone. I would visit mom one in a while and then at the diner to see dad. I was starting to have a hard time paying bills that were left over when Irene left, and I was not eating properly. I would buy a loaf of Italian bread and a pound of potato salad to fill me up every couple of days. I was too embarrassed to go to the diner. I didn't want dad to know how bad things were. My weight was 145 pounds. I dropped 15 pounds since Irene left. I was still having a hard time adjusting. I missed Petee terribly. She let me take him for a day but she had strict rules and I had to have him back at 6pm. I must say that she took good care of him. Rosemary had divorced Leo so they had plenty to talk about. Irene had gotten a job with a mattress or pillow manufacturing company in Jersey City.

September and October 1966 – Suicidal Feelings

One night I had a very bad depression and I was in the apartment alone. I was drinking heavily and took a knife and thought about killing myself again. Just then John Pierson came home and we had a long talk. I decided to stop feeling sorry for myself and start to do things again.

While at work one day I met a TWA stewardess who was in our office at the airport. She was lovely and we talked about an hour. She was from California based in Los Angeles. I told her when she flew in again to call me and maybe we could go to dinner. I had invited Lou, Carol, and Elaine Ferguson for dinner and I cooked. They came and I was very happy. I liked Elaine but she was going to Miami. I went to see Helen Higgins at 2 Guys and took the job part-time. All I did was pick up shoplifters, lock doors, and check on all security officers. I missed the fire department so much that I started to put applications all over the place.

Linda called me one day and said she was going to be bowling in Bayonne and I should meet with her. She would be with four girls from work. I went there with John Pierson and I ended up taking home Marilyn. We made love and I drove her back to her car at the bowling alley. Another of the girls that was there gave me her number. Her name was Mary. She was thin and quite cute. I called her and invited her over to my house one night. We had a couple of drinks and fooled around a little. We did not make love but I thought maybe the next time. She had a girlfriend named Margie who was dating an Italian guy named Joe. We got together a few times and one day I went over to Mary's apartment and met Joe coming down the stairs. He said you might as well turn around and leave now because after you go up you will see what the story is. He had been dating Margie about six months and did have sex with her where I didn't yet with Mary. I went up and Mary said you're not going to like this but Margie and I are in love and we will be living together. I was shocked and I left and went home. Personally, I didn't care for her much anyway. I went to the airport the next day and was told I was going to be sent to Idlewild because they were eliminating a station agent's position there. John had seniority over me so he was okay. They said I had about three weeks before the transfer. There was no way I was going to drive to Idlewild everyday in the NY traffic. That night when I went to 2 Guys I told Helen and she said she could promote me to full-time as an assistant security supervisor. I took the job and left Allegany immediately within a week.

November 1966 – Meeting Rose

My first week on the job as supervisor, Helen introduced me to a new hire whose husband had died. Her name was Rose. She was a tall, pretty woman 15 years older than me and blonde. Over the next few weeks we spent many hours together watching for shoplifters from a perch above the floor areas. Rose was very nice and told me about her husband Tommy who was a milkman and died of cancer. She seemed a bit high class and had money. She worked because she needed something to do. She came from a large Italian family; three brothers and five sisters. I was still mixed up over Irene and became close to Rose who I now called Rosie. After work she would take me to this bar and grill and buy me dinner. She knew my position and the hard time I was having. She told me her brother Steve was "mafia" connected but that didn't bother me because all Italians said that. Helen saw that we were an item so I could schedule Rosie on my shift. We always worked split shifts, night, day, weekends, holidays, etc. During November I was working many hours a day sometimes 12 hours. On Saturday I would go to the diner and work. Up to this time I never made out with Rosie. She was more of a companion. One night after we ate at Rockey's we were in the car and I was pretty horny. I started to kiss her and when I went to touch her she jumped and said no. I said to myself maybe too soon. Every time I went to my apartment in Bayonne she would call me and we would talk for hours. Just before Thanksgiving I took Rosie to my mother's house in Washington Township to introduce her to the family. The next day my mother called me and said, "Where did you get her from?" Rosie had a bit of an attitude like she was the Prima Dona of all, but at the time I needed someone.

On Thanksgiving Rosie took me to Belmar to meet her family. They were all there and all treated me nicely. Ten courses of food, wine, and her sister Ann's husband, Sonny played the piano and we all sang the old songs. It was nice but I could tell they all thought she was too old for me. The following week we were off on Saturday and Rosie wanted to make dinner for me. I said okay and that morning I did my laundry, got my car washed, took a shower then went to Rosie's apartment. She lived over a family that her brother Steve knew. That is how she got in there. I parked the car and went up the stairs. I had flowers with me. This woman was in the hall and asked who I wanted and I told her. I rang the bell and Rosie opened the door for me. I went in and the food smelled great. We had a couple of drinks then diner. We drank a bottle of wine and we did the dishes. We sat in the living room and kissed. I finally was able to touch her heart so I figured tonight was the night. After an hour on the couch she said I could stay over. She opened the bed and I got in after taking off my shirt and pants leaving on my underwear. Rosie came out of the bathroom and she had on bunny pajamas with the feet in them. We started to make out but every time I went to touch her between the legs she pulled my hand away. She said if we ever got married that is when she would do it. I laid on top of her and got my thrill. The next morning her phone rang and it was her brother Steve. He was yelling at her telling her and saying he was going to disown her because I was sleeping with her all night. The landlord downstairs called him. Rosie was very good to his daughter and had a special trust set up for her. Rosie never had children which I thought was odd. She had told me where she was married. They lived in Cliffside Park and her husband Tommy hung out a Manny's Gulf Station. I knew Manny because of the fire department. Anyway she had a fight with him on the phone. She said she was going to move out and get her own place. The next week she took a two bedroom apartment in Union City. I went with her and she bought new furniture "cheap furniture" for the apartment. She asked if I would move in with her and I said yes. John was going to move out anyway so I decided I would move out also.

December 1966 – Fire and Saving a Life

That night I was waiting for John to come home from the airport to tell him when I smelled smoke and someone yelling fire. I ran into the hall and saw smoke coming from the third floor. I ran down and someone said the fire was in apartment 3B and the guy was in there. I banged on the door and no one answered. I grabbed a fire extinguisher, the old soda and acid kind and broke the door in. I found the occupant in a room next to a room where I could see the flames coming from. I grabbed him and pulled him out into the hall. Then I went back in through the smoke and emptied my extinguisher on the bed fire. I went back out and someone handed me another and I was able to knock the fire down considerably to a smoldering stop. I was then having trouble breathing so I opened the window. I got some air then went to the kitchen and took a large pot of water and almost put the fire out completely. I hung out the window to get more air when the Bayonne ladder truck pulled up. They put up the ladder and I went down. John had arrived and saw me. We went back to our apartment and invited people in to get away until all the smoke cleared. The Bayonne chief came in to thank me for a job well done.

John and I decided we would move out and in a week we did. I moved in with Rosie. I took Rosie to Aunt Ann's and by now mostly all the family met her. They all thought she was too old for me but I didn't care. When I took Petee on my day off, we would go to the zoo in Staten Island and sometimes to mom and dad's. We always had fun when we were together. December was always a busy time for us at 2 Guys. I had a lot of overtime because of shoplifters. One thing I didn't like was Rosie kept a picture of Tommy on her dresser and one day she wanted me to go with her to the cemetery in North Arlington. We went and she introduced me to Tommy. I thought she was nuts but I played along. She told me that she had a mausoleum built above ground so Tommy could breathe. I should have taken this more seriously. A couple of weeks later I was bringing Rose home and we found the door to the apartment open. When I walked in the apartment was trashed. She started screaming and said the fur coat Tommy gave her was gone. So was some of her jewelry. There was no insurance and she was quite upset. I asked her if she locked the door and she said yes but she left the key under the doormat for her friend to go in and get something. How stupid is that? She was starting to get on my nerves so I told her I was moving to my mother's house. All I had was my clothes. I moved in and after two weeks I ended up going back with Rosie after her many calls. Mom was angry because she couldn't see me with Rose. I went shopping for Christmas presents and worked over the holidays. New Year's Eve we worked too.

January 1967 – The Divorce

I finally got notice of the divorce hearing in January 1967 and that day I walked past a restaurant on Journal Square and saw Lou and Irene having coffee. I was very annoyed with Lou over that. We went to the courthouse and the judge called on Irene to explain her complaint. She was asking for $60.00 a week alimony and $40.00 a week for Petee. I was only making $125.00 a week. She told the judge she didn't have a life because I was never home. Then I was called up and the judge asked me why I was never home. I told him I worked three jobs to pay the bills and keep the house. He asked if I belonged to any organizations that kept me away. I told him only the fire department and I had saved 14 lives so far. I told him I wanted my family back in tears. Finally he called the lawyers up and then he took a break. After 15 minutes he came back and called me up in front of him. He said, "Peter I am giving custody of Peter to Irene because she is a fit mother and that is the NJ law under the circumstances". "Would you be willing to pay $20.00 a week for your son?" I said yes and he said it would be set up with the Hudson County Probation department at Irene's request. I guess the lawyers came to this agreement before the judge made his decision about how much. Then he said there would be no alimony awarded in this case since Irene left under her own circumstances. The judge was aware of the reason why Irene really left. The fact that Irene said I was never home but didn't say why, the court decision and the divorce was granted and we all left. Later that month I was working for dad at the diner and Lou came in with Irene's attorney. They had coffee and Lou said I owed Irene's attorney $350.00 because he had to do extra work on the case. I told the attorney I had no intention of paying him anything. I said I paid Lou the $1,000.00 up front. He started to argue with me and I told him to drop dead. They left and believe it or not two weeks later he did drop dead of a heart attack. As soon as I got divorced I went to the Jersey City Police Department to get my gun back which Irene turned in to them when she left.

February 1967 Baby's Birthday

Irene told me she was having a birthday party for Petee and I could stop by if I wanted. I stopped by with his present and when she opened the door I saw Rosemary there. I kissed Petee and gave him his present then I broke down and left. I still couldn't get over the divorce, I really loved them both.

CHAPTER–EIGHTEEN
Rosie

Chapter–Eighteen – Rosie

When I got back to work I told Rosie what happened and she said, "Leave it alone." We had a bad snow storm coming one day and I had to close the Two Guys at midnight with Rose. It was already snowing hard and it was only 5pm. I told Rose to make a reservation at the motel down the block from the store so we could stay there that night. We had to open anyway. At 10:30pm we closed the store earlier because the manager said there were no customers and we better leave. So he left and Rosie and I remained for a while. We took a large canvas bag and went to the deli on the first floor. We took cold cuts, salad, bread, and two bottles of wine for the motel. We walked down to the motel in heavy snow and finally got into the room. It was toasty and we started to drink wine and eat. We didn't have pajamas so I said I guess we will sleep in our underwear. Rosie then said look in the gray bag over there. Inside she had taken a pair of her famous pajamas with the feet and pajamas for me, socks, underwear and a couple of sweaters. I started to realize every time we closed Rosie always had a bag with her. Now I knew why. I later found out everyone was stealing from the store. I was not happy with that and I told Rosie don't do it when I am around. We started on the second bottle of wine and I already was planning to try and have sex with her. Once under the covers I started petting and kissing but when I tried to take those pajamas off she refused to cooperate.

The next morning we went back to the store and she put her bags in the car. At the end of the day we went to Rockey's for a steak then we went home. We decided we would get married and Rosie said she would become Greek orthodox. I took her to St. Demetrios's church in Jersey City and she took the necessary steps and was baptized. I had been talking with dad about working for him full time when John retires soon. We decided to knock down the diner and put a new larger one there. Red told us the property owner had no problem with that. We went to Oakland, NJ to a place where they had used diners on blocks for sale. We bought a Nedick's Diner for $13,000.00. I took over and I got Jackie Ellison's uncle to knock the diner down in weeks. We got a contractor to set a new foundation so we could put the diner on it. We had a plumber set up to make the hook ups.

March 1967 – Rosie's Family

Rosie and I talked about moving to Belmar, NJ where most of her family lived. We both continued to work at Two Guys and I became the main Security Supervisor. I did the scheduling so I was able to do what I wanted. Helen Higgins had moved on. Rosie and I started to go down the shore a lot to visit her sisters Babe, Terry, Ann, and May. I never got to like Babe because she always thought she knew it all. Ann was regular and Terry was nice too. She had a teenage daughter who was always giving her a hard time. Terry's husband had died so she and her daughter were together.

Everyone lived within a block of each other. Babe was married to Andy who jumped at her command. He worked in a dry cleaning store. May lived in Union City and they ran a small grocery store and lived in the rear apartment. Rosie and I went there quite a bit to play cards at night when we could. They had two sons John and David. John Osborne lived with May and Clyde. They also wanted to move to Belmar. Rosie was getting to be a pain and I just couldn't figure her out at times. We argued a lot about stupid things. We had decided to quit and move to Belmar so we drove down and found a new garden apartment on 10th Avenue near the beach. It was owned by a Greek and the building was called Athenian Gardens. His name was Jimmy and we hit it off. He asked if I wanted to take care of the place, cut the grass and keep the apartments, about 16 apartments in all and be his manager on site. Instead of paying rent of $165.00 a month I would live free. Of course I said yes. We gave notice to the manager in Union City but had to give our $100.00 security.

April 1967 – Our Apartment

We moved into the new apartment on April 10th. We bought new early American furniture from Ethan Allen. We quit Two Guys because I started working full time working at the new diner. John, my father's partner, had retired at the end of February and moved to Greece so I became dad's partner. I also decided to sell my Chevy Malibu to Rosie's sister Connie in Massachusetts. Connie worked for Tom Mccann shoes in the office. I then bought a VW bug very cheap and I had a new engine installed. This was great because I would be traveling to the diner in South Kearny from Belmar every day. I supervised the construction. We were in a hurry because we had no money coming in.

May 1967 – The Construction of the New Diner

I went to the diner everyday to watch the work. The foundation was complete the second week of May and we made arrangements to have the diner transported to the site. This was arranged with the company we bought it from and made arrangements with the Hudson County Police because we needed an escort in front and behind. Since we knew the police chief there was no problem. We were very excited and finally we saw the police car and the diner on a large flat truck. It took three hours to get the diner on the foundation. The truckers knew exactly what they were doing. It looked great.

June through July 1967 – The New Diner

The next day the plumbers were making the gas and plumbing connections. We had an electrician making the electrical power connections to the diner. It wasn't too bad because the diner was all ready except for the hook ups. By June 30th most of the work was done. July and August we cleaned because the diner was sitting a couple of years. We had to purchase more pots, pans, dishes, etc. This diner was three times the size of the old one. I made up the menus and that went to printing. We ordered a sign and called our vendors in so we could start ordering supplies. Rose was on my back all the time asking why I spend all day up there and asking when we were going to open because we needed the money. Besides taking care of the apartments, I had a few painting jobs, too. I still had a problem with her because she would not have intercourse and I was getting upset.

August and September 1967 – Rosie's First Husband

I drove to Cliffside Park one day and stopped at the Gulf Station that Manny owned. I hadn't seen him since I divorced Irene. I told him I married Rose, Tom's wife. One of the employees said Tommy hung around the station with his white poodle a lot. He also said Tommy used to screw girls in his back room of the station every once in a while. He said his wife had a problem with sex. Well, that's all I had to hear. I knew then what I suspected all along. I was too embarrassed to leave her because my family would say I told you so. She really was a good person but her whole family always talked about their husbands and I didn't like that.

We got set to open the new diner with a grand opening on September 10th. Everything was set and Genny and her sister Dolores came in on Saturday to get set. Genny and Dolores worked for dad many years. They were great and Genny and I got a long very well. On opening day we were mobbed and mom was there and got in the way. Dad was yelling at her not to dry the saucers just put the cup on the saucer. We had an automatic dishwasher now so that helped, but mom didn't understand the operation. We had a wonderful opening and when we left that night we were all very tired. I drove home and Rose asked if I got any money. I said we just opened and we can't take money out each day. The next day I got to the diner at 3am and met dad. We realized now we had to get more help because we were going to stay open later until 11pm instead of 8pm. We tripled the business in one day from what it was before. I was in the kitchen making sauces and preparing the day's specials. We didn't know what to expect the second day. Well, we soon found out we were so busy because the people from the Western Electric Company were now coming in the diner because we had booths and more room. At the end of the day dad left and I went home to Belmar. As soon as I arrived Rosie said dad was in a bad accident and someone got killed. Dad was taken to Hackensack Hospital. We immediately left for the hospital and when we arrived he had already been taken home. We went to the house in Washington Township and dad was on the couch. When he saw me he started to cry. His mouth and jaw were all stitched up. He could hardly move. His teeth were knocked out and he had stitches over his eye. Dad was driving north on

Route 17 in Hasbrouck Heights and some man going south fell asleep and hit the divider and flipped over the wall and hit dad's car from the windshield back. The driver was dead at the scene. Dad was very upset because the man was young and he had a family. The doctor said dad should not work for at least a month or more. Mom called Lou Sorrentino and he came over. He said dad had a good case because it wasn't his fault. So Lou took the case on. I told dad not to worry I would take care of the diner. I wasn't home to bed since I had to get up in a few hours. I called my cousin Michael and asked if he could work part-time after he left his trucking job as a dispatcher. He agreed and I then asked Genny if she could get me a part-time girl. I was now opening the diner at 3am and closing at 11pm then driving to Belmar. I had to do all the prep work, soups, specials, ordering and do the daily receipts.

After a few weeks of this Rosie was complaining and I told her I must continue my job until dad comes back. I had no time for myself only Sundays then I would go to dads' to give him money and receipts. I told dad to keep mom away from the diner because she was more of a problem being there. I was beginning to get things under control.

October 1967 – My Dad's New Diner

The new girl Lois was very good. She was 23 years old and good looking so the truck drivers liked her. She was also fast and clean so I was happy. She would come in at 3pm when Genny and Dolores would go home. Usually the customers slowed down after 7pm and that's when I would do the books and get set for the next day. Michael came in at about 5:30pm to 6pm and he did the cleaning. Mom asked me to speak to dad's doctor so I called him. He told me he didn't think dad should go back to work for at least six months. That Sunday I went to dads' and we had a good talk. I told him we should put the diner on the market for a high price and see what happens. He agreed and so we did. We had a couple of offers during October but we turned them down. Lou also said if dad returned to work it wouldn't help his case, and he wouldn't get as much money. Dad had a lot of dentistry to be done since his teeth were broken.

It was around October when mom called me and said Barbara, Aunt Ann's daughter had run away and came home and told Aunt Ann who had bought a house on Van Rypen Avenue that she was going to have a baby with her boyfriend, Michael. Aunt Ann was rushing around to give them a wedding. It was at Frank's Italian Restaurant on West Side Avenue in Jersey City. Rose and I attended but I felt sorry for Aunt Ann because she would have wanted something better for her daughter.

November 1967 – The Sale of the Diner

Finally just before Thanksgiving another Greek wanted the diner. He tried to cut us down but I said no. I wanted enough money to pay all the bills and have plenty for dad. I didn't want anything because I could always get a job. I still wanted the Fire Department but being a volunteer in Belmar kept me going. I did make a good deal for dad because I got the bank to change the loan on the diner to the new owner. We produced our records for his accountant and they realized that dad was doing business since 1951. After the contract was ready the new owner would assume the current bills because obviously the food was in the diner and the balance of the new equipment which cost $3,500.00 was already there. The balance of the sale would be for dad and that was $25,000.00. I agreed t stay on with the new owner for one month. He would pay me under the table $150.00 per week.

December 1967 – The Holiday Season

When we closed just before Christmas I went home and Rose asked how much money I got from the closing? I told her I didn't want any since I never gave dad any money to be a partner. She went nuts and we had a big fight. I did my job for the new owner and one night Lois left when I did and we went into Down Neck in Newark for a drink. Down Neck was an Italian section off Ferry Street. When we left, Lois asked me to go to her house so I did. She really liked me and we started to kiss and the rest was history. I didn't feel guilty since Rose did nothing anyway. It had been a long time since my last time with a girl, and it was great. I went home with her a few times before I left the diner. I never saw her again after that.

January 1968 – My Painting Company

I started a full time job by opening a painting company. I had business cards made up and I bought some equipment. I already had a big job painting the inside of a 12 room house. I got the job through a friend who had a real estate agency. Since I was a first aid instructor I joined the Belmar First Aid Squad.

February 1968 – The Fire Department

I met a guy there by the name of Tom Kelley. He was also a fireman at Union Fire Company. He got me to join and on February 6th, I was sworn in and went to visit dad. He and mom decided to sell their house and get something smaller. Dad said he wanted to save some money in case Linda, one day, got married. Dad was not the same since the accident and that was a big house. He did get another Chrysler so he could drive again.

March and April 1968 - My Painting Business

Aunt Anna was living at my parent's house for a few months then she decided to get her own apartment again. The house was sold and mom, dad, and Linda moved into a garden apartment in Fairlawn. I started getting busy with paint jobs and Rosie's sister Mae, who finally moved to Belmar, helped me paint. I bought an old Willies Jeep Truck and had it painted and lettered Pete's Painting Company. I paid $300.00 and it was a floor stick shift but it served its purpose. That month the First Aid Squad decided to sell their old ambulance which was like a large panel truck. I bought it for $500.00. I had it painted and lettered. I bought several ladders and James, the owner of my apartment, gave me scaffolds and all kinds of painting equipment because he was going out of business. Tom Kelley was now working for me because, since he was a milkman, he got home about noontime. He had three kids so he could use the money. Since I owned the company I had my own schedule. I would take Petee once every couple of weeks if Irene let me. She used to tell me he was sick or had a cold and I couldn't take him all the time. Rosie and I made arrangements to get married on April 16 by the judge in the Belmar court. This was the same date I married Irene. Then we had a reception at her Brother Jimmy's house in Belmar. Mom, dad, Linda, Aunt Lil, Uncle Walter, and Aunt Dolores were there along with Rosie's sisters but not her brother Steve. I thought now we would have sex, but that turned out not to be so.

May 1968 – Police Department – The Beginning

A couple moved in below us, Joe and Marie and we became friends. The mayor in our town was John Taylor who owned the local hardware store. I became friendly with him because I purchased paint supplies and tools from him. He asked if I wanted to work as a police officer since I had the experience. I told him I would and he introduced me to Chief Larry Vola. I was sworn in and deputized as a special officer. During the summer Belmar was a vacation resort and they needed extra help.

June 1968 – The Pistol Range

The main crowds would start at the end of June. I went to the pistol range to qualify and began riding at night with the regular patrol. I liked the extra money and I was able to get more painting business because I was a cop.

July 1968 – A Visit with My Son

I picked Petee up one Sunday and took him to mom's. He always had a good time with us and dad loved him. I had gotten rid of the VW and bought a used

Cadillac LD. It was a beauty and brown in color. Rosie was a pain and always wanted me to hand over my pay check and what I made from the painting company. She was very domineering and always thought she was the big deal. Anytime we went to an affair she would always wait to be the last person to arrive so everyone noticed her. I had decided, in my own mind, that I would leave her, but I did not want dad to get upset. When I spoke to mom she said Linda met a fellow who was Greek at Sunset Springs in the Catskills and she liked him.

August 1968 – Working Two Jobs

I had three houses to paint and it was very hot. Working as a cop and painting plus answering fire and first aid calls day and night was very exhausting. I was making money and Rosie was taking it and paying the bills and giving me money for coffee and cigarettes. I did hide money when I got cash on small jobs once in a while. I would hide it in the basement where James let me build an office.

There was a big fight one night at Jerry Lynch's Bar on the beach. We answered the call for assistance from two other patrol officers and there must have been a dozen guys fighting. We tried to beak it up and we ended up hitting some of the guys with our night sticks on their head.

In those days you could to anything to stop a fight or defend yourself. Today you have TV cameras on you and you can't use excessive force. Today the bad guys get away with everything then they sue. I didn't take crap from anyone and if they were breaking the law, I made sure I took care of it. The chief at the end of the season said I did a great job and I should take the test in November for the Police Department. I was very busy painting and things were looking good. I hid as much money I could just in case.

September and October 1968 – An Affair

One night I was cleaning around the property and a new tenant named Jill came up to me to say hello. She was very pretty. She was married to a guy who I knew was a real jerk. It was funny every time she saw me; she always came over and spoke to me. Rosie was very jealous and I knew why. It was Halloween and I worked on the police force. I got off at 9pm and I decided to drive to the local lounge on First Street. When I walked in Jill was there so I sat next to her. She was one hot woman and we hit it off. She knew the score and we both left and went to my car. We started kissing and it was getting better so I said let's go get a room at the local motel. Then I realized everyone knew me so we drove to Bradley Beach and got a room. We made out and it was great. When I got home Rosie said she called headquarters and they said I got off two hours ago. I told her I hung around the station about an hour. The next week Jill's husband was stabbed in a fight and they were having big problems.

I stayed away from her because she wanted me to be with her. Finally they moved out and I was glad. I later found out they got divorced. At least I got laid once in a while.

Petee had a double hernia and I went to the hospital to see him. It was October 31st, Halloween.

November 1968 – Policing

Just before Thanksgiving Rosie's niece met me on the beach while I was working the board walk detail. We talked a little while and she told me a few things about Rosie. I didn't know, but she said Rosie had a lot of money in the bank and she had a special trust for Steve's daughter but she cancelled it when he didn't speak to her anymore. I don't think she liked her Aunt Rose much. She also said she thought Aunt Rose married me to show off a good looking young guy. I might make note that her niece had a few drinks even though she wasn't old enough. I never said a word to anyone about this. One day when Mae was painting for me she told me that her sister had money but she was always the downcast of the family. She also told me she had stabbed Clyde for fooling with someone years ago. I got along great with Mae. We fished under the bridge and had a lot of laughs. Mae was always honest with me. I paid her cash when she painted for me. The police department test was coming up the next week so I was busy studying. There were quite a few people taking the test for two positions. I took the test and a fellow named Harold Allen and I passed. They were sending us to the State Police Academy in March. I was very happy and couldn't wait to go.

We had Thanksgiving at Ann's house with all the trimmings. Clyde had gotten a job with the Public Works Department in Belmar through Mae's Sister Terry. Terry's husband who had passed away was a big deal in Belmar for years and Terry knew everyone.

The next week I picked Petee up and got the third degree from Irene, "Keep his jacket, hat, and gloves on, and make sure you hold his hand, and have him back by 6pm." I still say she was a good mother, just overpowering. I took Petee to Belmar and we had a good time. Rosie liked Petee, so that was a good thing.

Christmas 1968 – The Holidays

Christmas was coming and I had a couple of rush jobs. I also gave a party for the local old age home and Clyde and I were in the newspapers. Clyde played Santa Claus.

January 1969 – New Year's Eve with Rosie

New Year's Eve was as boring as ever with Rosie. We stayed home and had the downstairs neighbors for a drink and had some food and went to bed. New Year's Day we went to Uncle Walter's for dinner. Uncle Walter had a lot of people there from Aunt Dolores' side; her sisters, nieces, nephews, her brothers, etc. I was having a conversation with one of the girls and Rosie was getting annoyed. I took a walk with this girl and it was a beautiful cold day. The sky was so clear and blue. She lived down the shore so I told her I would call some day. She said okay. Rosie and I had a fight over this because she said the girl was looking me up and down and I was doing the same to her. We didn't speak all the way home.

The next day a local attorney called me for an estimate to paint the inside of his home. It was quite large and I came back to my office in the basement and figured it out. Rosie came down and wanted to know if I had any checks and I said no but I expected two during the week. The siren went off for First Aid and I ran to the station. It was a call for a woman in labor. Bill Goss, Sr. was driving and Phillip Greg came too. We got to the house and I went inside. She was on the bed and her husband said her water broke. We carried her out and I got in the back with her. We put her husband in the front. On the way to the Jersey Shore Medical Center I checked her and she was crowning; this is when the head starts to push out with each contraction. I yelled for them to stop so I could deliver the baby which I did. I had the baby breathing and she stopped screaming. I tied the umbilical cord off and we proceeded to the hospital. The placenta was coming out and I had blood all over me. We brought the baby in and everything was fine. I cleaned up some and I had to sign the birth certificate because I delivered the little baby boy. The girl was only 18 years old. I had to buy a case of beer for the squad because that was a tradition. Rosie was not impressed because my clothes had blood all over them. I continued my estimate and took it to the attorney. I got the job and I started it a couple of days later.

Mae and Tom Kelley worked that job with me. I wanted to get as much done as possible because I would be leaving the end of February for the State Police Academy. It was six weeks and I could only come home on weekends. I worked late some nights so I could get done and I would see Rosie pass by to see if I was really working. Any new jobs would have to wait unless Mae or Tom could do them. Since it was winter everything was inside. I had a list from the academy on what items I could bring like clothes, etc. Chief Vola already issued our revolvers and uniforms. I finished the job the day before I left so that was good.

CHAPTER–NINETEEN
Police Officer

Chapter–Nineteen – Police Officer

February 1969 – The Police Academy

Harold Allen and I would take one car. I would take it one week then he would take his car the next week. We arrived the first morning and there were thirty five of us lined up. I thought I was back in the Navy. Everything was military like. We were marched to our barracks and assigned a bed. After unpacking our clothes and essentials we stood at attention and went through an inspection. We were then marched to a large hall and our indoctrination began. They were very strict. We received our class schedules and were taken on a tour of the Sea Girt facility. The food hall was great and our first lunch was very good. We began the day at 5am with outdoor exercises and a three mile run. We then showered and stood for inspection. Each bed was inspected and it had better be right or you got a mark against you. The end of the first week we needed the weekend off. I had to study and keep a notebook which would be graded at the end. We had self defense and every other course you could imagine. Everything was intense and just before the last week they told us we had to do one more week of special training called operation combine for civil disturbances.

March through May 1969 – Police Academy Graduation

Everything was over April 4th and we graduated. Thirty three of us made it and three were dropped from the class. I had a week off then I went on patrol. I was on the night shift 4pm-12am which was good for my painting business.

One night on patrol on the beach I got a call that there were suspicious people under the boardwalk. I began walking below the boardwalk. I noticed three guys and a woman sitting on the sand. I asked them to step out and they did. After speaking with them I determined they came from Chile and just got here. Only the two boys spoke English, but the couple didn't. They looked very scared but seemed very nice. They came here to get jobs. The couple was married and she was pregnant. They were all in their late teens about 18-19 years old. I brought them to the police headquarters and made a report. The problem was they had no place to stay. The captain called Chief Vola and he said to let them go. I took them to the diner and bought them some food. Then I took them to a woman who owned a large rooming house. I had painted the place for her some time ago. She said she had a two bedroom bungalow in the back for $50.00 a month. The boys had two months rent in cash so they took it. It was furnished so everything was perfect. When I got off duty I went to their place in the morning and we all had coffee. Hector Soto and Gustavio Valencia had been fireman in one of the Santiago districts. I finally asked them if they knew how to paint and they said they did. I hired Gustavio and Hector and they came to work for me. The other boy had a friend in Asbury Park who had promised him a job so he followed that up. They were great guys and worked hard. I took them to get drivers licenses so they could drive my trucks. I was making good money now but I gave most of it to Rosie to pay for the furniture and car payments. I always hid some for myself because she was giving me only $5.00 a day for cigarettes and lunch. I also sent my $20.00 a week money order to the probation department in Jersey City.

June 1969 – The Plane Ride with My Son

I picked Petee up on Saturday morning and I asked him if he wanted to take a plane ride. He said yes and we went to Teterboro airport and for $20.00 I rented a single engine plane with a girl pilot and we flew around New York City, seeing the George Washington Bridge and a little of New Jersey for about an hour. Petee was thrilled. Obviously he never told Irene or she would have killed me. I needed a new truck because the Willies were breaking down all the time. I bought a new 1969 Chevy pick up with side panels, a rack for ladders and had a Western Snow Plow installed. Then I had it lettered. I would let the boys take the other truck home at night so they could go to the stores. They would use the trucks and do whatever I wanted for $2.00 an hour. I always gave them food and many extras. I always tried to work midnights or 4pm-12am but I had to work one week on a day shift.

July 1969 – My Experience as a Police Officer

We didn't have portable radios then, we had call boxes every few blocks on F Street. If you were working on the midnight shift it could be dangerous. One example was about 2am I was checking doors for the local businesses when I found the front door to the eye doctor's office open. I took out my gun and slowly opened the door. I didn't see anyone in the front office area but I heard someone in the back room. I thought the smart thing to do was wait until whoever it was left. I took a position behind the showcase so when the person came out he would be in front of me. I also put the lock on the door so he couldn't run out. After about 15 minutes the door started to open from the back room. I was sweating because there was no A/C on and I was also nervous. A large man walked out and as he approached the front door, I noticed he had something silver in his hand. The only light was from the outside street light shining through the front window. I yelled freeze and put your hands up. I scared him but he did what I said. I put him on the floor and he was yelling he owned the place. I handcuffed him then picked up the phone and called for help. Two cars were there in two minutes. The guy tried to say, "Let me up, I own this place", but I told him to be quiet. Sgt. Manetti and Officer Dan Monahan came in and we put the lights on. I was feeling good I made my first capture until Sgt. Manelli stood the guy up and said, "Harry, are you alright?" He looked at me and said take the cuffs off this is Dr. Goodwin. It is his business. I thought I would die. The doctor said his wife and he were out late at a dinner party and she broke her glasses. He dropped her off at home and came in to the repair them. He told me I was doing my job and he was glad I was alert. Sgt. Manetti and Danny were laughing and I went on my way to resume patrol.

August 1969 – Policing

The next day I was doing my reports and the chief called me in. He said I shouldn't have over-reacted and handcuffed the doctor. I should have listened to him first. When I left his office I thought what a jerk he was. That is not what they taught me at the State Police Academy and obviously the chief never went to an academy. The following week I was on days and the chief had put me on the walking beat on F Street. He said I should get to know all the business owners so I don't go around handcuffing our residents. I was pissed but I did my job.

About 3:15pm that afternoon I was at the crosswalk on F Street and 9th Avenue. I stopped all traffic to let the school children cross when I noticed a car pull out of the stopped traffic and head toward me on the wrong side of the road. I pushed the kids out of the way and kept blowing my whistle to keep everyone out of the road. The car approached very slowly and I stepped up to the driver side and yelled to stop. He stopped but then the car moved forward a little. I opened the door and turned the key off. I could smell the alcohol as I got him out of the car. One of the employer's from Taylor's Hardware came by and I asked him to pull the car over into a parking space then call the station for assistance. I asked the driver for his driver's license and he gave me a book of matches. He was so drunk he couldn't stand so I sat him on the curb. When a patrol car came I arrested him and took him in. He was a guy by the name of Finton. After I booked him, I gave him two drunken driving tickets 450 and 451 state codes. When I got off at 4pm I started to write my report. Captain Burns told me the chief said not to write my report until he sees me in the morning. When I went home I told Rosie and she said he probably wanted me to fix the ticket. Sure enough the next morning Chief Vola called me in and said Mr. Finton was a vice president for the local power company and the town was trying to get them to donate lights for the football field next to the school. I told him he almost ran the kids over. He said I should still consider what he said. I left his office and ran a background check on Finton and found out he had been in an alcoholic rehab and hospitalized in South Jersey a year before, and had two prior tickets. I decided I would not drop the charges. The chief knew he couldn't make me so I went to court that next Tuesday evening. The judge who married me was there and I knew he was also an alcoholic with the red nose and neck. Several other officers were present because they told me

I couldn't win this because of the political interferences. The city prosecutor was a good guy and always did a good job. I met with him prior to court and when he saw the history of this guy he said, "Don't worry just present the facts." The judge called me up and I presented the facts and his history. Mr. Finton could not deny this. The judge kept looking at me then found him guilty and suspended his licenses for two years, and told him to get back into the rehab and pay a $500.00 fine. All my fellow officers were happy, but we all knew I was in for it. Somehow the chief would get even. He put me on the walking beat all of August and September.

September 1969 – Policing and Maintaining My Painting Business

Actually I got to like it because I met many new friends. Midnight was the only shift I hated to walk, but I could paint during the day. Rosie was constantly on my back. She would even call the station if I didn't come directly home after work. Sometimes I would stop at a store or the fire house. I already made my mind up that I wouldn't have a steady girlfriend, but if I could find someone nice I would have sex. I was getting very horny now and one day I was painting a house by the lake and the owner stopped by to see me. He had moved back to New York for the winter and wanted me to paint the inside of his house. I was about four doors away from completing the outside. This was great. He showed me when he was going to kept the thermostat on so the house would be warm enough so as not to have frozen pipes, and gave me a key. After he left I had a great idea. Why not advertise to watch people's houses during the winter for a fee. I quickly went to the printer and in one day I had the flyers made. I had the boys go to all the houses in the beach area and put them under the doors. Since I was a policeman I know they would trust me. IN two weeks I got 27 houses which I would charge $30.00 a month. I set up a file for each folder with whatever instructions they had and put the keys with it. Twice a month I would check the house and leave a card inside with the time and date I was there. Rosie bitched because I was working too much.

One night while on patrol I stopped at Pat's diner for my lunch break about 3am. The waitress, a cute blonde began talking to me and we hit it off with each other. Her name was Susie and she lived alone in Belmar and was going to college during the day. She worked normally 7pm-11pm but sometimes when there was no school she worked the midnight shift. I began stopping in to see her often. One night when I was working the 4pm to 12am shift I told her I would stop in at midnight since she was working the midnight shift. I had a burglary in a store that night and when I got back to the station at midnight, I told the captain I wanted to go back to the scene and work with Detective Berger for experience. He said okay. That way if Rosie called they would tell her I was working. I went to the diner and she wasn't there so I left and on the way to my car she just pulled in the parking lot. She said they changed her schedule. She got in my car and we talked a little and I kissed her. She said let's go to my house so we did. She put on some music and the next thing we were in bed. It was great but I had to leave right way and she knew the reason why. I went back to headquarters and called Rosie to tell her I was leaving. I didn't feel guilty because she was not a wife to me and I knew someday when I got the guts I would leave her anyway.

Irene didn't let me see Petee because he was sick twice this month. I was starting to get depressed with my life. If it wasn't for working so much I would have gone nuts. Chief Vola didn't like me ever since the court case.

One Sunday I was on patrol and I got a call "Car 10". I answered and the sergeant said stop at Freedman's Bakery and pick up a package for the chief then get a newspaper and bring it to his house. I didn't know it then but this happened every Sunday morning whoever was working. When I walked up to the porch of his house he opened the door and took the bag which had Danish in it and the paper. He never said thank you just went back in the house. There was some kind of investigation going on with the state which I knew nothing about. I found out later he thought I caused it. I didn't know who caused it but it was about him. I later found out after I left the department it was one of the motorcycle cops.

October 1969 – Policing

Fall arrived and we changed into our dark uniforms. I spoke to Susie one day and she was home. I was working on a house near her so I walked over and I stayed about two hours. We had a great time. I needed this because I was really lonely. I was put back on the walking beat again but this time I was able to stop at Susie's house for an hour or so each night so that was good.

I was back on car patrol at the end of the month and was at the beach on one of those beautiful days and I met one of my uncle's nieces. She had a problem at home and just wanted to get away. When I got off at 4pm I met her and we drove to Bradley Beach where I parked. We started to kiss and we then went to one of the houses I was taking care of and we made love. We both said we would never tell anyone. It was our secret.

The holidays were coming which I dreaded. Rosie wanted to get a dog so she began to look. She found a place that bred poodles and we purchased a six week old male black toy poodle. We named it Fate. He was almost housebroken within two weeks. We bought him a bed and toys and even clothes. This became Rosie's baby which she would never have.

I finally was able to see Petee for a day and we went to the zoo in Staten Island. He was fine now and a wonderful boy. I dropped him off and I stopped to see Kay, Irene's mother. She told me she didn't know what Irene's problem was. She was not getting along with her and Irene wasn't getting along with her Aunt Helen or Cousin Dolores either.

November 1969 – Rosie Calls the Police

Back to Belmar because next week was Thanksgiving and I decided to go to Mom's. Rosie didn't want to go so we had an argument and I lost it. She called the police on me saying I threatened her. They had to send a car and by then she calmed down but the car came anyway. My fellow officers left and there was no report. I ended up working that day for one of the other officers who wanted off. After I got off at 4pm I went to Rosie's sister Ann's to eat. That week I saw Susie for an hour and she said she was moving to South Carolina where her parents had moved. After a love making episode I left never to see her again.

December 1969 – Snow Plowing

The second week of December we had a pretty good snowfall. I plowed about six driveways. Tom Kelley said I should get a snow blower and we could do sidewalks. I went to Taylor's Hardware and purchased a large blower. Tom made a ramp so we could roll it up the back of the pick up truck. That same week I became godfather for the Chilean's son. They had asked me long ago and I had said yes. They were leaving to go to Canada because his brother lived there. Gustavo and Hector stayed.

For Christmas Rosie and I went to Uncle Walter's and I called Irene to see Petee. I wasn't able to see him because they were going somewhere. Next week was New Year's and we had no plans. We stayed home and stopped at her sister Ann's. I had to go to work at midnight and we had extra people working because of the drunks, etc. Usually if a person was driving drunk and we stopped them, if they were from our town we would take their keys and drive them home. Drunk driving then was not like it is today.

January 1970 – Police Experience

I had a call at a bar on F Street for a fight. When I got there the fight was in the street. One guy was on the ground bleeding from a stab wound. People started running away. I grabbed one guy who had a bottle in his hand and he tried to cut me. I hit him across the face with my night stick and he was out. The guy who was stabbed survived but no one ever found out who did it. I had to arrest the guy I hit who also had a broken jaw and nose not counting the stitches he got. When I got home that morning I was so tired. I went to bed and woke up at 3pm. Rosie was annoyed as usual. With all the pressure I was under I was thinking of quitting the police department and moving away. I wanted to get on the fire department somewhere. I was representing the Belmar First Aid Squad for blood donor day on

January 13th. There was a large snow storm and Tom and I were busy plowing for two days. Rosie and I were talking about moving to Florida. She said we could stay at John Osborne's house in Lauderdale Lakes, a suburb of Fort Lauderdale, until we found a place and a job.

February 1970 – Mom and Dad and Their Apartment

Mom and dad were moving to an apartment in Park Ridge, NJ. Dad got a job as a cook at the Howard Johnson's on Route 17 in Hasbrouck Heights, NJ. Mom was working at Prentice Hall in Englewood Cliffs, NJ; Uncle Walter got her the job. Irene was giving me a hard time again and I wanted to take Petee on an overnight and she said no. She had bought a house on Roosevelt Avenue with the money left to her by her aunt. She was also seeing Ray Brew who she met near her house. Everything was going well except for me. On the spot one day I gave two weeks notice to the police chief and he said I could leave now, which I did. I was making a lot of money painting. Rosie called James, our owner of the building and told him we were leaving in March. She also told him that her sister, Mae and Clyde would take the apartment and job over. He agreed then we called a moving company and left the decision to Clyde when to get our furniture once we had a place in Florida. We didn't tell anyone we were leaving. I worked hard to finish all my paint jobs by March 1st.

March 1970 – The Move to Florida

I sold the ambulance truck and already got rid of the Willies jeep. I planned on leaving the new truck at the Chevy dealer with a note in it to take it back. They wouldn't have a problem selling it since I had a Western plow installed and all metal cabinets. I left the snow blower on Tom's truck so he could continue to use it. I owed about $75.00 to John Taylor. I sent him a check when I got a job in Florida. I felt Tom Kelley deserved to keep it and my customers. I told the boys and they said they would go to Canada. I gave them each $500.00 bonus. I finished all my jobs and gave Mae my client list and Tom Kelley's phone number. All taken care of, we left at 2am after I dropped the truck at the Chevy dealer and headed south. We stopped overnight and went directly to John's house because he had gotten married to a woman named Niawana who had two boys and a girl. John was working in the air conditioning business. They gave us a room and we settled in. The next day we went looking for a place. We looked at quite a few places all new. After a couple of days we found a duplex off Bailey Road in the unincorporated area of Broward County. It had two bedrooms, one bath, kitchen, living room and a small dining room. Our furniture would fit so we gave two months security and we could move in April 1st.

April 1970 – My Job as a Milkman

I called Mae and ordered the movers to pick up and deliver our furniture on April 1st or 2nd. The owner said we could put the furniture in before in case it came. I started to look for a job the next day. Rosie said to go to MacArthur's Dairy and become a milkman. I spent three days looking and I finally got a job at MacArthur's Dairy. I started immediately and trained for my route which was in the Harbor Island area of Fort Lauderdale. The man who took this route was going to retire in a month. I would go to the Dairy at 3am and usually got home at noon. It was like being in your own business. Once I got my route and truck, I started to research the fire department and began to get all the information. Florida was growing fast and soon there would be a need to hire firefighters. One week I worked with a guy who had the Margate, North Lauderdale area. We would stop at the Hess station in Margate and drop off milk. The young guy who worked the midnight shift was very nice. He always gave me a cup of coffee. On Thursday when we went to stop, there were police cars all over and we couldn't go near it. Later we found out that someone robbed the station and shot and killed the boy. We felt so bad because he was such a nice guy. The next week I got my route. At 3am I picked up my truck and loaded all my orders, milk, eggs, Danish, ice cream, etc. then I went to the ice house and filled the truck. I had no trouble and was done by 11am. I called the dairy in case anyone called in for something. I was back home by 1pm. Again I was asked by Rosie why I was so late. I told her everyday is different depending on the amount of orders. I was off one day during the week and Sunday. April 1st we got a call that the furniture would be here on April 4th. I called and had the electric turned on April 1st and also ordered the phone lines at the same time. On April 2nd we went shopping for food. I got home from work early on the 4th picked Rosie up and went to the apartment. The furniture arrived at 1:30 pm and by 4:30 everything was in. We paid the driver and began to unpack. Fate was running around the house exploring the area.

I was off the next day and we got everything unpacked. I went to work the next day and when I got home we finished everything. I hadn't gotten a check yet and I was over a month behind on my car payment. I had called the finance company and told them I moved and gave them my new address and said as soon as I got a job I would catch up. I asked Rosie if she could lend me the money and she said they could wait. When I got up the next morning the car was gone. I called the police and they said it was repossessed. I had to call a cab to get to work. Rosie was stuck also so when I finished work that day, I walked about two miles to Broward Blvd where I knew there were places that sold used cars with no money down. Funny as it was I had my first check with me. I spoke to the fellow that owned the lot and he spoke just like my father. I asked him if he was Greek and he said yes. We spoke for quite a while and I told him my problem. He said he had a small 1959 four door

Plymouth which was a six cylinder and he said I could have it for $500.00. I asked him if I could finance it and he said put $100.00 down and send him at least $25.00 a week until I paid it in full. He also said he wanted to see me in church on Sunday at St. Demetrious'. Well I drove home and told the story to Rosie. First she said she wouldn't drive an old car why didn't I show it to her first. I said I wasn't going to walk home seven miles and spend taxi fare again. I told her to go buy her own car. She had no choice but to drive it. I cleaned it all up and waxed it and I thought it didn't look bad. I had to take it to work every day. Rosie and I were fighting all the time.

May 1970 – Child Support Payments

I was falling behind in my payments to Irene and when I called to speak to Petee nine out of ten times he wasn't there so I started to call at supper time. She told the probation department I wasn't paying and they contacted me with a letter giving me a warning. I then got a job with Winn Dixie in Margate and worked every night part-time. I was able to take home dented cans and Winn Dixie breads that had expired.

That Sunday we went to church and we met Father Nick. I liked him right away. At the coffee and cake hour after church I saw Gus, the guy that sold me the car. He was happy we went to church. Between the two jobs I was always tired. I was still not getting anywhere with Rosie. I didn't have sex for the last few months. I was now going to look for someone just to go to bed with, once in awhile.

CHAPTER–TWENTY
Many Jobs

Chapter–Twenty – Many Jobs

June 1970 – The Dairy Delivery

One morning in June I was delivering milk to a special location on Las Olas Isles and it was a mansion. I was never there before and when my boss told me this was a special order and it was big, I got excited. He wanted it delivered between 10am and noon, milk, eggs, creams, ice creams, OJ, etc. about $200.00 in that order. I got there at 11am. There was a service entrance sign so I carried two racks in on my first trip and there were all kinds of people around the pool drinking champagne. I went in the kitchen and started to put my products in the two sub-zero refrigerators. This black guy came in and said hi. I couldn't believe it, it was Sammy Davis, Jr. and right behind him was Dean Martin. I was petrified and when I went to get my second load I took the rack and went back to the kitchen where two girls who were the kitchen staff helped me. They said Frank Sinatra was there outside, too. I wanted to see him so I took my empty case and walked out the rear kitchen door. There were about six women around a table, and another table with Champagne was near the pool. I saw Frank Sinatra talking with Sammy Davis but some guy said to me you are going the wrong way and shoved me out to the service entrance. I was thrilled to see them but I wish I could have spoken to them. I got home, ate lunch and went to Winn Dixie. I was speaking to this girl Carla who I had been friendly with and she said she was leaving to work for Publix across the street. They gave their part-timers a pension and more money. After work I went over to Publix and met Turner Booth the manager. After a nice talk he hired me and I notified John Winn, my manager at Winn Dixie I would leave next week. He said go now so I did. I liked working for Publix better. The store was cleaner, the people and staff were more professional. Carla and I started the same day and we sort of bonded with each other. She was a pretty girl about 5 feet 6 inches with black hair and a nice build. She came from Omaha, Nebraska with her parents and was going to Broward Community College. She was 18 years old and I was 30 but what the hell. Rosie was 15 years older than me. Summer was hot in Florida but I got used to it.

July 1970 – Marital Problems

Carla and I were getting a little closer but we hadn't done anything yet. She lived at home and didn't socialize much. I didn't have much time to myself because of working all the time. Rosie wanted a patio and she spoke to the owner. He said he would put in a patio and enclose it if I agreed to pay an extra $25.00 a month. We did agree and he had someone do it. It was near the end of July. Rosie and I had another big argument. I left the house and drove to Publix. I met Carla outside and she was leaving. I told her about the argument and she said let's go somewhere. She got in my car and we drove to a park in Margate. We kissed and petted but we didn't do anything further. We both wanted to have sex but the car was out of the question. I went back to Publix to work. I had an agreement with Mr. Booth that I could come and go when I wanted as long as I took care of the dog food. I would first punch in and out but worked at least four hours a day. If Rosie wanted the car she would drop me off and pick me up.

August 1970 – Another Affair

One day in August Carla told me her parents were going up to Nebraska for two weeks and she would be alone. I thought this was great. I would finally have sex. I went to work one morning and I was on Marco Drive and I knew we were going to have severe storms that morning. We had no A/C in the trucks and if it rained we had to close the doors and it got hot. .All of a sudden the wind picked up and it felt cool. I just got back in the truck and the wind was shaking the truck. I closed the doors and all of a sudden the truck moved. I thought it was going to tip over. It was dark and the power went out so there were no lights. Hail started to hit the truck and I saw a big tree in front of the truck fall over and hit a house. Within two minutes it all stopped. I opened the door and stepped out. I couldn't believe the damage. There were garbage cans, parts of fences, roof parts, shingles, trees and bushes in the street. People started to come out and we could hear sirens in the area. What had happened was I experienced my first tornado. I was stuck on that street for four hours until the city moved the debris from the street. I couldn't complete my deliveries so I went back to the dairy. The only damage was on the street. My boss Jim Luck didn't know about the tornado. I went home and went to Publix to work. Carla was working and she said her parents left today. We made arrangement to meet the next day before I went to work at Publix. I met her about 2pm and we went to her house. I was in her car and when we got there she said, "Get down on the floor and she drove up the driveway and opened the garage door with the electronic key and closed it behind us. We had great sex and after two hours she drove me back to Publix. We did this three times before here parents came back.

September 1970 – Back to NJ to See My Son

Rosie was on my back again and we had a bad fight so I left the house and drove to the airport. I had just cashed my paycheck so I had some cash. I called Irene because I thought I would fly to New Jersey then I could see Petee. Irene said not for the next few days. I decided to go somewhere so I took a plane to Boston on Eastern Airlines. It was about midnight when I got there. I decided to call my friend Joe Bustin who was in my wedding party with Irene. I hadn't kept in touch since I got divorced from Irene. He answered the phone and I told him where I was and the story. He said he would see me in the morning. So I sat on a bench and tried to fall asleep. All of a sudden I heard an announcement calling Peter Vallas dial 30. I went to a phone at the Eastern desk and dialed 30. I was connected to Joe Bustin who said he was coming to pick me up. I found out later Marcia told him, "You can't leave Peter there all night. He has a problem." Joe picked me up about a half hour later and brought me to his house in Cranston, Rhode Island. They gave me a bed in a spare room and I woke up early the next morning and went in the kitchen. Marcia made breakfast thank God because I was starving. We all talked for a while and Joe said I should go back, end everything, and go back to New Jersey. He dropped me off at the airport and went to work. I didn't tell him I only had $20.00 left. I finally called Rosie and told her where I was. She said stay there I don't want you back. I was going to go to the Greyhound Bus Terminal and get a ticket to NJ when I heard my name over the paging system. I answered the phone and it was Rosie. She said go to the Eastern ticket booth and ask for a Mr. Black. When I got there I found him and he said I had to sign for a ticket which was prepaid by Rosie. I didn't have a credit card then because of the car repossession. I got the next plane home, got my car and went to the house.

October and November 1970 – From Milkman to Management

Rosie said McArthur Dairy called because I didn't show up for work and they had to send Jim Luck, my boss to do my route for the two days I was away. I called the dairy and told them I had a problem and they said just come in and pick up your final check. Okay, now that I was fired I had to get another job. I went to the Lauderdale Fire Department and they said they didn't have anything open right now so I put my name on the list. One of the guys said the Citgo Station on Road 441 and 16th Avenue was looking for someone, so I went there. I met a guy named Russ Leoni. He was leasing the station with his brother. I spoke with them for an hour and they hired me. I began working immediately the next day. After a week of training; how to read the pumps, do reports, and mechanical knowledge, I was doing great. I opened in the morning, set the job schedules for the mechanics and Russ was there all the time. He had no place to live since he just came from NJ. He had a fight with his brother so he needed $2,000.00 to pay off his brother. Rosie was in the office and said she would give him the $2,000.00 if we were signed on as partners. He agreed and we were partners. I had no idea where she got the money and then she said he could stay in our spare room for $50.00 a week. It was an Italian thing so everyday Russ ate dinner at our house. Rosie washed his clothes and we worked together. I never got a pay check. Rosie would give me money for cigarettes and coffee, etc. amounting to $10.00 - $20.00 a week plus the $20.00 a week I had to send to Petee.

The fire department began to fuel its trucks at my station and I became friendly with Chief McKnight. He was having trouble with the union and some of the men. He said one day the town would have to expand and maybe I could get hired. Russ was having marital problems and I could see disaster ahead.

One day I went across the street for lunch at the Black Angus. The girl who waited on me was quite cute and I started to kid with her. Her name was Lucy and she lived about two blocks from the station. She started bringing her car in and at that time we always checked each car for oil, water, and air, not like today's gas stations. We found out that Russ was getting a divorce and he was having problems. I came in one day with Rosie because Russ said he was going to sell the station. Paul the Citgo Company representative was there with a guy by the name of John McGuer. Mr. McGuer wanted the station. He just moved here from NJ where he sold his station there. I was busy taking care of customers and was not involved in the meeting. I don't know what happened but Russ gave Rosie a check and Russ went home with Rosie, packed his clothes, came back to the station, took his tools, and drove away in his pick up. Paul introduced me to John who was about 60 years old. John decided to make me the station manager with an increase in salary. He told me to order new uniforms for the three part-time guys who worked the pumps, and I had a white shirt. I had to get a good mechanic so I put an ad in the paper and the next day a guy by the name of Roy came in and John and I interviewed him. We hired him immediately and the next day he came in with his tools. Rose wanted to get another car so we bought a used Mercury in good shape. She got tired of driving me to work everyday. Mom and dad moved to a rented house in Park Ridge. It was nicer than where they were. Linda and Tom were getting engaged on December 26th and they were going to have a party. We couldn't go because I didn't have the money. I spoke to Petee that week and he was fine. I was doing well as John's manager and he was happy with me. He didn't have to stay there all day because I was running things well. I started to do some mechanical work because Russ taught me. I would change water pumps, brakes, belts, hoses and other assorted things. I made friends with Chief McKnight and I got the contract to fill all the fire trucks. I even had the police cars and some city vehicles. I kept working at Publix but not as much. They still wanted me to come in when I could. We had met a neighbor Kostas Kokoris a Greek who had an air conditioning company. He belonged to our church St. Demetrios, too. They would come over for coffee and cake sometimes.

December 1970 – Petee, My Son

Mom and dad were in Park Ridge now and they were going to see Petee. I called Petee and we spoke for about twenty minutes. Christmas was quiet but as usual I was working all the time. Since Carla left Publix and went north to live with her sister in Nebraska, I didn't have anyone to have sex with. I stopped in to the Black Angus across from the station and spoke to Lucy. She was quite nice, about 24 years old and lived with her mother. Whenever I came in for lunch she would run to wait on me. Just before Christmas she came in to get her car serviced and I brought her into the office since it was air conditioned. I was kidding around and we kissed. I locked the door to the office and we made out on the couch. We didn't have sex but did have some fun. We said we would get together sometime somewhere.

January 1971 – Our New Home

On New Year's Eve Rosie and I went to church to a party. It was terrible and we went home. Some guy by the name of Dennis, who was a cop in Plantation and always came in the station, was telling me his live-in girlfriend left him and went back to Pennsylvania. She had his child and he said he was going to sell his house on 64th Terrace in North Lauderdale. It was a new house and he didn't want to give it to a real estate agency. I told Rosie about it and said she wanted to see it. The next day Dennis came in and he gave me the key to the house and said after work he would pick up his key. I drove home and picked up Rosie and we went to the house. It had two bedrooms, two baths, a living room, dining room, kitchen with an eat-in area, and a garage with a backyard. Rosie liked it so she came to the station and met with Dennis. We found out that he paid $25,000.00 so we offered him $19,000.00. He said okay and we went to his bank and in three days we assumed his mortgage. We made out like bandits but it was only because Dennis wanted to go to Pennsylvania after his girlfriend. He even quit his job. We were very happy about it. Rosie gave Dennis a $3,000.00 check and we took over.

On January 5th we cleaned the entire house. I rented a truck and the guys from the station moved us in. I had notified our owner but he kept the security deposit. I met our neighbor who lived north of us. Their names were Mary Ann and Joseph Colletti. To the rear of us was a retired couple Joe and Carol Mazola. Joe Coletti had an immaculate lawn and our lawn was lousy. Within a few weeks I had our lawn just as nice and we added a lot of new plants and trees. I loved to do landscaping so this was my new therapy.

February through April 1971 – Decorating Our New Home

Rosie bought drapes and a bunch of other things. Rosie was in her glory surrounded by Italians and Mrs. Mazola and she would be in each other's house having coffee everyday and even Mary Ann who was about 28 years old came, too. She had a boy, Chris, about three years old. During the next few months we were always together. We played cards at night and even ate at each other's house. I also kept in touch with Costas and his wife Virginia. He introduced us to Nick and

Harriet Catupous. Nick and Harriett lived around the corner from us and he did drapes, blinds, and curtains.

One night at Publix I was talking to one of the cashiers who I liked. Her name was Carol and she was divorced with a three year old boy. We sort of hit it off and she invited me to her house after work one day. I was getting off at 8pm. She got off at 4pm. I went to her house and we talked for an hour. I kissed her a little but I had to leave. The next morning I opened the station at 6am. We had a lot of work to do. We had six oil and grease jobs coming in, one water pump, and two brake jobs. At 9am I called John and asked him to come in to work the front desk so I could help the boys. He came right away. It seemed everyone under the sun was having problems that day. By 6pm I was tired and John had left at 4pm. I left one of the guys Harry to close at 11pm. He had done it before then I would read the pumps in the morning. I went across the street to get a beer at the Black Angus and Lucy was just getting off. I was filthy so I didn't bring her in the office. She was off on that Thursday and she said her mother was going on a two day visit to her friends in Orlando. Thursday about noon I went to her house and we made love until 2pm. I left and we planned to do it again tomorrow. I went home and Rosie said we should get shutters. I called a couple of companies from the station the next morning and they said someone would come Saturday morning. I had a couple of estimates over the phone already. Saturday the shutter man came and he had a good price. It was $675.00 so I gave him a $50.00 deposit. He said I could finance the rest with his finance company so I filled out the papers and on Monday he said the company would approve it. I had asked Rosie if she had the money and she said Mrs. Mazola would lend me the money with no interest until I paid her back. Little did I know Rosie gave her the money to give to me. I later found out after the divorce she had over $40,000.00 in Hudson City Savings in Union City, NJ and was getting a $225.00 a month check from her dead husband, Tommy from a union pension. If I knew this I certainly would have left her. I worked so hard to pay the mortgage and bills and she sat on her ass all day coffee clutching.

May through July 1971

Our anniversary was coming up so I said I was taking her to the Sheraton Hotel on the beach to a suite, then to an ice show. I told her I want this to be the honeymoon we never had. She said okay and that day we checked in after 12pm and had lunch then went to the pool. I ordered roses for the table at the dinner show. We had a few drinks and after the show we got in bed. After fooling around a little, I took her nightgown off. I went to put my finger in her vagina and she screamed no. After pushing her down I got on top of her and she screamed so loud and said she would call the police. I couldn't believe it. I got up, got dressed and threw three of the flowers on her and left. I drove home and later she came home by cab. We didn't talk for two days and then she said she was sorry but I had to understand.

I actually began to hate her but still I stayed. The next four months I worked the same and was starting to hide money. I couldn't hide too much but if I had an extra $20.00 or so I would at least get another pack of cigarettes if I ran out.

August 1971 – My Sister Linda

Joe and Mary Ann were over one afternoon and Mary Ann had on a short mini skirt. She was sitting with her legs crossed then she put her leg down. I actually could see her underpants. Rosie noticed and when they left we had a big fight because I shouldn't be looking at her.

It was the first week of August and I spoke to mom. She said Linda was getting married on October 24th and Petee was going to be the ring bearer. I was glad but when I told Rosie she was angry and said she wouldn't go to the wedding if Irene was going to be there. We had a big fight. I was livid and for the next two months I hated her more. John decided to sell the station and I started looking again. I spoke to Chief McKnight and he said for me to call the Division of Forestry because they always needed men.

September 1971 – The Service Station

I called and I went for an interview and was hired that day. I started two weeks later when John sold the station. I was stationed at Route 84 and trained for the next three weeks. My boss was Ray Bobo and he worked me hard. I learned how to run the bombardier which was like a tank. I learned all about forestry fire fighting, brush fires, and the everglades. Dad had called me and offered to fly us to the wedding. Rosie said no and I said I was going. She said then she was throwing me out of the house. I was stuck and I didn't know what to do. I worked everyday but I was not happy. I called Lucy and we met at the station when we got off. I told her everything and she said I should go and the hell with it. I tried to do it but I was stuck.

October 1971 – My Sister Linda's Weddinig

One Friday night I met Lucy at the station when I closed. We were in the back room on the couch and made love. I decided I would leave Rosie and go to the wedding. The next day I told Rosie I would leave and she said her brother Steve would have me killed. I had never met Steve and she always said her family was mob connected. I really didn't believe her but you never know. I called dad, mom, and Linda and told them I couldn't come. I am sure they were disappointed. I was very upset but I didn't have the money or the guts to do anything about it. I kept thinking about Linda and Petee and was very depressed.

November 1971 – Unpredictable Fires

At work Roy Bobo said he wanted me to take one of the fire trucks home everyday because there were many un-incorporated areas off Copans Road and Powerline which needed protection. Rosie drove me to work the next day and that night I parked the truck in front of my house. I answered a call one night at 1am of a house fire off Copans Road. When I got there flames were coming out of the front room windows. I had 500 gallons of water in the truck so I took the 1-1/2 hose and went in the front door. I managed to put the fire out just as a Sheriff's Deputy arrived. He wanted to know where the local district fire truck was and I said I didn't know. I pulled over to a hydrant and filled the truck then went back and put more water on it to make sure it was out. Just then a fire truck arrived from Pompano Highlands Fire Department. They wanted to know why I didn't call for help and I said the forestry did not have a night dispatcher. These were the old days. Today they would send a ladder truck, two engines, a Battalion Chief and a rescue.

People were complaining about the fire truck being parked at the house so I had to bring it back to the Route 84 station. Another day we had a large brush fire near the L16 canal. I was sent with two other guys to set a back fire. As I was walking through the brush I saw what I thought was a pile of garden hoses but they were moving. It was a nest of water moccasins. I turned and ran back to the top of the road. I was told I should go around them. Well that was when I decided the Forestry wasn't for me. I hate snakes and had no intention of living with them. When I got back to the station I gave two weeks notice. When I went home I had another argument with Rosie. It was good that I still worked for Publix as I would work more hours if I wanted.

December 1971 – New Job Opening

I was speaking to Costas one day and he said he would try to get me a job at the school board of Broward County. Costas had gotten a job with them and was well liked by the boss Vince Brown. Just before Christmas Costas told me to come over to the office and fill out the application and meet Vince Brown, Walter Pagott, and Leo Butch. They were all bosses. It was a good meeting and they said there would be an opening for an A/C apprentice in February.

On Christmas Eve I had invited Nick Catoupis and Harriet; Costas and Virginia over for snacks and drinks. I called Petee early and they weren't home. Christmas Day we went over to Joe and Mary Ann's and stopped at the Mazola's. Joe Mazola had been ill and he passed away into the New Year. Rosie was over there everyday to comfort her. He was taken to Brooklyn, NY for the funeral.

January 1972 – Security at Publix

I was asked by my store manager Mr. Booth to change stores. He said the manager at the Commercial Boulevard Publix needed me because I was always catching shoplifters and he had a problem. I got a 25 cent an hour increase and I said yes. I started at the Publix on Commercial Blvd. and boy was that store being hit! The first day I caught 12 shoplifters. The old people we would let go but the young ranging from 18-60 years old were arrested. I no longer had to stack shelves. I was made security manager still working any hours I wanted.

February 1972 – My Mechanical Experience

It was around Valentine's Day that I got a call from the school board to come in. I went over and Vince Brown said I could start as soon as possible so I did that next day. I was assigned to Morris Tucker, the older mechanic who was one of the best. I knew a lot about air conditioning anyway so it wasn't hard for me to catch on. Everyday we would go to different schools to do repair or service the A/C systems. We would eat lunch at the school cafeterias but Rosie wouldn't let me spend the money so she gave me a lunch box. When I found out we would only pay about $1.00 for the school lunch, which was good, I told her I would not carry a lunch box so I did get $10.00 a week to spend. She was a plain bitch.

One day I was at Fort Lauderdale High School and I met this girl Gail who worked in the lunchroom. She was quite nice and I wanted to see her again. The good part was we had a big job at this school (at least two weeks work) so we would eat there everyday. Gail was 33 years old and divorced, with jet black hair and a nice slim build. By the second week we knew a lot about each other and she invited me to her house sometime. She gave me her phone number and a week later I called her. I was hurting and I needed a woman bad. I went to her house after I punched out at Publix, which she lived around the corner from. I went in and she had a lovely place. It was a condo and her eight year old son was at her parent's house. We had a drink and we really got it on. This was better than any of the other girls I had. She understood what I was going through because she had a similar situation.

March 1972 – Seeking Fire Safety

During February and March I worked hard at the school board. They were expanding and I was working in the Superintendent of School's office on his A/C and we spoke to each other. I said to Mr. Benjamin Willis that I would love to get into the fire safety department. He asked why and I explained all my experiences in the fire service. He wrote down my name and thanked me for my interest. I had also researched who was in charge of that department and it was a Dan Demoro. I stopped in one day and introduced myself. We had a long chat. He said he had been asking for a fire inspector and safety officer for some time.

April 1972 – The Drug Free Program

On April 5th I received a letter from the superintendent, Benjamin Willis stating he was looking into the position for me. In the meantime, I ended up becoming the head of the Drug Program to fight drug abuse. I put on several programs in schools, churches, and local teen centers.

May 1972 – My Friend's Accident

One day we got a call form Niawana that John got hurt doing an A/C job on a roof and he was in Broward General Hospital. Rosie and I went there. He had lost an eye. He took an electrical surge and his son Randy saved his life by shutting off the power. The Jaycees later gave him an award.

May through July 1972 – Another Affair

About every two weeks I would see Gail. I called her one day and she said she wanted to get a hotel room at the Marriott in Fort Lauderdale. I worked around my schedule and we met for four hours. It was great. She had a bottle of champagne and cheese crackers. The good part was we weren't going to have an affair or get anymore involved other than good sex. I also met a new girl at Publix. She worked in the bakery department. She was a tall girl about 6' and very nice. There was something about her that turned me on. Her name was Michelle and on breaks we would see each other. She was 21 years old and was also going to school at night. She lived with a roommate.

One night Joe and Mary Ann invited us over to play cards and Joe got angry at Mary Ann and a big fight started. I couldn't believe what happened and we both went home next door. I was happy their children Chris and Dawn were sleeping. I still had a connection with the fire departments because I still was trying to get on the fire department. Florida had a lot of politics and there still were half volunteer and half paid departments all over Broward County. I was also good friends with the chief in North Lauderdale.

August 1972 – A Visit from My Sister, Linda and Her Husband Tom

Linda called me and said Tom and she were going to be in Longboat Key on the west coast and they wanted to visit us. I never met Tom so I was excited. Linda and Tom arrived and their rental car was covered with Love Bugs. We went out to dinner and had a great time. Rosie was her usual know it all, beauty queen. That day I will never forget because I went in the bedroom and I saw Rosie staring at the photo of her deceased husband, Tommy. I finally said please remove the picture. You are married to me now. After a big fight I heard her on the phone with one of her sisters. After she got off the phone she put the photo away.

September and October 1972

One day she got a call from her brother Steve's wife and she told Rosie she was coming to Florida and they would like to stop by. Rosie said of course and a few weeks later they drove up. Rosie and Steve hugged each other. I guess they were glad they made up. I finally met Steve and I liked him. They had lunch with us and we all took a drive to show them around. All went well and Rosie was happy. I was still miserable with her but I kept quiet. I spoke with Gail one day. I hadn't spoken with her in over a month and she said she now had a boyfriend and it was getting serious. We spoke and that was the last time I spoke with her. Now I wanted to get close to Michelle so at work one day I asked her if she wanted to get together sometime. I said I liked her and she said I am all yours if you want it. A week after I went to her place because her roommate was working. We had great sex and I was now back to having some sex in my life. I received a letter from the new Superintendent of Schools, William Drainer. He said he was considering me for the job for a Fire Safety inspector and would advise me soon.

November 1972 – Communication with Petee, My Son

Just before Thanksgiving I met with him and the interviewer was great. I still had connections with forestry and several fire departments and kept in touch. A new manager took over at Publix by the name of John Evans. He wanted me to keep my present job which I did. Thanksgiving was at my house and Rosie made a turkey. Mrs. Mazola came over and that was the day I called Petee and got him for a change. I missed him so much. I just wished I had a normal life with my son and a wife who cared. All Rosie cared about was herself, her dog, her cigarettes, and her neighbor, Mrs. Mazola.

December 1972 – Rosie and Her Expired License

One day she came home from shopping with a police car behind her. They got out and came to the door. I opened the door and she started yelling at me because she got stopped by the cop who was from North Lauderdale. Her driver's license had expired. She cursed me in front of the officer while that fucking little dog of hers kept barking. The cop couldn't believe her and said lady shut up. It is your license and you should know when it expires. He gave her a ticket just because of her big mouth. Christmas was its usual aggravating time. I couldn't wait until the holidays were over. December 29th I was in my den and I got a call from a friend at forestry. He wanted to know if I wanted to help with a rescue at the L-16 canal in Dade County because an Eastern Airliner L-1011 crashed and they had a lot of survivors trapped. I immediately left and went to the station and we got there about an hour later. We were advised by a trooper there was no room for more trucks. We got a ride on a rescue jeep to the scene. It was lit up by light from the trucks and also the helicopters. You could smell the jet fuel and it was hot and sticky. The plane looked like it was split in half. You could hear people yelling, "Over here, help!" and some other people yelling for help further away. I wouldn't go down in the swamp water because of the snakes and alligators. I stayed on top and gave first aid as they brought the people out. This operation continued through the night. One old couple just came out together holding hands. Some stayed in their seats. When dawn came I couldn't believe my eyes; there were many dead bodies. Most of the victims were in the middle to the first class area. My partner and I decided to leave and we got a ride back to our truck. When I got home I took a shower and fell asleep. When I went to work that day Morris Tucker said I was ready to get my own truck and when someone was sick I would take their calls. I liked the idea but it didn't happen every day. There was a guy that worked in another department who was a survivor of the Battan Death March. I enjoyed my conversations with him. What a hero he was. Costas finally left the school board to open his own business permanently.

January 1973 – A Visit from Mom and Dad

New Year's was another fight and another disaster. We ended up home and not speaking. I kept working days at the school board and part-time nights at Publix. I called Michelle and she said she had transfer papers to go to a Publix in Miami. That was the end of that girl. I had to find another but it didn't happen. Dad had a vacation coming from Howard Johnson's so I invited them to our house. Rosie wasn't too happy because she didn't like mom too much. They came and when we picked them up and brought them to the house they were pleased. Mom brought some large cans of crabmeat which she knew I liked. Rosie took them and said let me put them away before he eats them all. My mother said that was why she brought it. They stayed a week and did have a good time. After they left Rosie always had something to say about my mother.

February 1973 – My New Job at the Board of Education

Around the first of February, Vince Brown said the main office downtown was asking for letters of recommendation from my bosses. They all sent me the letter which was turned into the school board. I had to go see the Head of Security, Mr. Greeley who was retired from the F.B.I., for fingerprints and an interview. At the end of February, I was promoted to Fire & Safety Inspector and had my own office. Rosie had a fit because I had to use my own car. They gave me so much a mile plus gas and expenses, more money, and 8am-4pm hours. I had a white American Motors four door car which I bought. Rosie had the better Mercury. Rosie would have been happy if I were like her Tommy and had one typical job. I was not going to give up. I had "the fire within". My new job was to conduct fire inspections, investigations, trip and fall cases as well as all investigations regarding safety. Dan DeMauro was the director and I reported to him. I would go to my office at 8am and set up my work for the day. I got my new business cards and was listed in the school board directory. Dan was heavily involved in site plans and construction of new schools, so he couldn't do the inspections and fire safety like it should be done. He gave me an outline on what should be done at each school at least once a year.

March 1973 – Fire Safety

I didn't realize the power I had. I could walk into a school and pull the fire alarm and do a report on the evacuation procedures. I would check for blocked exits, hallways, doorways, etc. There were about 100 schools and offices in the county, maybe more. I also had to inspect the Chemistry Labs, cafeterias, kitchens, parking lots, etc.

April through June 1973 – School Safety Inspections

March, April, and May I put 100 percent into my job. I was ahead of myself and I had to get an assigned secretary to assist me. Letters were coming in from school principles and teachers. I was commended by Superintendent Drainer, and others. I still went to work at Publix off and on, and they were also happy. I had done an inspection at Stranahan High one day. I walked into the teacher's lounge and I saw three teachers leave. When I walked in I smelled marijuana smoke. They were allowed to smoke on breaks then, but not pot. I didn't report this because I knew many of the teachers smoked pot. I met a very nice teacher about 35 years old and very pretty. She had two blocked exits out of her room. I told her she must rearrange her room so there were at least two ways out. The bell rang and she didn't have a class next so I helped her rearrange desks, tables, and chairs and she was very happy. There was only one week of school left and I went in my office to check my mail. There was a letter from Stranahan High School from that teacher "Pat" that I helped. She wanted me to come to the school to see her because when school closed she was getting a larger classroom. She wanted me to help her set up the area so it would conform to the standard regulations. She ordered work tables and benches for her biology classes. I went there that afternoon and took a graph pad. She wasn't in her room so I asked where she was. The teacher there said she was in her new room on the third floor. I found her and we talked. I drew up a plan on graph paper so she could submit it to the school. It took about an hour and it was time to leave. I didn't have to go back to the office since this day was almost over. I mentioned to her it was cocktail hour and I was ready to go. She said, "Where do you go for a drink around here?" I didn't' know because I never went anywhere since I never had any money. I had $10.00 in my car and another $6.00 in my pocket. I said I know there are some places on Las Olas Blvd. so she got in my car and went to Las Olas with me. I parked the car and we went to the Riverside Hotel bar. We had a beer and had a wonderful discussion. She came from Vermont and had been a teacher two years at Stranahan. She had a bad marriage and was divorced two years, no children. I talked about Rosie and we got along very well.

After an hour we left and I drove her back to school. I kissed her and we parted. She also gave me her telephone number, and said she was going back to Vermont in two weeks for the summer to see her parents. The next week school was out and my job got a little easier. I would check out many schools for relocation of signs, new signs, and construction, draw up plans for new rooms or expansions. Rosie didn't like it because I had more freedom to get around and she couldn't watch me or know where I was at anytime. We had no sex and at this point I stopped any contact with her body because it didn't do me any good. She was an ice berg anyway. I was biding my time for the time being. I decided to call Pat and she was glad to hear from me. I met her at the school one day and we went to lunch. She was packing her things in the class before she left and we were able to do lunch. We had a couple of drinks and before I drove away from the restaurant she said, "Let's go to my place. I would like you to see it." I believe this was an invitation to see more than the condo. We arrived and went through the gate to her condo. It was very nice, clean, and well decorated. She made us a drink, put on some music, and we sat on the couch. She was leaving for Vermont the next day and was all packed. I helped her put some things in her car. Then we sat down again. I told her not to shut her air off because her condo would end up with mold. She didn't know that. I told her to put it on 78 degrees, and it would be fine. We danced to an old song I liked, "Could it be Magic" from the 1950s. We began to kiss and that is all she wrote. We spent an hour in bed and I had to leave. We would see each other when school started. She gave me her mother's number anyway. I didn't think I was going to be as busy as I was. Our next door neighbors Mary Ann and Joe sold their house and moved to a larger house in Margate. We went for drinks and coffee one night and it was lovely. After a few weeks it was obvious the new people next door were not taking care of their lawn. He was a rough guy from North Carolina; a real red neck with the confederate flag on the front plate of his pick up. His wife was heavy and very plain looking. There were no children so that was okay. We spoke to each other off and on but didn't get that friendly. I was taking care of my lawn and it always looked great. I had planted quite a few bushes and trees and the house looked great.

July 1973 – A Visit with New Friends

One Saturday we were invited to Joe and Mary Ann's house for dinner. We met their neighbors Al and Terry Fortunato. They were nice people and we had a good time. Another couple came later for a drink; a guy by the name of Joe and his wife, Genie. Joe worked with Joe Coletti and they were friends. His wife Genie and I hit it off. When I got home Rosie said, "I don't like the way you looked at Genie." I said, "You don't like the way I look at anyone." I went to work all summer doing inspections on the schools. Publix was busy as usual and I just kept picking up shoplifters. We were at Joe and Mary Ann's one night and Al and Terry called and told us all to come next door. We did and they had a couple visiting named Chris and Charlie McNally. Their son, Tommy was going with Al's daughter Denise. The McNally's had four boys, Charlie, Andy, Tommy, and Bobby. We all got along fine and would get together at each other's houses. We got to know each other during the summer because we would always have barbeques and play cards during the week. Everyone thought Rosie was a show off and a know it all but they got along with her anyway.

August 1973 – Another Affair

I had called Pat at her mother's but she wasn't home. I called back a few days later and spoke with her for quite a while. She was coming back on August 24th.

One Saturday night we were invited to Joe and Genie's house for dinner along with Mary Ann and Joe. When we went in Genie kissed me and we all sat down and had drinks. Genie liked to tease me and I could see Rosie getting annoyed. It was all in fun but Rosie would never see it that way. When we got home we had another big fight.

September through November 1973 – NFPA and Fire Prevention Week

I called Pat the next day and stopped by the school that afternoon. I went home with her 3:30pm and we made love. I stayed about two hours and left. I got home, ate something and went to Publix. I was busy at the school board getting ready for Fire Prevention Week in October. I had over 35 planned speeches at schools some with the Fire Department's Fire Prevention Bureau. By the end of September I had my schedule set and it was full. I had to do six schools a day. I had plenty of Fire Prevention materials from the National Fire Prevention Association and put everything in my car. Rosie knew I would be very busy so I would be late getting home then go to Publix.

I saw Pat twice in October because of my work schedule. She was great and knew all about Rosie and couldn't understand why I stayed with her. Well, I didn't know either. Rosie told me her brother Steve and his wife would be in Fort Lauderdale over Thanksgiving weekend so she was going to have them for dinner. The end of October I was going to my doctor for a check up and I told him about Rosie. He said I should tell her she needs a pap test then he would find out if anything was wrong. She wouldn't listen to me if I told her so I called her sister May in NJ. May knew my problem but would never tell anyone. She did call Rosie and through the conversation told her she should get a pap test at her age. The next day she asked about my doctor and I told her he was great. He also flew his own plane. She made an appointment and went on her own. I was working that day. That night I asked her, "How did you make out at the doctor's?" She said fine and that was that. The next day I spoke to the doctor and he said she got on the table and put her legs in the stirrups. When he went to examine her she screamed and refused to let him test her. He spoke to her about it and she said she doesn't want that kind of test. Well, that answered that question. He suggested she go to a psychologist but can you imagine me telling Mrs. Know It All to do that?

Just before Thanksgiving I got a call from Uncle Walter and he said Aunt Dolores, Debbie, and Diane were down so I invited them to come for Thanksgiving. Rosie had a fit and we had a fight. Steve and his wife came early on Thanksgiving and we got along fine. Rosie kept apologizing to them because Uncle Walter was coming and Steve said not to worry about it. When Uncle Walter came Steve and he hit it off and so did the two wives. Dinner was great and everyone had a good time. I was working hard with the school board and doing special classes for the teachers. Publix was always busy and the holidays were coming. We were invited to Joe and Mary Ann's one Saturday. Genie and Joe were there and I got a big hug from Genie. Genie was nice looking, a little thin but nice. We had a connection I think with each other. She told Mary Ann that she thought I was a good looking guy. Joe had told me what she said.

December 1973 – The Christmas Party

The following week Joe and Genie insisted all of us come to their house for a Christmas Party. I said we would go and that morning Rosie said she was sick. I said I would go alone and she said over my dead body. The following week before Christmas Al and Terry had their party and we went. Everyone was there and Terry put on a great spread. We had a party on Christmas Eve and it was smaller than the others and we didn't invite Genie and Joe.

CHAPTER–TWENTY ONE
My Father

Chapter—Twenty One – My Father

January 1974 – My Father

New Year's Eve we stayed home and went to bed early. I hated New Year's Eve anyway. I would call Petee twice a month and mom and dad twice a month. The first week of January I got a call at the school board to call home immediately. I wish they had cell phones then because I was on the road and my secretary tracked me down at Northeast High. She said call home, which I did, and Rosie said dad had a heart attack and it was bad. I called my boss and told him I would be out and that I was going to NJ. I called Publix from the school and told them the same then I went home. I told Rosie to call Delta for the next flight. She said, "Do you have the money for the tickets when we get to the airport?" I said we could write a check and she said there wasn't enough money. I called my credit union and got an emergency loan for $300.00. I drove there and picked up the money. Our plane was leaving at 7pm because it was after the holiday. Delta had to put us in first class. Rosie wanted to wait until the next day and I said no. There was a snow storm in New York and we landed at LaGuardia. Uncle Walter picked us up and we went directly to the hospital. Dad was 67 years old then and I was 34. I went in the room and he was unconscious with a breathing tube and hooked up to monitors. He was listed in critical condition. Dr. Alexander told mom the next two days were critical. We went back to moms for some sleep. Mom was totally out of control. The next day I stayed there all day. His condition was the same. I told mom to call the priest to give dad communion.

I spoke to the doctor in the morning and he said he didn't think dad would make it through the night. Mom went nuts so I asked Dr. Alexander for some pills so she could sleep. I spoke to Linda who was pregnant with Nickey and was sick, but would come down in the afternoon by plane, which she did. When she got there she saw dad and she was so dehydrated from throwing up I took her to the emergency room downstairs. I must say that Pascack Valley Hospital was the best. They were all so good to us and there was always someone with dad in the intensive care unit. Linda was examined and put on an IV. I spent hours going up and down from dad to Linda. We sent Linda, mom, and Rosie back to the house in Park Ridge. I stayed at dad's side all night. The priest came and gave dad communion and left. Dad didn't know anything. He was still out. I fell asleep in the chair outside. One of the nurses brought me toast and coffee at about 6am. Then she said came in and said to go in and see your father. I walked in and dad was propped up and he looked at me and started to cry. He said what are you doing here? I told him what happened to him. He said he was going to pick Mom up at work when he got a bad pain in his chest. He had just passed Pascack Valley Hospital so he turned around and drove in. He walked into the emergency room and that is all he could remember. They told me he walked in and dropped dead on the floor. He was immediately de-fibrillated and they brought him back. I kissed dad and we both cried. Even the nurse started to cry; no one ever thought he would be alive this morning. I quickly called home with the news. Obviously, he was not out of the woods yet, but it was a good sign that he was talking.

When mom came later I got her in the waiting room and told her not to get emotional and scream. I didn't want dad to get excited. After three days dad was moved to another room. I spoke to Dr. Alexander (a Greek) and he said dad had a clogged artery but he was too old for the new by-pass procedures. Dr. Alexander was old himself if that was the case. I wanted him to have the by-pass but mom said no. He also told me he gave him about five years if he stayed on his medication. He also said dad shouldn't drive anymore and it would be better if he recovered in Florida. Linda went home when Tom came down to get her. Mom said I should take dad's car since it was old and they would have to deal with selling it. Rosie and I left the next day and went back to Florida with the Chrysler. Dad was in the hospital another week and went home. I got home and went right back to work. I also called Pat and met her after school one day. Mom called and said dad had to quit Howard Johnson's. Mom quit her job at Prentice Hall to take care of dad. I asked Rosie about letting dad and mom come down for a few weeks so he could recover. She really didn't want them and said she would not take care of him. I told her mom said she would buy us two beds for the spare room. Finally she agreed and we made arrangements for dad to fly down first because mom was still packing boxes. They were moving to Syracuse. I picked dad up and brought him to our house. He was still weak but was glad he was here. After four days I checked his pulse. It was racing so I took him to the Florida Medical Center. He was admitted and put in the critical section. They had a Doctor Appleman who checked him out. He said dad was going into congestive heart failure. I knew enough that this wasn't the case. I told him to readjust his medication. The next day when I went back dad said he felt good but Dr. Appleman sent someone in to cut off a black growth on his chest. I called the nurse and she said that is what he ordered. I called him and he said it looked like a cancerous growth. I said who the hell are you to determine that? He was here for a heart problem. I took dad out of the hospital and I brought him home. After that he was okay and got stronger by the day.

February 1974 – Marital Problems

Finally mom arrived and everything was okay. Rosie kept complaining and I hated her more day by day. The next three weeks I was full of tension. Dad would walk up the road a little but I caught him smoking and got angry. After three weeks they went back and they moved to Syracuse to an apartment. I got back to normal but Pat moved to Tampa and got a job over there with more money. I met her the day before and she cried but I said we had a great time together and we should remember it as it was. Rosie's niece Debbie and her girlfriend wanted to move to Florida. They wanted to stay with us until they got a job. Rosie said yes. This was Babe's daughter. I liked her but I didn't like Babe, who was one of Rosie's sisters. They came and stayed with us for about a month. They got jobs at Red Lobster and then they left. They were just a couple of kids with a new adventure. They finally moved back to NJ. I was starting to think about suicide. I couldn't stand Rosie anymore. I had no one to have sex with. I had Rosie on my back and it was getting rough.

March through May 1974 – The Mazola Incident

One day Mrs. Mazola, whose son lived a few blocks away and did nothing for her, came over. She invited us over to meet her friends from New York. They were Mary and Nick Russo. We had a good time with them and started to invite them over after they moved here. We ended up being good friends. We met their families and went to each other's houses. Because they were all Italian and Rosie spoke five dialects of Italian they sort of accepted her. I know Mary Russo really liked me. Later on, Mary told me all Rosie talked about was me. She talked about me and Mary said that was what most of her family did was talk about their husbands.

June and July 1974 – Mom Moves to Syracuse

Mom called me and said she was really happy about living in Syracuse. Linda was due any day so she would stay until the baby was born. On July 5th a boy Nickey was born. Everyone was happy. I called Petee and he was funny. He never really knew me but we talked. I told him I would come up soon to see him. I was pissed at Rosie as usual and I said I was going to NJ to see my son. I took a plane to Newark and a taxi to Jersey City. It was late at night and I called Irene. I told her I was around the corner at Isie's Grocery Store and I wanted to see Petee. She said come over in one half hour. I saw Ray, Irene's boyfriend leave and walk down the street. I knew from her cousin Dolores that she met him and he was living with them. I could have caused a lot of trouble for them in court but I decided not to. When I got in the house Irene was very nice to me. We had a drink and she went into Petee's bedroom with me and woke him up. She said here is your father. He grabbed me and hugged me and I cried. He went back to sleep and I ended up sleeping on the couch.

The next morning I returned to Florida. Rosie grilled me to the end. I was happy and I just loved my little boy.

CHAPTER–TWENTY TWO
The Fire Departments And Rosie

Chapter–Twenty Two – The Fire Departments And Rosie

August through October 1974 – The Hospital

I was taking a course at Cornell University on security and on August 22nd, I received my degree. I hadn't been feeling well and I was ready to leave Rosie. I had a contact with Lauderdale Lakes Fire Department and they were going to hire me. I gave the school board notice and left to their surprise. I got ready to take the position when Rosie and I got into a big fight over my wanting to be a firefighter. We were in the living room and I picked up this ceramic rooster and threw it across the room smashing it to pieces. My nerves couldn't handle it anymore. I went to work at Publix and the next day was a Saturday so I decided to work all day. That night I spoke to Nick Russo and invited them over the next day for a barbeque. He said they would come over about 3pm. When they arrived Nick and I left to go to the Margate Publix to get some charcoal. On the way I started to get pains in my chest and told Nick to drive to Margate Hospital immediately. He pulled up to the emergency room door and I opened the car door and fell out. I didn't remember a thing after that. I had a major heart attack and two days later I awoke in intensive care. The nurse told me Rosie was not there but wanted to be called when I woke up. I had all IVs and machines on me just like dad had. I told the nurse not to call Rosie because I needed to get my bearings and clear my head. After about a half hour I told the nurse to call Rosie. I couldn't have visitors because I was in intensive care. Rosie came about an hour later. The first thing she said was, "See what you get when you lose your temper?" I didn't even bother to pay attention. I asked if she called my family and she said no. I couldn't believe it so I told her to call them but to tell them not to come down. I improved very well over the next 24 hours and was moved down to the 2nd floor.

That afternoon I had my phone hooked up. About an hour later the nurse came in and said she had gotten three calls from a Linda D'Jimas but Rosie said I was not to get any calls. I went wild because I was so angry. I had just been served my dinner when Rosie walked in. I said, "What business do you have stopping my family from calling me?" She said she thought I shouldn't speak to them yet. I threw the whole tray of food at her and immediately got a pain in my chest. Everyone came running in and they rushed me up to intensive care again. I didn't see Rosie for two days. I was back in the regular room the next day. I spoke to Linda and reassured her I would be okay. The next day the doctor ordered me to be transferred to Miami Heart Institute at Jackson Memorial in Miami. The ambulance took me and I was placed in my room. I was examined by a heart surgeon who reviewed my records. He said he was going to do a fairly new procedure called a cauterization in which they would put a tube into my femoral artery up into my heart to see what was going on.

That afternoon I was given some Demerol and an IV. Someone came in and shaved my groin. I was taken to the operating room where I found out I had to be awake for the procedure. The surgeon said he was going to pump me with a fluid during the procedure which would make me feel like I was burning inside. I was scared but this one nurse who I could only see her blue eyes kept holding my arm and wiping my head. It was quite an experience and I was returned to my room with a five pound bag placed on my femoral artery area so I wouldn't bleed.

About two hours later, Rosie came in with Nick and Mary Russo. Rosie went to the bathroom and Mary said I shouldn't let Rosie get on my nerves. Everyone knew she was impossible but they never said a word. I was taken back by an ambulance to Margate Hospital and was discharged two days later. The outcome was stress related with evidence of atheerosclerosis cardiovascular disease with coronary insufficiency. I was given medication to take for several months. I was back to normal at Publix but never told anyone about my heart. I had told everyone I had minor surgery. I had gotten a call from Chief Andrew Corso of the Pompano Highlands Fire Department which was run by Broward County. He was reviewing applications and wanted to interview me. I went to the station which was off Fed Hwy. near Deerfield Beach. I spoke with him for an hour and learned he was on the Hackensack, NJ Fire Department before taking the chief's job here. He hired me immediately and I started that Monday. The department had eight paid men and the rest were volunteers. He also hired a guy by the name of Howie Olshan. At the time of my hiring I had been going to Broward Community College to get my fire science degree. I was to be on call when I was off duty in case of a large fire. Howie lived a few blocks from me with his wife Shelly. We decided to meet at my house if there was a call and go together. I loved my job but these guys were so inexperienced it was awful.

November and December 1974 – The Holidays

The dispatcher during the day was an old man named Art Kuss. At night the captain on duty would answer the phone. There were two captains a kid named Greg Williams and Jim McDonald. During the day there was Bob Milkulskis, Howie, Ray, the chief and me. Ray was going to leave so a fellow I knew in North Lauderdale, Sal Russo, who I told to apply for the job, got it. Sal, Howie and I would meet at our house when there was a fire at night.

Christmas was the usual unhappy time for me. I missed Petee so much just calling him wasn't enough. I kept going to BCC to take all the courses offered including fire investigations and inspections. I had plenty of experience which was great.

January 1975 – The Brush Fire and My Promotion to Fire Marshal

New Year's day we had a large brush fire on Powerline Road and I arrived with Howie, and Sal. We spent an hour, then went home. New Year's Day I was home and we went to Mary Russo's. Her daughter Loretta, her husband, and her two sons were there. It was a nice day. Nick Russo played the guitar and other instruments. He used to be in the Gene Kruper Band, and Tommy Dorsey Band. He was talented and we all sang. I loved to sing and didn't have a bad voice.

Chief Andrew Corso, who by the way was an alcoholic, would leave the station at noon and meet the Volunteer Chief Bob at Crystal Lake Club and drink all afternoon. Andy, after work, would drink before he went home. The first week of January the county wanted an inspection program and told Chief Andy Corso to get a fire marshal. I was the only one qualified so he called me in. We had a long meeting and I told him if I take the job I wanted a captain's rank with it. That would mean more money. He submitted the proposal and they agreed to everything. I got my white shirts, black pants, and a new gold badge within the week. Captain Williams was pissed because I was new and he was passed over as fire marshal. I actually was second in command which Chief Corso wanted, so training, inspections, investigations, and on-site commands were all mine. It also meant Andy could drink all day. He had a white chief's car but would park it behind his favorite bars. He also had a two way radio and red lights installed on my car. I called mom and dad in Syracuse. They really didn't like living there. Mom said they decided to move to Eatontown, NJ near Aunt Lil. They planned to move in March. I still worked at Publix, but was dying to find a girl. I hadn't had anyone since March of 1974 when I was with Pat, whom I just don't go with anymore. Chief Corso said I had to get my state certificate so Bob and I had to go to school for eight weeks and go to Ocala to take a two day test. One was a written test, the other a physical, and we had an actual fire rescue in a burning building, pumping, pressures, etc. that we were tested on. We also had to go through a tunnel maze of smoke. I told the chief I didn't want to go to school and that I would challenge the test. If I didn't pass I would then go to school. The fire college said no so I called Olin Green, the State Fire Marshal who I knew from the school board job. He called the college and they approved it. Bob had to go to the school so I waited until he finished there then we both drove to Ocala, got a hotel room, and reported the next morning.

February through April 1975

I should mention that Bob was an alcoholic like Andy. We took the written test all morning then returned in the afternoon to take the second one which was on friction loss and hydraulics. At 3pm we found out our marks. I passed with a 91 and Bob failed with a 60. He was pissed. He used to be a paid fireman in Massachusetts before coming to Florida. When I got back he was already drunk in the room. He couldn't leave because I was driving and I had to do the physical testing the next day. I went to bed early because Bob passed out. The next morning I left, stopped for a good breakfast then went to the academy for four hours of actual firefighter tactics. I came back and took a shower. I returned at 3pm and found out I passed with a 95. I received my Florida State Certificate on April 15. Bob had to go to school all over. Howie and Sal had to go back to school, too. I helped all of them with studying at the station. They all eventually passed several months later.

May 1975 – Experience in Fire Inspections

I would start a new program where I would take an engine on inspections of the businesses. We also had a contract to provide the Fire Protection for Hillsborough. This also meant inspecting the high rises which were going up, one after the other. In the afternoon, I would conduct training classes for two hours. Andy was in and out mostly. Captain Jim McDonald was not liked by Andy or Greg. After 5pm, by the way, they could have beer which was in the refrigerator. I really didn't like this department but I wasn't going to give it up.

June 1975 – Brush Fire, I Had to Take Command

One day we had a large brush fire about four acres and close to a nursing home. When I pulled up the wind was blowing the fire right in its direction. I called over the radio and requested mutual aid from Lighthouse Point. I heard Andy call me and said he was in Fort Lauderdale and wait until he got there. I told the dispatcher to call anyway. I knew he was drunk, but I was on the scene and in charge. When Lighthouse Point arrived just in time, the flames were right up against the building. We had already evacuated most of the building. Two state troopers pulled up to help. Andy pulled up and when he was getting out of his car he fell over. The trooper saw he was drunk and asked who was second in command. I said I was. The fire was just about out so I told the trooper I would take Andy away. He let me take him. He could have arrested him. I took him to the fire house and put him on the bed. When the trucks came back after an hour, Andy got up and I made coffee. I told him what happened and he said, "You don't obey orders." I told him if I didn't do what I did the building would have burned, and if I didn't take him away the trooper would have arrested him. He didn't say another thing. Later he was in his office sleeping with his head on the desk. Finally he came out took a shower and left.

After this incident I was pretty much in control of everything with Andy's okay. I was at Publix one Saturday working and I got a call that Bob the chief of the volunteers died of a heart attack. This was Andy's drinking buddy. There was a funeral and Bob was never replaced. There were about 15 volunteers and most of them worked during the day.

July 1975 – Fire in the Hospital – The Oxygen Tank Investigation

We had a small fire at the North Broward Hospital in an oxygen tent. I sent the trucks back and I started the investigation. The nurse who was in charge on the floor met with me at an office behind the desk. She was very helpful. She said the boy who was in the oxygen tent was burned and was being treated. She said the tent was in operation at least two days with no problems. She said his father had visited him just before the fire but had already left. I didn't release the room for clean up yet because I needed to go through the bedding and examine the oxygen feeds to the tent. The nurse was Betty Kramer a lovely young girl about 25 years old. She was upset because she was just made head nurse on the pediatrics floor. The boy's father, who came to the hospital, said he was going to sue everyone responsible. I told Betty I was ready to examine the room and take photos. The door had a large sign on it stating "OXYGEN IN USE, NO LIGHTED OBJECTS OR ANY ELECTRICAL APPLIANCES". When I got in I checked the oxygen tank and it had been on at the time of the flash over in the tent. There was no real fire; just some scorching on the blanket and sheets. As I started to uncover the sheets and blanket I found a toy space gun; the kind when you pull the trigger colored sparks come out of the barrel. That's what happened. I also found a paper bag with a receipt in it from Eckhart Drug Store for the gun $1.29. It was dated that morning and the boy had only one visitor, his father. I photographed everything and Betty was very happy it wasn't the hospital's fault. I wrote my report as such and it went to the county. Unfortunately, the father didn't use his head. It was his fault.

August 1975 – The Investigation of the Oxygen Tank

A few days later I went back to the hospital to speak to Betty again because I needed more information on the times. She was off that day, but the nurse called her at home and she said she would come in. She lived three blocks from the hospital. I sat with her for about an hour. It was 12 noon so I asked if she would like to go to lunch with me and she said yes. We went over to a small lunch place. We really enjoyed each other and when we left she gave me her phone number and said to call her sometime. I said to myself, you bet, because I hadn't had sex in over six months. Andy kept on drinking and one day he asked Howie, Sal, and me to meet him at the Crystal Lake Club after work. We used to come to work in my car so we went there. He had to have been there a couple of hours before us. He drank vodka and soda. We each had a drink and Andy had two drinks to our one. He had his usual slur and glassy eyes. I had to go to Publix so we left him there. I finally decided to call Betty and she wasn't there so I stopped at the hospital. She was working so we went to the Café for coffee. I told her pretty much my story with Rosie and she appreciated my being truthful. She said she wouldn't go out with a married man but wanted to keep in touch. I gave her my card and we left.

Mom and dad decided to visit for one week. We went to dinner at Mary Ann and Nick's. One day I had Charlie and Chris, Mary and Nick over to see them. We all had a good time. Rosie wasn't bad this time. Charlie couldn't stand Rosie but, because of me, he behaved.

September 1975 – Bomb Scare at the Crystal Lake Club

One day I was home and there was a bomb scare at the Crystal Lake Club. I took dad with us with red lights on and when we got there I took charge. The building was evacuated and there was a wedding going on. I was inside with my men searching and when we cleared the building and went outside the band was playing and dad was right in with the reception party. Then I heard the music and realized it was Greek. Dad already was speaking Greek to some of the people. He couldn't wait to get back to tell mom. After they left things got pretty busy at the station. We had quite a few fires and I had 20 new high rise plans to review. One day I got a call from Betty. She wanted to see me. I met her for lunch and she told me she didn't want an affair but would like to see me occasionally. She was off two days later and at noon I went to her house. She made little sandwiches and a salad. We had a martini first then a second. I was standing behind her in the kitchen and she turned around and I kissed her. We went right to bed and had a good time. We did have lunch finally and I left. What a treat that was!

October 1975 – Training Teachers in the School Systems for Safety

October was Fire Prevention time and I had many schools to visit. I had my week schedule set up and several morning classes with teachers to train them how to use fire extinguishers. I had the men wax the engine the week before and clean them when we came back from each fire. The first morning I took the engine and we went to the first school at 8am. I told Howie to use the garbage can cover which we bought, and put some gas in it. The teachers were all around us with their fire extinguishers. We set the fire in the cover with a small amount of gas and each teacher had to put it out. After 12 teachers did this I told Howie to put everything away. He bent down and picked up the garbage can cover and screamed. The cover had been burning for a half hour and was red hot. He didn't think first. All the skin came off his hands. He had to go to the hospital to be treated then returned to duty. We still laugh over this today.

It was Halloween and I was at the hospital checking on an alarm that malfunctioned. I stopped in to see if Betty was in and she was. She was getting off at 4pm and she said to stop over. I said I would. I picked up a bottle of gin to bring with me. I took a shower at the station then left for Betty's house. We had a good time again then we talked for about an hour. I then left for home. Rosie was there waiting for the paycheck as she did every pay day. She would deposit the check but I had to pay the bills while she watched. She couldn't do it herself, God forbid she would have to balance a checkbook. I had a class at college that night and couldn't go to Publix. I was tired when I got home and went to bed.

November 1975 – The Fire at a Furniture Warehouse – Close Call

The next morning at 4am there was a fire at a furniture warehouse on Fed Hwy. It was a smoky fire and I got separated from my crew as I was leading them in when I fell over something and when I got up I couldn't find the men. The smoke was black. I made my way to a wall and followed it until I found an overhead door which I began to bang on. They heard me and started to cut a hole in it with the K-12 saw. My warning bell was going off which meant I had two minutes of air left. I kept banging as they were cutting through the door. I don't remember when my bell stopped but I disconnected my hose and put it in my shirt for extra air. I saw the sparks from the sawing and I don't remember the rest. After a little oxygen I was okay. That was a close call for me. I got home and I was filthy. Then I went back to work.

Thanksgiving we went to Mary Russo's and had a nice time. Her family was there, too. The next day Howie, Sal and I decided to do landscaping and painting jobs. We called it the "Personal Touch".

December 1975 – My Birthday

My birthday was on December 5th and Howie, Sal, and their wives came over for snacks and drinks. The next day at the fire station Andy came in and you could smell the remains of a night of drinking. He didn't say much, just nodded, got his coffee and went in his office and closed the door. This was typical of Andy Corso. I called Betty and she told me she was going north for the holidays. I wanted to see her because it was two months since the last time. She said she was busy and I should call her after New Years.

Christmas came and I was depressed. I spoke to Petee and I hung up crying. I missed him so much. Rosie was still a pain. No matter what I said or did, it was never right.

January 1976 – Martial Problems – Missing My Son

New Year's we went to Al and Terry Fortunato's house. They were Joe and Mary Ann's neighbors. Chris and Charlie were there, too. All Rosie did was complain about me as usual, but then again her sisters always did the same thing with their husbands. I went to work at Publix one evening and picked up six shoplifters while I was helping stock the canned food aisle. I always watched this aisle because shoplifters liked small expensive canned foods such as tuna, chicken, crab, etc. I got home about 9:30pm and we ordered pizza. I went to bed late because I was off on Saturday. About 3am I got a call that there was a structure fire at a rooming house in Kendall Green. On my arrival the house was fully involved. I did my investigation and found it started in a couch and was likely cigarettes.

February 1976 – Various Jobs

I resumed classes at Broward Community College in between working at Publix and some paint jobs. I called Betty and found the number to be disconnected. I stopped at the hospital and they said she left to go to a hospital up north. Well, that's the end of that. Work, work, work, it seems that is all I did but it was better than being home with Rosie. It got to the point where I couldn't stand her anymore. I started to think about leaving. My big problem was I had no money because she was in control of the money.

March 1976 – Saving Another Life

During the second week of March there was a bad accident one evening and I took charge of the extrication. It took over an hour to free the victim but we were able to save him. He had arms and legs broken as well as internal injuries. The front plate on his car said "ARRIVE STONED".

April 1976 – Went to See My Son

This month, we were going north because I wanted to see Petee. I had my vacation for two weeks and we left for NJ the second week of April. Rosie insisted on visiting her sisters in Belmar. We stayed for three days then planned to stop at Uncle Walter's then go to Linda's in Syracuse. First we went to mom's and stayed one day. I called to see Petee and Irene said I could pick him up, but bring him back by six. So the next day I drove to Uncle Walter's and called Irene. She said Petee was sick but I could go there. Irene heard Rosie in the background say, "I knew she would do that." Irene said I could come, but she didn't want to entertain someone with an attitude. I ended up seeing Petee who looked fine to me. I couldn't believe how big he was. I felt better and hoped I would be back soon. The next day we drove to Linda's and Nicky was in a cast because his legs were crooked. Linda's neighbor Sam had made Nicky a little bike with wheels so he could ride around the house. We stayed two days and headed home. As I pulled into our driveway Rosie said, "You better water the grass today before you go to work." I told her I would do it in the morning. I was still unpacking the car and went looking for her. Fate was running in the yard and I saw Rosie over at Mrs. Mazola's having coffee and probably telling her about the trip.

May 1976 – Boat Fire

May 1st, I went to work and called a meeting to catch up on things while I was away. On May 19th there was a boat fire on the intra-coastal waterway. It burned to the water line. I found the cause to be gas fumes in the bilge. Because we were Broward County Fire Department they had a contract with Hillsborough Beach for Fire Protection. From our station we had to travel a mile north to Hillsborough Blvd. past the Deerfield Beach Fire Department, go over the intra-coastal bridge then south on A1A. It would take up to 9 to 12 minutes to get to a fire.

June 1976 – The Fire Department Exhibition

During the month of June there was a Fire Department exhibition and convention on the west coast of Florida. Chief Corso said Captain Williams, the fire commissioner D'Simone, and two other men and he were going. They were going to take one engine too. I told the chief it was not a good idea to leave us with one engine and a brush truck to cover our area. He said it had been quiet and we probably wouldn't have that many runs. I couldn't believe what he said, so unprofessional. Well, I was left in charge for the weekend with four paid men and about 15 volunteers to cover 14 square miles.

Friday morning Andy left and at about 10:15am we received an alarm of a bedroom fire in Hillsborough Beach. Art Kuss, the old dispatcher didn't get enough information as to what building on what floor. I left with engine one and it took eight minutes to get there. As I pulled up I could see smoke coming from the 9th floor windows. I directed Engine One to be hooked up to the standpipe system. I also called for one pumper from Lighthouse Point and one pumper and a ladder from Deerfield Beach. I only had three men so I told Deerfield to drop a line from the hydrant to our engine and told the same to Lighthouse Point. I also radioed Deerfield to position the ladder to the north side parking lot. I ordered two high rise packs into the building which was being evacuated by management. Just as I was ready to go in, the windows blew out and flames were coming out. I called for two more engines and manpower. I sent one line to the fire floor. I went to the fire floor and located the apartment at the end of the hall. The door was open and after we hooked up to the standpipe with our 1 ½ inch line, we entered. Sal Russo and I had our Scott air packs on and we could see the flames in a fully involved bedroom. We opened up on the fire with first, a heavy stream then a fog. It was a quick knock down but the overhaul was about two hours. When I got in the apartment, I investigated the cause which was a short in a zip cord under the rug behind a couch, which ran to a flower lamp. The occupants had left to go up north for the summer, so the building manager was going to contact them. Several apartments had smoke and water damage, but we were lucky and we made a great stop even though we were short one engine.

July 1976 – The Valve

On Sunday, I went to the station and Captain Williams had a four-way valve on the truck which they brought back. He told us they got it at the convention and he laughed. The next day I asked Chief Corso about it and he didn't know anything about it. That day I looked for the valve on the truck and it was gone. I took a call that day from a vendor who said someone took a four-way valve and he was trying to find it. I said I would inquire, but didn't tell him I saw it. I went to the chief and he said to start an investigation. The next day, Captain McDonald told me he saw Captain Williams take the four-way valve off the truck and told one of the volunteers to hide it. He also told me one of the other commissioners and D'Simone was present when they took the valve from a display table and put it in the truck. I interviewed Captain Williams and he said he didn't take the valve and discovered it on the truck. I knew this was a lie. I went out to the truck room and found the valve behind some hose. I put it in the chief's office and notified the vendor who later came and picked it up.

The following week when Captain McDonald was on duty, about 11pm, and he said Captain Williams and two other men came in drunk and beat him up. This started what would end up in a lawsuit some time later. I made a report, about six pages, within two weeks after interviewing all who were involved. The commissioner refused to be interviewed. I gave the report to Chief Corso and he never mentioned it again. He should have taken some kind of action against Captain Williams but didn't. Instead he got tough with everyone. He wanted the trucks washed everyday, floors washed and waxed, etc. He also wanted the entire afternoons for training. In other words, the men and I were to be constantly on the move. Captain Jim McDonnell was very nervous because he knew they wanted him out. Andy would have gotten rid of me too, but he needed me and had no one to replace me. Now everyday at work there was tension. Newspaper reports leaked out and there were many verbal exchanges between each other.

August 1976 – Experience in Investigations and Inspections

Chief Corso avoided me unless he wanted me to drive the men harder. I received a call from Chief McKnight in the city of Lauderhill, Florida. He heard things were getting bad in the county and wanted to meet with me. I agreed to meet him on Saturday at his headquarters. Sal Russo and Howie were also worried about their jobs. Bob, the other firefighter who was also an alcoholic was Andy's ass kisser. He would tell Andy anything he heard. I met with Chief McKnight and he was very nice. He wanted me to take the test for the department because he had no one that had my experience in investigations and inspections. He also said he would need about four new firefighters. The problem was I was 36 years old and I would have to take the new physical; agility test which included rope climbing and running one mile under five minutes. I told him I would try. I went back to work on Monday and told Howie and Sal. I changed my training hours in the afternoon to three hours and all we did was practice for the test, which Howie and Sal said they would take also. Chief Andy Corso had no idea what was going on. He even thought I was getting tough with them. I was preparing them for the test. One day Captain Williams said Vallas I bet you couldn't climb the 200 foot water tower out back which was on the station property. The ladder was straight up to the top to the platform. I said okay and that I would do it at 5pm, only if when I come down he do the same and climb the tower. I had him on the spot but he said okay. At 5pm I climbed the tower and it was a bit scary but I got to the top and came right back down. I was soaking wet, but I had done it. I said to Williams, "Your turn." Everyone was outside including Chief Corso. Captain Williams went up and halfway up, he stopped. We yelled up to see if he was okay and he didn't answer. I told one of the guys to get a safety belt for him in case he was having a problem. He started up again and when he got to the top he lay down on the deck and didn't move. The chief said somebody go up and see if he is all right. I went inside the station and Bob came in and said no one wanted to go up. He said to tell the big shot he got up there so he can get down. Finally, I sent the safety belt up and someone got him down. I never said another word about it and neither did he.

I took the written test for the Lauderhill Fire Department on Saturday morning. On Wednesday Chief McKnight called me and said I came in first on the test. One other guy passed and six failed. He said the physical agility test would be announced in a few weeks. I kept training Sal and Howie for the next test. I began to run everyday and exercise also. After I would leave Publix at night, I would do my push ups and sit ups. That night I was awakened by an alarm on Powerline Road for a large brush fire. When I arrived the wind was blowing it towards a house and a farm. I told Howie to climb over the wooden fence and take a 1 ½ inch line with him. There were two wooden sheds between the house and Howie and I wanted him to spray them because of the sparks. The smoke was thick and I could barely see Howie. I had another line placed to cut off the fire several yards behind the house. All of a sudden I heard Howie screaming and saw him jump over the fence and fall on the ground. His helmet was bouncing ahead of him. I ran over and I heard this loud snorting. Behind the fence was a 300 pound sow who had been watching over its piglets when Howie was heading her way. He didn't see the sow and piglets until the sow went after him. I couldn't stop laughing but we had to get the fire out, which we did.

September 1976 – The Accident

September 1st about 9:15am a truck overturned on I-95 exit ramp. Sal Russo and I answered the call, which tied us up for three hours. I was still taking courses and completed an Allstate course and a NFPA course.

October 1976 – Hired as a Firefighter

The first week of October I went to the high school gym for the agility test. I climbed the rope and was first to make it to the top. I passed the test and the next Saturday I had to make the run. I was ready that morning and I ran the track behind the fire station and I passed. After that I had to pass the dive and swim test which I did pass also. The following week I took the medical test. They never found out about my heart attack and I passed 100%. The only thing left was the lie detector test. I went to the police department and they told me I passed. The questions they asked had to do with sex, stealing, honesty, etc. I was officially notified that I was hired and Chief McKnight said I could start in November. That Monday I told Andy I was leaving in two weeks and he said I could go now. I was happy to leave so I could have some time off.

November and December 1976 – A Salaried Firefighter

I started in November and went through the usual department training. I was back to being a firefighter and my captain was a guy named Pete Gannon. Everyone knew I was well experienced. After a few weeks Chief McKnight wanted me to review plans and do some inspections. This didn't sit well with some guys, but they didn't have the experience. There was an ongoing problem (politics) in the city and they wanted to get rid of the chief. The mayor was Gene Cipaloni and pressure from the union was putting Chief McKnight on the line. Captain Richard Korte was working on inspections. He was a good guy. When I went to work on Tuesday Chief McKnight was gone. Mayor Gene Cipaloni was looking for a new chief. He interviewed Chief Phil Brewster from Fort Lauderdale Fire Department who was retiring. After a few days he was hired. He had a meeting with Chief McKnight and the chief told him all about Rich Korte and me. After a few days I met with Chief Brewster and we hit it off. He said because of the union I would have to put more time in on shifts then he could move me up. I was very happy with the department even though some politics were involved. I was initially stationed at headquarters and saw Chief Brewster everyday. Sometimes he would call me in his office to look over plans.

January and February 1977 – Working Various Jobs

I had to change my schedules at Publix which was good in a way because on some days I could work eight hours a day and make more money. Sometimes when we got back from a fire to clean up I didn't leave the station until 8:30 or 9:30pm. Rosie would always call if I wasn't home by 8:15pm. I had it with her and decided I had to leave soon. I had to testify in Federal Court on an arson case from the county. I remember it was the Shangrali Lounge on Fed Hwy. a couple of years ago. After going over my credentials I qualified as an expert for the first time. The attorneys sent me a check for my one hour testimony for $65.00 plus expenses.

At this time that was great money and I decided I would go to all fire, bomb, and explosion courses and seminars. I was still going to college to get my associates degree in fire science. The fire department paid for most of my classes and I paid for some of my own seminars. It was in the middle of January and I paid $50.00 for a two day seminar in Miami on advanced fire investigations. The chief okayed it, and Rosie had a fit. She asked why I had to keep taking all these courses. She said, "You are on the department, you have a job so it is not necessary." I actually couldn't stand her anymore. I hadn't been with a woman in many months and I was very depressed. Mom and dad were going to come down for a week in March on the 11th. Howie and Sal had passed the written test and they were getting ready for the agility test. I showed them the track behind station two and after they got off duty they came to run the course. Finally they took the test and passed. Both started by the end of February. They were both very happy to get away from Chief Corso, and thanked me for all my help. I met Lt. Richard Schwartz who was the union president. He was a big guy and some of the guys thought he was too big to be in the fire department. I liked him and we became friends. There was some talk going around because Chief Brewster was asking me to do special things in fire inspections and investigations. It all amounted to jealousy. Captain Gannon had me transferred to Station Two under Lt. Don Shaw. This was a new station and I liked it. Whenever Chief Brewster needed me he would call the station and tell Lt. Shaw to bring the engine and crew to headquarters for training and then I would be in the chief's office with Lt. Korte going over inspection documents and plans.

March 1977 – Marital Problems Escalate

When I went off shift that day Rosie said Chris McNally told her that Joe and Genie had separated and Joe moved out. Genie was very nice. Genie was now hanging out at Al and Terry's house a lot. Rosie also said her sister Babe was coming down the same week as mom and dad. I was angry because I wanted to be with my parents and Babe was a trouble maker. She said she forgot dad and mom were coming. I knew otherwise because then she could go off with Babe and if I was working they would be alone. Babe came in two days before mom and dad. On March 11th I picked up mom and dad and went home. We had dinner and talked before we all went to bed. I was working the next day and left them with Rosie and Babe. When I got off at 8am the next day I had made arrangements for Howie to work for my next 24 hour shift this way I would be off a few days. We took a ride to the mall and I took them to lunch. That night we all went to dinner at the Red Lobster. I went to work the 14th and we had a big fire that afternoon and I was filthy. I got off at 5pm because I had Sal come in for me. I walked in the door at 5:30pm and everyone was sitting at the table for supper. Rosie said why are you so late? I said we had a bad fire; can't you see how dirty I am? Then she said, "Go over to Mrs. Mazola's she had a tree cut down today and put all the branches and logs out in the front of her house. I looked at my father's face and I said to Rosie to tell Mrs. Mazola to get her son to do it. He lives two blocks away and does nothing for her. Rosie said to me, "Just do it!" I told Rosie, "I've had it with you, don't ever tell me again what to do. I am taking a shower and then eat. Her sister Babe stood up at the table and said, "Don't you talk to my sister that way." I said, "Babe I want you out of my house by tomorrow and then I said to mom and dad, "I think you better go home too because I have some business to take care of." I took them aside in another room and told them I was leaving her. Dad said, "It's about time you became a man." The next morning I took mom and dad to Fort Lauderdale airport. Dad was happy and so was mom. I walked them to the gate and I will always remember dad starting to do a dance and we all laughed. Little did I know that would be the last time I would see my dad alive. I returned home and Rosie was leaving to take Babe to the airport. After she left I packed my car with all my clothes and personal things. When she got back from the airport and came in I told her I was leaving and wanted a divorce. She said, "I want the house." I told her, "Get a lawyer and you can have the house, the furniture, and the damn dog." You never just once when I came home say, "Hi honey, did you have a nice day?" She never said she loved me just waited for my pay check. I walked out and as I drove down 64th Terrace I threw my wedding ring out the window. I had $110.00 and no place to go. I went to Station One and that night I slept in the car. The next week I slept in the car and took a shower at the station. Everyone knew what happened but I couldn't sleep in the station because there was no room. I went to visit Mary and Nick Russo and I gave them $30.00 a week to stay with them until I found my own place. Rosie called the station one day and wanted to know when I would give her money for the mortgage, electric, water, etc. I told her, "No, that she had plenty of money of her own and I knew where it was - in Hudson Savings in Union City, NJ". She was shocked that I knew that. I hung up and two days later she called the station and said she had a lawyer and we should meet with her lawyer. I made a date and went to his office. I told him I would sign over the house and that is it. He said I should pay the mortgage and I said, "No, I don't care if I lose my job or lose the house". I was very adamant about it and I am sure he realized it was better for Rosie to take the house and everything else rather than lose it all. I called mom and dad and told them where I was. Mom and dad liked Mary and Nick so they were happy. I went over to Charlie and Chris's house one day and Little Charlie "19 years old" said he wanted to move out and maybe we could get a place together. I said great so we began to start looking.

April 1977 – Leaving Rosie My Second Wife

On April 2nd at 8pm I called mom and spoke to dad. He was laughing because he was watching Archie Bunker in "All in the Family". Mom was making baklava, and fenikia. Everyone was happy I finally left Rosie. At 11pm I was in bed and the phone rang. Captain Shaw answered the phone and I heard him say he would go and get him. He walked over to my bunk and said you have a phone call. I got up and answered the phone. It was Cousin Barbara. She said dad died about an hour ago. I heard mom screaming in the background. I was devastated. I said I would call back when I could get organized. I told the captain and I was crying uncontrollably. Most of the men got up and I went downstairs. I had no money and Al Sahiblich gave me a check from the union funds. I left and had a lot of trouble with my car getting to Nick and Mary's. My car was old and the transmission was slipping. Mary and Nick lent me a suitcase and I packed. Mary called Delta. I could get a flight to Atlanta then to Newark at 9:30am. I called Barbara with the information and so they could pick me up. I got to Atlanta and had a four hour layover. That was horrible but many cups of coffee kept me awake. I arrived in Newark and Barbara was there with my cousin Michael. They told me Aunt Lil was over to mom and dads and she left to go home. Dad was getting undressed and mom saw him gasping for air and he fell over in the bedroom. She called 911 and then called Aunt Lil hysterical. Barbara and Aunt Lil drove over and took mom to the hospital and they told her dad was dead. When I got to the house mom went crazy crying and screaming. I had to keep calm because there was a lot I had to do. I went to the hospital to identify dad. When I went in the morgue they took me to a gurney and I saw a white tag on his toe that said Vallas. I uncovered his face and it was dad. I kissed him and went outside, sat down and cried. I went back to moms and Lorraine, my cousin, took mom and I to the John Flagler funeral home where Uncle Bernie was laid out. We picked out the casket, put together the announcement and went back home. I spent the rest of the day making phone calls. I called dad's Greek Church in Jersey City; St. Demetrios to have the priest attend to the service. He refused because dad hadn't paid his dues to the church. I told the priest off there and called the Greek Church in Perth Amboy. I spoke with the priest and he said he would do the service. It was all about money. I don't think God would have approved of the way that priest in Jersey City handled it.

It was difficult handling mom but I kept things going. Linda came down the next day and we had the first viewing. I went to the funeral parlor by myself so I could get it out of my system and make sure dad looked okay. Then again, how good can you look when you are dead? At 2pm we all arrived and aside from mom nearly jumping in the casket all went well. The next day there were so many flowers even my Fire Chief Brewster sent a large piece from the fire department.

That night I almost had a heart attack. Irene and Petee came which was very nice and I was so glad to see them. So many people came and I was in a fog. Thank God Linda was handling mom. I made arrangements to bury dad in the Masonic section of Shoreland Memorial Gardens in Keyport. I had bought 2 graves the day before for mom. She only had a small insurance policy and it would cover everything. The next day we went to the church and the priest had the coffin on the altar open as is the Greek tradition. Everyone arrived outside the church and all of a sudden a terrific wind storm came through and blew dust all over us. After the service we went to the cemetery and dad was laid to rest. Everyone was invited across the street to the Shore Point Inn for the traditional fish lunch. Tom's Uncle Nick gave a tribute. Finally Linda was leaving and it was hard to see her go. Mom and I went home. The next few days I had to get the death certificate, take her to social security, and get rid of his clothes to the goodwill. I took a few things for myself, his rings, watch, and his Gillett razor he had when he first came to the U.S. I had to get back to work so I got a ride to the airport and took off. I was sitting in coach class and I guess it all got to me and I started to cry. The flight attendant saw me and asked what was wrong. I told her what had happened and she took me up to first class which was almost empty. She sat with me for quite a while and I must have had four scotches. She was wonderful, and I couldn't thank her enough. When I got off the plane Nick and Mary, Charlie and Chris were waiting for me. We went to the Russo's and had something to snack on and I had a few more drinks. I went to work the next day and mom had given me $1,000.00 so I could pay the union back and get a new car. That week I bought a 1977 Datson. My payments would be $112.00 per month. Rosie knew about dad but I never heard from her, not that I cared. I spoke to Charlie McNally, Jr. and we went looking for a place. We found a new apartment complex, two story, pool, and tennis, 2 bedrooms, large living room, kitchen, and balcony. It was just right. We both were able to collect furniture, beds, and all other kitchen pots, pans, etc. from the Russo's, McNally's, Fortunato's and friends. Charlie and I also spent some money for everything else. We moved in on April 24th to Rainbow Bend. I finally began to feel good again. No more pressure from Rosie. Charlie was working at the Holiday Inn at night on the front desk. I was working 24 on and 48 off.

May 1977 - Lecturing on Drug Abuse

On May 1st I did a lecture on drug abuse at St. Demetrios Greek Church in Fort Lauderdale for the Order of AHEPA, the American Helenic Educational Progressive Association. It went over well and on May 7th a letter was sent to Chief Brewster commending me.

I stopped at Al and Terry's one night and Genie was there. We talked a bit and I invited her over one night for a drink. It seemed odd because Rosie didn't like it when I was in her company when we were married. Genie came over that night and we both enjoyed each other very much. We began to see each other often and I was invited to her house also. I wasn't about to get involved with anyone on a permanent basis. I gave up my job at Publix finally because I was now making good money. Rosie's lawyer sent me a letter and wanted me to discuss some money for Rosie. I called him. He was a nice guy. I told him I never had sex with Rosie and I would also get my doctor to testify to that if she continued to ask for things. I can't imagine what she said when her lawyer told her what I said. She never contacted me again until the day we went for the desolation of marriage. I was now having a ball. I started to go to the Brickyard Lounge and I met many girls. One girl was a cop named Debby. I liked her and we began to get together often but she had a three year old girl so I knew I wouldn't get involved. Charlie was home one night and we both cooked dinner and then went to the Brickyard Lounge. We came home with a catch and we partied all night. I was having a good time and it felt good to be free at last, and having a pay check to myself. Charlie and I always split the expenses and we got along well. I called mom every other day but she was still having a hard time.

June 1977 – The Accident

Uncle Walter and Aunt Dolores called. They were at Disney World and wanted me to come up. I was off the next day so I drove and stayed with them overnight. The kids were in their teens and it was nice seeing them. I came home and stopped at Mary and Nick's. We talked for a while and then I left to go to the Rainbow Bend. Charlie was sleeping so I closed his door because the phone rang. It was Genie and she wanted to get together. I went over to her house and she made dinner. I stayed late but had to leave because I had to go on duty in the morning. It was May 4th and I was getting out of my car at the rear of the station when I heard a loud crash and saw black smoke in the sky. It was 7:45am. I yelled to the guys and we took off with the engine. It was at State Road 7 and Sunrise Blvd. A tractor trailer turned over and the cab was down in the embankment. Dan Wyatt and I tried to get the driver out who was screaming. The flames beat us back. We desperately tried to hose him down but the fire got the best of him and he burned to death. I had begun to write a book of Poems which I called, "My Own Reflections". When I was on duty I would always type a poem or two. I saw Howie at station one that day and he told me he was painting an apartment near Inverrary and the woman told him her daughter was coming down for one month and was going to stay at the Inverrary Country Club. She was 35 years old, blonde, and was a school teacher from Poughkeepsie, NY. He wanted to fix her up with someone Jewish. Howie said to call him when she came down at the end of June. Howie was going to have me meet with her. Every night I had off I was at the Brickyard Lounge having fun. Tony Chance, a singer and performer, was great and there was always a big crowd Friday and Saturday nights to see him.

Chief Brewster had called me several times to look at fires and plans. I was the unofficial fire investigator. Howie called me at the end of June and gave me the telephone number of Doreen Miller Kaye. I called her at Inverrary and made a date to take her to the beach in a couple of days. When I got off at 8am that morning I went home, changed and went to pick her up. I got clearance from the gate and found her apartment. She opened the door and what a pleasant surprise. She looked very nice. We talked a little and then we left. We went to the Pompano Beach fishing pier area because I used to go there. We had a nice time and she told me she was divorced and had a son Scott who was 14 and she was having trouble with him. She said she wanted to move to Florida someday if she could get a job with the school system. We started to leave and I took her to my house for a drink. I invited her to lunch the next day since I was off. The next day I picked her up and we went to lunch. I then took her home for drinks. We had a good time and made love. She was great and for the rest of the month we saw each other regularly. I stayed over at her place a few times, too. She took her mother, who I think liked me, but her father, Ned, I could tell didn't. I understood it was because I was not Jewish and there would be a problem but it wasn't my problem. My dad wanted me to marry a Greek, but when I married Polish and Italian he never said a word or was disrespectable to them. Doreen was her own free spirit but her mother had control. When she went back to NY we sent cards to each other and I called her often.

July 1977 – Saving Another Life

July 3rd I was at the beach when I saw a guy floating in the water. I dove in and pulled him to shore. I began CPR. A nurse came and we both worked on him and we saved him. Rescue took him away. I was notified later that I would receive an accommodation for saving a life on August 16th. I made my calls to Petee but he always sounded like he couldn't talk. I sent him some pictures of me and articles from the newspaper about me. I kept seeing Genie on and off but I also had a couple of other girlfriends that I met. It was near the end of July that another friend of mine Gary DeMaio, who I met through Charlie, called me. He was seeing this girl from

Elmira who was single and he had wanted her to come to Florida and stay with him at his mother's house. His mother and father were friends of the Russo's too. Her name was Mary Ann Copozzi. He asked me if she could stay at my house a couple of days because he was seeing another girl. I didn't like the idea but I said yes. He called me back and said I could pick her up at the motel where she was staying. I went over and she was very nice, a short girl, very pleasant, and well mannered. I baby sat for her a couple of days, took her to dinner and gave her my bed. I stayed on the couch. The day before she left she gave me a beautiful hanging shell chime. I took her to the airport. I felt bad for her.

August 1977 – Determination to Become the Best

Doreen said she might be down a couple of weekends in August. I was noticing some jealousy with Captain Pete Gannon. I don't think he liked the idea of my closeness with the chief. He never worked at Station Two so that was good. I was called in by Mayor Cipaloni to head the City of Lauderhill's United Way Program. Anytime there was a luncheon or meeting I was able to attend. The fire within kept burning. I was determined to become the best. I took advantage of every school and seminar. I even took courses in air conditioning, plumbing, and electrical to help me with inspections and investigations. Little did I know at the time that all this would make me a top expert one day in my own business. I had just completed another course at Broward Community College, and signed on to take another. I heard from Doreen. She was coming down on August 14th and staying at a different apartment at the Country Club until Labor Day. On August 14th she arrived and went to her apartment. I got off at 8am the next day and went home to do my chores. I saw her later in the afternoon. I told her the next day I was receiving an award for saving some guys life July 4th and would she like to go. The next day she came with me and I received the Certificate of Accommodation from the city of Pompano Beach. On the way back on the radio we found out that Elvis Presley died.

The rest of the month I hung out with Doreen until she left. On august 27th we had a house fire and Lt. Don Farmer, Don Shaw and I were injured. Farmer twisted his ankle, Shaw had smoke inhalation, and I had a burned knee. I later determined the fire was set. I left the next day for New Jersey to see mom and Petee. I drove up and spent two days at mom's, saw Petee one afternoon then went up to Doreen's. Genie was going to be in New Jersey that week also and she wanted to drive back with me. When I saw Doreen she had been with her friend Tony, who worked at the Culinary Institute. Doreen and Tony had been close friends for several years. I stayed at Doreen's for three days and it seemed like we might be getting closer together. I called Genie at her relative's house in New Jersey and told her I couldn't pick her up. She was angry. I didn't see her again after that. Genie was looking for a boyfriend and I wasn't ready for that. On the way back to Florida, I stopped overnight at South of the Border and called Doreen. She was with Tony when I called and I was having second thoughts about our relationship. I arrived home the next day and went shopping. Charlie came home and said he was having company that night. He asked me if I wanted to join in the party. I had no choice but I intended to go to my room early because I had to work the next day. Charlie was a lot younger than me. When his friends came there were three girls. Everyone was drinking and this one girl Debby seemed to like me. She kept grabbing me and I realized she was a bit drunk. About 11pm I said goodnight and when I went to my room she followed and got on my bed. We got undressed and got in bed and we both fell asleep. I got up at 6:30am and she grabbed me by the arm and pulled me down and we made love. The next day, after work, I found out she was 18 years old. I almost killed Charlie when he told me.

CHAPTER–TWENTY THREE
Investigations

Chapter–Twenty Three – Investigations

September 1977 -First Draft of My First Book

I started to write my book "My Own Reflections" and was also writing poems for the Sun-Sentinel. Chief Brewster called me in because they were having problems with false alarms at the Manors of Inverarry. I met with the Manor's director and he offered me an apartment free so I could work under cover and solve the problem. I accepted with Chief Brewster's okay. I told Charlie I was moving out and we sublet the apartment immediately. I moved in within a week. The chief issued me a portable radio so I would have contact with the fire department and the police department. It was a beautiful apartment and I was happy to be alone. I invited mom down for a couple of weeks and she said maybe sometime before the Holidays. On September 10th there was an article in the Broward Times by Dennis Powell, staff writer about my life saving 35 lives in 16 years. On October 14, 1977 I received a letter from Congress of the United States House of Representatives, Paul Rogers, MC commending me for saving 35 lives.

During these weeks while working under cover at the manor I called a meeting with the directors of the Manors and the Fairways of Inverrary who was also having problems. Pat La Cara, the manager of the Fairways wanted me to solve the arson problem and false alarm problems they were having. I was also contacted by the International Village Resorts Spa to give a program on Fire Prevention Safety 10am-3pm. The third week I finally had solved the cases at the Manors. Pat LaCara called me in one day to meet with her. She offered me a two story townhouse at the Fairways half price if I would move in to try and solve the problem there. I told her I would but not until November 1st. I had mom coming for a long weekend. I showed mom around the complex and she liked it. Mom left that Sunday and I called Pat and she said the apartment was ready if I wanted it now and I said yes. I moved two days later into a three-bedroom, two-bath, large living room, kitchen, dining room, and a 2nd floor gallery. Pat and I began to get close. She was married to Caesar who was supposedly involved with the mob in NY. He was a very big heavy guy. I just couldn't picture them together. Pat was beautiful and she worked for Leonard Steiner who was a partner in the Fairways as well as other complexes in New York City.

One night she let me into her apartment on the top floor of one of the buildings to conduct a stake out. Mr. Steiner gave it to her to use since she was the resident manager. They owned a house in Plantation but Caesar worked in NY. She made us a drink and we watched the complex and talked for two hours. I decided to call it quits for the night and as I left she kissed me. I wasn't quite sure how to take that but I didn't mind.

October 1977 – The Problems with False Alarms

Doreen called and I told her about the new apartment. I also told her she could stay here if she wanted when she came down. Mom also wanted to come down so I spoke to Pat and she had a nice two bedroom in Building 3 and would give it to mom for $200.00 less than the regular price. I told mom. She came down the next weekend and she loved it. She gave a deposit and went home. She hired a moving company and was going to come down in November. Captain Gannon was starting to complain because he was short one man when I was on investigations. I was getting to know some of the kids and the complex. Chief Brewster said when I got off shift to document my hours and he would give me compensation time for it. I already had 40 hours and he said add it to my list and hand it in each month to Rose, his secretary. There was a lot of bad publicity in the newspapers about the Fairways false alarms and I was determined to solve this problem. I was doing an inspection one day at the Executive House Condo which was built by Tony Provanzano's union funds as I was told. I saw Pat and she was with her husband Caesar and six other men one of whom was Tony Provanzano. When I went to leave one guy named Johnny pulled me over and said how could we settle this problem about sprinklers and other fire violations which I wanted done. These should have been done during the building construction and wasn't. He said I would be well taken care of if I could change things. Was this a bribe or what? I told Chief Brewster and he said to keep quiet and he would put the pressure on. It didn't work because Mayor Cipaloni went to Brewster to get off their backs. That was the beginning of the feud between them.

November 1977 – My Reward for an Investigation

On November 3rd Chief Brewster received a letter from Leonard Steiner commending me for my success in dealing with the child responsible for pulling a false alarm. On November 6th I received a letter from the White House and a commendation from President Carter for saving 35 lives in the past 16 years. I was now in all the newspapers again. On November 14th I received a letter from WAXY radio station honoring me. Mom came down and stayed with me and the furniture came a week later. Between working I helped her unpack, and took her to the stores, etc. She never drove so I had to take her everywhere. I was very busy and put in a lot of hours with the fire department. Chief Brewster was very happy with me and we got along fine. He did keep me busy because there were a lot of false alarms, and some arson's in the Fairways. I had lunch with Pat several times at the Executive House and I sensed she was very lonely.

One Friday night she met me at a place called "Hotsey Totsie" for a drink. We talked for two hours then we went back to the Fariways because there was another false alarm. I later walked her up to her apartment and when I got ready to leave we had a good kiss. I went back to my apartment and went to bed thinking I don't want to get involved with her because of the mob connection. There was a lot of money in her marriage and she had some rock on her finger.

November 28th early evening we had a large fire at the Inverrary Country Club Barn. The entire building and nine golf carts, a Volkswagen Beetle, a motorcycle, and 1,000 feet of fence burned with an estimated loss of $350,000. The state fire Marshal's office sent an investigator who ruled the fire accidental with no cause. After he left the scene I asked Chief Brewster if I could continue the investigation because the scene wasn't dug out and examined enough. He said go ahead. It was down in the floor area. I found evidence of spalling which is an indicator of an accelerant (flammable liquid). The concrete popped up and in this case it looked like a pour pattern. I ruled out electrical because I spent one week examining all wires. I also notified the state attorney's office, Ed Pyers who was the assistant state attorney and the investigator Jeff Lennox.

December 1977 and January 1978 - Fires

I did an arson cause and origin class at Plantation Central Station for Chief Donald Vander Linde. On December 28th he sent a letter to Chief Brewster thanking me. Doreen was coming down for the holidays and I was looking forward to it. The day before she got there I was in Albertson's Food Market and slipped on a string bean and fractured my ankle. They took me to Holy Cross Hospital and I was put in a cast. I had to take a week off but I went to the station each morning anyway. Doreen went back January 2nd to Poughkeepsie. On January 1st there was a fire in a trash chute at the Manors. I hobbled out of my car and did my investigation. I found a fire sprinkler at the second floor tied with a cotton cloth to prevent it from putting out the fire. In the debris in the chute were boxes with personal and corporate tax records from the City of Sunrise. I removed this material and brought it to fire station one for further examination. On January 2nd there was a fire at NW 55th Avenue and it was similar to the fire June 20th at the same quad-plex.

On January 4th I was appointed Fire and Arson Investigator for the department. I would be available to assist all officers in investigations at any time and would be called in for all fires involving large losses, injuries, and deaths. The police department was also notified. I now went on days and had red lights installed on my car and a radio. Near the end of January the Fire Marshal's office in Miami closed the book on the Inverrary Golf Cart fire stating it was accidental. They also said the information I had was pure bull. However my investigation went on and I submitted it to the state attorney's office. A couple of days later an investigator for the Broward County State Attorney's office said the fire was the work of a "professional arsonist". The assistant state attorney, Ed Pyers, head of the Special Investigations Division said, "There's no question it was arson."

I received an unknown threat on the telephone at the fire station and notified the police department. That is when I began to carry a gun. I was working day and night to solve these cases. One night I needed to get away so I went to the Hotsey Totsie Lounge for a drink. I met a girl there who sat next to me and we got along just wonderfully. She happened to be one of the Kennedy's. She wanted to remain unanimous and I understood. Just before we left to go to my house someone took a picture of us and it ended up being in the Sunshine State Nite-Life.

At the end of January there was a fire at 1769 NW 58th Avenue at Wimbledon Development. Captain Gannon called me to the scene. I found a gasoline can with newspapers around it. The fire wasn't big. After the engines left I began to investigate and interview neighbors. One saw two children run away into another building. I went to the second apartment. A woman opened the door and I saw two boys there. I showed my badge and asked to speak to them outside. They came out and after questioning them they admitted setting the fire. I spoke with the parents of both boys and called the Detective Bureau. We decided to put them in the City's work program for juveniles.

February 1978 – Fires

February 24th we had a fire at Sandal Grove Apartments on NW 18th Street in a utility closet. I found it to be set and began an investigation.

I was very busy planning for the Jackie Gleason Golf Classic at the Inverrary Country Club. President Ford would be staying there for the golf classic. Chief Brewster, Captain Korte and I mapped out emergency routes and all respective problems then we met with the police to finalize the plans. I met with Jackie Gleason and his staff because they were going to have a luncheon and break at the Executive House. I knew Jackie Gleason because when I was in charge of the United Way Program for the city I was in his house in Inverrary. The day I was there he was grouchy and drinking scotch. He told his wife to give me a check for $500.00. At the meeting he was very funny. He commented that his Rolls Royce Golf Cart that burned in the Cart Barn Fire had been replaced and President Ford would be riding with him. I would be on patrol in my car, too.

After all the plans were made we met with Secret Service to get special clearance IDs. There were a number of fires at the Inverrary Racquet Club about ten in all. After two days of investigations and stake outs I located a woman who said she thought the youngsters whose names (I cannot mention) were involved. I found the boy and he confessed and implicated the others who also confessed. Since last October the Lauderhill Fire Department had 79 calls. Arson was the cause of 17 of those trips.

False alarms; many of them deliberate accounting for 37. I had spent close to 1,000 hours investigating. I started to dust the fire alarms pull stations. The next day we had a false alarm. I walked around the crowd with my black light and found an 18 year old man, Randall Ringer who was visiting relatives. I arrested him and he was freed on a $2,500.00 bond. We also had 14 arson fires in the Manors after 72 hours of straight investigating. I took a reporter with me on an all night stake out. I finally caught three juveniles and turned them over to juvenile authorities. The Golf Classic began and on the second day when President Ford was at the Executive House there was a bomb scare and I was called in. I rushed to the Executive House along with the fire trucks. I went inside and showed my secret service ID. I told them I would be checking all first floor areas so he came with me. We went into the restaurant and there was Jackie Gleason and President Ford and others. I shook hands with President Ford and Jackie Gleason who knew me. He was joking about the bomb scare saying, "Wouldn't it be funny if it was in your new Rolls Royce". I told him I would take it for a ride and check it out and he laughed. I went on and cleared the building and left. What an experience. I needed a rest, but that wasn't going to happen. I was certainly working on investigations and had gained much respect from the police department. I received a call from Florida Power and Light Company to give a lecture in May. I was still trying to write my poems and wrote one for the fire department.

March 1978 – The False Alarm Investigation

I spoke to Doreen and she decided to move to Florida in June and live with me. On March 2nd we responded to a false alarm at the Fairways. It was the eighteenth false alarm there since October. I saw a crowd of kids and a 16 year old boy whose hand lit up like a Christmas tree. While I arrested him someone yelled to me that the 7th floor of building 4 was filled with smoke. I called the trucks back and pulled the alarm myself while I ran up to the 7th floor. The people who heard the alarm wouldn't leave because they thought it was another false alarm. I arrived on the 7th floor and smelled the smoke then as I approached apartment 4707, I saw smoke coming out. I grabbed a fire extinguisher and went in. There was a fire in the oven which I extinguished. The tenant Jack Wishnie had left the apartment because of the first alarm and wasn't there to turn if off. I was working with Detective Ted Beasley and Robin Anton on the February 24th fire at Sandal Grove. We received a tip and armed with a warrant from Judge Thomas Crocker, Jr. went to the everglades to a fence company and arrested a Timothy Lee Witko who was held in lieu of $10,000.00 bond for first degree arson. Things were looking up and I felt confident I would solve many other cases. The "Fire Within" was going strong.

March 1978 – The Divorce

I met Pat one night after work and we went to my house. We had a few drinks and the rest is history. The next day we had more false alarms always after school. I found a 14 year old girl whose mother was single and liked me. Her mother was talking to me at the pool one day and said her daughter knew what was going on. I asked her if she would talk to me and she said she wouldn't. I asked her mother if she could find out for me anything and she said she would try. I received a call from Rosie's attorney and he said the divorce date was going to be April 21st and Rosie and I should be at the court at 9am.

April 1978 – Bomb Scare

On April 12th there was a false bomb threat at Lauderhill Middle School. The police department came up with a name. I thought it was the same name belonging to a fire setter I had put in the juvenile work program before.

On April 13th we had a structure fire which I determined was set. On April 17th there was a set brush fire near the school. I started to collect the information. I spoke to West Magazine and they put an article in the paper requesting information on several fires. A lot of tips started to come in by telephone and I began to put it all together. April 21st, I went to court and met Rosie. We didn't say too much to each other but she wanted me to pay for the termite job at the house because she was selling it. I said it is your house now. The judge asked if we were sure about the divorce and we both said yes. It was over finally and I was very happy. I wanted to celebrate so I went to Yesterdays Restaurant on the water. My date was Debbie a paramedic I had met in the department. We had a great dinner and then went to the Brickyard. We got home at 1am and we both went to work the next day. I knew I wouldn't see Doreen until June. Besides, she still saw Tony so I didn't feel bad. I still stopped at Mary and Nick Russo's and Charlie and Chris's house. I had so much compensation time. I asked Chief Brewster for a week off in June so I could bring Doreen down. One of the firemen was lending me his pick up truck to move her. Chief Brewster said yes because I was doing such a great job. There were a couple of fireman who were very jealous of me and one fellow by the name of Cooper. Cooper was a snitch for Mayor Cipaloni and he hated Chief Brewster. Captain Gannon thought I was a threat for whatever reason. Lt. Don Shaw always told me everything so I knew what was going on. I was in the headlines almost once a week and was getting quite a reputation. I just finished another course at BCC. I don't know how I did all this. I was very tired now and I needed some rest. Mom was happy and made a couple of friends. I took her to the stores and to dinner sometimes. She felt more comfortable with me around.

May 1978 – The False Alarm Investigation

On May 6th I was able to connect a 15 year old boy to the April false alarm. He was placed in the Juvenile Work Program. I also caught two juveniles who set the April 13th structure fire, and I pressed charges against another boy who set a fire to an apartment building under construction on 52nd Avenue. This also tied in another boy who called in the bomb threat on April 12th. I was doing well and on Sunday May 7th Dennis Powell, staff writer from the Fort Lauderdale News placed an article about this. On May 25th a letter was received from FPL to the fire department and to Mayor Eugene Cipaloni about my lecture thanking them for my service. Since I was living at the Fairways I started to get to know some of the kids. I was always seeking information and names. I had a good list of suspects but I wanted to have enough evidence to get them arrested. When June arrived I drove to Poughkeepsie, NY and packed the pickup truck to the hilt. I covered everything with tarps and in two days Doreen, Scott, and I left. Scott had an attitude and mood changes. I liked the kid but he acted strange sometimes. He was into West Side Story and Ann Margaret. He also liked to perform and act. I felt sorry for Doreen because he always gave her a hard time. The trip down was rough with Scott because he didn't' want to move. We arrived back in two days and moved everything into my apartment. I returned the truck to the firehouse and picked up my car. I had to work the next day. Doreen had to buy a car and furniture for Scott and the living room. I had a dining room table, which Pat LaCara said I could keep. I never told Doreen about Pat. Pat knew she was moving in because I had to get an okay. When I went to work the next day I had quite a few calls to answer about my investigation. That night I knew I was getting close. On Friday evening someone entered the recreation rooms and vacant apartments and set the furniture on fire. Also on Saturday there were several more fires. I decided to start under cover surveillance on Sunday. I received assistance from three other firemen and the police juvenile division. Ian Friedlander was the police investigator and we worked together. Monday and Tuesday we documented every teen's movement at night. On Wednesday morning I held a briefing and told everyone that today is the last day of school so we set up the entire surveillance beginning at 3pm. I also requested an engine company to stand by when it got dark at a complex close to the Fairways. These kids had caused over $10,000.00 damage in the last week and I was about to get them. I was hiding in a closet adjacent to one of the recreation rooms and I discovered a fire in a restroom and saw six teens running from the area. I called on the radio for the Engine and all the others surrounded the area and we caught four boys and two girls. They confessed and implicated others. We also discovered drugs. The headlines the next day was "Juvenile Burglary – Arson Ring Busted by Lauderhill Fireman". I finally did it. We got the ring leader and more arrests were expected. The kids were saying they had nothing to do that is why they did it. We had 7 arrests that night and three the next day. This took a load off my mind. Chief Brewster was proud of me and made sure the entire department knew it. He wanted to promote me to captain and make my position permanent. The union said there should be a test and only qualified people could take it. The problem they had was no one but me was qualified. This controversy would continue for several months.

July 1978 – Deliberate Bombings

I had a meeting with Pat and told her the present social director did not cooperate with me and he didn't care about kids. She and Mr. Steiner agreed and I suggested Doreen to be the social director and I would be the assistant director free of charge. They all agreed and Doreen took over with a salary and a budget. On July 11th two apartments were destroyed by fire bombs. Both sides of the duplex at 5401 NW 18th Court were damaged. Bottles filled with gasoline were set on fire and thrown through the living room windows. This occurred between 2 and 4am. I now had another big investigation to do. I was still working on the Executive House problems and under Chief Brewster's orders. I threatened to shut the place down, and go to the state. Mayor Cipaloni again came to the station and told Chief Brewster and I to lay-off. That afternoon Detective Friedlander and I were talking in the police parking lot which was next to the fire station. Ian was about to walk away when we heard a wheeze sound and something hit the police car. We looked for a few minutes and found a bullet hole. It was too late to go after anyone because it must have come from a car passing on the street. From then on I was always on guard and carried my gun. Doreen was setting up a teen center and game room. On the wall of the remains of the previous game room was a sign which read, "Children Under the Age of 17 Not Allowed". Well, that now disappeared. Doreen set up programs from Yoga, Bingo, art games, pool parties and a fully staffed teen room all day. My mother Sophia was hired to be an assistant and answer the phones and log the kids in and out. The Fairways gave me 100 percent cooperation and soon there were no more problems.

August 1978 – The Citizen of the Day Award

August 4th I received the "Citizen of the Day" on Radio Station WINZ94AM. Also on August 4th I received a certificate commemorating August 4th as "Citizen of the Day" from Citizens Federal S&L. Chief Brewster called me in and showed me a letter from the police department commending me on the excellent work done by me. The letter said it has been a pleasure, and an educational experience to work with him and it is sincerely hoped that your department will be able to continue employing him in his present capacity signed by Detective John Pasmore, Juvenile Division.

September 1978 – Many Fires and False Alarms

I was working on about nine fires and false alarm cases at the beginning of September. One September 25th we had a bad lightning storm and a fire broke out on the 4th floor of the Greens of Inverrary, and the first arriving unit called in for help. Chief Brewster, Captain Korte, and I responded in the chief's car. It was a pretty good working fire so I suited up, helped Dan Wyatt set up the ladder truck and I put on my Scott air pack and climbed up to help. I entered the apartment which was burning and full of heavy smoke. Captain Gannon had seen me go in and he went in too. I had gotten down behind two firemen to back them up as we worked our way into the rest of the apartment. All of a sudden someone grabbed my mask and pulled it off. I struggled a bit then made my way back out but I took in a lot of smoke. Six firemen including me were taken to the hospital and all released several hours later. I went back and determined it was caused by a lightning strike. Two days later Chief Brewster said Captain Gannon put in his report that I panicked and jeopardized everyone else. I had been in more fires worse than this many years before he was on the fire department and never had a problem. This was purposely done to me and Chief Brewster and I knew something was up. There were several more fires to follow in the days ahead. One on the 10th floor of the Manors and on Sunday the 1st of four fires broke out at the Continental Garden Apartments on 1851 NW 16th Avenue. All these fires were set in the utility rooms. This was a busy month for me as you can tell.

October 1978 – The Turnpike Fire Investigation

On October 8th a fire was set underneath the Florida Turnpike overpass. When I investigated the fire I had no leads. Then we had a fire on October 10th and an onlooker gave me a description of a youth who started the fire under the turnpike. The onlookers told me the neighborhood where they thought the suspect lived. When I returned to the station I checked my files and found a picture of the suspect. I went to his house and knocked on the door. I found the 13 year old who confessed to some of the eight fires. He also identified a second juvenile. Checking my records again I found a 15 year old on my list of suspects. I found the boy and after questioning him, he said he had set the remainder of the eight fires.

The teen club at the Fairways was going well. On the weekend before Halloween, Doreen and I put on a parade for all the teen clubs. At the end of the parade in the complex we had a party for all of them. We had ice cream, cake, cookies, soda, and games. Doreen was dressed as Batwoman and I was Batman. We decorated a golf car as the Batmobile. Fort Lauderdale News and Sun-Sentinel staff writer, Lynn Demarest wrote a beautiful article about it on October 26th. It had two pictures of us with a Bat Mobile and the parade. She interviewed several of the teens who I arrested and heard what they had to say. Rusty and Sue were part of the gang and had set several fires and pulled alarm boxes. Rusty was now a cadet in the fire department program and Sue was a secretary of the teen club. The gang was caught by me and the ringleader was sent to reform school. Sue and Rusty were sent back to their parents. Doreen and I opened the new teen club. The Fairways gave us $2,000.00 for all new equipment. Doreen had a master's degree in psychology so she was perfect as a social director. This program had eliminated the problem at the complex.

October 1978 -A Missing Child

One day a two and a half year old boy was lost at the Fairways. His mother called the club and said she was afraid he might wander into one of the swimming pools or lakes. I banded about 25 kids at the club and set off four search parties. One of them found the child just 20 feet from the pool.

November 1978 – The Teen Program

One night I gave a first aid course to the teens. The next day one of our teens, Penny Dowling, saw an auto accident at Boyd Anderson's High School and rushed out to give first aid and stopped the bleeding. In addition, the youths also helped the older folks with heavy grocery packages, and serve hors d'oeuvres at the weekly bingos. Danny Falenbaum, president of the teen club said, "See, we had nothing to do, so there was a lot of vandalism around here." "What do Rusty and Sue think of the man who arrested them five months ago?" He is the best, that is all, said Rusty and added, "He helps us with our problems and always has enough time for us." Sue agreed and commented, "I hated him at first but he is the best."

A funny thing happened during the party. I had a fire call so I jumped in my car and went to the fire at another complex. When I got out of the car in the Batman outfit and radio in hand, I thought the guys would die laughing. Naturally the news picked up on this and had a ball. One night a few weeks later I was leaving the game room and decided to do a spot check of the complex about 10:30pm. I heard a noise coming from near the soda machines. I saw three men trying to jimmy open the vending machines with a tire iron. I said, "Hold it" and grabbed the tire iron holding my badge and radio in my hand. One guy ran and I called the police over my radio and kept the two guys against the wall. Arrested was Kallen R. Weaver, age 20 of Lauderdale Lakes and a male juvenile. A week later the headliner was, "Fire Investigator Wraps Up 32 Arson Cases This Year". This did not count the 30 or so false alarm cases I solved and four burglary cases.

December 1978 – The Fire Department

It was a good year. The chief was happy and so was everyone else. The riff between Chief Brewster and Mayor Cipolloni was getting worse. There was a new complex being built on 56th Avenue by a Cuban fellow from Miami. We wanted him to comply with up-graded fire codes and he didn't want to. He went to the mayor and the mayor said to leave him alone. This happened to be one of the problems the fire service has to contend with today. Politicians have to stop putting safety aside to benefit their carriers and do favors to get their votes and this doesn't include payoffs which existed then. Chief Brewster decided to leave because he truly believed that he had to do the job right or not do it at all. I was very upset because I believed the same thing.

January 1979 – Firefighter Politics

I went on a cruise to the Bahamas with Doreen. When I returned Chief Brewster was gone and we didn't know who the new chief would be but we heard it would be Cooper. Cooper was meeting with Mayor Cipolloni, his buddy. I was shocked when it was announced that Cooper would be the new chief. He didn't have much experience and certainly was not qualified.

The next day he called me in his office and said, "You're going back on "A" shift. We don't need a fire investigator on the job; we need someone to put the fires out." I went back on shift. Two weeks later I decided to leave and I gave notice. I had a lot of sick days left and about six months compensation time so for the next few months I still received my salary.

February 1979 – Changing Fire Departments

I received several calls from chiefs of fire departments asking if I was interested in working for them. I told everyone I needed time to think. I received a letter from Petee and it was written in a code. This never happened before so Doreen and I spent about an hour and we were able to read it. It was troublesome and he made a remark that things were not good at home. I missed him terribly and I was thinking of moving back to NJ. I also received a call from Walter Godfrey, a fire investigator who worked for William Alvine Assoc in NJ. He told me to send my resume to their office because they needed someone in NJ. I went ahead and sent it. In the meantime I had to think about what to do with Doreen. In the meantime I helped Doreen at the Social Club and mom was still working there. She liked it and it was good for her. She had a few lady friends, went to bingo and joined in on local events. When I told her I was thinking of moving back she asked, "What are you going to do leave me alone?" My head was full and I had to think everything over. The fire within was still in me and I thought I must continue in fire investigations. It was what I really wanted. I also knew I wasn't going to marry Doreen because her mother and father wouldn't approve, and I was not sure of myself either. I wanted to make a lot of money and I knew it wasn't going to come from the fire service. I called Petee and spoke to him a few minutes but he couldn't talk. Scott was finding himself with the Fairway teens but he was still a problem.

CHAPTER–TWENTY FOUR
Investigations And Rhoda

Chapter–Twenty Four – Investigations And Rhoda

March 1979 – In Between Jobs

March arrived and I was trying not to spend money in case I left. I made some money from Bingo and a few other odd jobs. I received a letter from William Alvine Assoc. saying the next time I came to NJ to let him know and he would interview me. I told Doreen about the job and she said go for it. I wasn't sure yet what I was going to do. One good thing was Doreen taught me how to properly speak the English language. More bingo, more pool parties, etc. and I was getting bored. I had a couple of offers from the fire departments but I would have to start as a fireman again. I was also asked to take a job with a hotel and casino in the Bahamas. I knew I could get a job but this time I wanted to make it big, but how? By the middle of March I decided to go back to NJ and take the job with Alvine Assoc. I told mom I would bring her up after I got settled. I told Doreen that if she wanted to come with me she could. We were outside the IHOP and she called her mother. I heard her asking her mother if she should marry me. After the call we went across the street to my place and she decided she wanted to stay. I made arrangements with Pat so Doreen could take over a new lease. I was going to leave about April 2nd or 3rd. I had about $875.00 in cash and only my clothes and personal things to take. I packed everything into my 77 Datsun and said good bye to mom and Doreen. Mom was crying but I assured her I would be back soon.

I drove about five hours and I turned around and went back. I arrived and it was Bingo night so I went to the hall. When mom saw me she started to cry. Doreen almost died and I will never forget the look on her face. After Bingo I went to mom's and we had a talk, then I went to Doreen and told her I came back because I wasn't sure about leaving. That is when she told me Tony was coming tomorrow and would be staying with her. Well that certainly answered my questions and I told her I would leave in the morning. I called mom and told her I was leaving very early. I left about 5am and drove to South of the Border. I also had $1,000.00 in cash which I put in a sock and put it in my toiletry bag. I got something to eat and drink then went back to my room to bed. I got up early and drove to my Aunt Ann's in NJ. I was driving up the NJ Turnpike when a New York Airways Helicopter crashed at Newark Airport. I saw the crash site as I passed and everyone on board was killed. I had something to eat at Aunt Ann's and they wanted me to stay there until I found a place. The next day I went to William Alvine Assoc. and met Bill and his wife Carol. Carol was part of the business and she seemed like she was the boss not Bill. Carol used to be Bill's secretary. Bill separated from his wife and married Carol who was much younger than he was. They liked me but they didn't want me to start until the fall. I told them I couldn't wait that long and that I needed a job. They decided to hire me immediately and told me to start next Monday.

April 1979 – The Heating Business And Meeting Rhoda For The First Time

I was glad and I was ready to start and make some money. Aunt Ann insisted I sleep in her room and she slept on the couch. I started my job and worked with Bill the first few weeks. Bill used to be in the heating business, oil burners, etc. then started to do fires. I noticed he really wasn't that good. I looked up an old friend of mine who was an attorney, James Demetrakis, Jimmy's father and my father were friends. Our families spent a lot of time together when we were young at the Catskills. His office was in Hackensack, NJ so I went there one day after work and saw Jimmy. It was great seeing him because I hadn't seen him since he was in my wedding party when I had married Irene. He told me he owned a large restaurant and lounge in Fort Lee, NJ named, "The Palisadium". It was on what used to be Palisades Amusement Park. Now the entire area was all condos. He said Wednesday and Friday nights there was music and dancing. That Wednesday I went there and I couldn't believe the amount of women there. I didn't' have a lot of money and this was a high class place, with a cover charge. I saw Jimmy and he introduced me to all his managers, maitre d', and bartenders and told them I was never to pay a cover charge and to always take care of me. I became the big shot at the Palasadium from then on. My drinks were always free except when I bought a drink for someone. I would always tip and take care of my favorites.

There was a new apartment complex opening in Hackensack, NJ on Prospect Avenue called Quail Heights. I went there and I rented a one bedroom apartment, terrace, kitchen, living room, and bath. I left Aunt Ann's and moved into an empty brand new place. I had a phone installed in two days. I had to see my sister Linda in Syracuse so the next weekend I went to see her. Linda gave me many utensils, pots, pans and she also let me use her MasterCard so I could buy a couple of suits for work. I had a charge card for one department store so I bought a bed with all the trimmings, a small table, two chairs, a couch, bookcase, stereo, and a work table. My life was coming together finally. I met at least four girls at the Palisadium already and would take them home occasionally. I was no longer hurting for sex.

I saw Petee at a baseball game and Irene drove by. I spoke to her and everything was civil. Petee was funny; he kept looking at me and I knew he wanted to get a hit but he didn't. I was happy I could be with my son finally and nothing else mattered. My job for the first month with Alvine was good. I was vice president of the northeast division. He had a nephew James Alvine who worked there. I liked Jimmy and we worked together very well. There was Bill Lichte who was his part-time engineer.

Bill retired from Bendex Aviation and he was brilliant. I never told Bill Alvine but my old landlord in North Bergen, Dino Korinis were good friends with Bill. They had worked together for years. I also began to realize except for boiler losses and heating Bill Alvine knew nothing. His wife ruled the roost. Then there was Ted Ryan who was a police officer in Montclair and worked part-time doing boiler inspections for Alvine. Ted was a heavy drinker and had some problems. Bill Lichte told me the only reason they hired me was because Alvine needed a fire expert on staff. I decided then that I would get all I could out of Alvine.

April 28th came and I went to the Palisadium. I had decided that night to eat a good dinner which I hadn't had for a long time. Tom, the maitre de sat me at a table right in the front. There were two men sitting at the table next to me. My waiter was Harry also a Greek and he knew who I was. I only had about $45.00 on me but I could sign the check if I wanted. I ordered a drink and as I was sitting there I noticed two girls waiting in line for a table. One of them was cute and I gave her a second look. I watched them sit at a table about 20 feet away. Harry, the Greek waiter came over and I ordered a glass of wine. While I was waiting one of the girls at that table came over to me and said, "I'm Judy." I am taking my girlfriend Rhoda out for her birthday and I thought you might like to join us. I said yes I would be glad to. She returned to her table and the two guys next to me said, "I don't believe she asked you when she could have asked us since there were two of them." Harry returned and I told him to move me over but make sure I get my own check since I didn't know them. Judy introduced me to Rhoda who was beautiful. She wore a suit and looked very businesslike. We all talked but Judy spoke the most. I think she really liked me but I was more interested in Rhoda. Rhoda didn't talk much but she said she was divorced after 25 years of marriage. She worked for Burrough's Wellcome in the diagnostics division in North Carolina at Research Triangle Park, but worked out of her house in Head of the Harbor, St. James, NY. I ordered a bottle of wine for the table on me for Rhoda's birthday. We had dinner and it was very nice. I got my separate check as requested from Harry. I only ordered a salad and an appetizer with the wine and my bill was $27.00. I paid cash and tipped Harry, and Judy paid their bill. The dancing started and they were going to stay. I told them I had to leave because I had to work early. I didn't ask for Rhoda's phone number because Judy and Rhoda were together and I felt funny to ask for just Rhoda's. I did ask if they came often and they said usually on Wednesday's and Friday's sometimes. I kissed them both and left. I only had about $7.00 and felt if I stayed I should buy them a drink. I went home a bit disappointed. I would have liked to have stayed.

May and June 1979 – I See My Son

On May 5th, I went to an International Association of Arson Investigators seminar. I started to live a little better. My bills were $112.00 a month for the Datsun, $30.00 a month for some furniture, and rent was $200.00. I also paid my sister back for my suits. The only nights I went out were Wednesdays and Fridays to the Palisadium. Saturday I would go to Molfetas, a Greek lounge and restaurant unless I had company for dinner at my apartment which was usually the case. I was now seeing no less than eight girls. I would have them over at least once every other night and accepted invitations to their places, too. I was having a ball. Work was good but I sensed something strange. It seemed I was training them and had a feeling they were using me. I was seeing Petee more often and I finally had him one day and we went to Journal Square to a drug store called Liss. It also had small lunch place and we sat and talked for almost four hours. We talked about everything and I tired to set him straight about life. I also told him his mother brought him up well and he should always respect her. I knew Irene was never a great communicator so I think that was the problem. The other problem was Petee was at that age of 15 and a typical teenager. His mother was very domineering and he was rebelling. It was a good talk and I felt good about everything. I was going to see Linda for the weekend and I wanted Petee to go with me. Irene said it would be all right. When I picked Petee up I told him we were going to fly to Syracuse and we did on a small commuter aircraft. We had a great weekend. Irene never learned of the flight.

I was working with Jimmy Alvine quite a bit and finally I started going on fires alone. I liked it much better and I was able to meet some of the insurance adjusters. They liked me and Bill Alvine got me to join the "Blue Goose" an organization of insurance claim managers, adjusters, experts, and engineers. They met once a month for dinner and a meeting, and I enjoyed the people. May 29th I received a letter from the Florida State Attorneys office thanking me for my work in Florida. I got along with Bill Litche, Alvin's electrical engineer, and we became quite close. I was also close with Ted and learned everything I needed to know abut boilers and furnaces. For the next few months I did many cases both engineering, structural, and fires. I also bought books on all these subjects for research and codes. Wednesday nights and Friday nights I was at the Palisadium. Saturday nights I always made dinner for some girl at the house. I didn't' have money to take them out so I would invite them over. I was having a ball. Mom called and said she wanted to move back and I told her to wait until I was settled in more. She still worked at the social club and went to all the events. I did know she should move back before the winter months if possible.

July and August 1979 – The Fire Investigation

I was busy during the summer with fires. I also met Richard Carucci, Captain of the Hackensack Fire Department and Chief Anthony Aiellos. I helped Richie on some fire investigations and did training for the department. Work was good but they weren't that busy. Bill started to send me to NYC to different insurance companies to solicit business some in the World Trade Center. I was able to get some new clients but it was still slow. Bill was talking about moving to Florida in the future and I was getting nervous. Carol Alvine was always complaining about everything.

One day Carol wanted to go with me to a fire and we arrived at the fire scene. It was a burn out and suspicious. I was doing the examination with Carol overlooking me. I had to go to the 2nd floor and the only way was to go up a partially burned staircase. I told Carol not to come up because it was dangerous but she insisted on coming up. After a couple of hours I took some samples to test for accelerants on the Gas Chromatograph. Carol was acting funny and kidding with me. It was almost like she was hitting on me. We drove away and stopped to get a late lunch. She mentioned that if there was more work to do we could have stayed over and was smiling. I had a date that night at the Palisadium and I wasn't going to miss it. We passed a Ward's Department Store and I stopped and bought a new stereo system which was on sale. I drove back to the office and she was telling me that Bill was older than her and not much fun anymore. His ex-wife was always on his back. He had a daughter, Diane, who I liked very much. She did the bookkeeping at the office and she didn't like Carol very much. After the trip Carol's attitude changed and she started to get on my nerves.

September 1979 – The Palisadium – Meeting Rhoda (Eleni)

One Friday night, the first week of September, I was walking into the Palisadium with a couple of girls and I heard someone say, "Peter." I looked and saw Rhoda who I hadn't seen since that night in April when her girlfriend Judy called me over to their table. I told the girls to go on and I sat down with Rhoda. We talked and then Judy came over. I danced with Rhoda and they were leaving to go to the Plaza Diner and invited me to meet them there with others. I went there and when we left the diner I gave Rhoda a kiss and we decided to see each other the following week. We met next week, and after dancing, I invited Rhoda and Judy to my apartment for breakfast. We had a good time and I invited Rhoda for dinner that night. She gave me her phone number and I was very happy. Saturday night I met Rhoda at the Plaza Diner and drove her to my apartment. I made a fish dinner and we had a lovely time. I then took her to Molfetta's for some entertainment and then back to the apartment. We made love and she stayed the night. The next day I took her to her car and she left. I was so moved by her; she was so sweet, beautiful, and a professional. I wanted to see her more so I called her when I could and when she was not out of town she would come over for the weekend. Petee met her and we took a trip to the farm in the Catskills for the day. Petee liked her and she liked him.

One weekend I went to Rhoda's for the first time. She lived on the Anaconda Copper Estate on Gate Road in Head of the Harbor. It took me two hours on the LIE to get to the Smithtown exit, then up to Head of the Harbor on Route 25A. It was like an Alfred Hitchcock movie when I got there. I went through the gate and the entire small road was covered over with trees. I started to think maybe she was crazy and was going to murder me. You talk about seclusion this was it! I found the driveway and drove up to the house which was in the woods. You couldn't see other houses. I thought what a spooky area. Rhoda was happy to see me and I was excited. She introduced me to her daughter Debbie who was also beautiful. Debbie was making chicken and we talked. I liked her right away. She was a fashion designer for Izod in NYC. Her boyfriend Mark was a bartender in Long Island. I don't think Rhoda approved of Mark but I remember my mother didn't approve of anyone I went with either. I stayed overnight on the couch in the den out of respect for Debbie. Rhoda wanted it that way, too. I went home Sunday and purchased some food for the week. The next day I was at work and Rhoda called me at 3pm. I took the call after Carol yelled at me and said "another personal call". That was the only call I had that day, and because it was a girl she said that. That was it; I decided I would leave Alvine soon. After thinking about it I decided to open my own business in the future. I told Rhoda and she said maybe you should. I was in love with her and if ever I got married again I would marry Rhoda. Then I thought, "Here you go again, Peter; slowdown." Rhoda and I spoke to each other almost every day and we would see each other as often as possible.

CHAPTER–TWENTY FIVE
Peter Vallas Associates, Inc.

Chapter–Twenty Five – Peter Vallas Associates, Inc.

October and November 1979 – Still Working for Alvine

The first week of October, I found a letter on my desk from Bill stating I jeopardized Carol's safety when we went to the fire in NY and they didn't feel I was qualified. I took all my things and left. Bill Lichte was right Alvine used me and then let me go. I went home and applied for unemployment. I told Rhoda I would like to start my own business, but I needed to get a job first. I made some phone calls to several places and had an interview with American Standard Testing Bureau in NY. They were very interested in me. The fire within was still burning. I stopped at Jimmy Demetrakis's law office and told him my intentions. He filed for my corporation as Peter Vallas Associates, Inc. I received it on November 9th, 1979. He also said I could use one of his offices to set things up. In the meantime Jimmy told me I should rent an apartment at the Stratford House on Overlook Avenue in Hackensack. I met with Mr. Charlie Luppino and his brother, Russ. They said they had a ten room Penthouse facing NYC. I looked at it and it was great. I called Rhoda and wanted her to see it. I went ahead and rented it immediately because Charlie Luppino said Jimmy Demetrakis said he would take care of me. I didn't even have to give a deposit. The rent was $600.00 a month and the building was going co-op in two months.

Mom came to visit for the holidays. I took mom to meet Rhoda and she liked her very much. As a matter of fact, this was the first time she ever liked anyone I dated. I was serious about Rhoda and stopped seeing everyone else. I was invited to Rhoda's for Thanksgiving. Mom was going to Walter and Dolores's and then to Linda's for Christmas. I started to make up advertisements, business cards, and a plan for the future business. I stopped collecting unemployment and filed for my private investigation agency license. I had no money so I spoke to Jimmy Demetrakis and he gave me $5,000.00 to start my business. Rhoda gave me an answering machine so I wouldn't miss any calls. I had a little office at Quail Heights. I couldn't move to the Stratford House yet because it was being repaired and painted, and floors were being restored. All of the floors were hardwood and had to be sanded and varnished. I took mom with me to the Garden State Plaza one day to buy a friendship ring for Rhoda. We were in a jewelry store and I asked to see a ring. Mom was walking over by the diamonds and called me. I went over and she pointed to a beautiful engagement ring. I couldn't believe it; she wanted me to buy it for Rhoda. I decided to do it so I bought it with time payments. When I got back to Quail Heights I hid it in the A/C unit. On the night before Thanksgiving, I left the office at 5pm and I took the George Washington Bridge then the LIE. It took over six hours because of the holiday traffic. I was so glad to get there. I had to get off to call Rhoda to let her know I was running late. We didn't have cell phones then.

The next morning I helped Rhoda chop onions, celery, etc and she couldn't believe I was so good. I told her I was a good cook and worked in my dad's diner. I was going to meet her sister Adele, who everyone called Dellie, her husband David and their two children Allen and Sheryl. Rhoda invited another couple, friends of Dellie and David's. Debbie was supposed to stop in, too. Rhoda seemed happy and so was I. The company came and we all had a good time. Rhoda's turkey was the best and still is. Debbie stopped by for a short time then left. I left to go home the next day to attend to my business. I had one case in November.

December 1979 – The Engagement Surprise

On my birthday, Rhoda gave me a party at the Palisadium and invited all my friends. Jimmy gave us bottles of champagne.

As we moved into December I spoke to Linda and I decided to get engaged on Christmas Eve. Linda was going to make a Christmas egg out of a Legg's container and I would put the ring in it and have Rhoda pick it off the tree. They were all nervous because it was going to be a surprise. Linda said what if she didn't want to get engaged? I said we'll see. I started to get a few cases and I was happy. I didn't spend the $5,000.00 I just used what I had to keep on top of things. Mom had gone to Linda's and Rhoda and I went up by car. Linda as usual cooked up a storm and everyone was excited about my surprise engagement to Rhoda. After some lovely Mezedes; the Greek appetizers, Linda said to Rhoda, "Since you are a guest you have to pick a gift first so go to the Christmas tree and pick the egg hanging there. She did and when she opened it and saw the ring she couldn't believe it and kissed me. .I knew then that it was the beginning of our new life together. Christmas day, dinner was special and everyone had a good time. My mom, niece and nephew Stephanie and Nicky were having a great time. Tom's Uncle Nick, his wife Bea, and his Aunt Andrimiki were there, too.

January 1980 – Spending the Holiday with Rhoda

Rhoda and I drove home the next day and we went back to work. I invited my friend Donald Caruso and his wife JoAnn for New Year's Eve. I had a little money left; about $35.00. I went to Pathmark and bought a small roast, snacks, and picks. I took my carriage next door to the liquor store to buy a bottle of wine. I had to leave the carriage outside and when I came out my bags were gone. I didn't know what to do. I went back home and got my checkbook which had about $50.00 in it. I went back and shopped all over again. New Year's Eve was nice and we had a good time.

The next day we went to Uncle Walter's for dinner. The next day Rhoda went out of town for a week on business. I received my NJ State Teaching Certificate and also a letter from President Carter thanking me for a couple of poems I had sent him. I was still working on my book "My Own Reflections". This was around the time of the big gas shortage which made things a bit difficult. I also moved into the Stratford House and moved everything in my Datsun 210. Rhoda decided to sell her house because I intended to buy the Penthouse when it went co-op. Mom had gone back to Florida to make arrangements to move in May or June. She wanted to go back to Eatontown where dad and she lived before he died. She also wanted to be near Aunt Lil. I had received a contract from American Standards Testing to do their fire investigations. Things were looking up and I started to advertise. Bill Alvine found out and he had a fit as was what was told to me by Bill Lichte and Ted Ryan. Carol said she would destroy me. I stopped by Jimmy Demetrakis's office for a check; part of the $5,000.00 he was lending me. I needed to buy a desk and some files for the new office at the Stratford House. Rhoda came back and stayed over for the weekend. We were going to get married in the fall but she said her company was going to celebrate their 100th Anniversary in June and all employers and their spouses were invited with all expenses paid. The only problem was they wouldn't allow boyfriends, etc. so we decided to get married May 11th on Mother's Day.

The next week of January 6th, I was paid a visit by the NJ State Police. They interviewed me for my license and asked if I had a phone in the company name. I said yes, and he said I must have it disconnected because I didn't have a license yet. This was a killer because now I had to call my clients with my personal number. They also said I couldn't do any investigations until I got my license. I was out of business. I called Captain Carucci at the fire department and he put me in touch with his wife's brother who was a big attorney in Hackensack with some pull. He said he would check the law out and see what he could do. A week went by and I received a letter from the State Police denying me a license because of a bad reference. I went to the attorney, Tom Giblin and he called the State Police. They did not cooperate so he filed papers against them for discovery purposes. I was still doing engineering cases because Bill Lichte and Ted Ryan were working for me without Alvine knowing. I was making some money at least.

Rhoda and I decided to have the wedding on Mother's Day, May 11th because the next week was the 100th anniversary. We would have it at the Penthouse on the terrace which was 100 feet long and 8 feet wide. We hired the singer from the Palisadium, Barbara Lang for the music and would have it catered. I was notified by the Stratford House co-op that I was approved and the closing would come shortly. Jimmy gave me the rest of the $5,000.00 so I had that to use for the closing if I needed it. Rhoda was giving me some money also to keep things going. Rhoda was preparing for a yard sale and she had someone interested in the house.

February 1980 – Family Visits with Rhoda

I had called Joe Bustin in Somerset, Mass. Rhoda and I were going to visit them over the weekend. They never met Rhoda and they insisted we stay over. We had a great time and that night Joe put a folding bed in the downstairs den for us. When Rhoda and I got in the bed it folded up on us. We laughed so much. I locked it in and we were fine. It was a great weekend and we went home to the Stratford House.

March and April 1980 – Rhoda and I Are Getting Married – Invitations are Mailed

Tom Giblin, my attorney called and said Alvine sent a letter to the State Police saying I was not qualified and he had fired me. He said he asked for a hearing before an administrative judge. I kept working the best I could. I saw Petee more often and we looked forward to our day together. Irene still treated him as though he was four years old and I could see trouble brewing. I didn't interfere. He was going to St. Aloysius Academy in Jersey City so I thought he was getting a good education. With the coming of spring, Rhoda hired a girl to take all of her things and conduct a yard sale one weekend. I had the closing on the Penthouse and it was now mine. Debbie was angry because she would have to move to the city and Mark worked at the bar in Smithtown. Debbie came one Saturday because Rhoda asked her to take what she wanted and that was when I met Mark. After speaking to him a few minutes, I knew why Rhoda didn't care for him. Debbie hardly spoke to her mother and they left.

Mom had moved from Florida and stayed at the Penthouse with her furniture in storage. Rhoda and I made the final wedding plans and the invitations had been mailed. Judy was going to be the maid of honor and Ray Mann was my best man. Everything was set. Rhoda told her boss we would be married so I was able to go to Research Triangle Park for the 100th anniversary. Debbie and Mark were not coming to the wedding. I knew Rhoda felt bad, but she couldn't do anything about it. We went on making plans for the wedding. Rhoda had set the closing at the end of April on her house. I had a call from the doorman one day and he said a man from the state was here and wanted to come up. I said yes and he came to the door. I let him in and he said the State Police told him I was attempting to start a business and thought I was collecting unemployment. I told him I cancelled unemployment when I started my business. He asked when was I incorporated and I said November 9, 1979, but I didn't do business until I cancelled my unemployment. He said it didn't matter as long as I had the corporation even if I didn't' make any money I should not have collected unemployment. A week later I was ordered to pay all the money I received back, which totaled $2,725.00. I was devastated because for some reason they didn't want me in business. My attorney finally got on the phone and made a call to the judge handling the case.

In the meantime, I took mom to Eatontown and she put a deposit on an apartment and would move in the second week in May. I made arrangements for the rugs to get shampooed and the apartment cleaned. Rhoda's house was sold and the furniture she wanted was moved to the Penthouse.

May 1980 – My Wedding Day to Rhoda, May 11ᵗʰ

One week to go and we were glad her son Michael was going to be there. Michael was attending Northwestern University in Chicago for his masters. He was always in school and was going to get his doctorate from the University of Chicago. Between family and friends there was going to be about 66 people. Mayor Ziza was going to marry us and we were having a Rabbi and a Greek priest from Teaneck for a special service.

May 11ᵗʰ arrived and we were up early. There were about 15 tables around the entire terrace. The caterers arrived and began to set up. Flowers were delivered and everything was moving along nicely. Mom and Rhoda got dressed and Rhoda looked absolutely beautiful. People started to arrive. I had the bartender serve drinks and the waitress serve hors d'oeurves. Music was set up and the weather was beautiful. Everyone at all tables had a beautiful view of New York City. We got married and the reception was out of this world. That week mom moved into her apartment in Eatontown and Aunt Lil was there to help. The following week Rhoda and I flew to Raleigh Durham, North Carolina. We were picked up by the company and taken to our hotel. Everything was done first class and the food and the tours were just wonderful.

When we returned home I spoke to my attorney and he said he had a hearing with the administrative judge and his decision was to grant my license. He said they shouldn't be keeping you from going into business because a former employer gave a bad reference. Two days later, I received my private detective agency license. I started a full campaign to all the insurance companies and sent out over 2,000 flyers to companies and attorneys.

The following week I got a call from the State Police and some woman saying they received a call from Alvine complaining I was working without a license and if I am, I must cease and desist immediately. I told her I was licensed and gave her my license number. She put me on hold and when she came back on the line she apologized for the error. Now the fire within was roaring wild. I personally made calls to the insurance companies and to claim managers. Business started to come in slowly and some of Alvine's clients came to me, too. I couldn't afford a secretary yet so I was typing my own reports and doing the investigations by myself. I worked days and nights including weekends.

June 1980 – Rhoda and My Job

Rhoda traveled a lot and when she was home we would go to dinner or I would cook because my office was a home office. Alvine was trying hard to give me a bad name, but that was a stupid thing to do. It showed his insecurity and it made him look bad. I joined the Blue Goose and that really made him angry. He didn't go to anymore meetings. The rumor was he was going to Florida next year. I was using Bill Lichte for my engineering and Alvine had no idea. I also made contact with Dr. Omar Battary who had a lab in Bellville, NJ. He and his wife Susan did testing of many things. They had a gas chromatograph to test arson samples and I made a deal to use them as a lab. I was getting it together and I was happy.

July 1980 – The Vasectomy

Rhoda was going to be in upstate NY for two weeks in July so I had a 4th of July party at the Penthouse, which was great. That week I went for a vasectomy and they told me I had to have nine ejaculations before I was clear. Then I had to bring a sample to the doctor for testing. Well, Rhoda was on her trip so I decided to meet her at the Treadway Hotel where she was staying. We went to Saratoga to see the races over the weekend and I returned home Monday.

The next week Rhoda returned and I had to do the last ejaculation. It was so funny because when I went to the doctor the next day I walked in the office and there were eight guys sitting there all with a small paper bags holding their samples. One by one we went in and they tested each of our samples. Mine was good, so I didn't have to worry anymore.

I was getting about five cases a week and I kept up my PR. I still wasn't taking any salary because I was putting the money back into the business so I could grow. Every month I was growing slowly but it was still positive.

August through October 1980 – The Need for a New Car

August, September, and October, I worked all the time. My Datsun 210 had over 150,000 miles and I really needed a bigger car. I couldn't afford a new car just yet. I made more flyers and kept sending them all over to keep my name in view. Each week I would get another case.

November 1980 – The Fire Investigation

During November there was a fire in Las Vegas, which killed 89 people at the MGM Hotel. I was called to go to Las Vegas. Everything was going well and I was very positive even though I put in a lot of hours. I took Petee on a couple of fires and I could see he was interested in the work. He was still young and 16 years old is a tough age. I was doing business, but not enough. I flew to Boston for an appointment with the head claims manager, Mr. Malconian at Liberty Mutual Insurance Company. I was brought to his office and served coffee. Mr. Malcovian came in and we shook hands. He asked what brought me there and I told him I was looking for business and gave him my handouts. He said, "Peter I don't know how you got an appointment with me because all our experts are hired by the local claims managers." We did have a nice conversation then he turned me over to the vice president of claims, Mr. Brown. Mr. Brown showed me around and I gave him a bunch of flyers and business cards. We shook hands and I left. I was a little down since I really didn't get anywhere, so I thought.

December 1980 – Getting Fire Investigation Accounts

A week later I got a call from Hal Reath, fire loss supervisor from Liberty Mutual in Saddle Brook, NJ. We spoke for a while and he assigned me a fire. No mention was even made about my visit to Boston. I think a call was made to Mr. Reath because I started to get more business from different Liberty Mutual offices. I was now using a girl named JoAnn to type reports for me. I was also having trouble with storage of evidence because of space. I found a basement office at 65 Hudson Street next to the building where Mayor Ziza had his insurance business. It was a basement office with a conference room, three offices, closets, and bathroom. The price was right and after cleaning and having new carpets put down, I moved in. JoAnn now had her own desk. I was still working on my Poetry Book and I got a literary agent, John Beddoe, He began the work on publishing the book. He obtained the copyright and printing would be in January or February.

January and February 1981 – Petee and My Office

I had Christmas Eve at the house and a New Year's Eve party for friends and family. January and February we had a lot of cold weather. I started to get plenty of boiler jobs and fires. Without Alvine knowing, Ted Ryan was doing boiler inspections for me and I would go to Bill Lichte's house with all the things I wanted tested. Things were working out slowly. I brought Petee to the office a few times to help when he was off from school.

My book was ready and I planned for a book signing on March 15th at our Penthouse with wine and cheese. Special invitations were sent out to family and friends. I told mom about it and she said her usual, "You're crazy. Why don't you get a job? What kind of silly business do you have going to fires, grow up." That was my mother, always trying to tell me what to do.

There was good news in January when President Reagan announced the return of the hostages from Iran. Rhoda and I went to the World Trade Center to meet them along with Mayor Koch. It was quite an experience. Sometime after that, I received a letter from one of the hostages Katherine Kolb thanking me.

CHAPTER–TWENTY SIX
Book Signing

Chapter–Twenty Six – Book Signing

March and April 1981 – My First Book is Published

The book signing came and we had 40-50 people in and out all afternoon. I was speaking with Richie Schwartz who was on the fire department with me in Florida. He was quite fat and I think they were trying to get rid of him. I asked him if he wanted to work for me someday investigating fires. He was interested so I flew to Fort Lauderdale and I decided to train him. He would work out of his house until we established enough business for him to leave the fire department. I visited my friend Charlie McNally and Chris. Charlie was dying of cancer and he had lost so much weight. He was very happy to see me. When I returned to NJ I prepared to solicit clients in Florida. About that time I heard Alvine moved to Florida to the Orlando area and opened an office. Bill Lichte was working for me as well as Ted Ryan. I would fly to Florida and stay at the Marriott Harbor Beach Hotel for one week per month to work with Richie.

May 1981 – Seeing Mom Once a Week

On May 21st, Chris called me in New Jersey to tell me Charlie passed away. He was in his 50s and I felt very bad. I was going down to mom's once a week and to take her shopping. I would pay for her groceries so she had some money for herself. Rhoda was just wonderful and we got along great together. Everything was perfect in my life and the fire within was burning hot. I was sending flyers all over the state of Florida, NY, and NJ. Richie was on shift so he would work 24 hours on and 48 hours off, then work for me on cases. When I would go to Florida I would see clients and work with Richie. I was actually experimenting to see if Florida would qualify for an office. I was also contemplating on a NY office somewhere.

June 1981 – "My Own Reflections" – A Book of Poetry

June 1st I received a letter from Hugh Carey and his wife, thanking me for the beautiful book "My Own Reflections".

July 1981 – Rhoda

I had a 4th of July party on the terrace with about 25 people and some of Dellie and David's friends. I was close to Dellie, Rhoda's younger sister, and David, who was an engineer for AT&T in Newark. One morning I was buzzed by the doorman who said I had a visitor who slept on the couch in the lobby all night. He said he was my son. He sent him up and Petee told me he ran away from his mother, my x-wife,

Irene. After speaking with him for an hour I knew he wouldn't return. I called Irene and told her he was with me and she said to bring him home or she would call the police. After calming her down I told her not to worry and that I would take care of him. I took him to work with me and Rhoda was very good about him staying with us. Rhoda had made arrangements to take me with her to California to meet her other side of the family.

August 1981 – Petee Begins Working with Me

In August I decided to have Petee stay alone and answer the phone and take any cases that came in. We would only be gone for one week. He agreed and everything went well. Rhoda's family was great and we had a good time. When we arrived home Petee was out but he set the table for us and had food for us to eat. As we approached the middle of August, Petee said he wanted to continue going to St. Aloysius in Jersey City. I told him it was too far away. He would have to take two buses every day and it would take one and a half hours each way. I know he was upset, but I also knew I was right. The next week he told me he wanted to go to Aunt Linda's in Syracuse and attend to school there. Linda called me and she said she didn't mind, so off he went. I am sure he wasn't happy but what could I do?

On August 26th I received a letter from Buckingham Palace from Prince Charles and Princess Diana appreciating my book, "My Own Reflections".

September through November 1981 – My First Meeting with David Redsicker

The next few months I was busy promoting the business and it still wasn't moving fast enough for me. On November 18th through 21st, I went to Norwood, Massachusetts to attend a seminar with the International Association of Arson Investigators.

One morning, while attending the seminar, I had my breakfast tray and couldn't find a seat. One fellow was sitting alone and he said, "Come and sit with me." His name was David Redsicker. He worked for the NY State Fire Academy. I told him about my business and I asked if he could do some cases for me in the upstate NY area. He lived in Saratoga and he said yes. This was the beginning of a wonderful relationship to this day.

One night while I was at the seminar, Joe Bustin met me for drinks and the next day I went home. I kept in touch with Dave over the next few months and hoped we could get more business in NY.

On October 10th I received a letter from His Holiness Pope John Paul II thanking me for my book, "My Own Reflections". Thanksgiving dinner was at our house and Rhoda made the best turkey ever.

December 1981 – Business is Growing Slowly

December was a little busy and I was very happy about that. I still hadn't taken a salary ye,t but it was getting close to my taking one. I was hoping I would start at the New Year. Christmas was in Syracuse at Linda's. Linda always was a great entertainer. I brought mom with Rhoda and I. Deli and David drove up too. Petee was there because he was still with Linda. He also worked part-time at McDonald's. After we returned home, Petee called and said he wanted to come back to New Jersey. I told him he would have to go to school in Hackensack and he said no. Linda said Petee was getting into trouble in school.

January and February 1982 – Petee Finishing High School

Petee then called and said he was in Jersey City and got an apartment with two guys who were going to St. Peter's College and he was going back to St. Aloysius. I was very worried, but what could I do? I spoke to him a couple of weeks later. He got a job at Tom McCann Shoes and at least he had some money. Cold weather was here and business was good. I started to pay off some of the local bills and my attorney, Tom Giblin, the $10,000 it cost me in legal fees to get my license. I decided I couldn't take a salary until I paid my attorney fee back and the $5,000.00 I owed Jimmy Demetrakis and wanted to pay him back. I was pushing 200,000 miles on my Datsun 210 and I knew I would start having problems with it. Rhoda always helped with paying the bills.

March 1982 – The New Car Needed for Fire Investigations

In March I had a fire case in Monroe, NY. On the way up my car started to drag and smoke going up a hill on Route 17 just as I was getting off the ramp. I pulled into a gas station and the owner checked the car. He said the valves needed to be replaced and he could rebuild the engine. He said it would cost about $800.00. I had no choice but to do it. There was a man who was a friend of the owner's and I asked him to take me to the fire. He did and I did the case, then he dropped me off in Monroe. I paid him and I took the bus to Hackensack. I rented a car for the next two weeks until the car was ready. When the owner called, he said he wanted cash only. I returned the rental and took a bus to Monroe. I called the station to get a ride and the owner said, "Take a taxi. Nice guy right?" I took a cab and picked up my car. It ran all right but I knew I needed to get a larger car very soon.

April 1982 – My New Car

The first week of April I traded in the Datsun for $800.00 and bought a new Cadillac Coupe DeVille along with a car payment. I was getting busier and I was dong fine. I entertained a lot. Rhoda's sister Adele and David always came to dinner on Sundays. I still went to mom's and took her for groceries. Aunt Lil would see her often also. Aunt Catherine was finally speaking to her sisters after the problem with Aunt Mary's will. Rhoda and I were seeing Cousin Doris and Willie. We even had a party and invited Aunt Ann, Uncle Mike and others. I always had some kind of entertainment.

May and June 1982 – Petee's High School Graduation

Petee was now going to graduate from St. Aloysius and Rhoda and I, Deli and David went to the graduation. After he received his diploma he said to me, "Dad everything you spoke with me about, was right. I am ready to come to work for you." Tears ran down my face and we hugged. I was upset because he didn't see his mother but I thought in time he would make up with her. Petee had a job with Pant's Place and he stayed there until I could afford to pay him full-time.

July and August 1982 – Petee (18 years old) Teaching My Son

During the summer I took Petee on cases when he was off and we had a good time. Sometimes he would stay in the office on the couch. He was getting involved with girls and was having a good time. I was always in the office at 5:30am doing reports and getting ready to go out on the road. Any cases in New York, Dave Redsicker would do for me. He continued to work part-time until I could put him on full-time.

September 1982 – The American Character Award – Saving Lives

I received a letter from Infocom Broadcast Services, Inc. notifying me that Senator Strom Thurmond, Dr. Norman Vincent Peale, and Rand Aroskog, president and CEO of ITT Corp invited me to receive the American Character Award on Tuesday, September 14, 1982 from 6-8pm at the Senate Caucus Room in the Russell Senate Office Building. This was in honor of, to date, the 38 lives I had saved in my career. What an honor and Rhoda and my sister Linda, my nephew Nicky were also invited with all expenses paid. I was told to prepare a speech for the event. Everyone was excited and I made the plans. I was getting a lot busier and Dave Redsicker was getting more cases to do. My name was getting around more and more. Petee was dong fine and I hoped someday in the future he could work full-time with me.

Well, it was time to go to Washington, D.C. for my award. Rhoda and I were flown to Washington D.C. and taken to the Ritz Carlton. Linda and Nicky arrived later. We had a beautiful suite and shortly after we arrived they brought a large vase of flowers and a cart with coffee, assorted pastries, cheeses, fruit, water, crackers, etc. What a spread! Mr. John Scott came to our room to introduce himself. He was the president of Infocom Broadcast Services, Inc. who was handling the whole affair. He said it was going to be a five-star event. The salute to me would be held in the Senate Caucus Rooms and would be attended by congressmen, senators, as well as representatives of the military and diplomatic corps. I also hoped President Reagan would appear, too. We all dressed up and went to the Senate Caucus Room at 6pm. We were placed at the head of the receiving line with Senator Strom Thurmand, Dr. Norman Vincent Peale, and Rand Araskog. First came the congressmen, then the senators including Bob Dole, his wife and all the others, then the military. It was quite exciting with the introduction and speeches. I gave my speech and received a standing ovation. President Reagan didn't come, but sent a letter of congratulations. We then had a large open buffet and spoke with many of the congressmen and senators. We also became very friendly with Senator Strom Thrumand and his wife Nancy. I was filmed for TV the next morning. The next day we were at the airport watching the TV and saw Grace Kelly was killed in a car accident. This pre-empted my appearances and I was not on National TV. It was a great experience to be honored like that in Washington D.C.

October 1982 – Promoting My Business

Back to work again. I started to send out more flyers. Bill Lichte had given me a list of about 100 clients and I solicited them immediately. I was getting busy and working seven days a week. I was getting more fires and that was what I wanted most. In the fall of 1982 I was making enough money to pay JoAnn, make my car payments, and pay for rent at 65 Hudson Street.

November and December 1982 – My Sister Linda

I loved Christmas and we always went to my sister's in Syracuse. She always put on a great spread. I took mom every year with us and it was a great family time. I loved Nicky and Stephanie, my niece and nephew. Watching them growing up was a thrill.

January and February 1983 – My First Paycheck from My Own Business

On January 4th, I received my license plate BPV10, I also took my first paycheck, as little as it was, but at least it was something. Actually it amounted to $120.00 per week. I could have taken more, but I always paid JoAnn and Dave Redsicker first. The weather was exceptionally cold in January and February, and I was very busy. My engineering work had doubled and I used Bill Lichte a lot as well as Ted Ryan on boilers, and freeze-ups. My company was established in 1979 doing fire, bomb, and explosive investigations and now we began to do engineering.

March 1983 – David Redsicker

I loved David Redsicker. He was not only a great investigator but a great guy. We discussed opening an office in New York for him to work out of so we took an office in Binghamton, NY on 211 Court Street. On March 17th, St. Patrick's Day we had our opening. I was very happy and now I would solicit New York State. In our building there were several attorneys, Stuart James, a forensic homicide private investigator, and another private investigator. At our celebration we had a party with food and drinks. A fellow came up to me and said he was a state of NY investigator and said I didn't have a license in NY State. I told him I didn't know I needed one and he told me what to do. Two weeks later I sat for the written test and received my NY state private detective agency license. I started a large mail out campaign in New York State.

April and May 1983 – David Redsicker Working Part-Time

David was working out of the office now and I was getting more cases. David was still part-time but we were able to handle it. I would go to NY several times a month to help Dave. I would stay over often. Petee came in the office one day and told me that he had bought a Honda. He had moved to Islin, NJ with his friend Eddy also16 years old and he had joined the Islin Fire Department. I wanted him to have fire experience.

June through September 1983 – The Merit Award

I receive an award of merit from the World of Poetry on June 30th, 1983. I was working very hard and I paid off Tom Giblin. Imagine it cost me $10,000.00 to get my P.I. license because of Bill Alvine. The good part was I was taking over most of his clients and Bill Lichte and Ted Ryan were working for me. I kept putting money back into the business so the company would meet the growing demands of my business. My Aunt Ann was not doing well with her breast cancer and we were very concerned. I had met a friend Phyllis "Claire" Robinson. She had lost her husband and had been involved in politics. She drove a Cadillac with the plate SAL 1. We were talking one day at Solari's Restaurant, In Hackensack, NJ, where I would go often. This was the local Italian hang out across from the courthouse and one block from my office. She said they were going to open the new Senior Citizens apartment in a few months and if I wanted she would get mom in. It would only cost her $150.00 a month. I thought this was great so I told her to put mom in for me. When I told mom she had a fit and said, "I will never go to a senior citizen home, are you crazy? You need your head examined. Your father would turn over in his grave." I told her she had no choice because I couldn't afford to pay for her food and expenses anymore. I finally convinced her and hoped that by June she would move in. The family criticized me but, that was too bad. I have been taking care of her since dad died in 1977 and thanks to Rhoda; I had a good life so far.

October 1983 – Solari's

On October 4th Aunt Ann died. We would miss her very much. Solari's became my after work hang out. John Solari owned the restaurant and Marco, his son, and Shelly, his daughter, worked there. I got to meet judges, attorneys, the police chiefs, etc. They all ate there and frequented the bar. Rhoda was traveling quite a bit, but we always liked entertaining on weekends. I started to give yearly seminars for the insurance companies. I was determined to be the best in the business and wanted to be a millionaire someday.

November and December 1983 – My Wife's Strength

My wife was a big part of my success because she never bothered me, let me grow my business, and never interfered with my business. It always gave us time together and we always went out to dinner on Saturday evenings. Sunday and holidays were always time for company. Rhoda and her daughter Debbie hadn't spoken to each other since we had the Penthouse. We felt bad, but hoped someday everything would be all right and they would get together again. Divorce is not easy for anyone and Debbie and her boyfriend Mark kept away from us.

Christmas came and we went to my sister's in Syracuse. It was great as usual and we then returned home the next day. We had a New Year's Eve party with friends, and Deli and David.

January 1984 – My Business is Growing

January started off great. By the 6th I had taken in 29 cases. Petee was working with me most of the time so I could train him. On January 7th Rhoda and I, with Captain Richard Carucci and his wife, had dinner at LaFinestra, an Italian restaurant. We knew the owner and his son Vinnie Masella, who lived in our apartment building. On Monday, January 9th, Rhoda was away in Pennsylvania until Thursday. There was a snow storm on Wednesday and I was concerned for Rhoda. I had been elected as president of the Board of Directors which I held until I moved in 1989.

On Saturday the 21st, I had dinner with Phyllis Robinson and she said anytime was okay for mom to move in because her application was approved and the building would be ready soon.

On Saturday, January 28th we were invited to dinner at Omar and Susan Battaryn's house for dinner. Omar was doing all my laboratory testing at his lab in Bellville, NJ. He had ten times more testing capabilities than Alvine ever had.

CHAPTER–TWENTY SEVEN
Business Trips

Chapter–Twenty Seven – Business Trips

February 1984 – My Son and I Working Together

Rhoda went away to Virginia in February and returned on the 3rd. Petee and I were very busy the next few months. I was only taking about $200.00 per week so I could keep Petee and Dave on the payroll. My total salary for 1983 was $6,150.00. Things were happening fast in the company and Richard in Florida was ready to start full time. I flew down and Richard left the fire department. I stayed at the Marriott Harbor Beach Hotel and had a party for him. I hired a limo and we went to the fire department so he could return his gear. I had two girls who took their tops off and walked him in with a champagne toast. We also rented a new office off Nob Hill Road, which would be finished in two months. I flew home and we were now looking for a new office which we needed badly. I purchased a new Chevy Blazer because the Caddy was getting too many miles. I decided to trade it in and bought a 1984 Mercedes. I always said that I wanted to have and do everything in life. I was already a professional artist, an author, and my business was growing. Petee and I went to Jimmy Demetrakis's office and I gave him the $5,000.00 I owed him. He couldn't believe it and said no one ever paid him back. He wanted me to keep the money, but I refused. He helped me with the money to get started and I appreciated it.

March and April 1984 – Preparing My Yearly Trip to Greece

I had planned a trip to Greece on April 19th to visit my family for the first time. Rhoda and I were very excited. We were booked at the Astir Palace in Athens. I also booked a cruise to Mykonos, Rhodes, Patmos, and Turkey. We bought presents for the women. Mom said to buy them cold creams because they didn't have those products there, so we did. We flew on TWA nonstop to Athens. When we arrived the baggage area was crazy. I finally collected all our bags and we went through customs. We were so excited. We had never met them before and we only had pictures. When we came out they recognized us at the same time we saw them. Everyone was crying. Velessairo spoke English so he was the interpreter. I spoke little Greek then but each day I got better. They welcomed Rhoda and we all went to the hotel. I ordered cheeses and drinks and when I went to get the bag with the gifts it wasn't there. I was so upset so I asked Velessairo to take me back to the airport which he did. I left Rhoda with my cousins Felitsa, Katie, and Marika with at least one who spoke English. At the airport I went in where the baggage area was and right in the middle was the bag on the floor. We went back and I gave out the presents.

The next day Rhoda and I found out that Athens had many stores and they all carried the creams. I could have killed my mother. Velessairo said he would come to the hotel before dark so we could watch the Good Friday Procession at Syntagma Square, just outside our hotel. Good Friday and Easter "Pasca" is the biggest holiday in Greece. Greece is a church/state country so it is a major celebration and very religious. Good Friday arrived and about 7pm. My cousin Felitsa's husband, Alex brought candles for all of us. The procession began at the church in the Plaka and it was led by the army, navy, air force, fire and police departments all marching to a slow drum beat. Then, came the priests and the church congregation behind them who passed the lighted candles to the crowds for them to light their candles. After the procession ended, I took everyone to the Hotel and treated them to a wonderful dinner to celebrate.

The next day Velessairo dropped off his daughter Angeliki, who was about 18 years old and her brother Sotiris 16. They took us to see the Acroplis and the Plaka. Just the history in Athens was very moving. This was where my father grew up before he came to the US. I was very moved by it all and so was Rhoda. Athens was very polluted from all the cars with their diesel engines, etc. but the government was working towards making it better. A very interesting thing happened while we were talking with Angeliki. She said she didn't like America or Jews. I asked why and she said a lot of people feel that way about capitalism. Greece had about 10,000 communists mostly kids, college age, and a different group who didn't like Americans or Jews. All my cousins did not feel like that including Sotiris. That night we were picked up and went to Felitsa and Alex's house for dinner and we danced until midnight.

The next morning they were to pick us up and we were going to catch the ferry to the Island of Salamina for Greek Easter. Velissairo picked us up and we went to the Port of Piraeus. We all met there and drove onto the ferry. This was exciting and as we approached the island it was beautiful. The fire within, made me look around for the fire safety conditions. There were none.

Everyone in Greece smoked and the boat was a disaster waiting to happen. I made notes about the 80 or so cars stacked next to each other on the half hour trip. The driver had to get out before the car was driven on the ferry because they were inches apart. If the driver stayed in the car there would only be enough room to climb out the window. All I could think of was what if there was a car fire.

We arrived at my cousin Marika's house which was on a mountain overlooking the Mediterranean Sea. It was a simple stone house with two bedrooms, a small kitchen, a toilet, and a large terrace. My cousin's son, Takis and his father Panayiotis were turning the lambs over the coals. Everything smelled wonderful and out came the ouzo. This was the real thing poured out of a large basket covered jug. Even the wines were in jugs, all straight from the barrels. This was heaven. We ate, drank, and we danced all day outside on the terrace. Most of the Greeks had summer houses on the islands and spent from April to September there. The winters were spent in their homes or apartments in the mainland. I took a walk up the mountain on the dirt road and the smell of the flowers was just wonderful. Looking out at the beautiful blue waters of the Mediterranean Sea and the white clouds drifting high above made me think someday I would live here.

Unlike in the US, the Greek people lived close to their families and ate together. The shop keepers, bakers, restaurants, etc. treated everyone as family. My cousin, Gus owned a fish market. We left to catch the ferry back because after 7pm there was no service. When we got to the Astir Palace we were exhausted.

The next five days Rhoda and I went to the Plaka to shop and did some sightseeing. We found the church where my father was baptized, "St. Catherine's". It was a 700 year old church in Plaka. I was thinking I would like to be married there someday. Each day we ate at different cousin's houses. After dinner we danced and danced.

On Wednesday the day before we were to leave on the cruise, I had Velissairo take me inside the Athens shopping area to buy a Bouzouki for my brother-in-law, Tom. I bought it and Velissairo would hold it for me until I returned. The next morning Velissairo drove us to the ship at the Port of Piraeus. Our first stop was the Island of Mykonos. I couldn't believe the color of the water; it was light green and you could see 50 feet to the bottom. The island was beautiful. We boarded the tender to the island and who greeted us was Peter the Pelican. A live pelican and yes, his name was Peter. All the houses on the hills were painted white. They were made of stone. The churches were the same; some with blue tops. We climbed up the steps around the houses and all the houses had potted plants and flowers outside. All the people said hello and were friendly. We stopped to have lunch at a small Taverner and of course I had ouzo and Rhoda had Retsina wine. We had four hours to inspect the island and we bought a few gifts. The fire within, made me ask about a fire department. They didn't have one. I was told the houses very seldom had a fire and if they did the neighbors would use garden hoses since they were all in stone, concrete, and stucco. They did have an old fire truck at the bottom of the hills which could go around the island. On another side of the island, the jet setters would go to the nude beaches. Everyone would be topless as was in most of Europe.

We boarded the ship and left for Rhodes. We had dinner and danced on the ship, the "Stella Oceanis" and we arrived in Rhodes in the morning. It was an old cruise ship but kept in pretty good condition. Of course, I had inspected all the ways out from our cabin to the life station, etc. It would never have passed inspection in the US. Rhodes was very nice and we walked along the pebble stone streets among the shops. We then took a bus to Lindos which was at the top of the island. It was beautiful but the winding roads with no guard rails made me nervous. We boarded the ship and had dinner. We then went to Kusadasi, Turkey the next day and saw the ancient city of Ephesus. What a sight to see because it was the beginning of civilization. We left about noon and stopped on the island of Patmos where St. John wrote the book of revelations. Rhoda and I rode to the top on donkeys. Again all the houses were white and the island was beautiful. We went into the cave where St. John wrote his book. What history and beauty in these islands. That night we had the Captain's Dinner and after we danced then retired to our cabin. The next morning we arrived in Athens and Velissairo picked us up. We went to his house for lunch then he took us to the airport. We had booked our return in business class but they didn't have seats for us because in Greek a V is a B and they had me under Ballas, so we had to take two coach seats in the rear of the plane. Never again would I take anything other than first class.

May through August 1984 – My Return from Greece and Back to Work

We arrived home and back to work. Dave Redsicker had covered the NJ office while I was away so he went home and May began as a busy month. In May, I received an award from the Hackensack Fire Department from Chief Aielllos for conducting the arson course for his men. Business was doing great and I hired Rose Monte as my administrative assistant. I knew Rose and she was a good worker. Even though I was taking a little more salary, I kept putting money back into the business. Petee was starting to go out on his own and he was doing great. We also had to hire a typist because JoAnn had left. Petee had left Islin and moved to Quail Heights Apartments on his own. Now he was near the office and he wouldn't have to travel. We also moved mom to the senior citizens apartment and got her settled. I was now traveling to Florida for one week per month. Richie and I worked together when I was there because I had to train him in all areas. I was working very hard and so was Rhoda. We were constantly traveling all over.

September 1984 – Investigations and Trials

On Labor Day, I had company and Judy Baronfeld, Rhoda's maid of honor, came to our house. There was a bad storm that afternoon and it rained very hard. I had four trials in the next two weeks so I had to study for each case.

On September 15th our lab owner Susan invited us for a trip on their boat in Northport, Long Island. It was great until they started to turn (called tacking) and the boat was going on its side. It scared the hell out of us until they stopped tacking and we enjoyed the rest of the day. That is when I decided I would never own a sailboat.

The first week of September my assistant, Rose Monte received a package of reports and photos from William Kunstler's office for me to review. He was defending an arson suspect and I told Rose to call his office and tell him I don't defend arsonists. When she did they said I would take the case because after I reviewed it I would agree with them. After reviewing the case with Dave Redsicker and Peter, Jr., I sent a letter on September 27th notifying them I would take the case.

September 24, 25, and 26th I attended a three day seminar with the International Association of Bomb Technicians and Investigators on advanced explosive technology.

Dellie's husband David was now doing engineering for me because he took an early buy out from AT&T. He still wanted to work so I gave him a job. He was always a little jerky, but because of Rhoda's sister Dellie, we worked with him.

October and November 1984 – NY Office Is Growing

We needed help in New York so David interviewed Bob Diamond who had left the ATF. On October 22nd, he came down for an interview. Rhoda's boss, Jim Roberts came down to my office to set up Rhoda's computer in my office.

October 10th, I went to Syracuse to a two day seminar on Advanced Explosives and Terrorist Activities. On October 11th, I had Rose Monte send a letter to Kunstler's office to secure a retainer, and arrange a meeting with the suspect, James Picozzi in Detroit and to conduct my investigation.

Friday October 26th President Reagan was in town. Now I sent David to Florida for some R&R and I went to the Binghamton office. Bob Diamond started to work for me and we gave him a new Chevy. Petee got rid of his Honda and now had a new Chevy Celebrity company car. We were investigating at least ten fires a week in NJ and about five a week in NY. The fire within was burning with great force. My dreams were beginning to come true. My assistant Rose Monte was doing a great job scheduling me between Florida and NY and everywhere else I would fly to.

December 1984 – Happy Holidays

December 5th I was 44 years old. On December 12th I had a Christmas Party at the Stratford House and on the 13th I attended the Blue Goose Christmas Party. On December 19th, it was my NJ Christmas Party and on the 23rd, the NY office Christmas Party.

Rhoda and I went to Linda's again and I had called Greece on December 25th. I wanted to visit them this coming year since I hadn't met all my cousins. On December 28th I went to an IAAI seminar in Binghamton, NY.

January 1985 – The Trials

On New Year's Eve, I had my usual party. Friday January 4th we had a snow storm. I was leaving for Orlando the next day because I was marketing the area. I returned on January 9th and had two trials and one deposition during the next week. I had a fire case in Barnstable County in Cape Cod in which an attorney and his wife died. I left Thursday, January 17th with my Mercedes at 4am for Cape Cod. Dave came down to work in NJ. On the way to Cape Cod my left hand became almost paralyzed. I was terrified and I started to look for a hospital. I spotted a doctor's office and stopped. I knocked on the door and the doctor came down from his apartment above and let me in. After examining me he said it looked like rheumatoid arthritis. I told him about the cold the night before and he said that might be the cause. He gave me some pills and I left. I worked the fire case with the police and went to my hotel. I still couldn't move my fingers. I was cold and hungry so I called Rhoda and she said I should go to the hospital. She was flying in the next day to Providence to meet me and we were going to meet my friend Joe Bustin and Marcia. Friday the 18th, the next day, I met Rhoda and we went to Hojo in Somerset, Massachusetts where we met Joe and Marcia. We all went together to Providence Hospital and I was x-rayed and examined. I was told again that it was rheumatoid arthritis. The next few days my hand returned to almost normal. On January 25th we went to Natalie and Jack's, who were Dellie and David's friends. On Saturday the 26th we went to Rhoda's friends Trudy and Al's for dinner.

February 1985

On February 1st I received a retainer on the Picozzi case and was to work with an attorney, Alan Silver on Prince Street in New York City.

February 5th, Rhoda was away until Friday, February 8th on business. Saturday February 9th, I attended a seminar on "Fire Death" at Rutgers University. On Tuesday the 12th I flew to Detroit to investigate the fire in Ann Arbor at the University of Michigan. Jim Picozzi picked me up and drove me to my hotel in Ann Arbor. I spent the day looking at evidence speaking with the fire marshal then I went to the university. It was beautiful. I left for the airport and it was snowing hard. I arrived at the airport and all flights were cancelled. I needed to get a hotel so I went outside and there must have been 200 people waiting for a taxi. I decided to walk around the terminal when I saw a Detroit Fire Captain walking towards the door. I stopped him and told him my problem and he took me in his fire car to the Holiday Inn. I thanked him and went in. The line was quite long, but I waited. The girl said there were only two rooms left and I got one. I went to the bar which was packed and had a hamburger and beer then went to bed. At 3am, I took a taxi to the airport and got on the plane to EWR. I called the attorney, Alan Silver and told him everything I found out and what should be done. He agreed and I told him I would fly back on Saturday, February 16th with my son. We arrived in Detroit and on Sunday the 17th we had a meeting all afternoon. On Monday we went to Hutchon's Hall. We spent three more days preparing for a March trial. Attorney Silver had hired a guy called "Tink", Josiah Thompson who was an investigator, and also wrote the book "Six Seconds in Dallas", who was at my disposal to dig up any information I requested. We returned home on Friday in fog and rain.

CHAPTER–TWENTY EIGHT
The Picozzi Case

Chapter–Twenty Eight – The Picozzi Case

"The Picozzi Case"

A little background on this case will enlighten you on the investigation which turned out to be a fantastic case. I never work defense cases. Being what some say, the most decorated firefighter in the US, and have put many arsonists in jail, and dedicating my life to the fire service, this case after I reviewed all the reports convinced me that Picozzi was innocent. The police and fire investigation was unprofessional and just plain bad. As a matter of fact because the university ran Ann Arbor, I feel they were biased. What happened was Picozzi, who was studying to be an attorney, was always subject to harassment by other students in his classes. He was short, had a mustache and was missing two fingers from his right hand due to a childhood accident. He had been picked on by Ned Miltonberg who in his later testimony admitted he felt animosity toward Picozzi. He called him pathetic and he stirred up trouble for Picozzi among both fellow students and faculty.

On March 8, 1983, early morning there was a fire in Picozzi's room. He was forced to go to his window sill and then dropped three stories to the ground breaking his back. He was also burned on the left side of his body. The fire department said Picozzi must have splashed gas in front of the inside of the door to his room then lit it on fire, which trapped him. Picozzi said he was in bed and heard a "whooshing" sound and saw flames by the door. He jumped up, pulled on his jeans and his boots and tried to go out the door and was burned in the process forcing him to the window then falling to the ground. When he was taken to the hospital and interviewed they took his jeans and boots to be tested for evidence of gasoline. The tests were negative. There was also no container found in his room with evidence of gas in it. They insisted he set the fire. Believe it or not, they did not charge him with setting the fire. The problem was after Picozzi's recovery the law school dean, Terrance Sandalow refused to give Picozzi a letter of good standing, which would enable him to transfer to Yale Law School, because they felt he set the fire. I thought what a way to destroy someone's life and dreams of becoming an attorney. Picozzi filed a lawsuit against the University of Michigan Law School for violating his civil rights and asked for several million dollars in damages. The US District Court judge ordered the university to give Picozzi an administrative hearing with an independent judge who was Robert Guenzel. The university attorney was Peter Davis and Picozzi's attorney was Mark Gombiner and Alan Silver. The principal attorney was from William Kunstler's offices.

Petee and I returned to the office on Friday February, 22nd in fog and rain. We had several fires and engineering cases to do the next month. We also conducted several tests in our lab with cups and gasoline for the coming trial. Rhoda and I were home together for a change and as always went to dinner. We were very happy and things were getting better and better.

March 1985 – My New Mercedes

On March 12th I received an additional retainer of $2,000.00 from Mark Gombiner which I requested prior to the trial. I was enjoying my new Mercedes very much and because it was a diesel I saved plenty on gas. On March 17th, Petee and I flew back to Detroit for the trial in Ann Arbor on St. Patrick's Day. We met with attorney Silver, Tink, and a paralegal wearing a white T shirt with no bra and had breasts like pointed paper cups. It was a bit distracting but we carried on. There was also a smell of pot, but I must say, these people knew what they were doing. The university listed 34 witnesses all of who were connected to the university including the students who hated Picozzi. The trial lasted four days, two of which I was on the stand. They had an expert, Marvin Monroe, a senior captain in the arson section of the Detroit Fire Department. He absolutely did not know much about fire investigations and even had a theory about a 4,000 degree fireball which was ridiculous. At the end of my first testimony the University of Michigan, attorney Peter Davis was so frustrated he said, "Wait until I get you tomorrow."

Tomorrow came and I simply destroyed him, so did Thomas Nolan, senior fire specialist who was another expert on Picozzi's side. My testimony proved Picozzi could not have set the fire because of the facts in the case. I showed that there was evidence of a small amount of gas on the sill of the outside doorway. Why didn't the fire Marshal take the elbow from the sink to test because he said Picozzi may have washed out the container that had the gas in it? No container was ever found so they said he may have used a coffee mug or one of about a hundred empty beer bottles Picozzi collected. Why would a person pour gas on the inside of the door, when it was the only way out? Picozzi didn't' own a car and yet a sergeant from the Ann Arbor Police said he located a gas station attendant and asked him if he sold a small amount of gas to a man missing two fingers. Obviously he prodded the attendant in a biased way and it was discredited by the department. One witness Ned Miltonberg, a former student who Picozzi thought set the fire admitted he didn't like Picozzi and everyone rather extensively picked on him. He called Picozzi "pathetic" and he did stir up trouble for Picozzi among both fellow students and faculty. Miltonberg said when he first heard of the fire he went to an associate dean for advice because he thought the authorities would think him as a suspect. Yet Miltonberg could not remember where he was the morning of the fire. My testimony disproved all the prosecutor's theories. There was one other event which I thought was great. Davis contended that Picozzi could not have put his boots on and pants in less than 45 seconds. Picozzi jumped out of the witness box and pulled on an imaginary pair of pants. He pulled on his boots, laced them up, and dashed to the middle of the courtroom in twenty two seconds. Pretty good Mr. Picozzi said Mr. Davis. It was also noted by the local paper that technically, this is an internal University of Michigan hearing to determine whether there is "clear and convincing" evidence that Picozzi set the fire. "Clear and convincing" is midway between the "preponderance of evidence" received for civil suit verdicts and the "beyond a reasonable doubt" standard for criminal convictions. I was very happy with Judge Guengel because he was very fair. Now with the trial over we had to wait about a month for a final outcome. The decision packs an incredible significance for both Picozzi and the University of Michigan. Petee and I returned to NJ. Petee had a court case on Monday the 25th and I had two trials on Wednesday the 27th.

April 1985 - My Yearly Trip to Europe

We were very busy and I had planned a trip to Greece to see my cousins and then to Israel, Egypt, and London. I also decided to send mom over and she would stay at Felitsa's house. Mom went over on April 1st and I had a trial on the 9th. Rhoda and I left for Athens on Thursday the 11th. The family picked us up and we went to the Astire Palace. That night was Good Friday and everyone came to our hotel for the procession. I took everyone to dinner later. The next day we went to Felitsa's for dinner. Mom was having a great time. Sunday we went to the Island of Salamina for Greek Easter and ate, drank, and danced. We returned to Athens very tired as usual, but it was great. Monday Felitsa and Alex drove us to Sounion about one and a half hours north of Athens. What a beautiful ride along the sea. We had a wonderful fish dinner overlooking the sea. On Wednesday I took the entire family to a night club near the airport for dinner and dancing. Food, drinks, desserts, and the bill came to $660.00. The next morning, Rhoda and I flew to Ben Gurion Airport in Israel. We went to the Tel Aviv Hilton, but didn't like it, so the next day we rented a car and drove to the Jerusalem Hilton. On the way there was a bus about one half mile behind us and it blew up. We drove fast and noticed all the bombed tanks and trucks on the side of the road from the Six Day War. Just before we got to Jerusalem we saw all the army jeeps and trucks heading the other way. That night we took a taxi to have dinner at Windows over Jerusalem, which was in the Arab section on top of the YMCA. The food was Moroccan and wonderful. We took a taxi back to the hotel and the driver tried to triple the price from what we paid to get there. I refused to give him the extra money. We got out of the car and an Israeli soldier stationed at the hotel came over because he saw me arguing with the driver. I told him what happened and he told the driver to take what I originally paid. The soldier then chased him away.

On Saturday the 20th, we drove through Israel to the Dead Sea and on to Masada.

This is where the Jews held off the Romans for three years. What a sight to see. That night we ate at the Chez Simon, a French restaurant which was also wonderful. Sunday the 21st we drove to Bethlehem and Hebron. We went into the manger to see where Christ was born, which was amazing to see this part of history, including the churches, many Greek Orthodox churches, and the people. That night we took Rhoda's cousins, who lived there, to dinner. In the morning I drove the car to the airport and dropped it off. We flew El Al to Cairo. When we arrived we had to pay for special tax stamps and also purchase $200.00 in Egyptian money. I told Rhoda I wanted to hire a driver for tomorrow to take us for the day. I found a guy who spoke English. His name was Mohammad. He was to pick us up at the Nile Hilton at 8am. The taxi drive to the Nile Hilton was nuts. Not only do they speed but they always honk their horn. The driver said if they hit a pedestrian they just keep going. I couldn't wait until we stopped. When we checked in, there was an Egyptian wedding going on. It was quite spectacular. When we got to the room it had a "Do Not Disturb" sign on it. I called down and they went in and no one was there so they began to clean the suite. It was a beautiful suite. We always liked plenty of room. We ordered a bottle of wine while we were waiting and I noticed a pile of dirty towels on the bathroom floor. Just then one of the men picked up a small towel and began wiping out the glasses. I went in and called the desk and an English speaking person came and he made them take all the glasses out and replace them. The next morning I called room service to order breakfast and they said "no fire, no fire". I said send something with coffee. I understood they must have lost their gas or electric in the kitchen. They brought some rolls and coffee and we went down to meet Mohammad at 8am. He did not show up. By 8:30am I asked the desk if they had anyone who could take us on a tour. He pointed to a large older man with a cane so I approached him. I told him I would give him $100.00 bill and he was extremely happy. He came with a black Caddy that had A/C so we were happy. We left and he took us where no tour bus would. We drove to an area where the people were washing clothes and dishes in the river. Our driver explained there was so much poverty in Egypt. We stopped at several stores then on to the Sphinx. What a sight to see, although Cairo was nothing but a dust bowl. Rhoda and I got on a camel and they took us out into the Sahara. The camel's head was covered with flies and Rhoda was having a fit. Rhoda is an absolute clean nut and the dust, flies, etc. upset her. When we were out in the desert the guy who was leading the camel stopped and he put his hand out because he wanted money. I still didn't understand the money part but I gave him a bill. He kept his hand out until I gave him a few more. I was worried he might not bring us back. We came back and the camels sat down and we got off. Our driver then took us to the pyramids and we went down underneath to the tombs. It was a little scary and the lights were light bulbs on a string. We saw the tombs and got out quickly. It was very hot and dusty but we wanted to see more. He took us to the Parade de

Grounds where Omar Sadat was killed then to his wife's home. It was a long day so back to the hotel we went. I made a reservation for dinner at 5pm. We were at the restaurant and the door was chained closed. We sat at the lounge which was also closed. I had a 5pm reservation. He said it was 4pm and it didn't open for another hour. Well, I almost died because I didn't know there was an hour's difference from Israel. It is no wonder why Mohammad was not there. I felt bad especially when I looked at Rhoda's face. The one thing about this wonderful wife of mine was she never got angry about anything. We ate dinner and went to bed. I was up all night thinking about the taxi ride back to the airport tomorrow morning. We were going to fly to London.

The next morning we got to the airport in one piece and got on our British Airways flight. Just before take off, the flight attendant walked down the aisle spraying. Rhoda didn't appreciate this but they had to do it so not to transport any bugs or flies to London. When we got on the runway, a large dust storm came and the pilot said we cannot move until it stopped. Looking out the window you couldn't see anything only brown sand hitting the plane. After ten minutes it stopped and we could see again. I was concerned because we went right to the end of the runway and got ready to take off. I thought what if the engines were full of sand? Well we took off and arrived at Heathrow at 12:15 and took a taxi to the Ritz in London. That is when I knew I would not rent a car. The hotel was beautiful and our suite was great. We went down for afternoon tea then walked around the shops. It was quite a place and very proper. The next day after sightseeing around London, Westminster Abby, the Palace and other historic places, we made plans to go to the theater to see Cats. We ate dinner at "Poons" a Chinese restaurant which was wonderful.

The next day April 26th, Rhoda and I did some shopping and went for "High Tea" at the hotel. That night we ate at the Ritz's fine dining. It was great with the best service. Everything was very delicate. I liked being dressed up with bow ties and Rhoda looked like a movie star. Saturday night we ate dinner at Interlove De Taibaillau, another wonderful place. The next day we left London to go home. Petee was going to Greece on Tuesday for his vacation. The next three weeks I was very busy and business was always getting better. Petee returned on May 17th on Tower Air. Back to work full steam. I thought it was great. Petee was only 21 and getting very worldly. I believed that I would do everything I could for my son so I could turn the business over to him one day, and retire.

June and July 1985 – The Gold Poetry Award

During June, I received my Golden Poetry Award which I was proud of. We were getting more and more cases as I kept up the PR and gave seminars to the insurance companies.

On July 4th I had a nice party with about 20 people. Our Penthouse overlooked New York City so we had a great view of the fireworks. We had a lot of lightning in July and we were kept quite busy. Rhoda went away to Pennsylvania July 22nd to the 26th. I had decided to lease a 1985 Cadillac Limo with TV, phones, bar, and all the trimmings. I kept it under my building and hired a driver, who was a little guy, named Melvin. He looked like Sammy Davis, Jr. I knew Melvin because he cleaned, washed, and waxed our company cars and the good thing was he didn't drink.

August 1985 – Rhoda's Driving Accident

Our first trip was Saturday night, August 10th and we went to dinner in NYC at the Regency. What a treat that I didn't have to drive and we could have a drink and watch TV on the way. Monday, June16th, Rhoda was driving in Norwalk, CT on the way to a sales meeting with Sue Rucci, another employee of Burroughs Wellcome Company when there was a big rainstorm. She was going down a hill and when she went to stop suddenly because she spotted a stop sign, she skidded across the road into a bunch of bushes and trees. When the police arrived and got them out, Rhoda had a small scratch on her head, but otherwise both girls were fine. The police gave her a ticket for careless driving and going too fast for the road conditions. When she came home on Friday I got all the information. The next day we had to go to my Cousin Dolores's daughter's wedding in Connecticut so we stopped by and I saw the sight. On Monday I went back and took photos and measurements. I noticed that from the top of the hill there were several driveways that entered the road and in front of each there was brown dirt and gravel that ran out on the road from the rain water. As I drove to the bottom about 10 feet from the road at the bottom was a stop sign, but you couldn't see it until you got on top of it. I was also an accident reconstruction expert and I knew right away Rhoda was not at fault.

September 1985 – My Investigative Report Regarding Rhoda's Accident

When I came home I prepared a report and blew up the photos to 8x10s and mounted them on a display board. Burroughs Wellcome penalized Rhoda because she had the ticket and it was a company car. She pleaded not guilty and a trial was set for September 5th, which was cancelled later to September 30th. I went back to the accident site again before the trial and I couldn't believe there was a city truck cutting all the branches off the trees that were blocking the stop sign. I quickly took photographs of them doing this. Then I went to the Department of Public Works and walked in the garage. I spoke to a man who was the supervisor and told him I felt bad they were cutting the trees. He thought I lived there and he said the police wanted the trees trimmed because it blocked the stop sign. I left and put everything down including his name. I processed the photos and mounted them. I was ecstatic because it had just made my case.

I continued back and forth to Florida to work and train Richie. Petee was doing great and business was on the rise. Every Saturday night my limo took us to NY or whenever we went to dinner. Bill Lichte was doing all our testing and it was great. September 30th Rhoda and I went to court in Newtown. The prosecutor met with us and wanted to know why Rhoda was pleading not guilty. I told him I was representing her as her attorney and expert. He said I couldn't do that because I didn't notify the court she was going to be represented. I told him I wanted to see the judge and a few minutes later he came back and said the judge would see us as soon as he finished all the other cases. Finally after an hour and a half he had me go into a room and I presented them with my case and showed the photos. The judge and prosecutor left and we went into the court room. Rhoda was then called and we stood before the judge. The judge then said to Rhoda, "All charges against you are dismissed for lack of evidence on the part of the police and prosecution. We were very happy and we went to the "Players Club"; George Pappas's Lounge & Restaurant in Hackensack to celebrate. This was one of my hang outs and we knew George and his wife Fran. We went to dinner in NY a lot particularly to "Bravo Gianni" an Italian Restaurant in Manhattan. Since I had the limo we went to places like Maxwell's Plum, Regine's, Mr. Chow's, The Plaza, Sherry, Netherland, and Sign of the Dove..

October 1985 - My Largest Payment for a Case

On October 3rd, I received a check for $15,000.00 on a big case I did. This was my largest check ever. I had several trials that month. In October I received my New York City gun permit. Now I could carry my gun in Pennsylvania, NJ, NY, and NYC. I had a deposition in West Palm Beach, Florida and I spent a week there at the office. On October 30th, I incorporated "Crystal Limo Inc" for Petee and me. This way we could make money when we weren't using the limo. On November 8th my brother-in-law and sister-in-law, Dellie and David flew to London for vacation. Rhoda, Petee, and I were going also on the 11th and 12th of November. I was giving a special training lecture at the request of the London Fire Brigade and the Institution of Fire Engineers on November 13th.

November 1985 – The London Fire Academy

On November 14th I was invited to the London Fire Academy to speak. I was driven around London by a fire investigator in the fire department car. His name was Steve Hanaford and in between all this, we went shopping and went to the theaters and restaurants. Petee was on his own at the Hard Rock and met a fellow his age Craig McIntyre, who he became friends with. We flew back on November 17th. The business was growing in Florida, NY and NJ. I still kept my PR, seminars, and continuous mail outs going.

December 1985 – The Company Christmas Party

December became a very busy month. Dave Redsicker planned a Christmas Party in Owego so Rhoda, Petee and I went and Dave had a horse and carriage pick us up at his house and took us to dinner at an apartment where the chef made a wonderful dinner. He ran his business there very privately. We then went to my sister's house in Syracuse for Christmas. I always had mom with us on the holidays. Tom made a Shadow Silver fox fur coat for Rhoda, which I gave her for Christmas.

January 1986 – Melvin My Limo Driver

January 2nd, mom went to the hospital with diverticulosis for a few days. Melvin, my driver was also taking mom to the Shop Rite. Can you imagine him pulling up to mom's senior citizen apartment with the limo? Aunt Lil came to stay with mom for a week and Melvin kissed Aunt Lil and mom when he let them off. Melvin always greased his hair so when he kissed them he greased their chins.

February 1986 – Meetings about the Business

Richie Schwartz came up to NJ for a week for meetings. On the 27th mom went to Syracuse to go to the doctor Linda had. Rhoda was away February 3 to the 7th so I went to Florida. We both came home on the 8th. On the 10th I had a big fire at a McDonald's in Buffalo, and there was another in Saratoga Springs. That night we had a big snow storm. I returned the next day at 9pm. I then went to Albany for three cases and a trial within the month February, and the weather was freezing.

March 1986 – Hiring a Structural Engineer

I had added a structural engineer, Mr. Moe for the NJ office. He was doing all our structural losses. Rose Monte was taking care of my next trip to Greece. I had Bob Diamond working for us and David told me his answering machine would say, Diamond Investigation's. I called him and he said that was the way he wanted it. I told him it should be Peter Vallas Associates. A week later he still didn't change it so I told David to let him go, which he did. I gave his car to Petee because it was new.

April and May 1986 – Mario Cuomo

April 9th, I received a letter from Governor Mario Cuomo that he enjoyed reading my book, "My Own Reflections". He said, "The book was an inspiration to those of

us who share your appreciation of life and your diligence in rewarding how we feel."
I also received another Gold Poetry Award and a Silver Award.

In April, I was beginning to look for a larger NJ office and laboratory. Things were getting tight and we needed space badly. I flew to Florida on April 25th and returned Sunday the 27th after meetings with Richie. On Wednesday, April 30th we went to Greece. Petee had been there already and he had returned on the 5th of April. Our visit with the family was wonderful. We went to Porto Heli for two days. The only problem was when we returned to the Astir Palace there was no A/C. When I asked they said they would not have A/C until June 1st. The windows in our suite didn't open so I called the Marriott on Syngrou Avenue, and took the Athenian Suite which was gigantic. We had the whole family one night for a party. There were 25 of us in all. I had the Marriott cater everything. We also had a bartender and waiter. It was great. We danced and ate plenty. On the 10th we returned to NJ. May was very busy too.

June 1986 – My Limo Driver

June 11th the limo was hired to pick up a friend Peter Cord, his wife, and children to take them to the airport. Melvin didn't show up so I drove the limo and picked them up in Bergen County, put their bags in the trunk and took them to the airport. Melvin later said he forgot. I was starting to look at offices and found one I liked on 42 1st Street. I signed a ten year lease and we took over July 1, 1986.

July 1986 – The New Office

We spent the next three weeks painting, moving in furniture, carpets, alarm system, and phones. What a job. I had a surprise 75th Birthday party for mom with about 25 family members at the Penthouse all catered. She had a great time. On July 29th the floors were done at our new office and we moved in July 30th.

August 1986 – Petee's Friend from England

On August 7th Petee's friend Craig from New Castle on Tyne, England called and wanted us to meet his father and mother. This was the fellow Petee met in London. We met them in Manhattan and went to dinner. We had a good time. They were wonderful. We had hired two more girls Yumara, and Mary.

September through November 1986 -Florida

Rhoda came with me to Florida to the Marriott Harbor Beach Hotel while I worked with Richie. My cousin Felitsa and Alex were going to Orlando from Greece. Rhoda and I hired a limo in Orlando and picked them up. We all went to a hotel in Disney World and stayed four days. We went home on the 9th of September. The rest of September was very busy with two trials and a deposition. Thursday the 25th Rhoda and I went to the Palisadium for dinner. Rhoda had to go to North Carolina to Research Triangle Park for meetings. I had nine meetings and two depositions in October. Then I went back to Florida.

I had seven trials during November so I was a bit nuts. You have to remember since 1979 when I started my business, I did almost all of the fire investigations so the fire within was burning like hell. We were making money and I was determined to do everything I wanted. Thank God Rhoda was working because she wouldn't see much of me.

December 1986 – Trials

December 1st and 2nd I had a trial each day. People don't realize you have to study for a trial and review reports and photos. Christmas we went to Syracuse and returned Saturday the 27th. Joe and Marcia came in from Somerset, Massachusetts and I took them to Manhattan to "Sign of the Dove".

January 1987 – Happy Holidays

New Year's Eve was another famous party at the Vallas's. January began with snow on the 1st and 2nd. We had a big snow storm on Thursday January 22nd.

February and March 1987 – Petee's Birthday

On February 3rd I took Petee and Rhoda out to Lon's Restaurant for Petee's birthday. It was great to have my two favorite people with me. Lon's was a great place on Route 17, New Jersey and we went there on Valentine's Day, too. I had purchased a gas chromatagraph to test arson samples for accelerants. That was $25,000.00. I took a three year loan and Stu James did all our testing.

One day I stopped at the Mercedes dealer in Paramus to service my Mercedes and while I was waiting I went in the show room and saw a candy apple red 560SL. I had to have it. On the spot I bought it and turned in my other Mercedes. My accountant Mike Mongelli was my good friend and asked, "Why do you want that? It is so expensive." I said, "I told you once before I was going to get everything I wanted out of life." I sent David Redsicker, his wife, and Petee to Florida for a vacation from March 13th to the 16th.

April 1987 - Sent Mom and Rhoda to Greece

April 11th I sent mom to Greece with Rhoda because I had to go to London to see Steve Hanaford who wanted to work for me. On the 16th I flew to Greece and

I had our usual Greek Easter on Salamina Island and it was great as always. On Wednesday the 22nd we flew to Vienna, Austria and stayed at the Marriott. It was beautiful. The next day I gave the driver, who had a black Mercedes, a $100.00 bill to take us through the mountains and the Black Forest for lunch. We also went to Mayerling where the romance among the Hapsurgs, an austro-hungarian Empress Elizabeth to Franz Joset happened. The crown prince and his lover died together over their love for each other.

On Saturday, April 24th we flew to Zurich, Switzerland and stayed at the Baur Au Lac (a very famous hotel). We saw Clorice Leachmann and her daughter there. The hotel was great. There was a parade the next day celebrating the end of winter. There was a big bonfire in the park and horseback races in full Swiss outfits going around the fire. On top of the stack of lumber about three stories high was a snowman about 15 feet high. What a celebration it was.

The next day, I went to the fire department and gave a lecture. In the afternoon we drove to Lucerne and took the cable to the top. It was breathtaking. We actually went through the clouds. At the top all you could see were the clouds below. We ate lunch on top and went back to the hotel. Tuesday the 28th we went to London to meet Howie and Shelly, my friends from Florida. Howie was on the fire department with me in Fort Lauderdale. We stayed at the Marriott in Governors Square. That night we ate at Mr. Chows. Wednesday the 29th we went to the theater and dinner. I brought some jackets and three pairs of Bally shoes which I still love. Rhoda's birthday was on the 30th and we went to the White Elephant on the Thames River. I bought her a beautiful necklace. It was a beautiful combination of rubies, diamonds, and pink sapphires and a few other stones.

May 1987 – Visiting Friends

Saturday the 2nd of May, Rhoda and I ate at St. James Club on our last night, then returned home on Sunday. The next Saturday we went with the limo to Venessa's on Bleeker Street and 7th Avenue, NYC. The rest of the month was busy and on the 29th Howie and Shelly came to NJ.

June and July 1987 – My Mother's Cornea Transplant

On June 1st mom went in the hospital for a cornea transplant. I visited her then went back to Florida June 12th. Petee came the next day because Father Nick's 40th Year Party was Sunday the 14th at 3pm, which I gave for him on a chartered yacht. Monday Rhoda left and I returned on Friday the 19th. The next week we gave our yearly seminar to 200 plus clients at the Fiesta on Route 17. July 27th I flew to Florida and entered into a business with Howie Olshan. The company was called "Totally Different" which sold all kinds of tee shirts with "Totally Different" on it. I also purchased a condo in Inverrrary at the Fairways where I had lived with Doreen in 1978. I was able to get a special price since I lived there previously. I bought a villa, 97-B, two bedrooms, and two baths overlooking the Inverrary Country Club Golf Course. I furnished the apartment beautifully with mirrored walls, tile floors, and new furniture. Now I could stay there and not spend so much money at the Marriott. I was also looking into getting a larger office in Florida.

August 1987 – Rhoda's Results

On August 11th Rhoda had a breast biopsy and we had to wait for the results. Dave Redsicker went to Florida for a long weekend and returned on the 17th. On Friday the 14th I was home and the doctor called and told me Rhoda had breast cancer. I couldn't believe it. Now I had to prepare to tell Rhoda when she came home. I told the doctor if she called the office for results, not to tell her. I didn't' want her driving with that on her mind. When she came home I remember her navy blue suit, she looked at me and asked if the doctor called. I then told her the news and she cried. I told her we would go together to speak to the doctor. A few days later we did and he said Rhoda could have a partial removal of the breast called a lumpectomy or a complete mastectomy with removal of all lymph nodes. I told Rhoda to get the complete mastectomy. I couldn't believe how brave she was in accepting all this. The day of the surgery my mother, Rhoda's sister, Dellie, and I were at the hospital when they took her into the operating room. Already I had a plant in my hand that someone sent. It is funny because I always called her my "Baby Wife" and as I went to the waiting room a nurse said to me, "Mr. Vallas we are putting your wife in pediatrics because we have no room but we will move her in a day or so."

My wife was about 5 foot tall and weighed 100 pounds so she looked like a kid. When she came out of recovery I was told everything went well. I walked with the gurney to pediatrics and she was put in a room with a 10 year old girl. After she was put in bed the girl was talking with Rhoda asking what was wrong. It was funny because the beds were so little. We let Rhoda rest and the next day the nurse told me they could move her to a regular room that afternoon. In the hallway there were kids playing with balls, carriages, dolls, anything you could think of. They came to get Rhoda who was feeling better and put her in a little wheel chair. We couldn't stop laughing. The next day she had 31 plants and flowers. They told me I had to take them out so I called the office and they sent my pickup truck over and moved the plants to the Penthouse. The doctor sent her home even though she had a drain in her. That day when I came home from the office I found her vacuuming the floors.

September and October 1987 – Rhoda Becomes Greek Orthodox

I flew to Florida and Rhoda came down on the 4th. She had called Father Nick and wanted to become Greek Orthodox. She stayed through Labor Day and then we returned home. She began to take lessons over the phone with Father Nick for a few weeks and we planned the Baptism for October 31st.

On September 24th we flew to Bermuda for some rest and relaxation. We stayed at the Marriott and it was beautiful. We had a beautiful dinner and danced. About 6am I ordered breakfast and at 6:15am there were all kinds of crashes and noises. I looked out on the terrace; we were getting hit with a bad storm. Someone knocked on the door and it was our breakfast. The man left the tray and ran. He said we were getting hit with "Hurricane Emily". I looked at Rhoda and said the hurricane was way out at sea what happened? What did happen over night was it turned and headed right toward Bermuda. We got hit hard and we ate breakfast in the bathroom away from the windows. We had no power or A/C. Windows were breaking in some of the rooms. After three hours the storm passed. I looked out and saw boats upside down, people outside by the pool which was filled with furniture, trees, and glass windows. I told Rhoda I was going down to the lobby and when I got down the stairway into the lobby; there were injured people mostly workers. I immediately identified myself as a firefighter and began to work with the injured. Someone brought me three first aid kits which I used for the first half hour. There must have been a hundred motor scooters which were blown into the lobby and in all different areas of the hotel. The roads were blocked so emergency vehicles could not get through. I treated about 15 people mostly for cuts and bruises except for a broken arm which I splinted. The roof at the airport had blown off and hundreds of homes and businesses were damaged.

That night the Marriott set up grills outside and fed everyone. They were wonderful, which was why I always stayed at Marriott Hotels. No matter where I go, I always choose a Marriott. In the morning breakfast was outside too. The roads were now cleared and that night a taxi driver took us to a fine restaurant on the other side of town which had power. It was a wonderful place and we had a good time. We returned on Sunday. Monday I flew to Florida, and mom and Petee flew down on Friday along with Linda. Saturday afternoon the 3rd of October, Rhoda was baptized by Father Nick in a tub of water with a white sheet over her body. After that we all went to the Greek Restaurant Ambrosia and we had a big party with music, a singer, and dancing. On Sunday we all returned home. On Friday the 9th Rhoda's son Michael Seltzer came in from Chicago, where he was going to Northwestern University, for a visit.

October 12th, I flew to Los Angeles to work a week to check out the insurance companies with the possibility of opening an office at some future date. I returned Friday the 16th. I stopped at mom's and told her I was thinking about opening an office in L.A. She said you need your head examined which I thought if I had my head examined every time she told me to, I would be broke. Rhoda and I flew to the condo in Florida on the 30th. Rhoda had to go to church and light a candle. She had to do this three times. I had spoken with Father Nick and told him I wanted to get remarried in Greece and have a real Orthodox wedding.

November 1987 - My Business in London

November 15th, I flew to London and opened an office with Steve Hanaford. We met with several engineering companies. I worked with Steve and met Murdock McIntyre for dinner. We went to Samuel Peeps for a drink and took a cab to the new Bene Hana's near Kings Cross. On the way there, there were many fire trucks "appliances" as they were called in England, which were flying past us. Murdock said something big was going on so we followed them. We got to the fire and it was in the underground at Kings Cross Station. We ran in and heavy smoke was coming from below. The fire within took over and I began to pull people off the stairs as they tried to escape. I met the chief and he thanked me, but one firefighter was killed. Murdock and I stunk of smoke but we wanted to eat anyway.

The next day I went back to the scene and that is when I met Prime Minister, Margaret Thatcher. I was down at the fire scene with a chief officer helping when she came down to inspect since so many people had died. I didn't know it then but a photo of me at the scene was on the front page of the NY Daily News. I left London on Friday the 20th. Steve flew over the next week and worked with Petee. I was in Florida the next week again working with Richie.

December 1987 – Family

Saturday December 12th, I took my cousin Donald and Phyllis to Bravo Gianni in NY. I was enjoying my limo very much. December was a very busy month in all offices. Again we went to my sister's in Syracuse and had a great time, as usual and returned home Monday the 28th.

January 1988 – New Year's in Florida

We went to Florida for New Years. I chartered a small 48 foot yacht for the New Year's Eve party and invited Murdock and Shiona who were in from London, Petee, Richie and his wife, and some friends. It was a wonderful evening and included fireworks. I thought someday I will have a yacht of my own.

January 6th I went to Liberty Mutual in Boston for a meeting with the head of claims. It was a great meeting and Mr. Robert Barber and I took a tour of the offices. I went back to the Marriott on State Street, and went home the next day.

February and March 1988 – The Diamond Ring Investigation

I had been investigating a large diamond ring for Rhoda which belonged to a woman whose husband had died. I had it appraised at $15,000.00 and I bought it from Ann Leesburg for $2,000.00. The next week I was at the Albany Marriott meeting with a new investigator who retired from the Kingston fire department, Jerry Kelder. Then to Vermont to Syracuse to my office in Binghamton then back home. I was on the road a lot those days but it worked out well because Rhoda traveled quite a bit also. In 1986 my salary went up again. Money was coming in and the NY and Florida offices were making money.

I spoke to Felitsa in Greece and asked her and Alex to be our best man and maid of honor when we were to get married in Greece. We set the date of April 16th because of Greek Easter. It is strange because I married my first wife Irene on April 16th and my second wife Rose on April 16th. I gave Felitsa instructions to plan the wedding. I made arrangements for my cousin Lorraine and Dan, Dellie, David, Petee, mom and Father Nick to fly to Greece for the wedding. I made reservations at the Marriott for all of them. I took the presidential suite for the wedding and had the Marriott handle all the arrangements for the food and bar. The general manager, Mr. Bonnie, and I were friends. I spent time on the phone with him and I was confident it would be okay. Felitsa hired the best Greek band and singer in Athens along with a belly dancer who I also knew from past trips to Greece. Felitsa made arrangements at the 700 year old St. Catherine's church in the Plaka. My dad was baptized there. She also ordered a black Mercedes to take Rhoda to the church. My son Petee was to give her away. She also ordered all the flowers for the church and the cake was made special. I would buy the rings when I got there. I also bought a Dodge Raider adding six cars to my fleet. As you can see I kept my salary low so I could increase the business.

On March 24th I went to visit Bill Lichte because he told me he was dying and it wouldn't be long. He had cancer and looked terrible. I was very sad. Bill died a few weeks later. I was busy with the business and trying to get all the wedding arrangements ready. It was going to cost me about $50,000.00 for everything. I had received another award from the World of Poetry.

April 1988 - My Yearly Trip to Greece – Rhoda's Greek Name is Eleni

On April 7th Rhoda and I flew to Athens to the presidential suite at the Marriott. Lorraine and Danny also arrived at the Marriott. Father Nick arrived in Athens at the Marriott on April 12th. On the 13th Dellie and David arrived but Rhoda didn't know they were coming. When they arrived at the Marriott Rhoda walked by the elevator in the lobby and was so surprised to see them. While Rhoda and I were with the family making plans, meeting with the chef at the Marriot, and getting our rings made, everyone else went on tours and to the Plaka. Petee arrived on the 15th with

Murdock, Shiona, and Craig. I went to pick up the gold rings which were engraved. My ring had the name Eleni engraved inside because Rhoda had to take a Christian name and her middle name was Helen. Eleni was Helen in Greek so her name became Eleni. My name was on the inside of her ring, Pantelis. Everything was set for the next day, April 16th. In the afternoon everyone was having a good time and very excited about the wedding. I had ten people from the US. Felitsa said my family was 20 but there were 10 other second cousins some I never met. The total came to about 35 people.

The day arrived and Rhoda looked beautiful. I had to be at the church before her so I was driven over by Velissairo. When I arrived I couldn't believe it. There was a red carpet running from the street down the stairway to the court yard and on into the church. Outside in the court yard was the entire family. Then the black Mercedes pulled up and it was covered with white carnations, what a sight to see!

Rhoda and Petee arrived with my camera man Greg McIntyre who video taped the entire wedding. The ceremony was traditional Greek and it was beautiful. Father Nick and the priest from the church didn't get along because Father Nick was doing the ceremony and some parts he did in English which the priest didn't like so he wouldn't come to the reception. Believe me Father Nick didn't care. After the wedding we went outside to the court yard to receive the guests. There must have been 100 people lining the street around the court yard taking photos and videos. When we got back to the hotel all the Marriott employees greeted us as we entered. I knew mostly all of them because we came every year. In my suite everything was set up beautifully. Girls were ready to serve Greek appetizers and the two bartenders were getting ready for the crowd. The band and singer were also there. This was one great celebration and everyone danced all night. Mom had a good time. My cousins and Father Nick asked her to dance and she would say, "I only had one man in my life and he was the best so she refused to dance." But that was mom. I made her dance with me and she said, "You're crazy." I felt bad because my sister couldn't come but then again I didn't go to her wedding when I had the trouble with my ex-wife Rose.

The next day everyone headed home. Eleni and I took a flight to Rome then on to Venice. We had a $900.00 a day suite, one in which President Reagan and Nancy stayed in at the Cipriani Island. Our luggage was not put on the flight from Rome so we had to wait at the hotel until the next morning. The place was beautiful and the food was spectacular. When the bags arrived we got organized and the next three days we went to the Murano Glass Factory and the City of Venice on a gondola. Harry Cipriani owned the hotel. We were at the bar in Venice, which was named Harry's Bar. Hemmingway was a friend of his too. I happened to be a Hemmingway follower so I always wanted to see the places where he wrote some of his books. We took a boat to Torcello where he wrote one of his books. We ate lunch at a little place and had homemade wine. On Thursday the 21st we flew to London then to

New Castle on the Tyne in England to visit Murdock and Shiona. They met us at the airport and when we got outside Murdock said, "I hope you don't mind but all I have is a pick up truck." There was one out front all dirty. As Eleni and I walked towards it, Murdock started to laugh and said no the car is over here. It was a Rolls Royce from the hotel and we drove in style to the beautiful hotel, Gossorth Park. We stayed a couple of days and even drove to Edinburgh, Scotland for lunch. On the 24th we left for the US. It certainly was a great honeymoon. Back to work and back to Florida.

May 1988 – Business and Depositions

May 11th, I was on to Vermont to a deposition with a return on the 12th. I had an appointment with Steve Hansen in a new place on May 13th on 125 State Street, Hackensack, NJ. A new three story building with a lot of room was just built. I had leased a small office for now.

Rose Monte had been getting an attitude and I told her to do something and she disagreed. I told her to do it anyway and she said, "I don't care, it is your name on the door." I fired her on the spot. I cannot tolerate disrespect. I immediately put an ad in the newspaper for an administrative assistant. I interviewed MaryAnn Kowalski, a school teacher who was perfect for the job.

June through August 1988 – New Hire in the NJ Office

I hired her and she began immediately. She worked with me at 125 State Street and on June 4th we moved in. I had received another Gold Poetry Award this month. Somewhere around this time Michael Mongelli and I purchased an apartment 16B, from our friend Vinnie Masella. Vinnie and his father owned the La Finestra Restaurant and the Lodi Modern Bakery. The apartment was completely renovated so Mike and I could rent it out which we did. Our new building in Florida was being built on 10260 Springtree Lake Drive in Fort Lauderdale. It was very large and Richie was happy. My only concern was he was getting very heavy. He was about 300 pounds and moving very slowly. July 4th Eleni and I flew to Key West for the weekend. July 1st I had received a call from Richie telling me five firefighters were killed in Hackensack at the Ford Dealership. All were friends of mine. That killed my weekend. We returned to New Jersey, Tuesday July 5th so I could attend the funerals. It was very sad.

October and November 1988 – The Fire Investigation

A few weeks later I was asked to do an investigation into the cause of the fire. Business was continually on the rise. We were very busy and I decided to expand our 125 State Street office to a large set of offices in the same building. Mary Ann took charge of that and I worked closely with her on the project. Eleni and I were in Florida for a weekend and we returned Monday. I had such a busy schedule, three trials, a trip to New Orleans and many fire investigations.

On November 2nd I had a case in Kansas City and had to stay two days. Eleni and I continued our trip to all the fine restaurants in New York City. I planned a vacation to Maui, Hawaii with Eleni. On November 11th we flew to Los Angeles and stayed overnight. The next day we left Los Angeles for Maui. The jet lag was rough so we ate in our room and slept. Saturday we looked around the area and had dinner at the "Sounds of the Falls" at the Westin. Sunday we had a suite at the Hyatt which was beautiful. That night we ate at Swan Court and it was great. Monday we went to the beach. I bought fins and a snorkel mask. We had a good day and we ate at the Peacock in Maui, a beautiful restaurant. On Wednesday we took Aloha Airlines to Oahu and traveled around the island to the Dole Pineapple Farms and then to Pearl Harbor, which was a very moving experience. I purchased a flag which was flown over the USS Arizona. We flew back and had dinner at Swan Court. The next day we toured the area and went shopping. We had dinner that night on a boat in the Pacific. This was a wonderful trip and we both loved it.

Friday we took a helicopter trip to Hana. It landed on the black sand beach; it was deserted. There was a jeep parked there with a cooler with lunch and a bottle of wine. I had set this up before we left. Eleni and I drove to Crystal Springs. Somewhere up the mountain we parked at one of the springs and had lunch. The chopper was to pick us up at 4pm so we drove back and parked. At 4pm there was no chopper and we began to get nervous. All of a sudden at 4:15pm we heard a put-put-put and the chopper appeared. He flew us around the island and hovered over a volcano and then returned to our base. Eleni was having a ball and she said this was one of our best vacations ever. Saturday we ate at Swan Court again because it was the best. On Sunday we went back to Los Angeles. We returned to New Jersey on Monday very tired indeed.

December 1988 and January 1989 – Buying Real Estate – Florida and NJ

Everyone should take a trip like that. Eleni was having some trouble bleeding and had to go to the hospital on Saturday December 3rd for minor surgery, a D&C.

Friday the 9th I had a fire at the Hensley Palace in the Bahamas at Nassau. Petee was going to buy our Penthouse because I was going to buy a house in Fort Lauderdale on Royal Plaza Drive on the water with a 60 foot dock and deck in the rear. It was a beautiful house with a pool in the rear and a large covered patio. Monday December 12th I closed on the house. Eleni had seen it a few weeks before and she loved it.

It was back to NJ for our Christmas Party at Lons Restaurant. Business was still growing and all offices were doing well. I hired Richard Wolfson as a new investigator along with another girl. I had to get a new computer, typewriters, and upgraded my phones.

Christmas was in Syracuse as usual with my sister. Monday the 26th I went back to Florida. I was still staying at my condo in Inverrary while we got all new furniture. I told Eleni I had her Christmas present in Florida and when she came down for New Years I would give it to her. What I did was buy a new Grand Piano for $20,000.00 and had it put in the living room of the new house. I also put a large red bow around it. On Wednesday December 28th Eleni came down for our company Christmas Party. I took her to the house and she was surprised. I was a member of the Tower Club in Fort Lauderdale and that is where I had the party. Friday Uncle Walter and Aunt Dolores came down for New Years. I took them to the Tower Club for dinner. I had a small party at the condo for New Year's Eve.

January 2nd we returned from Florida and back to work. January was another busy month. I had to interview some investigators because we were getting busy. I hired two more men.

February 1989 – The Pension Plan

On Friday February 3rd, I had a meeting with all employees to discuss a pension plan. I was already paying for my employee's hospitalization, which was a great benefit. I was also getting ready to go to Paris, Amsterdam, and London. On February 5th I went to Paris and stayed at the Hotel De Crillon. I contacted several clients to get business for Steve at my London office. On Tuesday the 7th I flew to London and met with Steve. We ate at Wheelers Restaurant and I went to bed. Wednesday the 8th Steve and I visited clients then I flew to Amsterdam. I ate at the Poseidon, a Greek restaurant. I visited two clients and made a list of others. I stayed at the Marriott as usual then flew home on December 10th. On the 13th I had a pension meeting and I took the 401K program for everyone.

Eleni had gotten an invitation from her daughter Debbie. She was getting married to Mark Remson. This was the first time Debbie contacted her mother in several years. We were excited hoping she would finally get together with her again. One Sunday February 19th my driver took us in our limo to Long Island to the wedding. When they saw each other they cried and I was glad that was over. I met Oscar Seltzer her ex-husband and we got along fine. I don't think Debbie realized it but very few people liked Mark. He was a bartender and thought he knew everything. He was the boss as they say. Debbie had a great job as a designer for Izod. She flew all over the world and I know Mark didn't like it. I think he was jealous of her.

March 1989 – The Florida Office

Officially on March 11ᵗʰ the Florida office moved to Spring Tree Lake Drive. Eleni and I were selling our furniture in preparation to move to our Florida home. Saturday the 18ᵗʰ my limo took us to Maximes in New York City.

It was back to Florida for the Grand Opening of our office. On the 27ᵗʰ I had a case in Texas. I will never forget I flew to Dallas and then took a small single engine plane to Tyler. We bounced up and down all the way and I threw up in a bag. We landed in what I thought was a field with tumble weeds and a shack for a terminal. I asked some guy where the taxis were and he said over there. He said there was only one. When I got to the, so called taxi, there was an old guy with a cowboy hat covering his face sleeping. I woke him up and he drove me into town. I had to inspect a piece of equipment from a fire. I already decided I was not flying back in that plane so I rented a car and drove to Dallas and stayed over night at the Marriott.

The next day I flew back to NJ. I always used Delta Airlines for everything. They were the best. I was giving a seminar at the World Trade Center at the Vista Hotel, which later was sold to the Marriott and on September 11, 2001, it was destroyed.

April 1989 – My Florida House

On April 12ᵗʰ, we flew to Florida. Eleni had retired so this was great. I was now running the Florida office and Petee took over all the others. I hired a landscaper to tend to the lawn and flowers. Eleni began her search for furniture, etc. I ordered a company to spray the lawn and interior. My friend Philip Vias was to clean the pool. I also ordered awnings for the terrace. Eleni had the Mercedes 560SL and I had two cars, a Buick company car and a new Cadillac that I had bought a week before. April 20ᵗʰ we had a big storm and a lot of lightning and no power. April 26ᵗʰ we flew to Greece on Olympic Airways. We went back to the Ledra Marriott to the Athenian suite. Sunday April 30ᵗʰ was Greek Easter and Eleni's birthday. Uncle Walter and Aunt Dolores were there too, and we had a great time.

May and June 1989 – My Mother Moves to Florida

We all went back to the U.S. on May 6ᵗʰ. Mom was also getting ready to move to Florida into my condo. Even though the condo was completely furnished she insisted on having her own bedroom set. So I sold mine and on May 22ⁿᵈ she came down for good. We were busy and Eleni was having a ball shopping. She went to the "Dakota" a decorator's showroom with many stores. You had to be a furniture dealer to get in and the people at Casual Patio gave us the pass because we bought our patio furniture from them.

July and August 1989 – Buying Furniture for Our Florida Home and My Office

Eleni wanted nothing but the best so I let her go for it. Just our patio furniture, which was made in Italy was $10,000.00. The whole bar and cocktail table was $6,000.00 and so on. Eleni was the best so I let her get what she wanted. The living room was being custom made.

On Friday June 9th Eleni and I went to Nassau to the Gray Cliff House. This is a very famous place. Our room was the same room that Winston Churchill stayed in and it looked just like it did then. Many famous people came here over the years. We had been a member of the Tower Club and went quite often. I would go to New Jersey one week per month. I discovered a roof leak after several rain storms so I ordered a new barrel tile roof.

On August 21st they started the roof. Business was great. Petee would fly down for a long weekend occasionally. I was traveling to Tampa to see clients. I kept up my PR as always all over Florida.

September through December 1989 – My First Yacht "Eleni"

October I went to the New Jersey office to work with Petee. We kept growing and growing and the fire was burning within. The boat show came to Fort Lauderdale the last week of October and Eleni and I went. We saw a 38 foot brand new Bayliner and fell in love with it. I gave a $10,000.00 deposit and they said I could take delivery in December. I picked out the electronics package and we went home. Again I always said I was going to do everything I wanted so I bought my yacht.

On November 9th it was my company's 10th Anniversary and I couldn't believe it. On November 16th my accountant Mike Mongelli and my secretary Mary Ann came down to Florida for a meeting. I made dinner at our new house and took them out to dinner also.

On December 1st I went to pick up the boat and had the closing at the Yacht Center in Pompano. After I signed all the papers they gave me the keys. I said I don't know how to operate this boat, and I don't know how to get home to my dock. He said I don't believe you bought this boat and you don't know how to run it. His name was Pete and I gave him $100.00 to take me home. He arranged for a pick up at my house and we left. He made me drive down the intra-coastal and showed me how to use both engines, how to steer, and how to turn. When we got to Fort Lauderdale I couldn't find the canal to my house. After going in and out of several canals, I finally saw Eleni standing on the dock at our house. We tied up the boat and Pete left. We were both excited I had my first yacht. I should note Eleni and I went to Coast Guard school for four weeks and graduated.

Sunday, December 3rd, I took the boat out with Father Nick, Uncle Walter and Dolores and we blessed the boat and christened it. On December 6th Uncle Walter and Aunt Dolores, Edith and George, Eleni, and I took the boat north on the intra-coastal and we stopped for dinner at Charlie's Crab. I was getting used to operating the boat. Christmas Eve Eleni and I took the boat to Lake Santa Barbara. I made dinner and we opened our presents. It was 37 degrees with 15 knot winds so we pulled anchor and went home. On December 29th my sister, Linda, Tom, my mother, my niece Stephanie, and my nephew Nicky took a cruise with us in the new boat "Eleni", and again had dinner at Charlie's Crab. The company Christmas Party was at the Tower Club and it was great. I always gave out the bonuses at the annual party.

January and February 1990 – The Holidays and a Visit with My Son

New Year's Eve we had dinner on the boat and saw the fireworks at Shooters and returned. This was a great evening with the family. Everyone had a good time. I even saw mom singing. I was very busy watching all the other boats and didn't drink because I was the captain and I had a great responsibility to my guests. When we got back I had my "Glenlivet on the rocks".

During January I was very busy both in Florida and NJ, but still took weekend trips with the "Eleni" to Miami and Palm Beach Marina. Petee came down on January 27th and we discussed business on a trip to the keys and dinner at Charlie's Crab. I traveled quite a bit during February.

One weekend my friend Joe and Marcia came down and we took them to dinner at the keys and ate at Monti Trainers. Richie had approached me several times since January and was having a problem with our assistant Laska. Laska had been working for Richie for about two years. Richie and his wife Diane were close friends with them. I told Richie, "You run the office so you do what you have to as long as it is in the best interest of the company." Deep down inside I think he just got tired of her doing what she wanted and Richie had no control. On Friday the 9th Richie fired her. My NY vice president, David Redsicker, and his wife Patti came on the 28th and stayed for the weekend. I always treated my staff to a weekend with all expenses paid. I was good to them all. When Richie went on vacation I always let him take the company car and paid for his gas, dinners, etc.

March 1990 – Promoting Florida Business

During March I visited Tampa clients to promote my engineering. I had one engineer on staff in Florida, John Louis, a retired professional engineer. On March

17th I flew to London on British Airways, on the Concord, flight 292. I arrived and went directly to the Marriott. I had dinner with Steve and went to my office.

The next day I had a meeting at Lloyds of London at 11am. The next day I had another meeting at Lloyd's at 5pm. I went to Wheelers for dinner with Steve. The next day I went shopping and stopped at the Ritz for high tea. I left on flight 292 British Airways to Miami. I loved the Concord because you could actually see the curvature of the earth and the flight was only three hours. March 26th I flew to my office in Binghamton, NY for a meeting. I returned Thursday.

Eleni and I had joined the Team Yacht Club and we met some very nice people. We had a trip planned to leave on Friday the 30th to Hawks Cay on Duck Key. It was our first long trip and there were eight boats going. We had a great time. Our closest friends were Jim and Eileen Marshall who were special agents for the U.S. Government.

Our trip to Greece this year was with Linda and Tom, Debbie and Mark, and Murdock and Shiona. We had one hell of a time going everywhere. I had rented a Suzuki van so we could all fit in it. Greek Easter was on Salamina and all we did was eat, drink, and dance. It was a great vacation for all of us. After we returned home I had a case in Key West and returned the next day. Petee flew down on Friday the 27th and on Saturday we took the boat to Palm Beach and had dinner at the Governors Club. Our return on Sunday had rough seas with 10-15 knot winds. When we came into Port Everglades we went to Bimini Boatyard for dinner.

May 1990 – Michael Mongelli, My Accountant

On May 4th Eleni and I flew to San Antonio for a long weekend and returned on Monday. On May 19th my accountant Mike Mongelli and his wife Lorie came for the weekend. We took the boat to Miami and stayed overnight, returning on Sunday, which turned out to be another wonderful trip. May 31st Petee came down because we were leaving June 1st for a boat trip to Bimini. We stayed until Sunday June 3rd. This was my first trip to the Bahamas and it was beautiful. On the trip back we hit a squall with high winds and seas for 20 minutes. That was an experience. On the 18th of June I went to NewJersey for depositions. Eleni flew in and we visited Uncle Walter and returned on Friday.

Debbie and Mark had bought a condo in Palm Beach and moved down from NY. Debbie had quit her good job in New York City to make the move. On June 29th Eleni and I went to Bimini again on a Floatilla, but it was a bad crossing - seas 4-5 feet and 15 knot winds. The next day we left for Great Harbor in the Berry Islands. There were six boats and we had a great time.

July 1990 – The Boat Accident

On July 3rd we were anchored off one of the islands and I was in my dinghy when Eleni said the group radioed that they were going to leave and go to another island for the night and anchor out. Mom had made us Greek food, and I had the refrigerator full. I followed with the Floatilla and at 5:30pm we arrived at Devil's Cay. We waited until the first boat went in. There were rocks and coral heads on both sides of the entrance. They called me and said to go in and as I proceeded in there was a large swell and I came down on a coral head. It went through the bottom of the boat and it began to flood. I called May Day and I put Eleni in the dinghy and the other boats took her away. One of the guys dove under the boat and he said my keel broke and I was hung up. I stuffed cushions in the hole but I had water up to my knees. A boat arrived and said they were from Basra, the Bahamas Coast Guard. The name on the boat was "Little Abner". They put a pump in the boat and said it was getting dark and they said they would come back in the morning. I told everyone I would not leave the boat until I could get a salvage company.

During the night I was eaten alive by mosquitoes. I drank a few scotches and ate some shrimp, which I was able to reach. The boat was now on an angle and the bow was down about six feet. I knew I was hung up so I wasn't worried about it going down. I was scared because they told me there were sharks in the entrance and I was told not to go in the water and if I had a problem to call "Little Abner" and they would come. I couldn't sleep. When darkness set in, I could see the other boat lights in the cove. When it got darker I was worried because I could hear the splashing of the water against the boat, and then heard things bump the bottom of the boat.

About 5am the boat began to slip and I thought it was breaking apart. I called May Day and Little Abner answered and said he would be there in an hour. When the sun came up Jim Marshall came over in his dinghy with several other dinghies. I passed over my guns, and all the clothes I could get and Eleni's personal things. When Little Abner came the two Bahamian guys took their pump and said they would stay with the boat until I got a salvage barge. One of the guys from the boat, "Nashville Cats" took me off my boat. Eleni had stayed on his boat that night with his wife. Jim Bleach the head of the Floatilla and who owned the yacht center where I bought the boat said the group was leaving Chubb Cay and I had to leave too. When I got on the boat and we pulled away, Eleni and I couldn't stop crying. It was a terrible emotional experience.

We arrived at Chubb Cay and I took a room at the small hotel. I made arrangements with the owner for a small plane to Miami in two hours and took a shower. The plane arrived in Miami in 45 minutes. I had to hire a taxi to take us to the house in Fort Lauderdale. I couldn't believe what had happened. I couldn't even talk on the phone without crying. I had to wait until July 5th to call the insurance company. That Thursday, July 5th, I called the insurance company, National Yacht and they said, "Read your policy, it says I must salvage the boat then they would send an adjuster."

I chartered a plane July 5th and flew to Great Harbor. I stayed overnight after making arrangements for someone to take me to Devils Cay the next morning in a small boat. At 6am we left and arrived in one hour. I couldn't find the "Eleni". We sailed into the cove and there it was; it had sunk. I could see it under the clear water. I took my clothes off and dove in. I couldn't believe what I saw. The entire boat had been stripped of all instruments, hardware, canvas top, including the stainless rails and pipes. The refrigerator, stove, furniture, toilets, and even the paneling were gone. I was sick and the fellow who took me there said the guys who came on the "Little Abner" were not from Basra. They stripped the boat the next day and pulled it off the coral head so it would sink. I asked him who they were and he clammed up. I returned after taking pictures and went home. I had never been so upset. I called the insurance company and they said I still had to salvage the boat. They said to call Moby Dick Salvage in Miami. They also said after the boat is salvaged they will reimburse me. I called and gave them the location and they brought the boat to Miami and pickled the engines. I called the insurance company again and they said an adjuster would go there and then they would contact me. After a few weeks they still did not call and they wouldn't call me back. In the meantime I received a letter and a book of checks from a bank in Delaware with a $100,000.00 credit line. I had already spoken to Jim Bleach and he said he felt bad about the boat so I could buy another and he would give it to me for cost. I owed $130,000.00 on the Bayliner, which I expected the insurance company to pay.

I picked out a 42 foot Mainship Mediterranean. I gave Jim Bleach a check for $90,000.00 from the credit line for a down payment on the $190,000.00 Main Ship. I figured when I get the check from the insurance company I would pay the loan off. All through July I tried to contact the insurance company and they didn't call back. I called my agent who handled my insurance. He said he left them a message.

August 1990 – The Boat Insurance

I was getting angry and decided to wait until August 1st to call again. In the meantime, I received a call from the bank telling me they cannot honor the $90,000.00 check because the credit line was $10,000.00 not $100,000.00. It was a good thing I kept the letter which accompanied the checks. The bank said it was a mistake. I told the gentleman I would call him back. I walked across the street to an attorney I knew, and she called him back. While on the phone with him I faxed him the letter. When she got off the phone she said they had to honor my check because it was their mistake. I was very happy but not for long. August 10th, I called the State of Florida to file a complaint against Nautical Management. After making calls, I reached someone at the department of insurance who told me there was a problem with that insurance company, but they couldn't discuss it.

The next day my agent called me and said Nautical Management went bankrupt. I almost died when I heard this. I called the insurance company again and found the phone disconnected. I called Moby Dick Salvage and they had the remains of the boat and had pickled the engines. They sent me a bill for $14,000.00 which I didn't pay. I kept calling everyone and soon I realized I was stuck and had to pay the Bayliner loan of $130,000.00 and the loan for the Mainship and the $90,000.00 to the bank. What a mess this was. On August 24th I picked up the Mainship and brought it home.

On August 31st, Murdock and Shiona, Eleni and I took the Mainship which I called "Eleni II" on a cruise to Freeport but hit a squall 25-30 knots. This was a surprise for Murdock and Shiona because it was their anniversary and what they didn't know was that Petee and his girlfriend, Emme; Craig and Claire; (Shiona and Murdock's son and daughter) would be at the hotel for a surprise in Zanado. We had a good time except Petee and Emme had a bit of a tiff. She was from Columbia and had a very bad temper. I didn't particularly like her.

September 1990 – My Son and His Girlfriend

On September 3rd Petee and Emme sailed back with us to Fort Lauderdale. We cleared customs at Pier 66 and went home to my dock on Royal Plaza Drive. Eleni and I took trips on the weekend and did enjoy the yacht very much. The sad part was I had to make the payments on the old boat that sank.

Work was busy in Florida, NJ and NY offices. I still went to NJ one week each month to work with Mary Ann and Petee. When I returned to Florida I traded in my Caddy for a new four door Mercedes. I had increased my salary because of the boat loss.

October 1990 – Our New Orleans Trip

On October 23rd Eleni and I were invited to New Orleans because her company gave her a retirement party along with a Mississippi Steamboat Cruise. We had a great time.

November 1990 – Avoiding a Shootout

We returned on November 4th and I was back to work on Monday. My friend Jim and Eileen who also had a boat met us at Port Everglades early on November 9th for a boat trip.

For my company's 11th anniversary we went to Dinner Key in Miami. On Saturday we decided to walk to Monti's for dinner. Jim and Eileen always carried their guns since they were special agents and I always carried mine since I was licensed as a private investigator and had a carrying permit. As a matter of fact, I was licensed to carry a gun in NJ, NY, NYC and PA. As we were walking through a path covered with trees we saw a car parked under one of the trees and two guys were watching us approach. We split up and told Eleni to stay a little behind us. I think the two guys saw our moves and decided not to attempt to rob us as I am sure they were going to. Can you imagine if they approached and the three of us pulled out our guns and shot them?

One night in November, I took Uncle Walter, Aunt Dolores, and her sister, Ethel out to dinner at the Tower Club. While eating Ethel began to choke on a piece of meat. I jumped up and used the Heimlich maneuver and saved her life. Another saved life to be added to my list. This was #41, I saved.

On November 25th Uncle Walter, Aunt Dolores, and mom joined us for a cruise to Bayside in Miami. We returned for dinner at Charlie's Crab.

December 1990 – The Holidays on My Boat

December 1st I had the Christmas Party at the Ocean Grand in Palm Beach. Eleni and I flew to NJ on the 3rd and returned on the 6th. Petee came down with Emme and stayed at the Riverside Hotel for a few days and we took a couple of day trips. During the night another girl called Petee in the room and Emme went nuts. I think this was when Petee decided to let her go. He went back to NJ and I planned New Year's Eve on the boat. I cooked up a storm and invited Walter, Dolores, mom, Debbie, Mark, and their friends, Lauren and Rob, Murdock and Shiona, and their daughter, Claire and her boyfriend, Steve.

January 1991 – The Holidays with Family

New Year's Eve came and we all had dinner on the boat and went to Shooters for the New Year fireworks. Again I couldn't drink because I was driving. It was loaded with boats and I decided never again on the water for New Year's Eve.

Murdock and Shiona had moved to Jupiter to a condo but still had their house in New Castle, England. Almost twice a month we took a cruise with Murdock and Shiona and sometimes with Danny and Lorraine. January 10th Eleni and I flew to San Juan because her old company Burroughs Wellcome was having a meeting and her best friend Susan Rucci was going to be there. We didn't tell Susan we were going there and when we got there she was surprised.

The next morning about 5am I went to the casino and it was roped off. I spoke to some guy who told me they were shooting a movie. While speaking with him Dennis Hopper walked up and I said, "Hello". He then walked into the casino and he said something to another guy who came back to me and asked, "Would you like to be in a movie?" I said, "Yes!" They told me to just walk back and forth between the slot machines when they gave me the okay. There were many others that were going to do the same thing. After an hour of waiting the time came and the lights went on and we all walked around like we were gamblers on the slots. Dennis Hopper walked in front of us and after five minutes it was over. I asked what the name of the movie was and they said "Double-Crossed". I told Eleni and then we went shopping, then to dinner. We left Puerto Rico on Monday the 14th. Tuesday the 15th I hired Powers and McNalis, attorneys to investigate my loss with the "Eleni".

February and March 1991 – Boat Insurance Fraud

February was a busy month and I heard from Attorney Powers. I went to his office for a meeting. He told me Nautical Management was not licensed to sell yacht insurance only insurance for commercial boats. He said I could sue my agent because he was the one who placed the insurance with them. I told him to go ahead and I gave him a $3,000.00 dollar retainer.

Tuesday the 12th of March I flew to the Cayman Islands to do a fire case and returned the next day. I received a call from Generali Insurance in New York who insured DeLongi products from Italy. We successfully represented them in a few cases. They said they would like me to meet the VP of DeLongi in Milan. Mr. Claudia Bonavito said he would meet with me and we set the date for Tuesday April 16th. On March 22nd PVA, Inc. a Florida Corporation was opened and we became a licensed engineering firm.

April 1991 – Our Trip to Europe

On April 8th Eleni and I flew to Athens then to Rome. We were going to attend my cousin Velissairo's daughter Angeliki's wedding. We did our usual visiting and of course we stayed at the Ledra Marriott. On Saturday the 13th we went to the wedding. The reception was at her new husband's restaurant in Peristeri. It was a typical Greek wedding. In Greece the invited families bring their kids so it was noisy and busy.

On Monday Eleni returned to the US and I flew to Milan, Italy. Tuesday I had my meeting with the VP of Generali. It went very well and I knew we would get all their business. In the afternoon I had an appointment to speak at the fire station in Milan which I did. They made lunch for me and awarded me with a trip to La Scala where the operas are held. It was beautiful. I never saw such a beautiful place. After the performance I went outside and the captain left. I stopped in the square for a drink and met some people at the table outside. We had a great time and finally about 1am I returned to my hotel.

The next day I flew home to the US on April 17th. On the 24th I flew to Birmingham, Alabama to do a case and returned the next day. April 26th Angeliki and Alkis flew in from Greece on their honeymoon. They stayed in NJ with Petee and were taking some side trips. I had to fly to Nassau in the Bahamas for a case and returned the next day.

May 1991 – Cases in the Islands

On May 8th I flew to St. Thomas for a case and returned May 9th. Tuesday the 14th Angeliki and Alkis arrived in Florida. They went to dinner with us and stayed in Miami. They took a trip to Disney World for a couple of days and returned on Friday the 17th. On Saturday we took them on a trip to Dinner Key on the Eleni II and returned the next day. They left Miami the next day and returned to Greece.

Eleni and I planned a trip to Hawks Cay for the Memorial Day weekend. We left on Thursday May 30th and on the way off Key Largo I lost my steering. I called the marina at Key Largo and made arrangements to come in using only my engines. I got the boat in and pulled it alongside the dock. One of the dock attendants crawled in the engine room and found that two bolts had fallen out of the steering arm. He replaced them, but it took two hours. We stayed and had dinner then saw the original African Queen and went to bed. The next day we continued on to Hawks Cay. We had a visit from John and Linda Evans, our friends. John used to be the manager at the Publix where I worked in the 70s. He took us to his house and we went with him on his boat, and then to his friend's house for dinner. We returned at 2:30am. We left that day and returned home.

June 1991 – My Mother and More Trips with Eleni

During the month of June I was busy working and traveling. We went to mom's occasionally for dinner and she was fine for age 80. She had bingo and went on outings with the people there. She kept company with a couple, Monroe Kaplan and his wife Ann. They even took her shopping.

Richie was doing well but he was still very much overweight. Everything was going great. I was making money and Eleni had finally bought everything she wanted. We loved having company especially for dinner. The kitchen was large and cooking was great because we had gas. The only trip planned with the boat was on June 28th with Jim and Eileen with their boat the Dolphinas and us. We went to Palm Harbor in Palm Beach on June 28th. The next morning we left for Xanadu in the Bahamas. We hit a storm and rode it out. After we arrived we had dinner on Jim's boat. The next day there were heavy winds, 50 knots and heavy rains. I had a lot of leaks to tend to.

July 1991 – The Storm

On July 1st we left for Great Harbor and 30 miles out we hit a terrible storm with 6-10 foot waves and heavy rain. Jim's anchor dropped down and he radioed me that he had to slow down. I couldn't turn to help him in fear of capsizing. After he crawled out on deck he finally secured the anchor; soon after the storm passed. We stopped to get organized then continued on to Great Harbor. I pulled in the slip using only one engine. We went to a small restaurant we had eaten at before when I had my sinking yacht episode. The cracked conk was the best. I have to say one thing, Eleni was one brave woman. Nothing ever bothered her even during the storm. She would sit and read. Her big treat was the cracked conk.

July 4th we ate at Tamboo's and had the buffet. This island was the best and we really enjoyed everything it had to offer. Jim and I made the necessary repairs and we helped each other. A note about Jim is that he is a great guy, but has a short temper. He would get annoyed at the smallest thing, but we learned not to pay much attention to him. On July 5th we returned to Xanadu, which was a better trip than when we originally came.

On July 7th we returned to Fort Lauderdale and had to wait two hours at Bahia Mar Marina to be cleared by customs. July 9th I went to New Jersey and returned on the 12th.

August 1991 – A Visit with Petee, My Son

On August 3rd Mary Ann and her husband, Frank came to Florida and Petee and his girlfriend Anna (one of many) came too. On Saturday August 3rd we took them to Dinner Key for dinner. The next day we returned home from a nice trip. On August 9th we went to Bimini with Mark and Debbie. It was a good trip. The rest of the month I did many fire investigations. Back from NJ I planned a trip with the Floatilla. August 31st Jim and I, with the rest of the boats, left for Miami. We stayed overnight and the next day we went to Faro Blanco and had dinner at Kelsey's. It rained hard that afternoon and Jim's canvas top leaked and he went nuts. The next day we left for Key West to the Gallion. We stayed there and ate at several places. Eleni and I ate one night at the Marriott.

September 1991 – The Boat Trip

On the 4th of September we ate at Louie's Backyard which was excellent. We left Key West on September 5th and went to Hawks Cay. When we left on the 8th my stern line got caught on my prop. I had to dive several times to cut it off.

When we went to Miami, going out the port, we hit heavy seas but returned safely.

October 1991 – The Boat Insurance Lawsuit

October we used the boat once because I was very busy. Attorney Powers told me he filed suit and people were put on notice. I traveled quite a bit in October; all over the place. I had company for dinner on Sundays. Eleni and I always went to dinner on Saturday nights alone. We never had anyone stay over at our house to this day. I always made sure the spare room was a TV room and an office.

On Saturday October 17th, Eleni and I flew to Los Angeles and stayed overnight at the Beverly Willshire and saw her family. The next day we flew to Alaska then to Hong Kong. It was a 23 hour flight, but we traveled first class and it was great. Landing in Hong Kong was also an experience. We came in for a landing and it was dark but the lights of the city were beautiful. We came down between two mountains, and at the end of the runway was the water. If you overran the runway you could end up in the water. We landed and cleared customs and took a taxi to the Regent Hotel. We had a beautiful suite overlooking the city. We had to sleep because of the jet lag, so we ate at the hotel and went to bed.

The next day we went to see the city and took a boat over from Kowloon. It was quite a cosmopolitan city. The men and women were all dressed and everybody had a cell phone. We did a little shopping and that night we had dinner at the Mandarin Hotel.

The next day Eleni and I were picked up by the fire department and taken to fire headquarters by the chief. We were then taken to meet Director Batterymarch of the fire department. He welcomed us and had one of his officers take us around to see their operations. I couldn't believe the command center. There were many stations; at least 50 of them with each having large computers and a red revolving light on top of each station. All their trucks and cars had computers in them. When there was an alarm, the officer would put the red light on and a supervisor would go to that station and take charge. They actually worked the fire from their stations sending whatever was necessary to the scene. It was quite impressive and then we were taken to see all the equipment. I gave a lecture in the afternoon then we went back to the director's office where he presented me with a hat and tie. We were then returned to the hotel and after lunch Eleni and I went up to the ladder streets. We walked up to the shops on steps which looked like large ladders. Eleni was looking for a gift for someone and made the merchant open at least six large boxes and we unpacked them to see each one. After she saw all of them she said thank you. She didn't like any of them. The guy went crazy because we weren't buying anything. I told Eleni to get out and keep walking. I then told the guy to put our name on one box and we would return tomorrow. He started screaming so I left and ran down the block to Eleni and we quickly disappeared. We did buy two beautiful vases, which we had shipped home and one for Linda, my sister. That day I made arrangements to take a boat on the South China Sea to "Macau". This was in Red China and occupied by the Portuguese and had a large gambling casino. The next morning we left on the hydro foil to Macau. There were many fishing boats 40-60 years old and the fishermen wore large hats. I thought I was going through a time warp.

We arrived in Macau and I immediately found a taxi whose driver spoke English. I told him I would give him a $100.00 bill if he stayed with us all day. This was like giving him $1,000.00. He took us to some beautiful places to see and to lunch on the side of a mountain in what looked like a castle. The lunch was wonderful and the people were great and very hospitable. After lunch he took us to a small town where the center square was like a circle. Eleni and I got out and went shopping. I bought a large samurai sword and a very old picture of Mo-Sang-Tou. Today this is very valuable. After a couple of hours we came out of one of the shops and there was a commotion in the square. I looked and saw the police arguing with my taxi driver. They wanted him to move his taxi and he refused because he was waiting for us. Eleni and I ran up and we drove back to the boat. When we got back to Hong Kong we had dinner at the Peninsula.

October 24th we shopped again and had lunch and prepared to leave the next day. What a great trip. We returned and stopped in Anchorage to refuel so we shopped a little and then onto Los Angeles. We took a suite at the Bel-Air Hotel in Beverly Hills, the top place in the US. The usual people who ate there were the Reagan's and most all of the movie stars. We loved it and we left on Sunday back to Florida.

November 1991 – The Bahamas Case

On November 6th I flew to Nassau in the Bahamas for a case and returned on the 7th. On Saturday the 16th I flew to Montreal to promote the company and also to do a case. I returned on Thursday 21st and spoke with Uncle Walter because he was not very well. He told me he didn't have much time left. I flew to New Jersey for two days and visited him in the hospital. We had a good talk and he said Dolores would be well taken care of. I parted and I cried in the hall. I knew I would never see him again.

CHAPTER–TWENTY NINE
The Nanny Case

Chapter–Twenty Nine – The Nanny Case

December 1991 - My Uncle's Death

On December 2nd he passed away. I didn't' go to the funeral and I haven't gone to one since. Two things I didn't like anymore, weddings and of course funerals. Weddings were a big party so the families can show off and see who is wearing what and who is dressed better than whom. I called it the gossip show. The same with most funerals that was where you see everyone you have not seen in years.

December 1991 – The Nanny Case

I had given a seminar in the Riverside Hotel. On December 5th Petee was down for my birthday and we got a call from the NJ office. It was from an attorney in NYC, Laura Brevetti, who wanted us to represent a nanny who was accused of setting a fire which killed a 3-month old baby, Christie Fischer who was in her charge. The nanny was 20 year old Olivia Riner who was a live in nanny and was placed by Au Pair Services. We flew to our office and along with David Redsicker and Arthur Jackson; we conducted an investigation at the Fischer's house at 5 West Lake Drive, Thornwood, NY. After a very intense investigation, we determined the nanny; "Olivia Riner" did not set this fire. We did a great investigation and we were looking forward to the trial in July of next year.

On December 19th Eleni's son Michael came to visit us and stayed at the Riverside Hotel until Sunday December 22nd then returned to Chicago. Linda, Tom Nicky, and Stephanie were down for the holidays staying at mom's. We took a cruise on the 29th for lunch and all attended.

January and February 1992 – Business Meetings and IENGA

New Year's Eve was at the Tower Club. The first week of January we cruised to Miami for lunch and back to Dania for dinner at Martha's. On the 5th the family returned to Syracuse. January again was a very busy month. I now had six employees in the Florida office.

On January 20th I went to NJ for a meeting and returned on the 24th. I had several fire investigations in the Orlando area and returned February 3rd. Sunday February 9th Eleni and I flew to Los Angeles. We stayed at the Beverly Wilshire. I had a meeting February 11th at the Beverly Hills Fire Department. I gave a talk and took some photos. We had lunch at the Beverly Hilton and dinner at the Beverly Wilshire. Wednesday February 12th we flew to San Francisco and stayed at the Marriott. It was a bad day with high winds and rain. I had rented a car and we had planned to drive to Oakland to inspect the fire scene which destroyed a few hundred homes and killed several people. We drove across the Bay Bridge and went to Sausalito. We ate lunch at Gabriaci's overlooking the Golden Gate Bridge. We then went to fisherman's wharf which was very interesting. Friday February 14th we drove to Napa Valley and I visited with the Napa Fire Department. After that we drove to several of the wineries then on to Sonoma Valley and did the same. I purchased several cases of wine to be shipped home. That night we ate dinner at the Regis Restaurant in San Francisco. Saturday February 15th we took the boat to Alcatraz. This was quite an experience. We actually went in and saw the cells of Al Capone and other famous prisoners. That night we had dinner at Ernie's Restaurant with a friend of Eleni's, Nancy Fisher, which was great. Sunday we went aboard a US Submarine and chalked up another great day. I remember looking at my beautiful wife as she was getting ready for bed then looked out the window at the lights of San Francisco. It happened to be the Chinese New Year. I thought I came a long way since 1979 when I started my business, and as I said before was going to do everything I wanted in life. I never saved much money and I really didn't care. I watched so many people work all their lives and when they retire they end up dying. My philosophy was to do everything you can in life because you never know when the end will come.

On Tuesday February 18th I had a meeting with Ralph Ciarlo of the Forensic Accounting Association. Mike Mongelli wanted me to check this firm out because he received a solicitation from them and wanted to know if they were legitimate. The meeting was very interesting and little did I know then that I was to make a lot of money in the future working with them. Yes the business was legitimate. They would train accountants how to do forensic accounting investigations and special cases for firms and insurance companies. My conversations with Ralph Ciarlo revealed his partner, James Hogge, ran a training program for First General, which was for contractors. Ralph was interested in me because I had a company that did investigative engineering, fires, accident reconstruction, etc. He asked if I was interested in joining a team with him if he decided to open a company for the Investigative Engineering Assoc. I told him I was and would send him all my literature and resume. On Tuesday February 25th at 2pm I met with Ralph. I signed a contract with him and agreed to present a three day program and classes for $1,000.00 a day plus expenses. This began an association which still exists today. The Investigative Engineering Assoc. was born. I worked with his office and we developed a three day training program and the manuals were printed. I started to give classes once a month to engineers who came from all over the US. I also received word that my old girlfriend Doreen's son Scott passed away at age 21. I was made the senior advisor instructor for IENGA (Investigative Engineers Association). Again, "Who said you cannot get ahead in life?" In this country anyone can make it. All you need is the will to do it, and hard work, and I only had a high school education with numerous college courses. I had begun to look for another Florida office. We were outgrowing our Spring Tree Lake Drive office.

March 1992 – Vacation and Theft

On March 10th I looked at a place at the MacKenzi's Industrial Park near the Fort Lauderdale airport. I met with Summer Robinson, the owner, and he said he would build an office to suit my needs. I agreed and within weeks we moved to a much larger compound. We had more storage area with overhead doors, offices larger than before, and we were closer to I-95, the turnpike, and the airport. In the month of March I had gotten in touch with my godfather's son Jonathan Stathakis who was a producer in Hollywood. He wanted me to meet several people to possibly do a movie about my career and cases. He set it up for me to come to Hollywood on Sunday the 29th. I was very excited.

Eleni and I took a trip with the Eleni II to Miami Beach Marina at South Beach. We met some friends Bob and Lauren and we walked the beach stopping at an outside bar & grill after dinner. I always carried a men's pocketbook as I called it. They used them in Europe all the time. In it were my credit cards, driver's license, a gold Cartier pen and pencil set, etc. and of course my gun which I always carried. We sat down at a sidewalk table and I placed my pocketbook on the ground near my foot. A few minutes later a gypsy type woman was creating a fuss in front of our table and we all looked. She then left suddenly and we all thought she was crazy. All of a sudden I realized my bag was gone. She created a diversion, "the oldest trick in the book" and I fell for it. I ran to see if I could find her but I couldn't. Obviously someone else behind me took it. We called the police at 8:15pm and they didn't come until 10pm. I was so upset. It ruined the day. Eleni and I went back to the boat and called my credit card company to report the theft. The next morning I had to drive without a license to go to the office. At 8:15am I received a call from a Florida Power and Light office in Miami. They told me one of their men found a Publix bag with my credit cards in it. I immediately drove to Miami to their office. When I got there they called this worker, who was a lineman, to the office and he told me he pulled up to a pole about one mile from the office that morning, about 6am, and saw this Publix bag. He looked in and saw the credit cards, driver's license but no gun, and no gold pen and pencil set. He saw my business cards and that is when he went back to his office and called. I was thrilled and I thanked him and gave him $50.00. I got back to the office and realized the only thing missing was the gun, and the gold pen and pencil. I guess after seeing who I was and my private detective license they didn't want to touch the credit cards. Saturday morning my new Amex, MasterCard, and Visa cards were federal expressed. Thank God because I was leaving the next morning for LA. Eleni and I received a call from my brother-in-law; David who said Dellie, Eleni's sister who was diagnosed with lung cancer a few months ago was not doing well. I left Sunday the 29th for California and stayed at the Beverly Wilshire. Jon met me for dinner at a great Greek restaurant. The next day Jon took me to several agencies for meetings. On Tuesday the 31st I met Mike Greenfield who would be my agent in Hollywood. We also met at the Vidmark Agency and everyone seemed to be interested in me. That night I ate at Dean Martin's favorite place, La DoceVita Ristorante on Santa Monica Blvd. All I can say is, "It was the best." While sitting at my table Sidney Portier came in and sat across from me. We spoke briefly and I ordered. We said a few more words when I was leaving. What a nice man. I later learned many more stars went there.

April 1992 – Another Family Death

I returned to Fort Lauderdale on April 1st and Eleni and I went to dinner at Sheffield's in the Marriott Harbor Beach. This was our favorite fine dining restaurant in Fort Lauderdale. Early in the morning about 2am, April 3rd the phone rang and it was David. He said that Dellie died a few minutes ago. We made arrangements immediately and flew to NJ that afternoon. The funeral was Sunday April 5th. Michael and Debbie also flew in. It is funny that at the funeral Dellie's friend Elaine, whose husband died a year ago, kept holding David's hand. She was a very heavy woman, larger than Dellie was. She flew up from North Carolina for the funeral. Something was strange about David. David and Elaine were whispering to each other. I mentioned this to Eleni a few days later, but we didn't think much more of it. We were now looking for a new office in Binghamton because someone bought the building at 211 Court Street. I had to fly back to NJ because Time Warner called and wanted an interview with me. I met the next day, April 10th with Nancy Diamond in NYC. This was about doing my life story. I returned to Florida and on April 16th our anniversary, we had dinner at our other favorite place, the Rainbow Palace. This was not your typical Chinese Restaurant. It was oriental and the owner Eddy and his partner Kenny were great people. There were flowers on the table; very high class and expensive but the best. We still eat there to this day.

We were going to Key Largo to a private club called, Ocean Reef with the Yacht Private Club on April 25th. That morning we met outside the inlet and went to Ocean Reef. One of the members of our club was a member of Ocean Reef so we could go. Jim Marshall, my friend didn't like Ocean Reef because it was mainly for the rich and he refused to go. That night we had dinner, dancing and a buffet which was the best I had ever had. They served lobsters, crabs; all the best! This place was great. I filed an application and already had my two sponsors. The initiation fee was $10,000.00 and $2,500.00 a year membership.

We returned Sunday night and it was back to work. Eleni's birthday was April 30th so I decided to go to Palm Beach with the Eleni II. Jim and Eileen came with their yacht, the Dolphanis. Petee came down and I took them all to dinner at the Ocean Grand Hotel. This was the Sun Fest weekend and we had all kinds of entertainment and fireworks. Debbie and Mark came to the boat one night too. We returned on May 4th.

May 1992 – Lloyds of London

When we returned I received a call from Lloyds of London that they wanted us to do a fire on a British Schooner in Singapore Harbor in China. The British used the ship for R&R for its officers. I decided to send Petee. It was a 27 hour trip from Los Angeles. When he arrived he was to meet with the chief of the fire department for the Port Authority. When he got to the hotel he fell asleep. I received a call from them and they said he never arrived. He was out cold from jet lag and didn't even hear the phone. Finally he awakened and did the job. Petee returned on May 8th to Florida and he stayed at the Riverside Hotel.

On Friday May 15th Petee went to New Orleans on a case. I was notified that I was accepted as a member of Ocean Reef so we planned to go on Friday, May 22nd and pay our fees and get our cards. I was busy going over the case in Shangahi with Petee.

On Friday, Eleni and I left for Ocean Reef. What a beautiful exclusive club; well it should be for that kind of money. It even had a small airport, golf course, hotel, restaurants, and stores. It had its own fire and police departments. The pool was beautiful and they always had a band on the weekends. On Saturday and Sunday we took the "Baby Eleni", our dinghy, out and I did some diving. One night we ate at Carysfort Restaurant, which was our favorite. Sunday we took the "Baby Eleni" out for a two hour trip, had lunch at the Raw Bar and I made dinner on the boat. We returned home on Monday. We also had a trip to Key West on May 30th with the Yacht Club. I really enjoyed the yacht and it also gave me some relaxation. May 30th we left for Hawks Cay. That night we ate at Porto Cayo.

The next day we went to the Gallion Marina in Key West. Key West was quite a place. It had its own identity and many bars including Sloppy Joe's where Hemmingway hung out. We took a walk over to the Hemmingway house and took a tour through it. Even the cats were there as they were in the Hemmingway years. I was a great fan of his. We had dinner at the Marriott that night. The next two nights we ate at the Louie's Backyard; a great place to eat.

June 1992 - IENGA

June 5th we went to Faro Blanco and ate dinner at Panchos. That next night we ate dinner on Jim's boat. We had squalls at about 3:15am for two hours. On the 7th we returned home. I taught classes on June 9th through the 11th for the Investigative Engineers Assoc. (IENGA). Petee flew down on June 18th and we went to Ocean Reef. On Sunday we returned and stopped at Fowley Rocks to do some diving then went home.

July 1992 – Ocean Reef in Florida

Eleni and I went back on July 4th weekend, which was another great weekend. Almost every other week we would go to Ocean Reef. I was still going to NJ and back and we were growing fast. July 7th, I received a call from Petee that we won the trial of the nanny and she was acquitted at 11:23pm, July 7th. I was very happy about this. I will be addressing this case in full in a later book. We had great publicity and we were very happy. We also did a segment on the Discovery Channel on fires in automatic coffee makers. I also had three trials in July in NJ. I returned from New Jersey, Friday the 31st.

August 1992 – R&R

I was exhausted from the trials and decided to sail to Cat Cay. Cat Cay is South of Bimini and a place you could clear customs before going to Nassau on the Berry Islands. It was a private club which had a restaurant, bar, and a small airstrip. It was beautiful and I did some diving and exploring there. The next day Eleni and I left for Ocean Reef. I had purchased a golf cart; a Rolls Royce and had the name "Golden Greek" painted in gold on both sides. This was so we could get around Ocean Reef because it was quite large.

CHAPTER-THIRTY

Hurricane Andrew

Chapter–Thirty – Hurricane Andrew

August 1992 – Hurricane Andrew becomes a Threat

Eleni and I spent time using the "Baby Eleni" our dinghy, and eating at the Carysfort. On the 10th of August we left for Little Palm Island, a private island where many of the movie stars go for R&R. They had thatched huts, no phones or TVs. We had dinner there but we really didn't like it very much. The next day we left for Hawks Cay. We had dinner at Porto Cayo. The next day we ate at the Galley Restaurant and had great lobsters. On the 15th we went to Ocean Reef for two more days and returned home on the 16th. On August 22nd my cousin Felitsa's son Costa arrived with his new wife Eleni. We went to dinner at the Tower Club. We began to worry because Hurricane Andrew was building and heading for us as a category 3. I drove to Costa's hotel and got them a limo to take them to Miami to get out of the storm's path. The next day was panic day as the storm grew to a category 4. I spent all day putting up the shutters and I moved the Eleni II to the middle of the canal and tied it to both sides. I took the dinghy back and put it on my dock then filled it with water. Eleni had made a chicken then we went to mom's to stay there. There were high winds all night about 70-90 miles per hour. The condo was fine because we were blocked by other high rise condos.

The next day, Eleni and I, headed back to our house. Mom had no power when we left. I couldn't believe the destruction as we approached our street. Las Olas Blvd was covered with trees and I drove around many wires and trees, but I got to my street. We lived on an island at Royal Plaza Drive. The street was covered with debris. I drove over driveways and lawns and got to our house. I had shutters so the house was okay but my pool was filled with dead birds, trees, bushes, and shingles from other houses. My wooden fence was blown away. The Eleni II was fine sitting out there in the water. Another strange thing was that our power was on so clean up began early. I did have one tree, which fell on the roof but it didn't damage it. I had $18,000.00 worth of damage to my landscaping which was not covered by my insurance. Benny, my gardener took three days to remove all the debris. I then had him plant new bushes, plants, and some new trees around the house. I moved the boat back to my dock behind the house and it was covered with leaves and mud. It took me a whole day to clean it.

On August 25th I called Ocean Reef to see if the employees were all right. I found out that their dormitory was very badly damaged and they had very little food and supplies. One of the girls had a small baby so I went to Publix and spent $500.00 for food, water, baby diapers, and all kinds of supplies. I went to my office and took a small generator to the boat. Eleni and I loaded the boat and on August 30th we left for Ocean Reef. We entered Hawks Channel and a lot of the markers were gone. I took a heading and set the loran for Ocean Reef. We saw roofs floating in Biscayne Bay. I think every tree on Key Biscayne was down; wood and all sorts of debris were in the water. I used extreme caution to get there. When we arrived I pulled along side the fuel dock and I was greeted by Hugh, the dock man. He was a great guy, Fito the dock master was also there. They asked if I was crazy going out there and I said you sound like my mom. When they saw what I brought they had tears in their eyes. I delivered all the food and supplies and Hugh took the generator. All the girls and guys thanked us and some were crying.

My next venture was to find the "Golden Greek" (my golf cart), which had blown about ¼ mile away. I found it upside down with the top smashed. I turned it over and it ran so I drove it to the golf cart garage and left it to be repaired. Eleni and I had something to eat and we sailed back to our home.

September 1992 – My Yacht, the "Eleni II"

September was a very busy month. I was in Alabama and Jacksonville on cases. On September 18th we took the Eleni II to the Boca resort for one night.

October 1992

I had a lot of cases in the Florida office so I helped Richie out by going on the road. I was in Birmingham, Alabama for a trial and returned home on October 1st. October 4th I flew to Nassau and returned on the 5th. October was just as busy and we went nowhere until October 31st. We went to Fisher Island with the Eleni II and there was a Halloween Party at the Vanderbilt Mansion. We had a good time and returned November 1st.

CHAPTER–THIRTY ONE
Looking Back And The Boat Accident

Chapter–Thirty One – Looking Back And The Boat Accident

November 1992 – Success

Monday November 9th was our 13th year anniversary. That morning as usual I was up at 5am and made coffee. I went out back and sat by the pool. Just beyond the pool was the Eleni II at the dock. I thought back to when I arrived in New Jersey in 1979 and bonded with my son Petee and met Eleni. I knew I was determined to make it big someday and a few thousand cases later the fire within was still burning. I was now getting closer to the top. I had a great wife and I was so proud of my son. All three of us grew together the past 13 years and as I looked around at the house and my yacht, I knew that this was the result of hard work and a dream.

Many family members on my mother's side always talked about me saying Peter will never amount to anything. He is always chasing fire trucks and was divorced twice already, etc. One of my cousins always told me, who was saying these things. Well as I look around now you could say I fooled them all because I became the most successful and wealthy person in the family. I never held a grudge and have financially helped some of them after they "got divorced". The sun was coming up and I walked out to my yacht with my coffee. I was feeling like a million dollars.

November 14th I flew to Dallas for a four day seminar with the National Fire Protection Association. Wednesday the 18th I flew to Los Angeles for meetings with Jonathan Stathakis and my agent, and then returned home on November 21st.

December 1992 –The Holiday with Mom

I made reservations at Ocean Reef for New Year's Eve. Eleni and I sailed to Ocean Reef for my birthday. We picked up the Golden Greek which had been repaired and drove around the island looking at the houses, which were being repaired from the damage of Hurricane Andrew. I returned and flew to NJ then I went to Pennsylvania for two days on a case then went home.

Christmas was at mom's house then we left for Ocean Reef on December 28th. The next two nights we ate at Carysfort which we loved. They always had a piano player and we were friendly with the manager, Bo Sanchez and the bartender, Anita Lingenfelser.

January 1993 – The Storms

Debbie and Mark arrived by car on the 31st of December for New Year's Eve. The event was black tie and we had a great time dancing to the music of the Peter Duchin Orchestra. The power went out on the marina later and we ran our boat on our generator for the next two days. On January 3rd the weather was bad and we decided to take the intra-coastal home. Going through Angle Fish Creek the wind moved the boat over while Eleni was driving and we hit the rocks. We took on water which the bilge handled. I couldn't get any speed because of the vibration so it took us eight hours to get to my dock at home. I called Cape Ann Towing and they towed the boat to Lauderdale Yacht. Both props and shafts had to be repaired for a cost of $4,300.00.

Petee came down on the 15th and we went to Ocean Reef. Petee and I spent two days of meetings and returned on the 16th. Back to work for both of us to New Jersey. I returned from a busy week and on January 24th Eleni and I went to Sheffield's at the Marriott Harbor Beach. This was another great fine-dining restaurant. Our Captain was Carlos and our waiter was Charles. We always laughed about the time Carlos dropped the tray of food on my head.

February 1993 – Business is Successful – Many Fires

February we were very busy with many fires. I was driving all over the state doing, sometimes two or three fires a day. I was doing most of the big fires because Richie was heavier than ever. I had a call from several clients indicating Richie didn't go up into an attic or on a roof to look for evidence of fire extensions. I liked Richie so I just did the cases where I knew there would be a problem. Another thing I noticed was that Richie's wife Diane had complete control of him. She ran the roost. Diane also let her daughter, Doreen, get away with everything. Richie was always glad when he had to go away on overnights or to NJ just to get away from her.

Eleni decided to go to Greek School this month and began classes at the St. Demetrios Church. I kept going to arson classes and bomb seminars and always kept the fire within burning. Even though I conducted one to two thousand investigations I continued to learn every day.

March 1993 – Petee's Many Years of Experience with Investigations

Petee had been investigating fires for fourteen years now and had become one of the best. March 2nd I flew to Los Angeles for meetings with Jon Stathakis about doing a movie of the week and possibly a series. I stayed at the Bel Air Hotel two nights and went on a tour to Culver City, Paramount, Columbia Pictures, and several agencies.

One night I ate at my favorite restaurant La Doce Vita. Another night I ate at the Bel Air Hotel and Elizabeth Taylor was there. I had arranged for Eleni to meet me in Las Vegas on Friday, March 5th at the Mirage. That night we went to see Julio Engleis. We went to the Flamingo to gamble and stopped at Bally's. I always started with $500.00 and always played the dollar slots. I was about $2,100.00 ahead when we returned to the hotel. The next evening we went to see the Sigfield's performance with the white tigers. After the show, I gambled and won another $700.00. We returned on March 8th and I went back to work.

I had a call on Monday the 8th from a person in Washington D.C. who represented a certain federal agency. We had a classified discussion and I flew to Washington D.C. a couple of days later. I met him in a hotel and spent about an hour together. After our meeting he paid me cash for my trip and I returned home. I cannot discuss the agency or what I was going to do not even to Eleni.

I spent a week working on a case in New Orleans and turned in the results immediately. It was a fire and bomb related investigation with a lot of tension. Mom had made friends with Monroe and Ann Kaplan when she first moved to Florida. Ann had died and mom and Monroe were seeing each other. Monroe drove so he would take mom to dinner and to the stores, which was a big break for me. He was a nice man and they both got along fine.

I was hired to do a fire investigation for one of my insurance company clients in North Florida. I did the investigation at the scene and saw that the fire destroyed the kitchen. I spoke with the owner and she told me the fire department took the toaster oven from her house. I then went to the fire department, who I won't mention, to get the toaster oven and test the remains in my lab. Our job was to determine what caused the fire. If we found it was caused by a product defect, the insurance company could go after the manufacturer to recover their money because it was their evidence. I advised him that this was not a set fire and we must recover the toaster oven. He refused to give it to me and said, "You private guys don't know what you are doing. We hire fire investigators who are in charge and are well trained." Little did he know I had 32 years experience in fire investigations. He was only about 25 years old. I asked to see the chief and he told me to leave.

I called the assistant chief the next day, and he said to come and get the evidence. I drove the 101 miles back and when I got there the same fire lieutenant said they threw it out, and the garbage was picked up. I had never seen such an unprofessional, uncooperative fire department. I have been training fire departments for years on fire investigations and wrote many articles, which I still do to this day to help train new investigators. I found out later that this lieutenant never had training other than watching other people over a two year period.

March 18th Eleni and I went to Ocean Reef until the 23rd; a great relaxing time as usual. The 24th and 25th I had to teach the Investigative Engineering Assoc. (ENGA). Friday mom had her friend Monroe and Eleni and I for dinner. We got a big kick out of them. I thought it was great and they were both happy even though she would tell him what to do.

Chapter–Thirty Two
The Boat Court Case

Chapter–Thirty Two – The Boat Court Case

April 1993 – The Boat Court Case

April was to be my trial on the loss of my boat. I made my usual plans to go to Greece on April 16th. The trial started in Broward County Court with Judge Fleet presiding. The trial carried on to Friday the 16th, our wedding anniversary, and that night we were leaving Miami for Greece. Jim Marshall came to the trial and would take us to the airport. During the trial Judge Fleet was paying little attention by doing paperwork rather than listening to what was going on.

On Friday morning he said we have to end this case early because I have to be home before sundown for the start of the Jewish holiday. At around 3pm he said, "I'm dismissing the jury Mr. Vallas and you should be suing the state instead of the insurance company". Even though the agent put me with a company that wasn't even licensed to sell yacht insurance, he dismissed the case. This is the same judge who pulled a gun in his courtroom and was reprimanded and put on civil trials taking him away from criminal cases. I was devastated and I had to pay the bank $130,000.00 for a boat I didn't have.

Jim drove us to the airport and I was in shock. Poor Eleni was upset too, but what could I do? This judge should have been thrown out of the court system. We arrived in Athens the next day. The one good thing was we always flew first class so the food and drinks were unlimited. We had a good time but our holiday was overshadowed by the court decision. We were at our usual stay at the Ledra Marriott, visited the islands, and had many dinners with my family.

May 1993 – Liabilities from the Boat Incident

We returned home on Sunday, May 6th. I had to pay my attorney $20,000.00 and he said I would need $3,000.00 if I wanted to appeal. I was so angry but I was stuck with the decision. Then the insurance company wanted me to pay for their expenses of $21,804.83 for the recovery of their attorney fees and court costs. I ended up settling up with everyone, which cost me $40,000.00 plus I still had to pay a $130,000.00 note on the boat.

June 1993

Business was still going strong and I increased my salary to adjust for the loss a bit. I was back in New Jersey a week to work with Petee and Mary Ann. I began to sense some frustration between Petee and Mary Ann. I don't think Mary Ann liked having Petee as a boss. On the 20th Eleni and I went to a party at Cousin Michael's house for Barbara Ann's daughter, Allyson. We stayed at the Eatontown Sheraton.

The next day we saw Aunt Lil for the last time. We stopped at my cousin Barbara and Ted's where she lived. She told me her time was getting short. We hugged and kissed; it was sad. I heard people on the second floor but no one came down to see me. Eleni and I flew back to Florida Monday and I had to teach three days for the Investigative Engineer's Association. I loved teaching these classes because I got paid well and it was great. We continued to take our yacht to Ocean Reef whenever we could.

July 1993 Contract for a Movie and a Book on Investigations

I had to go to Los Angeles for more meetings with Columbia Pictures and returned on July 2nd. We took the Eleni to South Beach for the weekend and had dinner at La Forge. On the 14th of July, Petee and I went to L.A. to meet with Jeff Saganski, VP of Columbia Pictures. We discussed a contract for a movie and book. We returned on Sunday the 18th and felt very positive about our future contract.

We stayed at the Peninsula Hotel on Little Santa Monica Blvd. in Beverly Hills. On the 25th mom and her friend Monroe drove to Ocean Reef and met us. They stayed overnight and we had dinner at the Islander. Eleni and I got a kick out of the two of them. They left on Sunday for home and we did too. Mom and Monroe had a good time and I took a picture of them walking and holding hands. Earlier I told mom they made a nice couple and she said, "There was only one man in my life and that was your father." Monroe just looked at me and smiled.

On Friday the 30th, I bought a new Mercedes; black in color. Now we had the red 560SL Mercedes convertible, which Eleni used and I had the new one.

August and September 1993 - IENGA

On the 23rd I flew to New Jersey and then on the 25th to New Orleans for an IENGA convention. My last night on August 26th I got to my room and found a large package on my bed. I opened it up and it was a large certificate. It was an International Honorary Citizen Award from the City of New Orleans along with the key to the city. This was for the undercover case I did and for my own safety it was given in private.

On August 27th I had to fly to Los Angeles for more meetings and returned on September 3rd. Saturday the 4th our friends joined Eleni and I for a trip to Naples to the Ritz Carlton. The next day we went to the Hilton Resort in Palm Harbor. We spent a couple of days and I went to Tarpon Springs and returned Wednesday the 8th.

I was now interviewing for a new engineer for the Florida office. John Lewis was retiring and I needed to replace him. My friends from England Shiona and Murdock opened a new kitchen business in Boca Raton and we met them one evening and went to dinner at Le Vie Masion. September 18ᵗʰ I hired a new professional engineer, Paul Getty, who turned out to be great and to this day we are still good friends and work together. On this date my dear Aunt Lil passed away. She was a sweetheart and I was going to miss her.

Eleni and I still traveled by boat to Ocean Reef every few weeks and always had a good time. My cousin Costa came in from Greece and Petee and he came to Florida and we all went to dinner at the Rainbow Palace.

October 1993 – Eleni Goes to NJ to Work with Petee

Saturday October 2ⁿᵈ Eleni flew to New Jersey to work a week with Petee to do some marketing. Peter picked her up and took her to the Marriott. That night they went to the city for dinner. The rest of the week they did marketing in Pennsylvania. On Friday she returned home to Florida. On October 3ʳᵈ I received a check from Columbia for $12,500.00 on my contract. On Saturday Jon Stathakis and his girlfriend Barbara came to the house and we went to dinner at Le Dome. The next day we took them on a cruise to Charlie's Crab on the intra-coastal.

After discussions about the movie contract with Jon I flew to L.A. on the 15ᵗʰ and returned on the 17ᵗʰ. Saturday I was at the Bel Air Hotel and saw Elizabeth Taylor at the bar and said hello. She was with another woman so I didn't say much more than hello. I loved the Bel Air Hotel and its history. Hollywood always put me in the best places. My room was $1,200.00 a day and my expense account was $400.00 to $500.00 a day. I met many movie stars at this hotel such as the Reagan's who lived nearby, Tony Curtis, Barbara Walters, Milton Berle, Walter Matthau, Tony Randal, etc. I was also at the Oscar's Party at the Beverly Wilshire and met Jack Lemmon, Jack Klugman, Goldie Hawn, Cher, and many others. It was quite an experience and I will never forget it. I was provided with a limo to take me back to Bel Air. I think my half hour conversation with Walter Matthau was the best. He was a regular guy and he introduced me to Tony Randal who spoke to me for about 15 minutes. One thing I noticed is that he had very large feet. His shoes were gigantic. On October 17ᵗʰ I started a corporation called Valiant Films with an address on Rodeo Drive in Los Angeles so that I could put all my deposits in the corporation. The writer for the script was Philip Rosenberg.

I still could not believe how successful I had become. Eleni and I were on top of the world. Thank God she was such a beautiful and understanding wife. We always compromised and rarely had an argument to this day. If we did, it was because of my Greek short temper and I adored her very much. I was in business fourteen years now and making money. I still had this vision to do everything I wanted rather than save money. I never realized I had great business skills including marketing. I kept working and training Petee as we grew. He was doing a great job and enjoying life also. He was a real lady's man and had some of the best girlfriends, but he always said he would not get married or have children. He was the ultimate "playboy" enjoying life.

On October 22nd, I took the Eleni to Ocean Reef. The seas were rough; four to five feet and the winds at 30 knots. It was a lousy trip but we got there safely. The next day I rented a car and we went to Boca Chica Lodge. The return trip to our house was great. Petee came down for the boat show and we had a good time.

November 1993 - Eleni Helps with Marketing the Business

November 1st, Eleni drove to Tampa to do marketing for the company and returned on Friday the 5th. My long range planning was paying off and I kept up the marketing with Eleni and Petee and was moving the company ahead.

On Saturday November 13th, I flew to Phoenix, Arizona to a National Fire Protection Assoc. meeting. I returned on Tuesday November 16th. Thursday my Aunt Dolores and her sister Ethel arrived to spend time at their time sharing apartment. On Sunday November 21st, I flew to New Jersey to meet with a writer from Columbia Pictures. I returned on Tuesday November 23rd. We had Thanksgiving dinner at our house with Aunt Dolores, Ethel, Mark, Debbie, Monroe, and mom.

On Monday Eleni went to the west coast of Florida and worked the Sarasota and Fort Myers area. On November 23rd, I signed with Columbia Pictures for my rights to a movie about my life. On the 29th I began receiving checks. The first check was for $12,500.00.

December 1993 -My Birthday Party

Saturday December 4th was my birthday dinner which was at Brook's Restaurant attended by Dolores, Ethel, Jim, Eileen, Monroe, mom, and Eleni who got a little silly. The next day we went to the Symphony Guild Christmas Party. Monday I left for a week to New Jersey to work with Mary Ann and Petee. I could still see tension with Mary Ann and Petee. I decided that I would not interfere since Petee was running the office. He had to learn how to handle all the problems of the business. I had a Christmas Party at our house on Sunday the 18th. On the 20th of December I had the company Christmas Party at Largo Mar.

December 23rd I received $3,148.00 from CBS Entertainment. On December 23rd, I also flew Monroe and mom to Syracuse to spend the holidays with Linda. Eleni and I also flew in, and I got mom and Monroe a hotel room at the Marriott's Residence Inn along with us. We had a great Christmas Eve and Christmas Day then we all returned to Florida, Sunday December 26th. New Year's Eve was at the Largo Mar with Debbie and Mark; and Jim and Eileen.

January 1994 – Marketing My Business

We hadn't used the Eleni II at all during December so we planned to go to Ocean Reef, Monday January 6th. That day the seas were bad and the trip was sloppy. I planned to work on the New Year's marketing and the expansion of the company. The wind was very strong all weekend about 30 knots. The weather was good, but the seas had white caps and were running 4-6 feet, but we kept on and arrived in four hours. On Sunday, January 9th, I had to rent a car to drive home and leave the yacht at Ocean Reef because the seas were too dangerous, 30 knot winds and seas, nine feet.

I flew to the New Jersey office and worked all week. Sunday, January 16th Eleni flew to Orlando to do marketing and stayed at the Marriott. I drove up on Friday, January 21st and took a suite. When Eleni and I were together we always took suites with two baths. We met my friends Vinny Masella and his wife Laura. They took us to their New York Modern Bakery to see the facility then we had dinner that night at the hotel. Sunday we drove home. Monday I went to Miami to meet Jon Stathakis about our movie and book contracts. I also spoke to my agent Mike Greenfield who we called Greenie. They set me up with a meeting in Tampa with a writer Patrick Carr. He was to write the book with me called "Fire Proof". This was set up with Columbia Pictures. I liked Patrick and was happy to have him on board. I returned Saturday the 29th and Eleni and I went to LaDome for dinner.

February 1994 – Movie and Book about My Investigations

On February 7th I also signed a contract with Fifi Oscar Agency for another book. Things were looking good, but my agent said Hollywood is strange sometimes. It could take five years to start a movie but you get paid anyway. I also met in New Jersey with Larry Ferguson who was going to write the movie script. Larry wrote the script for the "Hunt for Red October". I was very busy and I couldn't return to get the "Eleni II".

On Valentine's Day, I took mom and Monroe, Debbie and Mark, Lorraine and Danny, and Jim and Eileen to Largo Mar for dinner. The next day Patrick Carr was in from Tampa and we took him to Largo Mar. Because I was a member of Largo Mar Resort, I could always bring guests. It was not a public place so outsiders could not just come in to eat. It was a great place. Again I was very busy with work and finally on Friday the 18th I rented another car and drove out to Ocean Reef. On Saturday the 19th I left Ocean Reef alone on the Eleni II on a trip I will never forget. The Port of Miami; the inlet was so bad I couldn't get in so I continued up the coast to Fort Lauderdale. The seas got worse, nine to twelve feet with nothing but white caps and the wind was 25-30 knots. There were small craft warnings. I threw up twice and was peeing in my shorts. I couldn't leave the bridge. I was hoping to be able to go into Port Everglades inlet and if I couldn't, I would have to leave the yacht to save myself.

I arrived at Port Everglades and went out so I could try and go straight in. The wind was blowing from the Northeast so I hugged the north side of the inlet and went in full steam. I don't know how I did it, but I got in safely while the Coast Guard Helicopter was overhead. When I got to the house and docked I was exhausted and I had water inside and out. It took me eight hours which was normally a four hour trip. I couldn't even wash the boat until the next day. It took me the whole day to clean and dry out the "Eleni II". It was quite a job.

March 1994 – The Eleni II to Ocean Reef – Our Favorite Place

On Saturday February 27th I left to work in New Jersey and returned March 2nd. We had a visit from Eleni's cousin, Sheila and her boyfriend Rudi. On the 10th we took the Eleni II to Ocean Reef and returned on the 13th. On the 19th, Vinny and Laura, our friends who owned the New York Modern Bakery were staying at the Largo Mar so we went to dinner two nights and took them to South Beach with the Eleni II. We had a good time and they went back to Orlando on Sunday the 20th.

The next day I had to go to Charlotte, NC on a case and returned on the 23rd. Monday the 28th I had special tickets for Miss Saigon at the Center for Performing Arts. It included cocktail hour and a dinner and was a black tie affair. It was wonderful. Our life in high society was great. My determination to make it big was becoming a reality. We belonged to several private clubs including the Tower Club, Largo Mar, and the Exclusive Ocean Reef Club. We also were members in the Symphony Guild, which held parties in some of the multi-million dollar mansions.

April 1994 – Time to Visit Greece

Our friends, Joe and Marcia came in on the 7th for a few days and we took them out on our yacht and to dinner. I went to New Jersey on the 11th for a week to work with Petee. I returned for our anniversary on April 16th, which we celebrated at the Rainbow Palace with Jim and Eileen, mom and Monroe, and ended with up with a ride in the intra-coastal with the Eleni II.

Jon Stathakis came in from Hollywood and we had dinner at Largo Mar. We discussed the movie contract over dinner. I liked the idea of getting paid for doing nothing, but that is Hollywood! I was busy getting ready to go to Greece on the 27th. I had several meetings with Richie who was still acting strange. I received a call from my New Jersey office and they forwarded me a letter from one of my engineers, Tony Laws. It was written by Richie telling him he was going to open a business and John Lewis was going to work for him and he wanted Tony to work with him, too. He also said I was always spending money and he was insinuating he was going to leave me and start his own business. I thanked Tony for telling me and I called Richie for him to meet with me immediately and I showed him the letter. He was embarrassed and I told him I taught him everything he knows, gave him a good job, a car, paid his gas, hospitalization, and even let him go on vacation with the car and use the company's gas. I said to him, "After eleven years you decide you want to go on your own?" I was angry and told him to get back on track and let him know how good he has it working for Peter Vallas Associates, Inc.

On the 27th ahead of Eleni because we used points to fly first class, I left for Greece first, then Eleni flew the next day to London on British Airways and then on to Greece. We met at the Ledra Marriott. Sunday we took the ferry to Aegina for Greek Easter at Nitsa and Russo's. We had a great time and returned on the last ferry back to Athens. All week we ate at each of the cousin's houses and had lunch at our favorite place Hermion in the Plaka. One night we ate at the Kona Kai in the Marriott.

May 1994 – Paul Getty and Richie; My Employees

We returned to the U.S. on May 11th. I had a busy schedule in May because I had meetings in San Francisco and Los Angeles. I was still nervous about Richie, but I had Paul Getty in the office so I felt better. I left for San Francisco on May 14th and stayed at the Marriott. For the next few days, I met with a writer and did some marketing as well. No matter where I went, I always made some cold calls on insurance companies. I also spent some time at the San Francisco Fire Department with a lecture at one of the stations.

On Monday the 23rd, I drove to Los Angeles to meet Eleni who was flying in to meet with me. I had caught a virus and wasn't feeling too well. I rented a beautiful Villa at the Peninsula. Eleni arrived and the next day Eleni's son Michael met us and we took him to Mr. Chows for dinner. Wednesday Eleni and I went to Rodeo Drive to shop. I also opened an office for Valiant Films on Rodeo Drive for my movie business and opened an account at Wells Fargo bank. That night we had dinner at the Bel Air Hotel and saw our friend, the piano player, Ron Merritt. He had put out some CDs and gave us one. We had a wonderful dinner as usual. It was dinner for two with drinks and came to about $500.00.

Thursday the 26th we drove to Long Beach then had lunch on Sunset Blvd. That night my agent Mike Greenfield "Greenie" and Jon Stathakis, Eleni, and I had dinner at the Peninsula restaurant, which was one of the best in Los Angeles. Saturday night, Jon took us to dinner at the Café Athena, a great Greek restaurant. Sunday, we returned home to Florida very tired. On Monday morning I went to the office and found a letter taped on my office door. It was Richie telling me he resigned. He cleaned out his office including my list of clients and other forms to copy from. One of the fellows across from my office said he saw Richie putting things in his car with his wife Diane. I was very upset because after all I did for him, I really think his wife put him up to this.

June 1994 – Meetings with My Son

Petee flew in on June 2nd and we had several meetings and of course we ate in our favorite places such as Pisanos, LeDome, Largo Mar, and Sunday I made dinner and invited Murdock and Shiona. It became a tradition for me to cook every Sunday and invite company. I always loved to cook and it was a great stress reliever.

Monday June 1st I was sitting at my pool and my right arm and hand got numb. I thought it would go away, but after three hours Eleni and I went to the Cleveland Clinic for me to get examined. They took an x-ray and the doctor said I must have pinched a nerve. He put my wrist and hand in a plastic brace and said to sleep with it on, and the next day, it should be okay. I did what he said and the next morning it was a little better but when I put my left foot on the floor I could hardly feel it touching the floor and I fell. I immediately called the Cleveland Clinic and they told me to see a Dr. Hanson. I went there and he took x-rays of my back and later told me he wanted to do a spinal tap. He thought I might have a problem in the spine. I came home and was very upset. Eleni and I went to LeDome for dinner and my friend, the barmaid told me that I went to the worst place and that she had a problem with Dr. Hanson. She told me to go to the Mayo Clinic and that they were the best.

The next day I called the Mayo Clinic in Rochester, MI. They said they would call me back in 15 minutes. They called back and said they could get me in the Mayo Clinic in Scottsdale, Arizona right away. I said okay and on June 18th, we were to leave for Scottsdale.

June 12th Eleni went to Syracuse to do marketing for Peter Vallas Associates. She went to Buffalo, Rochester, Albany, and Syracuse and came back Friday the 17th. Saturday we left for Phoenix and went to the Marriott Camelback Resort. We spent the weekend driving around and it was quite beautiful. Monday the 20th I was at the Mayo Clinic at 7am to begin testing. All morning I went from one test to another. I have never had such a detailed and complete going over in my life. I had a consultation at noon with Dr. Timothy Ingall, a neurologist, and Dr. Hassan Loutfi, a heart specialist. They wanted to do a test the next morning on my heart, which was to put a tube down my throat and then put a TV camera to my heart. I was very nervous and they were very gentle about preparing me for the test. They did more testing during the afternoon and we went back to the hotel. The next morning I went back to the Mayo Clinic and was brought into the testing room. I had an IV in me and was surrounded by TVs. Then the test began. They sprayed my throat and told me when they put the tube in, to pretend I was sucking in a strand of spaghetti. I did as they told me, and down it went. I was given a sedative but I was able to watch everything on the TV. After a few minutes I started to feel sick as they slowly removed the tube. After a few minutes more, I settled down and met with both doctors. They told me I had a hole in my heart, known as atrial septal defect, and had this all my life. Atrial septal is a defect characterized by incomplete closure between the two upper chambers of the heart. There was also a clot which was in my brain stem. They gave me a prescription for Coumadin to keep my blood thin. I later found out that the clot could move and I could die. I did not want heart surgery to repair the hole. I never had an operation before and decided to take the alternative; to stay on the Coumadin.

On Friday the 24th we moved to downtown Scottsdale to the Marriott suites. We ate Mexican food, which was the best, and another night we ate at Swan Court at the Hyatt. I had to use a cane because I had no feeling in my left foot and my fingers were numb.

We returned home on Tuesday the 28th and Petee came down. We went to the California Café to eat. Petee and I spent a few days discussing my condition and our future plans for the company. I was having a little trouble using a cane and it was giving me some back pain. I was never one to take pills, even aspirin, so I took nothing for the pain. Eleni was my greatest support. She never let me feel sorry for myself and never babied me. I continued to do my work when I had to do a fire, and I would take Paul Getty or someone else with me. I did have a young boy working as an apprentice but he decided to leave and I later I found out he went to work for Richie. John Lewis died so Richie didn't have him and Tony Laws also died. Richie opened up under Richard Schwartz Assoc. and obviously copied my operation. I personally knew he would never make it down the road. He could not provide the quality of work I could produce. I met him once a couple of years later and he was even fatter than he was when he was with me. At the present time as I write this book, Richie Schwartz is now working as a public adjuster.

CHAPTER–THIRTY THREE
Arizona

Chapter–Thirty Three - Arizona

July 1994 – Physical Issues

July 4th I had a barbeque at the house, and Jim and Eileen came over. I decided to try and use the Eleni II for the first time since my stroke. I took the yacht on a cruise with Eleni on the Intra-coastal Waterway and Jon Stathakis was in so he joined us. I was able to do everything because on a boat there were plenty of places to hold onto.

Petee and I continued to evaluate the Florida office. We decided to undertake a study on the business and would evaluate our findings by October. I flew to New Jersey on the 13th of July and returned on the 15th. I took mom and Monroe to LeDome for her 83rd birthday. The rest of the month I was very busy doing fires and Paul Getty was busy with engineering. Intra-coastal Realty called and wanted to show the house, which they did. We had the house on the market and we had been talking about moving to Arizona.

August 1994 – Thinking and Planning About the Future

On August 5th we took the Eleni II north to Soveral Harbor Marina in Palm Beach Gardens. We had dinner the next day with friends, Mary Ann and Joe Colletti, at Carmine's Restaurant. I left the next day for the Boca Resort. I was doing a lot of thinking and planning about the future. That night Eleni and I had dinner at the LaVeMasion and returned home the next day. Now that I had become an "entrepreneur" my mind was always focused on new ideas and ways to improve my businesses. I now owned Peter Vallas Associates, Inc. PVA Engineering, Inc., and Valiant Films, Inc. Every thing had been a success so far, and I intended to keep it that way. PVA, Inc. of Florida was on its own as well as PVA Engineering of Florida. I also owned Vallas Enterprises, Inc. to handle my other ventures such as teaching, book sales, and other projects.

Eleni and I ate out almost every night at Pesano's, LeDome, and Rainbow Palace. Sunday August 19th mom had Monroe and Eleni for dinner and I drove to New Jersey. Petee and I had several meetings and we decided to let Paul Getty take over our Florida office and we worked out a deal with him. After much thought I had figured we were expanding at a fast pace in New Jersey, New York, and Pennsylvania, and billing was much higher in the north. I was making about half a million a year in Florida, after expenses. I decided we should put the money where we could expand even more. We would still make money in Florida from fires and I was teaching at IENGA for good money once a month. This ended up being a smart move.

I had noticed mom was forgetting things a lot lately and I thought something was wrong. On Saturday August 20th, Eleni and I flew to New Jersey to the Marriott. The next day, Petee and his girlfriend, Lee had us over to his Penthouse for dinner. Monday we went to the office and then to the Sheraton in Eatontown. That evening my godchild, Debbie visited us and we went to dinner. The next night my cousin Barbara and Ted came to dinner with us at the hotel. The next day we went to dinner with my old friends, Carol and Lou. Lou was my chief from Matawan Township Fire Department in the 1960s.

On Friday the 26th we went to Atlantic City to Trump Palace. We met Eleni's cousin Flo and Sid. On Saturday we took my cousin Lorraine, Danny, Bernice, Loretta, and Danny Jr. to dinner at Roberto's Restaurant. Sunday we drove to the Dupont Hotel and had lunch with Susan and Peter Rucci. Then we continued on to Springfield, Virginia to visit our friends Steve and Sharon. Both were special agents with the government. They were good friends of Jim and Eileen Marshall who were also agents with the boarder patrol. We stayed at the Sheraton and had dinner at the local steak house. The next day we went to Savannah, Georgia to the Marriott. We ate dinner along the river and the next day we went home. Eleni and I always enjoyed our trips. For me, I was back to work.

September 1994 – David Resicker comes to Visit

On Wednesday, September 7th, my New York vice president David Redsicker and his wife Patty came down and stayed at the Riverside Hotel. We had meetings the next few days and of course dinner at a different restaurant each day. Sunday as usual I cooked dinner and our friends from Ocean Reef, Anita and Robert came over. The next week I taught an engineer's class.

Our real estate agent called and said they had an interested party for our house in Florida. They came to the house and they liked it very much. On the 18th we had an open house and on the 20th of September Eleni and I left for Ocean Reef. We hit a storm and squall but we made it in all right. We had dinner and the next day we left for Hawk's Cay on Duck Key. The waters were blue green around Hawk's Cay and you could see the bottom. It was beautiful. We stayed a couple of days and on the 23rd we left for Ocean Reef. We ate dinner that night at the Islander. The next morning we went to Miami and had dinner at Monti's. In the morning I made omelets and waffles. We ate dinner at Christine's. The next day the 26th we left for home. It was a great relaxing week and I was able to run the boat for the first time since my stroke. I was moving about the boat well, since there were so many rails to hold on to.

October 1994 – Valiant Films, Inc.

Saturday, October 1st and Sunday, October 2nd we went to the Boca Resort. The water was calm and Jim and Eileen came with us for the weekend. We returned on Sunday night. On October 3rd I started Valiant Films, Inc. to handle the movie business. Intra-coastal Realty, Beth Bauchamp called and said the person who was interested in the house wanted it and was going to pay cash. He came to see the house again the next day, and he put a deposit down and signed the contract. Eleni called the movers and arranged to have them pack next month. I also decided to close the Florida office and let Paul Getty take all the business.

On October 16th Eleni flew to Columbia, Mo to field train an engineering firm for IENGA. She returned on Friday the 21st.

November 1994 – Business and Pleasure

November became a very busy month. On November 2nd, I went to Tampa on a case and returned on the 3rd. On the 6th Petee and his friend Sandra went with us to Charlie's Crab on the yacht for dinner. On Saturday November 12th Eleni did field training for IENGA in Tulsa, Oklahoma and returned Friday November 18th.

On November 25th I drove to Baton Rouge, El Paso, then to Phoenix, Arizona and on to Los Angeles. I met with my agent in Beverly Hills and with Jon Stathakis. We met at my office, Valiant Films, on Rodeo Drive.

December 1994 – Our New Home In Scottsdale, Arizona

On the 2nd of December I drove to Scottsdale to the Marriott Suites. Eleni called and said the house was sold. Now we had to find a new house in the Scottsdale area so Eleni flew to Scottsdale the next day Sunday, December 4th. I spent the day with a Remax agent. Virgil and Eleni saw many houses. December 5th was my birthday so we went to the Boulder's for dinner. The next day Eleni went with Virgil while I went to the Mayo Clinic. When I got back to the hotel I saw Eleni come in with this great big smile on her face. I knew immediately she found a house. She said, "Tomorrow Virgil will take us to the house which was in Fountain Hills about five miles northeast of Scottsdale."

That night we ate dinner at Palm Court, which was a very fine place. The next day December 7th all three of us went to Fountain Hills up a mountain to Cerro Alto Drive. It was a beautiful home built on two acres of land. There were five levels built into the mountain with a four car garage, a negative edge pool with a waterfall; it was magnificent. Virgil said a couple had built the home and had a $20,000.00 sound system built in and four extra phone lines for computers. The window from the sitting room and living room were huge overlooking the mountains and valley below. There was a large covered patio with a beautiful stone bar and sink. The second patio was adjacent to the kitchen. The living room was about 35 feet long and a dining room adjacent to that. The kitchen was all granite and open leading to the den, living room and dining room. There was a large drawing room, which I would use as an office. It had two large guest rooms at each end of the house; one on the upper level, and one off the kitchen. Each one had a private bath and shower. The master bedroom bath had a large Jacuzzi and a large walk-in shower with two overhead showers, and adjacent to them was the toilet. The master closet was as big as a normal sized bedroom. There was also a bath just outside the master bedroom with a door leading to a stairway down to the pool and outside was a hot tub. On the wall in the master bedroom was a control panel, which operated the pool temperature and hot tub. There were also lights outside and everything was automatic. The top of the garage was finished and could be used as a lookout towards the four peaks.

Virgil said the people never moved in because they had lost their jobs with one of the large banks. Both were vice presidents. I was told to make an offer because they hoped to get $800,000.00 and it wasn't selling. I told Virgil to offer $500,000.00 and see what happens. Thursday the 8th Virgil called and said they accepted. Eleni and I were so excited. I called CitiBank who I did business with for 15 years including my last mortgage and they approved it immediately. We set the closing for January 6th, 1995. We left Scottsdale for home on Saturday December 10th. We stopped in Amarillo, Texas and the next day we went to Dallas to see my cousin Dolores, Ann, her husband, and daughter Erika. We took them to dinner and the next day we went to Pensacola, Florida and on to Fort Lauderdale. We called for the moving company and made the arrangements for the packers to come on December 28th and 29th. We would move out on December 30th. December 18th, I had to go to New Jersey and Petee and I met each day and I returned to Florida on the 23rd.

We had Christmas at mom's with Debbie, Mark, Monroe, Lorraine, Danny, and Jim and Eileen. On the 29th the packers came and worked all day. Friday the 30th we closed on the house and the last thing put in the truck was the Mercedes 560SL. I had moved my yacht to Jim's house until I could return and move it to a marina.

January 1995 – The Move from Florida to Scottsdale, Arizona

We spent New Year's Eve at mom's then left at 4:30am, New Year's Day for Arizona. We stopped at Baton Rouge Marriott overnight and the next day we made it to El Paso. Tuesday the 3rd we went to Scottsdale Marriott. We closed on the new house on Friday, January 6th. Saturday and Sunday we began house cleaning. Everything was brand new including all new carpeting. We had a central vacuum system which was good. Monday, January 9th the movers came and it took all day. Tuesday we had the locksmith come to change all the locks and we had an alarm company come and add a pad in the master bedroom. We also had window breaking alarms installed.

On Wednesday, January 11th, we had our new washer and dryer delivered and installed in the laundry room. Thursday we had the windows measured for blinds. We ordered a culligan water softener and began to purchase some new pieces of furniture including furniture for my office. I spent $10,000.00 just for my office but it was beautiful. We also ordered new furniture for our large family room. As you can see we were very busy. We had the gas company hook up both fire places, one in the family room and one in the master bedroom. I also ordered new landscaping to be done, very plain, no grass. I had small stones spread about, new trees and cacti and many new plants in the front entrance. The rest of our property was left in its natural desert surroundings. I left for Florida on Monday January 23rd. Eleni was busy and on the 25th the blinds were hung. We had cabinets installed in the garage, and we also had the garage air-conditioned.

In Florida, I stayed on my yacht at Jim's and on January 28th I moved the boat to Lauderdale Marina then flew home and we had dinner at Palm Court. On the 30th we went for our Arizona driver's licenses and new tags for the cars. We were busy all week getting eight telephones and having the chandelier installed in the dining room.

February 1995 – My Son Comes To Visit our New Home in Arizona

Petee came in on February 6th and we went to dinner at Palm Court. He loved the house and took many pictures. He left on Thursday the 9th. On the 15th my cousin Chickie was in Scottsdale and we met her for dinner. All week we were busy with service men and deliveries. Sunday we went to the Greek Church then we went to lunch at the Quilted Bear. We spent the next week with all the landscapers working three days and we had a gas grill installed outside. Sunday the 26th we went to church and it was very nice but the members were very cliquish.

March 1995 – The Mayo Clinic

Twice a month I kept going to the Mayo Clinic for check ups. On the 3rd of March we had all new shower doors installed. Then on Sunday the 5th I flew to Florida. One thing we had noticed was a few "scorpions" began to appear. They looked like little lobsters on the wall and were on the ceiling. We called a pest control company and they said during the construction they probably nested in the walls. We had the entire house sealed on the outside and treated on the inside. October 7th I moved my yacht to Pier 66 for the week and returned the yacht to Lauderdale Marina. I returned from Florida on the 12th and we went to dinner at Chaparral's. March 16th, Eleni and I already found the finest restaurants in the area and we enjoyed them very much. On the 16th Jim and Eileen arrived to spend a couple of days with us before going to his daughter's in Mesa. We had a good time and they left on the 18th. The next day we had severe lightning, which was common this time of the year, so we contacted a company to install lightning rods on the house.

On the 19th I flew to New Jersey and worked at the office with Petee. On Wednesday the 22nd I flew to Florida and stayed on the yacht, then flew home on Sunday the 26th. The next week we did a lot of shopping. Sunday we went to church at Holy Trinity's, had lunch out and I made dinner at home. Again the next week was busy with service people, deliveries, and shopping.

April 1995 – Applied for Arizona Private Detective License

Saturday the 8th we ate dinner at Chapparal's. I had applied for my private detective license in Arizona so I could operate in this state. Eleni and I did plenty of shopping and we ate out a few times a week. The Mexican food was wonderful. We also ate at a place called El Trillo. They made wonderful dinners with fresh game such as rabbit, elk, buffalo, quail, etc. fine tuning everything. I called it the PVA western white house.

All month I worked about the house, which is when we began to discover the night life in the desert. The first time we heard the un-godful screams, it sounded like a baby being killed. The next day I spoke to the neighbor up the block and he told me that was when a coyote gets a rabbit and the rabbit screams when it is being eaten. He also told me the rattlesnakes come out at night and we should always look out before we leave the house and when we return. If we hear the rattle just freeze and eventually it will leave. If you move, they can strike at 125 mph and the distance is how long they are. Anytime we see one we should call the fire department and they will come and capture it then take it away. I also began to feed the rabbits every morning in back of the house in a small clearing. It was always light out at 4:30 in the morning because in Arizona the time never changed. There was no daylight savings time so the clocks were always the same. I would buy rabbit food and when I went out, they would line up, about ten of them and I would spread the feed on the ground. After about a month they were not afraid of me. When I would go to New Jersey, Eleni would put the rabbit food out for me when she got up. One morning when I went out through the garage door, I saw a large mountain lion lying next to the house. He looked at me and I looked at him. He stood up and walked down the mountain. I guess he was waiting for the rabbits. It was a beautiful animal, light golden with white lines. After he left the rabbits came with a dozen quails around them. I fed them and it seemed there were more animals showing up. Before I left for New Jersey I would fill one jar with food for each day so Eleni would feed them. Saturday night we ate at the Chaparral Restaurant in the Marriott Camelback Hotel.

Sunday was Greek Easter and I had prepared a great dinner with lamb, spanakopeta, tiropetes, dolmades, potatoes, carrots satziki, and keptedes. We invited some friends and it was a good day.

Monday the 30th, I returned from Florida and took care of things around the house. We would still see a scorpion or two on the ceiling and we didn't like that.

May 1995 IENGA and Eleni's Marketing Skills

On May 7th Eleni went to Minnesota to train a new IENGA member. IENGA used Eleni because of her marketing experience and paid her well. I spent the week at the shooting range and received my firearms carrying permit. Eleni came home on Friday the 12th. Saturday night we went to Chaparral's for dinner. Monday I returned to New Jersey to work at the office. On Saturday the 20th Eleni picked me up at the airport and we went to dinner at Palm Court.

The next day we went to church and it was Eleni's name day. Greeks always celebrated name days more so than birthdays. We began to realize that Arizona was not for us. Everything was still, hot like a microwave oven, plenty of dust, snakes, scorpions, and all other desert animals. Our house was a mansion with beautiful views of the four peaks, but I could see Eleni didn't like it very much. On May 26th our friends Shiona and Murdock came and stayed with us. We wined and dined them. We went to Old Town, and we hit the Indian Reservation Casino, which was only three miles from home. Tuesday the 30th we went with Murdock and Shiona to Camelback Mountain. Murdock had a business client to see. Their names were Diana (who had been the wife of Dale Nightingale, who had a very famous radio program and had passed away). After we left Murdock and Shiona we went home.

June 1995 - The Eleni II

June 5th, Eleni flew to Des Moines, Iowa to train another IENGA member and she returned on Friday the 9th. Saturday we went to dinner at Chaparral's. Sunday the 11th I flew to Florida and told Jim and Eileen they could use the Eleni II to go to the islands. June 12th, I picked up my boat at Jim's house and took it to Pier 66 Marina, slip A-10. I cleaned the boat and on June 15th I took it up the intra-coastal for a ride alone. The next day I left the boat at Jim's and returned to Arizona on Sunday the 18th. Eleni and I had dinner at Palm Court. We discussed putting the house up for sale soon.

Linda and Tom and my mother came to visit on Wednesday the 21st. They loved the house. Thursday the 22nd we all drove to Sedona in my land rover. Sedona was a beautiful place with red rock canyons. The next day we went to Old Town and had lunch at Laudry's Pacific Fish House. That night we went to dinner at Chaparral's. The next day we drove to Las Vegas and they all loved it. We had two suites at Treasure Island and mom had her own room. Tom gambled but lost and I won $1,600.00 on the slots. The next morning we drove south and stopped at the Boulder Dam. What a sight to see, then continued on home to Fountain Hills, Arizona.

On the way, mom complained about her foot. It was all red and swollen and I thought she might have been bit by something, which was not uncommon in Arizona. We took her to the emergency room at Scottsdale Hospital. She was given medication and we went home. Tuesday the 27th they all returned home. It was great having them. The rest of the week Eleni and I went shopping and had lunch at the Quilted Bear.

July 1995 – The Brush Fire In Arizona

Sunday, July 2nd Eleni and I went to our friend's, Jon and Ann Stathakis's wedding and reception at the Sheraton Crescent Hotel. The next day we went to their house for brunch. Tuesday July 4th Jon Stathakis and Barbara came to the house for dinner. On Saturday the 6th, Eleni and I returned to the house from Palm Court and we had our first scare due to a large brush fire heading our way from Rio Verde. The sky was lit up for miles and you could smell the smoke all around. I noticed burning ambers and went up on the roof with my hoses and wet it down for the night. The next day our street was lined with fire trucks and the "Hot Shots" helicopters and planes were dropping water to stop the fires, which even now were within a half mile of our house. Finally the fires were under control by nightfall and we didn't have to evacuate.

Tuesday July 11th, Eleni and I drove to the Grand Canyon for the day. We stopped in Flagstaff at the Little America Hotel and stayed over. The next day we left for Las Vegas to Treasure Island and had suite 3076. We had dinner at Moongate and I won $600.00. The next day we stopped and had lunch in the Land Rover then went home. That night there was a big sandstorm and our satellite went out. The next day DSS came out and the windstorm had pulled a bolt out. Sunday it was back to Florida for me. On Thursday the 28th Eleni met Diana Nightingale in Arizona. Back in Florida I took the boat up the intra-coastal for a ride. Jon Stathakis came over the next day and we discussed my meeting with his director about setting fires in his new movie. We took the boat to Charlie's Crab for lunch. On the 27th, Eleni had lunch with Susan Simmons, wife of Bob who lived in Scottsdale. Bob Simmons was from IENGA. I returned home on Friday the 28th.

August 1995 – Eleni and I Took Many Trips

On August 8th Eleni and I drove to the Petrified Forest then went to Flagstaff and stayed at the Little America Hotel. The next day we drove to Las Vegas to Treasure Island. We had dinner at Moongate and that night I won $1,100.00. The next morning we drove to Palm Springs and stayed at the Marriott Desert Springs Resort. The day after, we went to the Indian Casino and had dinner at LG's Steakhouse. I lost about $400.00. Saturday the 12th we went home. Sunday the 13th we had dinner at Chaparral's with Diana and Bob Atwood. I was getting excited because I passed the casting for the movie "Exit" and it was to begin shooting in Fort Lauderdale on August 15th. I flew to Florida and the movie people paid my expenses for the hotel. It was quite an experience. It was a B movie about a hostage situation in a topless night club. I was Chief Peter Vallas of the fire department. They hired a couple of topless dancers from the local clubs and I got them a fire truck from the Lauderdale by the Sea Fire Department. Jon Stathakis was the producer and we had a lot of fun doing it. Since this was my first movie, I learned plenty. It was normal for some of the girls to walk around topless or nude. I memorized my lines and the shooting was great, so was the Wrap Party. I returned home on Friday. I was now in the Screen Actor's Guild because I had a principal role and speaking part. Money for the role was $1,250.00 a day if you were in the Guild. On August 28th, I went to New Jersey for a week then back to Florida on September 1st.

CHAPTER–THIRTY FOUR
Scottsdale Az
Murder Investigation

Chapter–Thirty Four – Scottsdale Az Murder Investigation

September 1995 – Eleni's Family

Eleni's son Michael, and girlfriend Shelley came to visit. We took them to dinner and on Sunday September 3rd we went to Sedona for the day. On Monday the 4th they returned to California.

On Tuesday the 5th, I received my private detective license from Arizona. I was also working on a contract with Avon Books. I had met a girl at Gardner's Tennis Ranch who told me her brother was shot to death at the Hyatt in Scottsdale and there was a $50,000.00 reward to find the killer. I gave her my card and a few days later I received a call from her father. I went to his office and discussed the case with him. He gave me all the information he had in a cardboard box and I looked at it. I could see from the father that he was devastated and wanted justice. In short, his son was out with another fellow; a good friend of his. They were at a lounge and he had words with another guy. They both left he lounge and drove up Scottsdale Road to the Hyatt. On their way, a car cut them off. They continued on, to the Hyatt parking lot. The two boys got out and were confronted by a guy who began firing and hit both boys. The shooter escaped. The fire rescue took the two boys to the hospital, but they were already deceased. Now I went to the Scottsdale police and spoke to a detective. He told me that sometime after the shooting a female called the police asking for a detective to talk about the shooting. She was told she had to call back in the morning as no one was in. She never called back. He said he couldn't give me any more information as the case was still under investigation. I suspected that she may have been the girlfriend of the shooter. I received all the information, and told the father that he must tell the police to question the girl once they identify her. The police didn't know in the beginning that the girl who called that night was connected to the case.

Several months later according to the newspaper, the girlfriend of the shooter told the police her boyfriend killed them. I did not receive any word even though I told the father the girlfriend was the key and it should be followed up. I never heard from him again. September 4th, I was contacted by a reporter, Robbie Sherwood from the Scottsdale Tribune. She requested an interview with me because she heard about my background in fire investigations and the movies. We met at her office and had quite a discussion. She requested a photo and sent a photographer, Tony Blei to take a picture of me.

On Wednesday the 6th, I went to New Jersey to meet with Petee. I returned home on Friday the 15th. On Monday my friend Vinny Masella and wife Laura came to visit with us. We went to dinner at Palm Court and the next day we took them to Sedona. On Monday the 18th they left to go back to Orlando, Florida. Eleni and I decided to go to Vegas again so on Wednesday the 20th, we went to Treasure Island. By now I was classified as a high roller so we always got a large suite and special privileges. We had dinner at the Moongate at the Mirage, which we liked very much. On Thursday we had lunch at the Flamingo and dinner at the Mirage. That night I hit several jackpots on the slots netting $3,560.00. Friday we returned home. Saturday the 23rd, I received my concealed weapons permit then Eleni and I went to Chaparral's for dinner. Petee was doing a wonderful job running the business. We made a great pair. Money was coming in and I was well over three figures. I always paid for mom's expenses and sent her money so she was happy. She was also living in my condo in Inverrary so she didn't have to pay rent. Eleni and I were very happy and we were certainly enjoying our life. I was one who never had any money or a life and I was doing everything I wanted. I always said when I make it big I will get everything. I never saved; I always spent because I felt when I die I would have done everything I wanted.

On September 24th the Scottsdale Tribune had a two page article with photos about me. It was a great article. Wednesday the 27th Eleni and I drove to Santa Fe and spent the night at the Hilton. The next day we left for Colorado Springs and stayed at the Broadmoor Resort. This was also a wonderful place and had great food. I loved buffalo so I was in my glory.

The 29th we left for Aspen, Colorado and stayed at the Ritz Carlton. What a beautiful place. The drive to Aspen was over the Continental Shelf in a snow storm. There were many cars off the narrow road, but I had the Land Rover which was great. Actually, they had closed the road after we started up, but we made it okay. We rode the chairlift to the top and shopped during the day.

October 1995 -Eleni Gets Her Gun Permit

Sunday October 1st, we left for Durango. We stayed at the Best Western because there were no fancy hotels there. It was nice and we had dinner at a lovely place. Tuesday the 3rd it was time to go home. We had a wonderful time and this part of the country was just beautiful. Sunday, the 8th, I flew to Florida and noticed mom was forgetting so much and I was worried. I knew she was in a demented state and I watched her closely. I returned to Arizona for the weekend and Saturday, Eleni went for her concealed weapon permit and class. She did very well as a matter of fact; she scored two points more than I did when I took the test. I bought her a 357 magnum, which is what she wanted. The gun was bigger than her, but she was a good shot. Sunday the 15th I went to New Jersey and returned home on Friday the 20th. I did many things around the house the next week and when my landscaping company came we added some new plants. Friday the 27th Eleni went to Findlay, Ohio to train IENGA members and returned home on Friday November 3rd.

November 1995 – Peter Vallas Associates, Inc.'s Anniversary

Saturday, November 4th, we had dinner at the Chaparral and Sunday, lunch at the Quilted Bear. I began to notice I was gaining weight, which was a sign of success, I guess. On Wednesday the 8th I had to go to Tampa on a case and returned on the 10th. The 9th was our 16th anniversary of Peter Vallas Associates, Inc. The company was growing at a fast rate and my son was making a big name for himself. Sunday the 12th I had a dinner party at home for the staff at the Gardner's Tennis Resort.

The next two weeks we ate out at our usual favorite places and Sunday the 19th we went to church. Tuesday the 21st my cousin Chickie and her husband Leon came to stay with us. One day I cooked and we drove to Sedona. We always took our company to Sedona because it was a beautiful sight. That night we took them to dinner at El Trillo. The next day was Thanksgiving and Eleni made her famous turkey dinner. She made the best turkey than anyone. Saturday the 25th, we all went to dinner at El Trillo's. El Trillo was a small restaurant in Scottsdale, which specialized in buffalo, elk, and many other wild game dinners. It was great. They even had rattlesnake, which was plentiful in Arizona. On the 26th they left and I flew to Florida. I went to Jim's house and left with the Eleni II for a day's run to Miami alone.

December 1995 – Eleni II and Arizona

I brought the Eleni II back to Jim's on December 1st and returned to Arizona. We went to Palm Court for my birthday on December 5th for dinner and this was Eleni's gift.

On Friday the 8th I went to the New Jersey office. Petee and I had a lot to do with company business. Mary Ann was not happy with Petee being the boss. She kept calling me with complaints. I told her she had to accept that because Petee was taking over the operations as CEO. Mary Ann used to be a school teacher before I hired her. One thing she did was she always did her job well and I liked her. December 20th Eleni flew to New Jersey, but her plane was three hours late. We stayed at the Marriott in Park Ridge, NJ. The next day we took Eleni's cousin, Flo and Sid to dinner at Solari's Restaurant in Hackensack. This was my favorite place since 1979 when I started my business. The owner, John Solari and his son Marco, who worked for his father, were good friends of mine. Mom had been up at my Uncle Walter's for a few days and Eleni and I picked her up on Friday December 22nd and drove to my sister's in Syracuse, NY for Christmas.

Christmas Eve was always wonderful at Linda and Tom's. She was a great cook and loved to entertain. Eleni and I were staying at the Marriott at Carrier Circle and Monday the 25th Eleni got the flu and was very sick in bed. Tuesday December 26th she stayed in bed again. We all went to Linda's for dinner and I came back early. Wednesday, Eleni was still sick but came to Linda's for dinner. Thursday Eleni was still sick, but came to Linda's for dinner again because Bernice and her husband Bob were there. Friday Eleni was a little better but stayed in bed. Saturday our friends, Joe and Marcia arrived from Massachusetts and also stayed at the Marriott. New Year's Eve the party was at Linda's. About 30 people showed up and it was great. January 1st we had a brunch at Linda's then mom went back to New Jersey. Eleni and I went back to Arizona.

January 1996 – Moving out of Arizona

January 11th, Eleni and I had lunch at the Black Angus and discussed selling the house. Friday the 12th we called Virgil from the real estate office who sold us the house, and he put it on the market. Saturday we had dinner at Palm Court. I had taken up a new hobby of finding stones and polishing them. I walked around our two acres between the Saguaros because the snakes were all in for the winter. I really enjoyed it at this time of the year. We even had light snow occasionally. I was still feeding the animals even some by hand. They loved it when I would talk to them in the morning and it was funny that they would be all outside in my special clearing at 4:30am. I was always an early bird. I loved mornings watching the sun come up and nature at its best. Even the rodents would visit me. I had one pack rat that would take food from my hand. When I was away, Eleni would throw food out to them but never go near them. Imagine having a wife like that to feed my animal friends. She was the best.

Sunday, January 21st I went to Tampa to discuss a book deal with Velnet Click Productions and returned several days later. January 29th we went to dinner with Dr. Jon Stathakis and his new wife Ann whose wedding we attended.

February 1996 – Helping Family Members

February 4th, I left for New Jersey as a new Delta million miler. Delta was the best and I always flew first class and over the years I got to know most of the flight attendants. I remember when I had nothing and now my life had changed so much. Eleni and I always flew first class and when we went to a hotel it had to be the best suite and always with two bathrooms. I know a lot of the family on my mother's side talked about me, but it was jealousy. There were several cousins I helped out with money when they needed help and I never asked for it back. One cousin in particular who got divorced as most of them did, I helped quite a bit. Today's day and age that is what they did, get married, have a kid or two then get divorced and have the ex-husbands pay. Not that these guys were all bad but they were stupid. My son Petee always said he would never get married and would not have kids. He was living the life of a rich bachelor with many girls. He was great looking and just like his father in many ways. We were like kids when we were together and always, as a pair, the life of the party. After quite a while he was finally getting along with his mother at my insistence. Irene had married again to Raymond Brew and they had a son, Ray, Jr. It was funny back a few years ago before I met Eleni, I had been seeing Ray Brew's sister for a while and didn't know it was Irene's husband's sister. Life goes on and so does my adventure.

February 4th, I went to New Jersey. Eleni had an open house that day. I flew back because we had an open house for agents and served food. Eleni and I disappeared to the Quilted Bear for lunch. February 9th we went to Rolland's for dinner and the next day I had my photographer Sylvio and Lynne, his wife, for dinner. Paul Getty, my engineer and his wife Olivia were going to come to dinner but she injured her leg. About Paul; he was a great guy who when I hired him knew nothing about investigative engineering. He loved Arizona and always said he would live here someday. February 15th I was back in New Jersey. Things were the same with Mary Ann and Petee. Petee received a letter of resignation from Mary Ann's daughter who worked for us and was close with Petee for some time. I think she was so sure Petee would not let her go but he did. I had a rule that if anyone left me, they would never be hired back.

Eleni decided to work at the Mayo Clinic in Scottsdale as a volunteer. I was still going there because of my stroke and I was still using a cane because I had no feeling in my left foot. I was asked to make a promo film for the Mayo Clinic which I did. I returned home from New Jersey on Saturday February 24th and we went to dinner at Rolland's. Sunday we went to church then went home.

March 1996 – Preparing for Greece

The first two weeks of March I stayed home to do things around the house. I rested and went in the pool and in the hot tub quite a bit. March 10th I left for Tampa and returned on March 30th. We were preparing for our annual trip to Greece. We went shopping for gifts for the family, which we always did.

April 1996 – My Physical Issues

On April 7th, my sciatica nerve started to give me trouble and I was hurting. April 10th we flew to Cincinnati then to Athens. We arrived on the 11th and were met by cousin Felitsa. We then went to Felitsa's where Linda and Tom were with Katie and Velissairo. That night Eleni and I went back to the Ledra Marriott to get some sleep. April 12th we drove to the Plaka to St. Catherine's church where we were married. Good Friday, April 13th we went to St. Antonio's church in Peristeri then to dinner at midnight at Felitsa's.

Sunday, Greek Easter began and the whole family went to Aegina to the home of Felitsa's son's girlfriend's family. The lambs were on the coals and everyone took turns turning them. What a day; great food, wine, and dancing. We drove the car back to the ferry then to the Marriott. Linda and Tom were staying at Felitsa's. Coming to Greece every year to visit my cousins was a thrill; we were so close. Life in Greece was to eat, drink and dance. Food was the priority and no matter where you walked you could smell the breads being baked and all the wonderful odors of spinacoptia, tripotia, baklava, etc. I really got a kick out of all the men sitting outside the stores and Treverna's smoking. The subject was always about the Turks. The Greeks had been fighting the Turks for 800 years over a pile of rocks. I think it was all gossip. My dad's partner John Sophanis was a Turk.

Everyday we ate at someone's house. Wednesday the 17th we went to Alkis and Angeliki's, Katie's daughter's house. They were all great cooks and even the tomatoes in Greece were the best. Usually at lunch we would eat in the Plaka at Hermion Restaurant outside on the terrace. This was one of our favorite places. I was still having trouble with my back, but I was getting along. Friday the 19th Linda, Tom, Eleni, and I met a friend of mine, Cecile and her boyfriend from New Jersey. We all had lunch at Hermion in the Plaka. Saturday the 20th Linda, Tom, Eleni, and I took the hydro foil to Spetsus. We had a great day then returned in the afternoon to Athens.

Spetsis is probably the greenest of the Saronic Gulf Islands. It is covered with many pine groves. It used to be called "Pityou SSA" (Pine-Tree Island). In antiquity, cars are not allowed on the island. Bikes and mopeds are available. Spetses's town is called "Kastelli", which meanders along the harbor and inland in a lazy way. There are beautiful mansions with high walls and greenery. As you stroll along the waterfront, there are many horse drawn carriages to take you around. The beautiful beaches and blue green waters are mesmerizing. Spetses restaurants are just wonderful. I just love it there. At Lazaro's Taverna they have the best homemade retsina in kegs. Again all you do is eat, drink, and dance.

We took a taxi to the Marriott where Tom discovered he lost his camera. All the photos he took were lost and he was very disappointed. Sunday the 21st Linda and Tom flew to Syracuse, NY. Monday Eleni and I went to cousins Katie and Velissairo for lunch. Tuesday Velissairo and Katie picked us up to take us for a drive. I wasn't feeling well that day but we went anyway. On the way back I told Velissairo to pull over because I was going to be sick. Little did I know he would pull over next to an outdoor ice cream place and when I opened the door I threw up in front of it. There were at least 25 people sitting at the outside tables. I was so embarrassed. They took us back to the hotel and I went to bed and had terrible diarrhea and was sick until Saturday the 27th. When I felt a little better on Sunday, we had lunch in the Plaka and dinner at Velissairo's house. Tuesday the 30th was Eleni's birthday and I invited the family to the Kona Kai Restaurant in the Ledra Marriott.

May 1996 – Returning from Greece

Wednesday May 1st, we left Greece and arrived home in Arizona on Thursday May 2nd. It was a long trip, but in first class it was wonderful. Sunday we went to church and then lunch at the Biltmore Fashion Park. The rest of the week we stayed home and rested. Saturday May 11th was the anniversary of when we first got married 16 years ago and we went to dinner at Palm Court. Monday the 13th I flew to Florida for business. I decided to move the Eleni II to the Marriott Marina in Fort Lauderdale on May 16th. It was better because they had a restaurant, bar, tiki bar, and pool. I flew home Friday the 17th. On May 30th we went shopping for a new car and bought a new Mercedes S320, color black. We ate out for the next week.

June and July 1996 – The Casino

On June 3rd we went to the casino and I won $750.00. Sunday June 9th, I went to Florida to my yacht. I moved it to slip 23 which I liked better. Saturday the 15th Eleni flew in and Debbie, her daughter and Mark, her husband went to dinner at the River Watch. Father's Day, mom and her boyfriend Monroe, Jim and Eileen, and Debbie and Mark went to dinner at Brook's Restaurant. Tuesday we had dinner with Paul Getty and his wife Olivia. Wednesday the 19th our friends from Scotland, Shiona and Murdock, and Eleni and I went to dinner at Brooks. Eleni and I cleaned the boat and Saturday, we flew to Arizona. June 30th, I flew to New Jersey for three weeks on business. When I was away Eleni would work at the Mayo Clinic and shop. I came home Saturday the 20th after traveling to my NY and NJ offices. It was good to be home. We didn't have any hits on the house and we continued to eat out and lived a pretty high lifestyle. The adventure was still going on.

Petee flew in and we spent the day in the pool then dinner at Rollands. We had a meeting mostly about Mary Ann whose attitude was getting worse. I told Petee, "Do what you have to do because you are running the office." I trusted my son with the business and always felt he would learn by his mistakes, not that he made many, but he and I had the reputation of being the best when it came to fire and explosion investigations. I was very proud of him and I never knew who his next girlfriend would be but they were all good looking.

August 1996 – Time With My Son

We took Petee to Sedona on August 1st then to Lake Pleasant. That night I made lamb shanks for dinner and Petee returned to New Jersey on Monday.

Saturday the 10th we were going to dinner at Tomaso's and there was a power failure in the valley so we ate in Fountain Hills. Sunday, I left for Florida. Eleni had a house showing in Scottsdale. On August 14ᵗʰ Eleni flew to Florida and we had dinner at the 15ᵗʰ Street fish house with Paul and Olivia Getty.

The next day Debbie and Mark came to the yacht and we sailed to Hawk's Cay. Saturday the weather was bad so we didn't take the yacht to Key West, instead we rented a car. Sunday the weather was bad and was going to get worse so we left for Miami. On the way near the channel by the bridge, we got caught with a lobster trap. The line was wound around the props. I steered the yacht under the bridge and dropped the anchor. I dove under with my knife and it took me one hour to cut loose. The tide dropped and when I went to start the engines they wouldn't start. I called Sea Tow and about an hour later they arrived. Both water separators were clogged and he had to replace them. It cost me $250.00. We headed to Miami on the inside of the intra-coastal waterway through Biscayne Bay during two heavy storms with lightning. Mark was as useful as tits on a bull. Debbie sat with me on the bridge and watched the charts and markers. We arrived wet, but safely at the Miami Marina. We cleaned up and had dinner at Monti's. The next morning we had good weather and returned to the Marriott Marina. I washed the boat and then we ate at the Rainbow Palace, the best Chinese restaurant that exists with French service, flowers and tablecloths. It was very expensive. For two, with drinks the bill would come to about $175.00 but the best Chinese food I had ever had. Tuesday we had dinner at the Marriott, but "hot headed" Jim walked out. Jim always had a short fuse, but he was a nice guy. Jim and Eileen had both retired from the U.S. Boarder Patrol. We were good friends for a long time, but I didn't go after him. Wednesday the 21ˢᵗ, we had driven to Brook's and Eleni and I flew home the next day.

September 1996 – Marketing Promotions in NJ

On September 15ᵗʰ, I flew to New Jersey and on Saturday the 21ˢᵗ Eleni flew to New Jersey and we stayed at the Marriott in Park Ridge. Eleni worked with Petee doing marketing in Connecticut. On Friday the 27ᵗʰ Eleni went to visit her parent's graves. On Sunday the 29ᵗʰ Eleni flew to Syracuse to work for Petee on marketing in Buffalo, Syracuse, and Rochester, NY.

October 1996 – The MSH Entertainment Contract

October 5ᵗʰ Eleni flew back to Arizona and I flew back on the 6ᵗʰ of October. I left for Los Angeles on the 8ᵗʰ and Eleni flew in on the 12ᵗʰ and we stayed at the Peninsula Hotel.

Sunday we went to Michael's house and met with Shelley's family. Monday we had lunch at the Stage Door Deli and dinner at the La Doce Vita in Beverly Hills. Tuesday the 15ᵗʰ Eleni returned to Arizona with me; a 6 ½ hour drive. October 19ᵗʰ, we had dinner at Palm Court and then we went to church.

On October 24th a representative from a book publisher came to Arizona for a meeting with me. October 27th I flew to Florida and worked on the yacht. On October 28th I had discussions with Bob from MSH Entertainment about a contract for another movie. I flew to Los Angeles and signed a contract with MSH Entertainment. They gave Petee and me 30,000 shares of stock in MSH.

November 1996 – Back to Work

I came home on November 13th. The next day I had a case in Mesa and did it in one day. Friday Linda's friends from Syracuse, Nancy, Ernie, and Brenda came to our house for lunch. November 25th, I went to the Mayo Clinic in Scottsdale for tests and again on November 27th.

December 1996 – Physical Issues and Meeting with Petee

I was going for my colon x-ray on Monday the 2nd so I had to prepare. I had the test and on December 4th and a heart exam. Thursday December 5th I was 56 years old and I can't believe how time flies when you are having fun. December 6th, I flew to New Jersey to meet with Petee then I flew to Florida. Eleni flew in on December 22nd and was staying until January 4th. We had dinner with Mark and Debbie that night at the Marriott.

Monday, December 23rd, Eleni and I had dinner at the Rainbow Palace. Christmas Eve we had Cess and Todd, friends of ours along with Joe and Mary Ann Coletti. Christmas day I had mom, Debbie, and Mark to the yacht and took them to dinner at Largo Mar. The 26th my friend Philip picked us up and took us to my cousin Lorraine's. Philip wanted to date Debbie Cahill, my goddaughter. Friday the 27th Petee and Raymond "Irene's son" and Petee's half brother came to see us. Saturday Petee and Raymond came to the boat and met Lee, one of Petee's girlfriends. Later we had cocktails on the yacht. Sunday, Petee and Raymond went jet skiing and then lunch at the Marriott and they all went back to New Jersey. I liked the Marriott Marina. I had met a guy named John Cordes and his girlfriend Susan. John was a bit rough and a heavy drinker. He had a 53 foot Hattaras a few slips away from me and he just had it refurbished. Monday the 30th we had dinner at Pisano's with our friends, Veronica and George Thorne, then went to their house on Las Olas Isles where we used to live.

January 1997 - The Holiday

I had a party New Year's Eve at the Largo Mar and invited mom, Debbie, Mark, Lauren and Rob, Lorraine, Danny, Philip, Debbie Cahill, Paul and Olivia. It was a great night. New Year's Day, Eleni and I went to Brooks for dinner. January 2nd we all went to Lorraine's for dinner including Philip. Philip and Debbie Cahill spent a lot of time together. January 3rd I took Eleni to see the 54 foot Hattaras that John was going to sell. Philip came over to discuss buying a house or condo in the future and we went to the Tower Club for dinner. January 4th Eleni flew back to Arizona. I was again negotiating with MSH for book rights and they gave me another 5,000 shares of stock. I flew home to Arizona and Eleni and I had dinner at "The Other Place", sister of the Quilted Bear. The next week we ate out at the Palm Court, Chaparral, and LaLaconda. Paul and Olivia Getty came to stay with us for a week. The next day I made a big breakfast and we all went into the Town of Fountain Hills. We had dinner at Chaparral's. The next day I lent Paul my Land Rover so he and Olivia could drive to Sedona. Paul had a piece of property there. They returned the next day and again we had dinner at the LaLaconda. Sunday the 19th Paul and Olivia left. Monday I had to go to Tucson and returned to have dinner at the LaLaconda again on Sunday the 26th then I went to the NJ office, and then to Florida.

February 1997 – My Sister Linda

Linda came to visit mom and stayed at my condo. Eleni flew to Florida on the 1st and I took both of them to a private Symphony Guild Party. Linda stayed on the yacht that night. Sunday, Linda left and Eleni and I met with Sid and Flo, and, Debbie and Mark. Monday we took mom to dinner and we had an argument because mom was starting to get dementia and was getting difficult to deal with.

February 3rd was Petee's birthday and he was 33 years old. He was doing a great job and he loved it. We had dinner with my godmother Hazel, her brother Tom Manos and his wife Kelly. Mom came to the boat on February 4th and we took her to Piasanos. I always took mom grocery shopping every week which was an experience. On February 6th, I had a fight with my sister Linda on the phone over mommy and I hung up. The pressure I had with mommy was getting bad. She would call me ten times a day yelling about going back up north. I felt bad after I hung up from Linda, but we spoke later and things were okay.

I was still speaking to John Cordes about possibly buying his yacht. I told him I had to sell mine first. Friday, February 7th we took Lorraine and Danny to dinner at the Marriott and Saturday Eleni flew home. I returned to Arizona on the 13th. On Valentine's Day we went to Palm Court and Saturday we ate at LaLaconda. I was gaining weight wearing extra large shirts with a 40 inch waist, and weighing 220 pounds. We were eating out so much. Eleni never gained a pound. She was always about 100 pounds. Sunday I left for Florida and on February 28th we had another open house in Arizona.

March 1997 – A Visit with Paul and Olivia Getty

March 1st Eleni came to Florida and we had dinner with Paul and Olivia.

Monday Eleni and I went to Palm Beach to look at the Marinas then we went to Worth Avenue. That night Philip met us at Brook's for dinner. Tuesday, I met with John Cordes and Susan. John had a buyer for the Eleni II and we discussed my buying his yacht, "Spotless" and spotless it was. We had dinner at the Rainbow Palace. Originally I paid $190,000 for the 42 foot mainship and, I, after eight years sold it for the same. Friday March 7th I closed on the 54 foot Hattaras and changed the name from Spotless to Eleni. Eleni flew home March 8th and I had to move all my things to the new boat. Then I went to New Jersey and returned home on March 15th. Diane Sullivan who worked for us a number of years took over Mary Ann's job as Petee's assistant. Petee decided to have my Land Rover picked up and brought to New Jersey on the 21st of March. Saturday the 29th, we returned to Florida and began to shop and buy new things for the yacht.

April 1997 – Taking Care of Mom

Wednesday, April 2nd Shiona and Murdock paid us a visit on the boat. The next day Eleni and I had dinner at the Tower Club. Friday I took mom to get her hair done then to Publix for her shopping. Saturday Eleni and I ate dinner at the Rainbow Palace. Sunday the 6th Lorraine, Danny, and Jennifer, their daughter stopped by the boat. Eleni and I liked the new "Eleni" and had the yacht name painted and added new decorations to our taste. Eleni returned home on April 8th to Arizona. I stayed until April 14th then went back to Arizona. That week we had dinner on the 17th anniversary of our wedding in Greece at the LaLaconda.

Saturday the 19th we had dinner at the LaLaconda and Sunday I flew back to Florida. I had a lot of things being done to the yacht. Eleni flew in on Saturday the 26th and we had dinner at Largo Mar with Debbie and Mark. Sunday the 27th was Greek Easter. I made the traditional dinner and invited Lorraine, Danny, John, and Susie.

May 1997 – Eleni's Birthday and Mother's Day and the Lottery

On April 30th it was Eleni's birthday and we went to the Tower Club. Saturday Eleni returned to Arizona and I stayed. Mother's Day was the 11th of May and I took mom, Debbie, and Mark to Brook's. The next day I returned to Scottsdale. I missed my Dallas connection and I got home four hours late. Wednesday the 14th we had people to see the house, then we went to the LaLaconda for dinner. May 16th Eleni had her trigger thumb operated on and then came home. The next day we had dinner at the LaLaconda.

Sunday I was back to Florida. Eleni had her stitches out Friday the 23rd at the Mayo Clinic. I was busy making changes on the boat. This was another great adventure and Eleni and I loved it. Eleni flew in to Fort Lauderdale on May 30th,

Memorial Day. We had a beach barbeque with John, Susan, and her son Robert. On Saturday May 31st, Debbie and Mark came to the boat. Sunday, Eleni and I went to dinner at Brook's.

Monday June 2nd mom called and was screaming that she won the lottery. She had all six numbers and the drawing was $16 million. I told Eleni and I jumped in the car and raced to the condo. I was so excited I was shaking. I kept saying $16 million, $16 million and already I was spending the money. I got there and mom was almost crying. She handed me the ticket with the numbers 5-7-27-30-32-37. Then she said they were the numbers she played and she showed me a piece of paper with the same numbers on it that she wrote down when she went to Publix. I almost died. Yes, those were the numbers she wrote and it matched the ticket because she played them. They were not the numbers in the newspaper. I could have killed her and she already called everyone before I got there. She still didn't believe me until I showed her several times. I went home pissed as they say. Eleni had a good laugh.

June 1997 – Boat Problems

June 3rd, Eleni and I left Bahia Mar Marina for Ocean Reef Club in Key Largo. When I got out in the ocean both engines were overheated and the alarm went off. I slowed the boat to idle then returned to Bahia Mar Marina. I called a diver and he said the entire bottom was filled with moss and barnacles. I was pissed that John lied to me, when he said he had the bottom done. The diver cleaned it, and the next morning Eleni and I left. The weather was beautiful and we ran at 18 knots through Hawk Channel. The ocean was calm at two feet. We arrived at 11:15am. We had dinner at the Islander and had drinks with our friend, the barmaid Anita.

The next day we went to the pool, had lunch at the raw bar and dinner at Carysfort. Friday, June 6th we left for Bahia Mar Marina. It was a good trip until we hit the Fowley Rocks and the ocean got sloppy. We arrived at our slip E-358 at 11:15am, and I washed the boat. It ran just fine but I still needed more time to get used to it. The rest of the week Eleni and I ate at the Rainbow Palace, and Bahia Mar Marina. Eleni left on June 8th and I stayed another week to work on the boat. Sunday, June 15th I returned to Scottsdale. I had purchased a new car to keep in Florida next to the boat. It was a four door, color gold, Mercedes.

Monday I went to the Mayo Clinic for a check up. Tuesday we ate at La LaLaconda and again on Thursday. I flew back to Florida on Friday the 20th. June 30th Eleni returned to Florida. I had to go to New Jersey for a meeting with NBC. I returned the next day, July 1st. We had dinner with John, Sue, and John's daughter, Christina and her husband Michael. Wednesday night Eleni and I ate at our private club, the Tower Club. July 3rd we took the yacht to Palm Harbor Marina in Palm Beach.

July 1997 – The Fireworks

We ate dinner at Dempsey's. July 4th, Joe and Mary Ann Coletti came to the yacht to watch the fireworks. Saturday night we ate at Jo's in Palm Beach with Debbie and Mark. Sunday the 6th we met Kelly and Tom and had dinner at the Mediterranean Café. July 7th we returned to Bahia Mar Marina and had dinner at Largo Mar. Eleni returned to Scottsdale Wednesday the 9th. I returned on July 13th.

The 14th I had an appointment with the Mayo Clinic for my heart. We had dinner at LaLaconda. The next day I returned to Florida. One thing I loved about living on the yacht was it was so peaceful. I always got up at 4:30 or 5:00am, made coffee and went up on the bridge to watch the sun come up over the ocean. It was great to feel the trade winds blowing from the ocean and watch the palm trees swaying in the breeze. Cocktails in the evening, was also a favorite event. My adventure continues.

July 27th, Eleni flew to Florida and we had dinner at Largo Mar. Largo Mar was also a private club and very beautiful located on the ocean. I now belonged to three private clubs, the Largo Mar, $1,000.00 initiation fee; $100.00 a month, the Tower Club was $2,000.00 initiation fee and $200.00 a month fee; and Ocean Reef the most exclusive; was $10,000.00 initiation fee, and $2,000.00 a month. Even the Bush's came there. George W. Bush liked to bone fish there. Again the adventure continues. Monday the 28th we went to the Rainbow Palace. The 29th we had dinner at George and Veronica Thorne's house. July 31st Dave Redsicker and his wife, Patty flew down as well as Petee and Diane Sullivan. This was a company staff meeting and they all stayed at Bahia Mar Marina in the hotel.

August 1997 – The Trip to Ocean Reef

August 1st we left for Ocean Reef. They all stayed at the hotel. At 1:30am there were bad storm winds at 35-40 knots. During the day we sat around the pool for a meeting, and had drinks, of course. It was a great time. August 3rd we left for Bahia Mar Marina and the trip was good. Everyone went back to NJ and NY and Eleni and I went to dinner at the Rainbow Palace. Wednesday the 6th Eleni went back to Scottsdale. Sunday the 10th I flew back to Scottsdale because I had a 7:30am appointment at the Mayo Clinic. Then we had dinner at the LaLaconda. Wednesday we went to Old Town in Scottsdale and had lunch. Saturday the 16th I returned to Florida. Tuesday I got my hair cut at Tony's, who was my barber since the early 1980s. He was a great guy and was the lead singer with the "Jersey Shore Band". He had a rough time back in 1993 when his wife left him and she too sang in the band. He lost his business and went to work for Lou's Styling Den. He was still working with Lou all these years. This was a place where you loved to go. We did nothing but laugh and tell stories. I would love to have a sitcom about these two guys. The next few days Ray Blake, my mechanic and Scott Moore worked on the boat.

On the 21st Petee went to Europe and to Greece. Eleni flew to Florida on August 24th and we ate at Bravo's. Eleni and I decided to move the boat to the Town of Palm Beach Marina. August 28th we took the yacht to Palm Beach. We loved Palm Beach Islands, the Kennedy's compound, and all the rich. Worth Avenue was filled with Rolls Royce's, beauties, and movie stars. Our adventure was continuing. Eleni and I had dinner on the yacht that night. The next day we went to the Governor's Club; sister to the Tower Club.

September 1997 – Fire Investigations Continue

We had dinner with Debbie and Mark at Dempsey's. Friday the 5th we had dinner at Casablanca owned by a Greek friend of ours. Saturday Eleni returned to Arizona. September 8th I did a fire investigation in West Palm Beach for Petee. All these years I was still doing fire investigations all over the U.S. where ever and whenever I was needed.

September 14th I flew home and went to the Mayo Clinic for testing the next day, and on the 17th had an MRI at the Mayo Clinic. That week we ate at the LaLaconda twice. I flew back to Florida September 20th. I cleaned the pool even though it was self cleaning, put salt in the water softener, and worked with my landscapers to change some bushes. We had dinner at the LaLaconda.

Eleni ordered our Christmas cards as we always did every year early. I flew to Florida on September 20th. I brought the yacht to Spencer's to have the bottom cleaned and painted.

Mom was starting to get bad. Her friend Monroe called me and said she was going nuts. She stopped going out and would sit by the window every day. I went to Publix and did her shopping for her. I was checking the condo and went into the spare room and noticed towels on the floor near the second bath. The water was shut off in the toilet and I asked her why? She said she didn't do it. I called our plumber and he said the toilet was stuffed up with panties. I could see she was getting worse with her dementia.

Monday I went to the firing range to practice which I did every six months. I was licensed to carry a gun in Florida, NJ, NY, and PA. Tuesday I made a reservation for New Year's at the Palm Beach Yacht Club, which was the 4th PVT club I joined. I got my boat back and cleaned the outside. A few days in the boatyard and it was full of dust. At night I would make my rounds at the cocktail hour to the Tavern owned by a Kennedy and Taboo, Chesterfield's and a few others. I got to know everyone in all the restaurants and clubs. It was quite an experience.

October 1997 - Dining

Eleni flew in to Palm Beach, Sunday October 5th. We went to dinner at Dempsey's.

Monday night we ate at the Tavern. The bartender "Peter" was around for years and used to sing at night. I sang there once in a while, too. Wednesday we ate dinner at the Yacht Club. Thursday, the 9th cousin Lorraine and Dan drove up to the boat and we took them to dinner at the Tavern. Friday our friends Shiona and Murdock came to the boat and we went to the Tavern. Saturday, October 11th, Eleni and I went to the Governors Club for dinner. Sunday October 12th Columbus Day we went to the Marriott Marina in Fort Lauderdale and had lunch with John and Sue.

Eleni left for Scottsdale on Tuesday. Sunday the 19th, I flew back to Scottsdale. This week we ate at a new Chinese restaurant and a Mexican restaurant El Tortitos. Friday, October 24th, I returned to Florida and Petee flew in to meet me. We went to the Tavern for dinner and hit the clubs. Petee stayed until Monday then returned to the office in NJ. Eleni flew in on Tuesday the 4th and we ate on the boat. Wednesday we went to the Tavern for dinner. Thursday we went to the Yacht Club. As you can see we ate out in the best of places.

November 1997 – Debbie and Mark, Eleni's Daughter and Son-in-law

Friday, November 7th we ate at the Brazilian Court Club. Saturday I made dinner for Debbie and Mark on the yacht. Sunday Eleni and I went to mom's with her groceries. After our usual argument between mom and me, Eleni and I went back to Palm Beach for dinner at Casablanca. Sunday the 9th was the company anniversary; 18 years. We had dinner at Casablanca again. They always had great Greek food and belly dancers.

Monday we had dinner at the Tavern with Tom and Kelly Manos, and the next day Eleni returned to Scottsdale. November 15th I went to mom's to shop for her as I did every week. She had been acting crazy on the phone and now she was writing checks and they were bouncing.

The manager from "Citibank" called (they are the best) to tell me her checks were overdrawn. What was happening? She would pay the bill such as Bell South and the next day she would pay it again with the receipt so she was paying all her bills twice. I took her checkbook away and she screamed and cried for an hour. When I left she called me twenty times a day. Eleni flew in on November 24th because Debbie was to have her twins. The next day, November 25th, we were at Good Samaritan Hospital in West Palm Beach and at 2:49pm Jordan was born and at 3:03pm, Hayley was born. Eleni and I scrubbed and put on our gowns and we went in to see them and we even held them. The thing that bothered me most was Mark before the babies were born, he came out in the hall after the delivery yelling that Debbie wasn't pushing enough and if the babies were damaged it was all her fault. That is when I realized what a nut this guy really was. I knew he was lazy because he wouldn't even take the garbage out for her. Debbie did this and Debbie did that. He didn't even know what a screwdriver was.

I left the hospital to go across the street to the Yacht Club and Mark came with me. We ordered a drink and he proceeded to tell the bartender that Debbie was responsible if anything was wrong with the kids. I was ready to knock his teeth out but rather than cause a problem I shut my mouth. From that moment on I had no respect for him. My wife didn't like the way he treated Debbie either.

Thanksgiving Eleni and I went to cousin Lorraine's for dinner. Friday the 28th we were invited to dinner at the Sail Fish Club in Palm Beach. We were invited by a couple who was on the yacht next to us. They too lived on the island in Palm Beach. She was a movie actress many years ago and we became friends. Her name was Rayleen and her husband's name was Mike. Saturday, Debbie and Mark came to the boat with Jordan and Hayley.

Sunday we went to mom's and she was still yelling about her checkbook. I had a bill from Deer Park Water Company for $78.00. I asked her what it was because it was so high. She said it was for her water. I thought to myself if she drank that much she would drown. I went in the spare room and on the floor were 62 gallons of water. I called Deer Park and they cancelled her account. Lorraine had called me that week because mom said she stole her jewelry. I went to mom's and along with her friend Monroe, we found her jewelry in a cloth under the mattress. I knew something had to be done soon, but I didn't know what. Eleni left for Arizona, the plane was late, and she arrived in Scottsdale at 1am.

December 1997 – The Wedding

Wednesday, December 3rd Eleni mailed the Christmas cards. Thursday the 4th my long time accountant, Mike Mongelli came to visit on my yacht. He slept on the couch in the lounge because he had claustrophobia. We discussed business then we went to dinner each night. He returned to New Jersey, Sunday the 7th. Tuesday the 9th I returned to Phoenix.

Saturday, December 13th, Eleni and I drove to Los Angeles for Michael's marriage to Shelley. I had a meeting with Jon Stathakis and MSH Entertainment. We had a suite at the Ritz Carlton at Marina Del Ray in Los Angeles and we ate dinner there. The next day was Michael and Shelley's wedding at the Marriott in Marina Bay. It was outside on the deck and it was cold. After the wedding reception, which was great, Michael played the guitar and Shelley sang. Michael is a professor at UCLA in statistics. Shelley is also in education. After the reception we went to Cooper's Tavern named after the "Cooper" who stole money and jumped out of an airplane and was never found. Michael played along with other friends in a jam session.

Monday Eleni and I drove back to Scottsdale, which took about six hours.

Tuesday I flew to Florida and on December 20th Eleni arrived in Florida. Can you imagine all that money spent back and forth to Florida for the both of us first class? We did get upgraded to first class most of the time, but still it was a lot of money. I think I knew all the attendants and they certainly took care of me. We had dinner on the boat and Debbie and Mark brought the girls over. Monday I did a couple of fire investigations and was also teaching at the Palm Beach Fire Department. The fire within was still there.

Christmas Eve I had a party for eight. Christmas Day we went to mom's, then back to the boat and Debbie, Mark, and the girls came for dinner. December 26th Eleni and I went to Stressa for dinner. Monday the 29th Eleni and I went to Fort Lauderdale and stopped at moms. No comment, then to dinner at Il Tartufo. I knew the owner, Gianni and he had wonderful food and a beautiful place. It used to be the Banyan's because it had two giant Banyan trees in front. Gianni did the place over and it was beautiful. The next day we ate at the Tavern. New Year's Eve we went to the Palm Beach Yacht Club. It was too crowded and some guy with a cigar burned Eleni's dress by accident. New Year's Day I made dinner on the boat "Mexican style", which was great.

January 1998 - Debbie, Eleni's Daughter

January 2nd Debbie and Mark took us to dinner at the new Gingerman, which shortly after went out of business. Mark was such an exaggerator. He thought he was a big shot, but still I kept my mouth shut. I always thought one day Debbie might smarten up and get rid of him.

Saturday, Eleni and I ate at the Tavern and on Sunday we ate at Stressa's. January 5th Eleni went back to Phoenix. I was working a fire on the 8th in Sunrise, Florida and I did a fire in the Keys on the 12th and the 13th. I returned on the 14th and had a meeting with Paul Getty. I returned to Phoenix on Sunday the 18th. Monday, Eleni and I ate dinner at Mr. C's and Wednesday we ate at the Biltmore Resort and on Thursday we ate at a Mexican place. Saturday I flew back to Florida and Eleni flew in and we had dinner at Dempsey's. Monday we ate dinner at Stressa's. Tuesday the 27th Linda, Tom, and Nick went to mom's.

On Wednesday we took Linda, Tom, Nick, Lorraine, and Dan to Il Tartufo's for dinner. The next day Linda, Tom, and Nick came to the boat and we had lunch at Chuck and Harold's. Nicky then left for Tampa. That night we all went to the Tavern for dinner. Friday Debbie brought the kids to see Linda and Tom on the boat. That night we all had dinner at the P.B. Yacht Club and the next day they flew home to Syracuse. That night Eleni and I had dinner at the P.B. Tavern with Nancy and Bob, the president of MSH Entertainment. Sunday I made dinner on the boat for Debbie and Mark, and the girls.

February 1998 – Problems with My Mother and Damage on the Yacht

February 2nd we had a big storm, winds 40 knots and heavy rain. I had some damage to the canvas on the bridge. We went to dinner at P.B. Tavern that night. Eleni returned to Arizona the next day. I was having so many problems with mom. I went to an Alzheimer's class for four hours to try and understand how to be a caregiver. It was helpful, but I think a few more scotches would have helped. She kept saying someone was stealing her rings and jewelry and called me everyday. She wasn't eating much and I found the toaster oven burned one day. The problem was even worse than before. Eleni returned on February 14th and we went to the Governor's Club for dinner. Sunday I made dinner on the boat. Monday we had dinner at Stressa's. Tuesday I did a fire investigation in Fort Lauderdale then in the afternoon Debbie worked and the girls came to the boat. I could see things were getting strained with Mark. I overheard Debbie telling her mom how Mark does nothing to help her.

Wednesday we ate at the Palm Beach Tavern. Friday the 20th we ate at the Raindancer and Saturday at the P.B. Yacht Club. We loved eating out as you can see, and we always got the royal treatment. Eleni returned home on February 23rd.

March 1998 – The Scottsdale House

On Thursday, I told Eleni to go buy a St. Joseph's statue and bury it upside down next to the house. Everyone said if you do that the house would sell. The same day back in Florida I went to HRS to discuss mom's situation. It was a good meeting and I knew what I had to do. The first week of March I did two fires and on March 9th I returned to Arizona. I worked around the house putting salt in the water softener, cleaning around the pool, etc. That week we ate at Mr. C's and Tonte Verde then on Saturday the 12th I returned to Florida. Eleni showed the house that week and I worked on the yacht. I had dinner with Philip at the Greek Isles in Fort Lauderdale on March 19th. Eleni arrived at the boat on March 23rd and we had dinner at Stressa's. Tuesday we had new blinds installed on the yacht and we had dinner at Paul and Olivia's house. Thursday we took Lorraine and Danny to the Governors Club for dinner. Eleni and I were busy this week getting new blinds, and a new top on the yacht. Friday, Eleni and I ate at the Palm Beach Tavern. Saturday we ate at the Palm Beach Yacht Club. Sunday I made dinner on the yacht for Debbie, Mark, and the girls. March 31st Eleni returned to Phoenix.

April 1998 – Business Meetings

Eleni had two house showings on April 2nd. My vice president in the NY office, David Redsicker, and his wife Patty, and Petee and Diane Sullivan from the NJ office came to Florida for business meetings. They stayed at the Colony Hotel. Saturday night we all went to dinner at the P.B. Yacht Club. Sunday we all ate at Aqua Terra; a restaurant owned by Charlie Palmer.

Monday everyone left and I had the yacht pulled to have the bottom cleaned and painted. I took a room at the Palm Beach Hotel for four days and picked up the boat on Thursday the 9th. I worked on the yacht the rest of the week cleaning and waxing. Eleni returned to Palm Beach on our wedding anniversary, April 16th. I had sixteen roses, the same as the ones she had on our wedding day. We went to Debbie's and that night we ate at Aqua Terra for dinner.

The next day, Saturday the 18th, Eleni and I went to Fort Lauderdale for a mini boat show and we went on Jorge and Betty's yacht at Pier 66. We then went back to Palm Beach for dinner on our yacht. The next day was Greek Easter and I cooked to the hilt, roasted lamb, potatoes, carrots, stuffed grape leaves, Zaziki, cheeses, olives and of course baklava. We invited Debbie, Mark, and the girls, Lorraine, Danny, Jennifer, Catherine, Stephanie, Ces and Todd, Philip and Jeannie. We all ate plenty and had a good time. On Monday the 27th Eleni returned home to Phoenix. Petee flew in for a meeting on the 30th. We also met with Bob and Nancy from MSH Entertainment. Petee returned to NJ on the 3rd of May.

May 1998 – Visiting My Mother

I went to mom's and as usual she was nasty and sitting by the window. I did her shopping but she was always eating the sweets and not her regular food. I now had to check on her twice a week and it was a pain driving from Palm Beach to Fort Lauderdale. On the 7th mom called me and she was crazy on the phone. She was going back to her family in NJ. I told her they were all dead, but she didn't understand.

I returned to Phoenix on Sunday the 10th. Eleni had her former coworker Paula Halpern at the house for two days and she had just left. Tuesday we went to downtown Scottsdale to Mr. C's and they were closed due to a fire so we ate at the Peking Palace. Thursday the 14th I had to go to the Mayo Clinic for another check up and that night Eleni and I ate at the Mexican Restaurant. Saturday I returned to Florida. I couldn't stay away long because of mom. She was always forgetting things. May 23rd Eleni returned to Florida. I had investigated three fires that week. We ate at "Charlie Palmer's" Aquaterra Restaurant that evening. May 26th was Jim Marshall's birthday and he had been in the hospital. We ate dinner at his house. The next day we ate at the Palm Beach Tavern. Thursday we had dinner with Tarsi and John, friends of ours, who owned many Wendy's, at the Mediterranean. Friday I had trouble with my radio on the bridge so I removed it and took it to Larry Smith's Electronics for repair. We went to dinner at Aqua Terra that night. Saturday Eleni and I ate at the Governors Club and she returned to Phoenix the next day.

June 1998 – The Christening

On June 1st, my friend Jim had an operation and I went to see him. I went to mom's and shopped for her. I worked on the boat all week and went to the captain's meeting for the boat club on the 9th. I had to replace an A/C unit on the boat on the 12th. June 21st, Eleni returned to Florida and we ate at Aqua Terra. We ate out all week at our usual places and on Friday Eleni brought Michael and Shelley to see the boat because they were staying at Debbie's. The girls were being christened at St. Michael's church in Palm Beach, Sunday June 28th. We took everyone out to the Aquaterra for dinner; all 14 of us. Sunday was the christening and we all went to a little reception at Concordia East and I made a salad and other things.

July 1998 – My Training Classes and Fire Cases Continue

July 1st Michael and Shelley, and Debbie, Mark, and the girls came with us to dinner at Stressa's. The next couple of days I cleaned the yacht and cooked for July 4th. On the 4th Debbie, Mark, the kids, Jim and Eileen were on the boat for the fireworks. Everything was good. The next day we ate at the Aqua Terra. Eleni flew home to Phoenix on July 6th. On Thursday the 9th I did a fire investigation in La Belle, Florida. I was averaging about two cases a week and still training fire departments. I realized that being a success meant hard work and that was what Petee and I continued to do and it all boiled down to the fire within. I had planned a trip to Lucaya on Grand Bahamas Island. We always liked it there especially since they had a casino. I began to prepare for the trip, waxed the hull, fueled and stocked up on provisions. I also invited Philip Vias to come along. We were going to leave early in the morning on July 22nd. July 17th I had Broward Fire Equipment re-inspect all fire extinguishers and our automatic extinguishing systems. Petee returned from Greece on July 19th the same day Eleni returned to Florida. I always couldn't wait for her to return so we could be together and go to dinner. There was a captain's meeting on the 21st and on Wednesday the 22nd at 8:30am.

Eleni, Philip, and I left the Port of Palm Beach for Grand Bahamas Island. We took a course of 111 degrees to Freeport, approximately 78 nautical miles. The weather was clear but crossing the gulfstream can be a challenge. The gulfstream is one of the great currents and flows north. It moves about 20 miles offshore between 3-5 knots. I set my course for Freeport and made the necessary adjustments. As we began our crossing the winds picked up and the seas went from 3 to 5 feet to 7 to 10 feet which made our trip a bit rough. Once we crossed the Gulf Stream, I adjusted my course to Bell Channel. We stayed offshore about two miles to avoid the shoaling on both sides of the approach to Bell Channel. We arrived and the seas were 2 to 4 feet as we went down the center of the channel. I told Eleni and Philip to prepare the lines and fenders for docking, and put up the Yellow Quarantine flag. I radioed the marina and received instructions to tie up at Slip 606 and await clearing of Bahamian customs. We waited about a half hour to clear and the customs officer was arrogant as usual. In all the trips I made over the years it was the same except at Cat Cay. Then you had to tip him besides. He checked my guns and ammo, our passports, then I gave him $50.00 and he left. I was now able to take down the yellow flag and put up the Bahamian Courtesy Flag. I fueled up with 227 gallons in the tank. I burned about 32 gallons an hour mainly because of rough seas. I washed the boat and then had to repair a failed bilge pump. I always carried spare parts in case we needed them. The first night we ate at the Ferry House and we all went to bed early. Thursday we went to the pool and had lunch at Fat Boys and dinner at our favorite Ruby Swiss. I always hired a limo from our Bahamian friends, Mary and Willard Halpern drove us to the Princess Casino and after to the marina. I would never drive in the Bahamas because they drove on the opposite side, same as London. We won $400.00, and on Friday we ate at the Ferry House again. Saturday we ate lunch at Zorbas, a Greek place, and we met a friend of Philip's from Fort Lauderdale. I invited our members of the Yacht Club for cocktails on our yacht. That afternoon we went to the Princess Casino and we met our travel agent Carol and Larry from Total Travel. That evening we ate at Luciano's with the club.

Sunday we left the Bahamas at 7:30am and the weather was good and the seas were 2-3 feet. We arrived back in Palm Beach at 2pm and I called customs for clearance. Then we went to dinner at Aqua Terra. When we got back to the boat, we discovered a leak coming from the rudder packing gland. I called Ray in Fort Lauderdale and he immediately came and repaired the gland. Then I pumped out the water. Monday the 27th I installed a new bilge pump and Eleni was cleaning up. We had dinner on the boat that night.

Tuesday we went to mom's with her groceries then we went to Philip's apartment and then went to OPA Taverna in Hollywood for dinner. Wednesday, we went to dinner at Brook's with John, Sue, his daughter Christina and her husband Michael. Friday, July 31st Eleni returned to Phoenix and I went to mom's because she kept calling and yelling at me. Then I went to Lil Reds for lunch. I returned to Phoenix Sunday the 2nd because I had a PSA test of 4.5 and had a biopsy scheduled at the Mayo Clinic the next morning. I was a nervous wreck on Monday, but they knocked me out and I didn't feel a thing.

August 1998 - Cancer

Tuesday, August 4th, Eleni and I went to the Bamboo Club for dinner. Wednesday

I did things around the house and we then went to dinner at Ray's Pacific Rim. Thursday morning the 6th, I was in my office and the Mayo Clinic called and told me I had cancer consisting of five tumors in my prostate. I went cold and told Eleni. I had a meeting the next day to discuss what treatment I would take. We ate dinner home and I was quite upset. I had a few Glenlivet scotches and went to bed. Friday, I went to the store and bought a few books on prostate cancer then saw the doctor. He suggested I have a radical operation and wear a colostomy bag temporarily for eight weeks. My alternative was to have radiation seeds put in my prostate or total radiation. We went to dinner at Gardner's Tennis Ranch that night and I returned to Palm Beach the next day which was the 8th.

Monday the 10th I had mom sign a release for her life insurance policy to cash in her policy because if I had to put her in a nursing home, they would get the money so this way she would have it. It would only be $9,000.00, but at least I could put it in the bank. I researched all week on my cancer issue and decided to get the radiation. Eleni flew in on Monday the 17th and we ate at the Palm Beach Yacht Club. It was lobster night. Eleni and I discussed my decision about the radiation and she agreed with me. During the week we ate at the Palm Beach Tavern, and at Carmines, and I worked on the boat on Friday the 21st, then Eleni and I went to mom's to shop for her, then we went back to the boat.

I must say that Eleni was very good to mom and I would never forget it. Some daughter-in-laws would not want to be bothered, but Eleni was great. When I was out of town Eleni would drive to Fort Lauderdale to shop for mom. On Monday the 24th, I went to the cancer institute to get set up for my treatments. On Wednesday the 26th I had my first of 38 treatments of radiation. Eleni returned to Arizona on Sunday the 30th. I had to go to the hospital everyday except Saturday and Sunday and I began to get tired everyday.

September 1998 – Mom and Monroe

Eleni arrived in Florida on September 15th and Monday Debbie and the girls came over for a visit and that night we ate dinner at the Palm Beach Tavern. The next two days we ate on the boat. Thursday we ate dinner at Aqua Terra's. Saturday the 19th Petee came in and we went to the Palm Beach Yacht Club. Sunday the 20th Petee and his friend Karen had dinner on the yacht. The next day he left for New Jersey. Tuesday Eleni and I went to mom's and Monroe was there. We stayed for awhile then went to a captain's meeting and then went home.

A storm was approaching which would become Hurricane George. On Wednesday the 23rd, Eleni and I moved our yacht to the Bluff's Marina in Jupiter which was a safe lagoon. We prepared for the storm at Slip F-9. My friends Kelly and Tom Manos came to the boat and we went to Nick's Tomato Pie for dinner. That night and early morning we had winds of 50-70 knots but the yacht held up fine. The next night we went to Carmine's for dinner. Saturday the 26th we brought the boat back to Palm Beach and had dinner at the Palm Beach Tavern. Sunday, Eleni went back to Arizona. I went for my radiation every day and Wednesday I went to mom's and to Tony's for a haircut. Mom was getting worse and I knew it wouldn't be long before I had to do something.

October 1998 – The New Car

On October 5th, I brought a new Lincoln and got rid of the old Mercedes. I did a fire investigation and taught a class at IENGA. Eleni arrived from Arizona on Saturday the 10th and we had dinner at Aqua Terra. Sunday Debbie, Mark, and the girls, and Lorraine and Danny, came to dinner. Wednesday, Eleni was in bed with a virus along with Jordan, Lorraine, and Debbie. Thursday I went to mom's and made dinner on the boat. Friday we saw Debbie and I knew she was having trouble with Mark. She was taking good care of the girls but Mark wouldn't do anything to help her, not even take out the garbage. That night Eleni and I went to dinner at Aqua Terra's.

I decided to get a new carpet for the lounge in the yacht and I had my carpet man over on Saturday the 17th. Then we went to Casablanca for dinner. Monday Eleni went to Debbie's to watch Hayley, while she took Jordan to the doctor. Tuesday we ate dinner at the Mediterranean and Wednesday at Aqua Terra. I was really tired from the radiation which had ended that week. Saturday night we ate dinner at Casablanca and Sunday I made dinner on the boat. Saturday the 24th Eleni returned to Arizona. Eleni called and said someone came to look at the house on Tuesday for the second time. Hopefully we would have it sold soon.

November 1998 – 19 Years in Business

On Friday the 6th the people came back to look at the house again. I was busy on the yacht installing a new water pump and cleaning. November 9th marked my 19th year in business. I couldn't believe it. I had investigated about 9,000 fires over this period and still had the fire within.

November 11th I went to mom's and she was yelling and screaming that Lorraine was stealing her jewelry and sneaking in the apartment through the attic. She was getting impossible to handle. I had to leave because I was having a new wooden floor installed in the pilot house. Eleni flew in on Sunday the 15th and I picked my sister Linda up at mom's (Linda had flown in from Syracuse, NY), and we went to dinner at Aqua Terra's.

On Monday I made a buffet on the boat and had Linda, Debbie, Mark, the girls, and Lorraine, and Danny. Tuesday I took Linda to the airport and Eleni and

I had dinner on the boat. Thursday the 19th Eleni and I began our search for an assisted living home for mom. We ate at Aqua Terra's that night discussing the problem with mom. Saturday the 21st I made dinner on the boat with Jim and Eileen. I made ossa buca and it was wonderful. I planned Thanksgiving on the boat with Debbie, Mark, and the girls. Thanksgiving was great and the bartender, Spencer and his girlfriend, Valerie stopped by for a drink. Spencer and I became friends and he was a great guy. A couple of years later, I found out he was killed while scuba diving in the Keys. As he came up from below his head was cut off by the props.

On Friday the 27th, Petee came down and we went to the breakers where he met up with his girlfriend Karen. We all went to Casablanca for dinner. The next evening we all went to dinner at Aqua Terra, then dancing at the Chesterfield Hotel. Sunday we took them to the airport then Eleni and I went to dinner at Stressa's. I really liked the Palm Beach scene and I think Eleni and I knew we would like to live in Palm Beach on the island someday. It was millionaire's row and was the best town in the US. Houses were in the millions and the world's most famous people lived here. We always ate at the best restaurants, such as Café L'Europe, Brazilian Court, the Breakers, and many others. Worth Avenue was another Rodeo Drive and very festive during the Holidays. I guess since I was living on my yacht at the town of Palm Beach Marina and visited all the bars and restaurants, it was far beyond what I ever thought I would accomplish in life.

I remember in 1975 my ex-wife Rose and I drove here and walked around. I remember her saying, "Look at all these rich bitches." At that time I was working three jobs and we would only eat out once every two weeks at the Red Lobster early bird. Now here I am among the rich and could spend whatever I wanted. Eleni and I loved it here and I knew we would move to Palm Beach.

December 1998 – Moving out of Arizona

December 2nd Eleni flew back to Arizona. We did have a deposit on the house and Eleni had United Movers for an estimate on packing and moving to Palm Beach even though we didn't have a place. We thought we could keep everything in storage anyway until we found a place. I called my good friend Philip Vias, who was a real estate agent, and told him we wanted a condo on the Ocean in Palm Beach. The week of the 7th to the 12th Eleni was busy with the engineering inspection, which took five and a half hours including termite inspection, pool inspection, etc. Sunday the 13th Jim and Eileen, and their daughter Patti came to the house to discuss her handling a garage sale at her house. On the 15th I flew to the NJ office then to the NY office to pay my employees a Christmas visit. We had about 21 employees then and the company Christmas party was going to be in NJ on the 17th. Petee and I were very good to our employees with large bonuses, gave them hospitalization, and a 401K plan.

The Christmas Parties were always at a large restaurant with entertainment. Eleni flew in that day too. The next day we went back to Palm Beach. Philip showed us many condos but the one we liked was on the ocean with an ocean view. It was owned by an elderly couple who were moving to an assisted living facility. We hit it off. He was an ex-Navy man. We had them on the boat for a drink. We also took them to dinner at Palm Beach Tavern. This was not normal when you are buying a house but I always did what I wanted.

On Wednesday the 23rd, Eleni and I went to the Café L'Europe to celebrate after putting a deposit down, and signing a contract when they accepted the offer. We were happy. The condo was very big with no windows only glass doors from one end of the apartment to the other, approximately 3,000 square feet. The condo had a large master bedroom with a large walk in closet, extra large master bath with shower, and separate bath tub, with a make up table and two sinks. There were two other bedrooms and two other baths; the great room was huge, about 35 feet long and 20 feet wide with a built in bar. The kitchen was not as big as I would have liked it, but it was good. We had two separate entrances and it was on the 7th floor. The name of the building was the Barclay. There was beautiful landscaping and underground parking with two spaces. This was one of the largest apartments in the building.

January 1999 – Thanksgiving on the Boat

Christmas Day I went to mom's early and returned to the boat and had turkey dinner with Mark, Debbie, and the girls. New Year's Eve Eleni and I went to Aqua Terra and back to the boat before midnight. Eleni returned to Arizona on January 6th to prepare for our move to Palm Beach. I had been busy with Ronald Kessler, an author, helping him with his book about Palm Beach. When it was published "The Seasons" I was in the acknowledgments with Donald Trump, and others.

While Eleni was in Arizona I had to see the doctor and prepare the boat before I left for Arizona. I arrived in Phoenix and Eleni and I went to dinner at the Chaparral. The next few days we packed all the important items we intended to take in our car. The packers came on Wednesday the 20th and Thursday the 21st. They did a great job. Friday we had the packers for a half day and we had an inspection of the house that afternoon. Saturday Jim Marshall's daughter Patti arrived with her husband and a truck, and removed everything for the yard sale. Monday the 25th the movers came and loaded the truck. They left at 4pm and we stayed at the Scottsdale Hotel overnight. The next day we went to Phoenix and closed on both houses; our Fountain Hills home, and the condo in Palm Beach. Then we drove to Tucson and stayed overnight. The next morning we left Tucson and drove to San Antonio and stayed at the Marriott. We left the next morning and drove all the way to Pensacola, Florida. Saturday we arrived in Palm Beach at the boat at 3pm.

February 1999 - Our Condo in Florida

The next day we went to the condo and found the people still didn't have everything moved out. They were told to be out the next day because our truck was to arrive on Wednesday the 3rd. We let them move the rest of their things out on the 1st, and 2nd. We felt bad because they were old. Finally on Wednesday the truck came and everything was moved in. Thank God we had our yacht to live on until we unpacked, changed the locks, and ordered a new refrigerator, cleaned, etc. for the next two weeks. We also ate out in our favorite places every night. I had an electrician replace the old fuse box with a new breaker box. I began painting the condo and we ordered the west wall of the great room to be mirrored.

Petee called me and said we were doing a Discovery Channel program which would air on the 26th. It was about the "Nanny" case. We were still living on the yacht, until we had all the work done at the condo. We also had two telephone lines added and the cable company ran new cable all over, even in the kitchen.

March 1999 – Eleni's Daughter, Debbie

March 3rd, I gave a class for IENGA. Debbie had gotten a job at a beach restaurant called John G's; famous for its breakfast. Mark was a lazy guy so Debbie had to work. Eleni helped by baby sitting for the girls so Debbie could work. We had moved to the condo and we were doing a lot of shopping and we were having the kitchen done with a new stove, cook top, and new floor. The glass company came on the 12th. Jim and Eileen stopped by and we went to dinner at Aqua Terra. Al Gore was in Palm Beach so traffic was disrupted. Sunday we invited Danny, Lorraine, Philip, and his date for dinner. Wednesday I went to mom's and she was bad and said she was leaving to go to NJ and live with her family. She was getting worse to handle day by day.

Thursday the 18th I flew to NJ. Eleni had the piano man to tune up the piano. I was busy working in NJ and on the 21st I was at the NY office then returned to Florida on the 23rd. Eleni decorated the whole condo. She was busy ordering new faucets and fixtures and counter tops. On the 29th Danny and I replaced the kitchen ceiling tiles. I was out on a fire investigation all day and returned late and ordered Chinese food.

April 1999 – Raymond Brew, Petee's Half Brother is Brought into the Business

Petee and I had a discussion about hiring Irene (my ex-wife's son) Raymond to work for us. I knew Ray and I thought he was a good kid so we hired him. Petee wanted to get Raymond away on his own because Irene was always on his back and Petee wanted him to grow up so this was a good thing.

In the month of April, Eleni and I had all new glass shower doors installed. I was busy all week baking, cooking all kinds of Greek food for Greek Easter. Sunday the 11th arrived and we had Debbie, Mark, the girls, Lorraine and Danny, Jim and Eileen, and Philip and Jeanette for dinner. Everything was great except Mark started trouble with Debbie and they had a fight. It was interesting after they left because everyone said they never liked Mark. He was always a smart ass. Eleni and I never interfered with them or took sides. I believe this was the beginning of the end.

April 16th Eleni and I were married 19 years. We went to dinner at Aqua Terra's. The end of April we had two new A/C systems installed. Sunfest was on Eleni's birthday and Petee came down. We stayed on the yacht to watch the fireworks. Mark, Debbie and the girls came with friends. Bernie and Lorraine came too.

May 1999 – The New Condo and the Family

Saturday, May 1st we went to dinner with Petee at the Ritz Carlton. Sunday I made dinner for Paul, Olivia, and Petee. Petee returned to NJ. The rest of the week we were still busy with the new condo. I went to mom's and she was still a problem but at least I was able to keep her calm and bring food. I began to make meat loaf, chicken, and other things because I didn't want her cooking. Sunday was Mother's Day and I baked a cake for Debbie because she was working at John G's. I think she liked the waitress job because the tips were good. That night John, Suzie, her son, Robert and another friend, Betty came to our house for hors d'oeuvres then I took them to the Café Celini for dinner. The next week we ordered new carpet.

On Wednesday the 19th I taught a marine fire investigation and bomb class at the Palm Beach Police Department and the Florida Marine Patrol. I also had an examination at the Cancer Institute and saw my regular doctor. May 29th I made dinner for Jim, Eileen, Philip, Howie and Shelly. I was pretty much having company for dinner on Sundays as I liked to cook. During the week we always ate out at the Palm Beach Yacht Club, Palm Beach Tavern, Aqua Terra, etc.

Friday the 21st the electrician worked on our new bathroom. I did a couple of fire investigations this month and I almost had to shoot someone. I was already licensed to carry a gun in FL, NJ, NY, and PA. While doing one of my investigations, I was digging through the rear bedroom of a two story home when I heard someone move behind me. I turned and saw this guy with a crow bar over his head. I jumped out of the way and pulled my gun. He turned and ran. I chased him a block, but then decided not to go any further because it was a bad neighborhood.

May 25th the new carpets were installed and the carpenters returned the next day to finish. I must mention Eleni had always been immaculate and a clean nut. I always offered to have a maid but she was stubborn. She was also a perfectionist about everything so clean up was always a major project. It never bothered me because I always let her do what she wanted and we always compromised about things. We only had a couple of arguments in all these years we were married. I think that was what leads to a good marriage. I would go to the boat almost every day to clean and work on projects.

June 1999 – The New Condo in Florida

June 1st the tile man put a new floor in the guest bathroom and we had to get a new toilet. Then we had the entire bathroom mirrored. Saturday Eleni and I went to the Ritz Carlton for cocktails and dinner.

The next week I put the sealer on the new floor. Saturday the 12th I was making bread with my bread machine. The bread burned and caused smoke in the hall. Wednesday the 16th I flew to NJ. I had to do two fires in NY and on the 17th I did a fire in Long Island. Monday, the 21st Eleni picked me up at the airport and we had dinner at home. Wednesday the 23rd Linda and Stephanie flew in to stay at mom's. The few days Linda stayed at mom's made her realize how bad she was getting. Linda went home on the 28th.

July 1999 – Visits with Friends, Employees, and Family

On July 4th we had Paul and Olivia for dinner at the condo because the weather was bad. The next day we went to mom's then to Las Olas Blvd in Fort Lauderdale to shop. We had lunch at Mango's. Eleni bought a vase then we went back to the condo.

On Friday the 16th the plumber came with the new toilet but he came too late because the condo association does not allow workers in the building after 5pm. He came the next day and finished the installation.

Sunday the 18th Jim and Eileen came to the boat and we all prepared to leave on Monday the 19th for a week long trip to see the shuttle take off. Monday we left Palm Beach at 10am and arrived at Fort Pierce Marina at 2:30pm. We ate at the marina. The next morning at 8:30am we left for Melborne. We saw many dolphins along the way, and they would ride alongside the boat for miles.

We arrived at the Melborne City Marina at 1:45pm. I had to back the yacht in because they had a very short slip and we had to board down on the deck. We ate dinner at the Chart House and it was great. The weather was good so far and the waters calm. Wednesday we left at 8am and arrived at Kennedy Point Marina in Tittesville at 12:15pm. This was the worst marina so far and I decided we would never return again. We ate on the boat that night. The space shuttle launch was delayed so we left the next day at 8:15am and arrived at the Grand Harbor Marina in Vero Beach. The marina was good, but they didn't have cable or any restaurant. We ate on the boat and went to sleep early. Friday we left at 8:05am for the Outrigger Marina in St. Lucy. We arrived at noon and had lunch on the boat. This was another lousy marina and very close in area.

Jim cut himself and was treated by Dr. Vallas. We ate at the marina restaurant and went to bed. Saturday I filled the tanks. It cost $392.00 and then we left for Palm Beach at 8:05am and it was a good trip. We arrived home at 1:30pm. Eleni and I went home and made dinner. Sunday I went to wash the boat and returned to make dinner. Debbie and the girls came over to visit at the condo. I could tell something was wrong because Debbie was referring to "Mark" as a "banana head". I did hear her say she would come home from work and he would be sitting there with the garbage overflowing and dishes in the sink and did nothing. He never helped her with anything including the girls. Eleni and I just minded our own business.

The rest of the week, I worked on the boat. Saturday the 31st Debbie, Mark, and the girls came for dinner. The next week I was on the boat every day working and cleaning. I never hired anyone because they never did a good job so I did everything myself. Saturday night we ate at the Pasta House, which was part of the Breakers Hotel.

August 1999 – Eleni II Repairs

August 9th I took the yacht to Rybovich Boat Yard to have the bottom cleaned and painted and get new intake valves. I also made arrangements to move the yacht to the Bluff's Marina in Jupiter. I always liked that marina. It was in a lagoon off the intra-coastal waterway and protected from storm surges during hurricanes. Saturday the 14th Jim helped me move the boat to the Bluff's Marina from Rybovich. Eleni came and we went to dinner at Nick's Tomato Pie.

Monday it rained and we went home to the condo. My friends Vinny and Laura were staying at the "Breakers" on Friday the 20th and I picked them up and we had dinner at the Palm Beach Tavern. Saturday we picked them up and we went to Spoto's for lunch. We later met them at the Breakers Bar and then had dinner at the Florentine Room. The next day I went to mom's and found the toaster oven all burned. I asked what happened and she said she didn't do that. I cleaned everything up and threw it out. I stopped at Home Depot to get cable connectors to hook up and install a flat TV in our kitchen. We had a storm "Dennis" but it wasn't bad.

September 1999 – The Eleni II – Cable Service

September 2nd the cable people came to the boat to hook us up for service. Eleni and I met Paulette and Peter, my Cousin Doris's daughter at the condo and went to the boat for lunch. We stayed on the boat and on Monday Debbie, Mark, and the girls came and we took them to Nick's Tomato Pie for dinner. Tuesday we returned home. I was going to mom's at least three times a week now to check on her. She was calling everyone at all times telling the cousins she wanted to move back to NJ.

Monday the 13th we had to evacuate because of Hurricane Floyd so we went to Jim and Eileen's in Fort Lauderdale. We ate dinner there and I checked on mom. Tuesday it hit but not bad, so Wednesday morning we returned home. On Friday I had new shutters made and installed on all my glass doors. Now, not only did I have the accordion shutters covering the outside of my 80 foot terrace, but now the inside of the terrace was done also. Now, no storm could affect or do any damage to our condo.

Saturday, the 18th I did a fire investigation in West Palm Beach and that night Eleni and I went to Casablanca's for dinner. Sunday I made dinner for Jim and Eileen, and Lorraine and Danny. The 22nd I left for Fort Lauderdale to teach for IENGA. The IENGA people would always get me a hotel room for the four days I taught. I returned home Friday.

Saturday, the 25th, Eleni and I met Petee at La Forge Restaurant in Miami, then we went to the Delano Hotel where he was staying. Monday the 27th the shutter men were done. I made cookies for the girls as I usually did. Petee had planned a PVA retreat for our key employees. Thursday the 30th we picked up Dave Redsicker, my vice president from the NY region and his wife Patti, Amy, my administrative assistant in NY, Petee and Shelly.

October 1999 - Hurricanes

Friday October 1st, I picked them all up at the Colony Hotel and took them on a boat ride in the ocean. They went swimming off my rear swim platform and had a good time. That night we went to Casablanca for dinner. Saturday we had a big meeting at the Colony Hotel. That same night we all went for cocktails at my condo then to dinner at the Four Seasons in Palm Beach.

Sunday the 3rd, everyone left. I was busy the next week cleaning the boat and I also did two fires. Hurricane Irene, a category 1 was on its way so on the 14th, I went to mom's then checked the boat and put extra lines on it. Friday the 15th Eleni and I went to Celini's for dinner and the storm hit. We drove in our underground garage just in time. You couldn't see with the rain and the wind at 75 mph. The next day it was over and I had to go to Dallas, Texas then to San Antonio to do a fire investigation. I returned from San Antonio on the 20th. I was very tired so we stayed home for dinner. Saturday we went to mom's then Eleni and I went to Janeros in Palm Beach for dinner. It was lousy and we would never go back again.

Sunday the 24th I flew to NJ on my routine run to my offices and my accountant Mike Mongelli, who had been taking care of all my finances since 1979. He was a great guy. He had a large firm and did everything by the book. I had a busy week with Petee and returned on Sunday the 31st.

November 1999 – Greek Night

I worked on the boat and cooked all week. Eleni and I had prepared a "Greek Night" for 45 people at the condo. Sunday arrived and Philip tended bar for me and Nicole, one of the waitresses at John G's served the hors d'oeuvres. It was a great party and everyone had a good time. They loved the Greek food. November 9th was our 20th year anniversary of PVA.

November 16th, I did a fire in Fort Pierce then returned in time for dinner with Jim and Eileen. The next day I put up the Christmas decorations including the tree. November 20th Debbie was having a big problem with Mark again and decided to get an attorney. On Tuesday the 22nd she had to call 911 for the police because of him. Thursday the 25th the girls were two years old. Eleni and I were invited to Lorraine and Danny's along with the girls, Debbie, and Mark but Debbie decided not to come because of her situation.

Friday at 2:30am I left for my NY office in Binghamton, NY. I stopped overnight just outside Washington D.C. and the next morning I was in Binghamton until Monday the 29th then went to the NJ office.

December 1999 – My Birthday Celebration

I worked until Saturday the 4th and picked up Eleni at the airport. She flew in for my birthday December 5th and we had dinner at the Stony Hill Restaurant. Our company Christmas party was going to be on my birthday at Solari's Restaurant in Hackensack. It was also the 20th PVA Anniversary party. Petee hired out the entire restaurant for the affair. I had been eating there since 1979 and knew John, the owner, and Marco his son very well. All the guests from out of town were staying at the Great Western Inn in Hackensack. Other guests were Irene, my ex-wife, Raymond Brew, her husband; Raymond Brew their son, Tony, Shelley and her husband Andy all attended the party. The music was great, the speeches were funny and it was a great party. Eleni's cousins, Flo and Sid, and Sheila were also there together with Olivia and Paul, Jim and Eileen, and Debbie Cahill, and we met Gloria, Petee's new girlfriend.

The next day Linda, Tom, David, Patty, Amy, and Petee had breakfast at the Heritage Diner. Eleni and I left to drive home and we got to North Carolina the same day to a Fairfield Inn. The next day we got home at 12 noon. That weekend I had Aunt Dolores, her sister Ethel, and Cousin Debbie Farley for dinner. The next day I had Philip, Lorraine, and Danny for dinner. Tuesday the 14th I had to teach for IENGA and returned home from Fort Lauderdale on Friday the 17th.

Sunday, Debbie and the girls came over. Tuesday December 21st Shelley and Michael had a baby girl Sarah Adalia in Los Angeles. On Christmas Eve I had Jim, Eileen, Lorraine, Danny, Philip, Debbie Cahill, Dawn, Danielle, Catherine, Debbie, and the girls for dinner. Christmas Day we went to mom's and brought dinner for her, then we went to Jim and Eileen's for dinner. Monday the 27th we went to Jim and Eileen's then we all drove to Adventure Mall in Miami to buy caviar and foie gras.

January 2000 – The Holidays

New Year's Eve Eleni and I stayed home. I hate New Year's Eve and so I made filet mignon and lobster tails along with the caviar and foie gras. New Year's Day I had a big dinner for Lorraine, Danny, Jim and Eileen, and Philip. I made roast pork with stuffing, vegetables, and German sausage soup with homemade deserts. We had a great time.

January 3rd, I went to the doctor to prep for my colonoscopy. Because I was on Coumadin I had to be admitted and put on Heparin IV. I had two polyps removed and was released on Friday the 8th. I had to give myself two Heparin needles in my stomach every day until January 15th.

I had been asked to run for the board of directors of the Barclay and I agreed. There were a lot of problems with some of the people, but I decided to run. I was elected January 24th and after much screaming and nasty phone calls I quit on January 25th. I didn't need this aggravation. Saturday, January 29th Eleni and I went to a Greek restaurant in Boca Raton with Paul and Olivia. I stayed on the boat for a few days to work.

February 2000 – Petee's Birthday

February 4th Petee was 36 years old. I couldn't believe it. We had built an empire and the fire within continued. Peter was going to buy an apartment 16B at the Stratford House from me so we had the closing set for January 25th. Wednesday the 9th of February there was a large explosion in Manalapan. I was there to do the investigation along with the State of Florida and ATF. I spent eight hours there. It was a propane leak which caused it.

On Friday the 11th Lorraine, Danny, Loretta, and Danny Jr. came to dinner. I made lamb shanks, onion soup, vegetables and salad. The 15th to the 18th I taught classes for IENGA. After the Friday class I drove to Jacksonville and stayed overnight at the Marriott. I left Jax at 3am and arrived at the Park Ridge Marriott at 5:45 pm. All these years I always stayed at Marriott's because they were the best and safest. I remember a funny story which happened at the Marriott when I was in Oklahoma City after the bombing. I went to my room about 10:30pm after a few drinks at the bar. As I entered the room I spotted the pizza sign on my desk. I called room service and ordered a pizza and a beer. After it was delivered, I took off all my clothes and sat on the bed eating the pizza and watching TV. When I was finished, I went to put the tray outside the door. I was in a corner room so I opened the door and leaned out to place the tray on the side when the door hit my foot. I jumped and the door closed and locked. There I was stark naked in the hall. No one was in the hallway so I could hide behind the ice machine. There was a space behind it and the soda machine. The elevator was to the right of this space and it had a house phone. I took a chance and stepped out and called the desk. I told them my room number and they said they would send security. I waited about fifteen minutes and no one came. All of a sudden I heard the elevator bell and a man and his wife walked by the ice machine. I yelled out and told them my problem. After a confused look they both laughed and he brought me a towel. I called the desk again and they said security came but I wasn't in my room. They sent security again and after a good laugh he opened my door.

After a busy week in NJ, I headed back Sunday at 3am and drove straight through to Florida arriving home at 9:30pm. I had hit several heavy rain storms in Florida which slowed me down. This trip to NJ was also strange. Petee let me stay at his penthouse one night because he was going to be away in NY. I had been at Solari's that night and came home to the apartment about 10pm. I got undressed and got in his bed. About 20 minutes later I thought I heard the door down the hall and thought Petee came back and he was going to scare me. I had my gun under the pillow but I was sure it was him. I heard steps then someone came into the room. I heard some sounds then someone got in the bed and I felt an arm on me. I turned and came face to face with a girl who was naked. She screamed and jumped up and said, "Who are you?" I said I am Pete's father. She ran in the bathroom with her clothes and I put my pants on. When she came out I was in the living room. After she got over the embarrassment we laughed and had a drink. Petee had given her a key but never told her he was going to be away that night. She finally left and I went to sleep.

CHAPTER–THIRTY FIVE
The Suicide Investigation And Ienga

Chapter–Thirty Five – The Suicide Investigation And Ienga

March 2000 – Debbie, Eleni's Daughter and her Twins

March 3rd Eleni's cousin Flo and Sid came for dinner. I made shrimp Mykanos. Debbie and the girls also stopped by that night.

March 6th Eleni and I took the boat to Fort Lauderdale. The wind was 10 knots and seas were 2 feet. When I approached Port Everglades I was close to shore and waited too long to go out further and hit a hole. I heard the props hit and then came the vibration. We pulled into Bahia Mar Marina for the night. I had the props pulled by ABC diving. We went to dinner with John and Susie. We stayed at Bahia Mar Marina the next few days and had dinner at the Rainbow Palace with Jim and Eileen. The props were returned and we went to my cancer doctor for a check up.

The 14th through the 17th I taught an IENGA class. That weekend my cousin Bernice and Lorraine came to the house for dinner. Bernice was Lorraine and Barbara's sister. A couple of years ago her husband committed suicide under strange circumstances. My company, since we had grown did death investigations too. I did the investigation for her and found some troubling information. Their insurance company didn't want to pay, but after I got through they finally did. She was a sweetheart but I didn't like her new boyfriend Bob who she allowed to move in with her. He was a drinker and very obnoxious. I think everyone just put up with him. Bernice had two great boys.

I wasn't feeling well for a few days and I was in a hurry to get home from the boat to the condo and I got stopped by a state trooper on I-95 doing 75mph in a 55mph zone. I took the ticket; the first one in 30 years. I signed up for the four hour traffic school so I wouldn't get any points. Petee was in Chicago on the 27th and I was in Stone Mount, Georgia giving a seminar. I stayed two days and drove back with Nancy, one of the girls from the office who drove up with me. Two days later Ralph Ciarlo, my boss at IENGA died suddenly.

April 2000 – Family Problems

Friday the 7th, Eleni and I went to the funeral parlor. On April 11th Debbie was crying because Mark was giving her a hard time as always. His foul mouth in front of the girls was terrible.

I went to mom's that day and she was just terrible. She wouldn't eat and kept fighting with me. I knew I had to do something with her before she hurt herself. She hadn't been out of her condo in six years. Saturday, April 12th I went to traffic school for four hours.

April 16th, our wedding anniversary, Paul and Olivia came to dinner and I made veal stew. I also ordered a complete set of Dell computers, fax, scanner, and speakers for all of my workers. I did a large fire in Miami on the 20ᵗʰ. On April 25ᵗʰ through the 28ᵗʰ I taught an IENGA class. I had Greek Easter on the boat on the 30ᵗʰ with Jim and Eileen.

May 2000 - Doctors

May was a busy month for doctors and chores. Eleni and I stayed on the boat the week of the 15ᵗʰ. We ate at Roly's two nights. We returned home on the 21ˢᵗ. I had to go to mom's three times a week in response to her mad calls. Eleni's lovely friends Lucy and Bob from NY, came for a visit. They were very sweet people and I liked them a lot. I did another IENGA class from May 31ˢᵗ through June 1ˢᵗ. Then I flew to NJ for a meeting with my accountant, Mike Mongelli.

June 2000 – An Employee Leaves

On Tuesday the 6ᵗʰ, Shelly left PVA and we had to find another administrative assistant. I also did a couple of fire investigations in May. Petee went to Greece on the 1ˢᵗ for vacation so I watched the office. June 11ᵗʰ I went to my NY office for a meeting and returned the next day. Shelly returned on the 13ᵗʰ. I had a big fire in Paterson all day on the 14ᵗʰ.

Eleni flew in on Saturday the 17ᵗʰ and we had dinner at Esty Street; a great restaurant in Park Ridge, NJ. Petee's new girlfriend, Gloria lived a couple of blocks away. Father's Day, the 18ᵗʰ we had a party at Gloria's house in Woodcliff Lake, NJ. We returned the next day to Florida. Linda flew in to help me with mom. Things were critical.

Debbie had a party on the 23ʳᵈ and we were all there. Debbie and the girls finally left Mark aka "Jackass" and moved to a townhouse in Lake Clark shores in West Palm Beach which she purchased. She had filed for divorce and now felt good. She couldn't take his foul language in front of the girls, his screaming, and yelling, and him never helping her.

July 2000 - Mom

July 5ᵗʰ Linda gave mom a shower. It was terrible. She had "BM" stuck all over her. Thank God for my sister. We fooled her by saying Blue Cross was going to cancel her insurance unless she had a physical. We took her to my doctor, Dr. Fortier in West Palm Beach. After he examined her she didn't know her age, what day or year she was born. She was totally out of it. Since I had power of attorney, and full charge of her medical decisions, I had the doctor commit her under the Baker's Act to the Good Samaritan Hospital. They had to strap her in the bed and gave her a needle with some drugs. I was so upset to see her this way. She was 89 years old. Linda and

I went to many nursing homes in the next few days. They were all terrible, smelled, had roaches, and I couldn't stand it. We finally found one in West Palm Beach called Darcy Hall. It was very nice and quite large, had a full medical staff, nice food hall, and it was clean, too.

On July 7th I took Linda, Debbie, and Eleni to the Casablanca for dinner where we discussed mom. July 8th mom was taken by ambulance to Darcy Hall. She was incoherent but was relaxed. She didn't know us so we left her at Darcy Hall to rest. The next day we went to the nursing home then to Lorraine's for dinner. The next couple of days we had a lot to do at the condo in Lauderhill. I cancelled mom's cable, paper, and of course took most of her things to the goodwill. I also put the condo up for sale.

I had a meeting with Jeff Saganski from Columbia Pictures over dinner. I also had a fire investigation that day. I had a meeting on the 13th with the Palm Beach Fire Department regarding training. Linda returned to Syracuse the next day. I was able to see mom everyday because she was only minutes away from Eleni and I. On the 17th I did a fire investigation in Pompano and on the 19th another case in Palm Beach. Mom was starting to adjust to her new surroundings. She kept saying, "When am I getting out of here?" Her 89th birthday was on the 23rd of July. I ordered a large sheet cake for her, large enough for the whole nursing home. It was big enough to serve about 100 people. The 25th through the 28th I had a class to teach in Fort Lauderdale for IENGA.

August 2000 – The Boat

I went to the boat on August 3rd through the 5th and got fuel in both tanks. Tuesday the 8th, I had a lunch meeting with Jeff Saganski at Bici's in Palm Beach. Petee came down on the 11th and I made lamb shanks for dinner. The next evening we all went to the Café L'Europe. My cousin Chickie arrived in Orlando at Disney World, and I planned to meet her. I had a fire to do on the 14th. Eleni and I drove to Orlando and stayed from the 17th through the 19th and took the family to lunch. Sunday the 20th Chickie returned and we drove home. The next week I had an IENGA class from the 22nd through the 25th in Fort Lauderdale. Hurricane Debbie arrived but did little damage in our area. The rest of the month I worked on the boat.

September 2000 – Petee and Gloria Come for a Visit

September 1st, Petee came down with Gloria for a meeting and we ate at the Four Seasons Friday and Saturday we had dinner at Café L'Europe. We were on the boat for this weekend so on the 3rd we took the boat out for a cruise in the ocean at 10am. We returned after lunch on the boat about 2:45pm. We went to Nick's Tomato Pie that night. The next night we ate at Bici's. Petee and Gloria left for home Tuesday the 5th. On the 8th I did a fire in Palm Beach. My NJ and NY office were taking in about 25-30 cases a day. I was handling Florida and Georgia. I had an American Legion meeting on the 12th. I was always a member and a member of the VFW too. Since I was a Vietnam Vet, I became involved. A lot of the World War I and II and even the Korean Vets were dying.

On Friday, September 15th, I went to Orlando to do a fire investigation. Hurricane Gordon was heading for the west coast of Florida and we had high winds and rain.

October 2000 – Physical Issues

During the first week of October, I had a severe diverticulosis attack. I got over it in two days. October 10th through the 15th I had to teach an IENGA class. We had very high winds that week which finally ended by Saturday the 14th. On Saturday the 14th at 7:15am Eleni, Lorraine, Danny and I left for Key West with the first stop at Ocean Reef. The weather was good but I had a problem with my generator. We arrived at Ocean Reef at 3:15pm. We stayed Sunday, Monday, and Tuesday eating at all the fine restaurants.

Thursday we left for Key West at 7:10am. Petee, Gloria, David and Patti Redsicker, and Shelly were going to be there for a company retreat. There was also a big festival going on that week. We arrived at the Hilton Marina at 2:50pm. I had a very bad tick attack and my back was out. I had to use a wheel chair because I couldn't walk far. That night we all got together and went to dinner at Mango's Restaurant. I couldn't eat at all. Danny pushed me in a wheelchair the entire way and back. On the way back, the streets were packed with parties. As Danny was pushing me a girl stood in the way falling on me and she pulled up her top showing me her breasts. Then she put a set of beads on me and left. I thought Danny would die. Actually, everyone saw this, but it was party time.

The next day we took a walk down Duval Street, which was always an experience especially Sloppy Joe's. I had been here many times because I was an Ernest Hemmingway fan and this was his town. That night we took a taxi to Backyard Louie's. It was great as usual, but I didn't eat much. I was still in pain. Sunday the 22nd the crew left for NY and NJ and the rest of us ate at the Hilton. There was bad weather coming so we had to leave in the morning. We left at 6:30am to get fuel at the Texaco. We filled up by 7:30am with 305 gallons. We headed out to Hawks Channel when we heard on the NOAA radio to expect gale force winds and rain. The wind already started to pick up and I told everyone to get off the bridge, go down below, and sit down. About an hour out we hit one storm with 47mph winds and the seas were 8-10 feet with all white water. The next two hours I was glued to the wheel.

Danny came up only for a cigarette, which took him a long time to light up. The rain was so hard I couldn't see, but I managed to stay on course. I was soaked because I had to keep the front window open. I was also peeing and threw up once. I called down below and everyone else was fine but there were three major water leaks. This was the worst trip I had ever had. I think God was testing my seamanship. As we neared Rodriguez Key it cleared a bit and I saw a coast guard orange helicopter circling my yacht. They radioed me on channel 16 and said they were looking for six people whose boat flipped about two miles ahead. They wanted me to watch for orange life jackets. I called Danny topside to help me watch because I was busy handling the boat in the rough seas. Every once in a while we would spot orange lobster pots, but no people.

The coast guard called again saying four of the six people were recovered, but the father and son were missing. We hit another bad storm, the winds were hitting us at 50-55 mph for another hour and we finally approached the Ocean Reef Channel. I entered and pulled into the fuel dock. I took another 300 gallons of fuel. I pulled into slip E-1. The girls were still cleaning up the leaks with towels. I was still shaking and couldn't wait to get a Glenlivet 12 on the rocks. We all had a couple of drinks and went to eat. I don't have to tell you but we all slept well that night. The next day the weather was still bad and was to continue for a few days, so we stayed for several more days. We ate at Carysfort, the Islander, and the Raw Bar. On the 28th the seas were 4-5 feet and the wind was 15-20 knots. We left at 7:15am and arrived at 2:30pm at the Bluffs. It was a trip to remember. The rest of the week I worked on the boat repairing the leaks, and fixing the generator.

November 2000 – My Sister Wants to Move to Florida

On November 8th Linda and Tom arrived to look at houses. They decided to move to Florida. They were staying at my condo that I had given to mom. We looked at many places the next two days. Friday the 10th we met an old friend, Johnny Pyle and his wife Elaine at Il Tortufo in Fort Lauderdale for dinner.

The next day Linda and Tom came to Palm Beach and we went to Amici's for cocktails then Café L'Europe for dinner. Sunday, I made dinner at our Palm Beach Condo with Lorraine, Danny, Linda and Tom. Earlier I had to ride in the Veteran's Day Parade with the American Legion. Then we all went to the Greek Restaurant OPA for dinner. The next day Linda and Tom returned to Syracuse. Eleni and I went to the boat for the weekend. I met with Philip Vias at my Fort Lauderdale condo to put it on the market. We spent Thanksgiving at Debbie's new home with Lorraine, Danny, Jim and Eileen, Deb Cahill, and Philip. It was a great day for all of us and the girls. Tuesday the 28th through the 31st I had to teach for the IENGA in Fort Lauderdale.

December 2000 - My Surprise Birthday Party

I came home Friday, December 1st. Saturday Eleni gave me a surprise birthday party at Café Cellini. The guests were Debbie and the girls, Howie and Shelly, Jim and Eileen, Lorraine and Danny, Bernice and Lorraine, Tony and Margie, and, Paul and Olivia. It was a great party. Tuesday Eleni and I went to the Yacht Club Marina meeting. Wednesday the 6th I moved the yacht to another slip at Bluff's, slip A-6. I liked it better.

Tuesday and Wednesday I stayed on the boat and I had the phone line and cable TV installed at the dock. Eleni and I stayed on the boat until Saturday then went home. We had to move our terrace furniture inside and tape all our doors with plastic to prepare for the concrete restoration on the building. Wednesday the 20th we moved to the boat until the work was done. It was a $20,000.00 assessment. Eleni and I did some Christmas shopping then stopped at mom's. I would stop at mom's about four times a week. She was still adjusting, but was okay.

Christmas Eve Eleni and I went to Casablanca for dinner. I gave Eleni a beautiful diamond bracelet and she was happy. Christmas Day we went to mom's and then Christmas dinner at Lorraine and Danny's with Jim and Eileen, Dan's mom, Zelda, and Philip. The next few days I made dinner on the boat and Friday the 29th we went to the condo to check on things. The 30th and 31st was very cold. We ate at 1352 Restaurant and went back to the boat. I had to put the heat on in the boat because it was so cold. It was about 60 degrees and down to 55 degrees at night. When you live in Florida as long as we did it was like freezing.

January 2001 – The Holidays

The first week of January we went to the condo, washed clothes, and checked on the apartment. I had work done on the boat's generator, but I was told it had to be replaced. We decided to take a trip to Ocean Reef in Key Largo on the 11th. I had bought a new golf cart when Danny and Lorraine were with us on the last trip. It was designed like a caddy and the color was purple. I had "Papou's Toy" put on it. It had a radio, storage, cooling fan, windshield and top. I paid $16,000.00 for it. My old golf cart was a white Rolls Royce. I kept it at Ocean reef and used it when we drove around the island. We had a good week at the pool and ate at each of the restaurants at night. We left on January 19th. The seas were 3-5 feet and the winds 15-20 knots. A little sloppy but we stayed on the outside in the ocean. Just before the Palm Beach inlet we hit a rough wave and the boat went on its side and began to broach. I hit the engine full speed and was able to right the boat up. It was a very close call. We had a lot of interior damage. Dishes broke, the couch and chairs in the lounge were all to the port side on top of each other. Lamps broke and in the master bedroom the TV flew across the room and broke the glass on the dressing table. We got back to the dock and felt very lucky. It took two hours to clean up. The next three days it was very cold again. I had people repairing the glass and a few other things. Saturday the 27th I left for NJ at 6am and drove straight through arriving at 11:30pm. I spent the week with Petee and returned February 3rd.

February 2001 – Debbie, Eleni's Daughter

I worked on the boat all week and Eleni had to baby sit for the girls one day. February 13th through the 16th, I had an IENGA class in Fort Lauderdale. On the 17th, Saturday we went to Debbie's and I cooked dinner. Eleni slept over so she could baby sit the girls Sunday because Debbie had to work at John G's. Later we met Lorraine at the boat and we drove to Vero Beach to visit Aunt Dolores who had a bad fall and was in a rehabilitation facility. Later when we returned we ate at Roly's. Again I had a problem with my generator. I made arrangements to replace it which was a major $16,000.00 job. The 26th and 28th they dismantled it.

March 2001 – The New Generator for the Eleni II

March 1st they began to install the new generator. That night we went to Paul Getty's party at 5:30pm. After two weeks the generator was in and running on the 14th of March. On March 23rd we met Petee and Gloria at their hotel in South Beach, and then we had dinner at the La Forge. I finally sold the condo in Fort Lauderdale and closed on the 27th. Our condo in Palm Beach was full of dust from the concrete drilling. We were both upset but we couldn't do a thing. The dust had gotten into my closet in my office. Thank God we had a yacht to stay on. We just couldn't have stayed in the apartment.

April 2001 – My Book

On April 3rd I met with author, Ron Kessler about my book at the Chesterfield Hotel in Palm Beach. This was the same place where I met Rod Stewart. The meeting was good and we discussed a possible deal. Petee finally hired a new assistant Lorraine Grieco; a very smart girl and very efficient.

Friday the 6th Eleni baby sat for Debbie while she went to court about Mark. The rest of the week I went to the condo every day to clean the mess. For Greek Easter, Jim and Eileen came to the boat for dinner. I had a class for IENGA in April from the 24th to the 27th in Fort Lauderdale. Saturday Eleni went to sleep over at Debbie's to baby sit on Sunday while she worked. I went to Debbie's to cook dinner when she came home, and we celebrated Eleni's birthday a day early.

May 2001 – Debbie's Divorce

May 7th Debbie received her divorce from Mark. She was very happy. I was busy sending papers and information to the Greek Consulate in Atlanta, Ga. I wanted to get my Greek citizenship. I was still walking with a cane since I had my stroke because I had no feeling in my left foot. This condition was also causing pain. I was also bleeding from the rectum on and off. I went to the doctor and he said I was over radiated from the cancer treatments and my colon area was causing it. It would happen unexpectedly and I was not a happy camper. I was getting sick of doctors but I had no choice. We continued to go back and forth to the condo checking on the dust and cleaning.

Friday the 11th Debbie had a problem with her garbage disposal. It had to be replaced with a new one so I got under the sink and asked her to give me a pot so I could drain the water as I removed the old one. I filled the pot and handed it to her from under the sink. The water was dirty and smelled because it was there all week. She took the pot and all of a sudden water was pouring down in my face and I got soaked. She forgot I had removed the pipes and poured the pot of water in the sink. Well, we had a good laugh and a good story to tell.

Mother's Day I went to Darcy Hall to see mom, then I had Lorraine and Danny for dinner. I made grilled pork chops that day. Wednesday the 16th I flew to Las Vegas to the Monte Carlo to give a seminar for IENGA. On Saturday the 19th I had Eleni fly to Los Angeles and meet me at the Marriott at the Marina Del Ray. Shelley, Michael, and Sarah picked her up. I had rented a car in Las Vegas and arrived at the hotel after Eleni arrived. That night we went to Michael and Shelley's for dinner. Sunday we had a brunch at their home with all the family. We had Shelley and Michael for lunch at the hotel and that night Eleni and I had dinner at the Casa Del Ray.

Tuesday we both flew back to Palm Beach. Thursday we had a luncheon with the American Legion at the Breakers Hotel. Monday the 28th I went to Debbie's at 5:30am to baby sit. Usually once a week when Debbie had to work on Sundays I would go there at 5:30am and Eleni would come later. We would take the girls to Publix and I would make dinner when Debbie came home. I loved the girls and I would play with them, take them to the pool, and take them shopping. Saturday we went to Fathoms for dinner. It was horrible and this was one of the Breakers restaurants.

June 2001 - IENGA

I taught an IENGA class from June 4th through June 8th in Fort Lauderdale. Eleni began cleaning everything. Saturday Petee and Gloria came down and we went to dinner at the Café L' Europe. On the 14th I did a fire investigation at the Boca

Resort. Saturday we went to Debbie's and barbequed steaks that day for dinner. I was having trouble with one of my fingers, which had a large bump. I went to the doctor and had surgery on Tuesday the 19th. The condo was finally cleaned and the terrace washed. Now we could return home. Saturday the 23rd we went to a Greek restaurant, Ambrosio's in Boca Raton. Sunday we went to church.

On the 25th I had new shutters installed on all my glass doors, and had all A/C vents cleaned. Now, finally, after all the concrete work was done we put our furniture back on the terrace. Saturday we ate at Casablanca.

July 2001 – The Boat, Ocean Reef, and My Golf Cart

July 2nd Eleni and I moved all the rest of our things back to the condo. July 4th we went to Debbie's for a barbeque. July 6th we left at 6am for Ocean Reef. We had a good trip with 1-3 foot seas. When we arrived I put 257 gallons of fuel in the tank, and then went to slip E-1. That night we had dinner in the Ocean Room. Saturday we went to the pool and we had dinner at the Country Club. We loved riding our fancy golf cart to the Country Club, which was about one mile from the boat. Sunday I had to get a new battery for my generator. We ate at the Ocean Room that night. Monday and Tuesday we relaxed and ate dinner both nights at the Ocean Room. On Wednesday the 11th we left at 5am for home arriving at our dock at 1:30pm just before a big storm. The next day we returned to our condo.

Friday the 13th I received a call that my cousin Doris. De Bona's husband Willie died. He was a great guy and we had made wine and had many good times. Saturday I began to remove the wallpaper in the kitchen and later we went to dinner with Lorraine and Danny at Ambrioso's. The next few days I removed the rest of the wallpaper and painted. On the 20th I had all new electrical boxes installed. I also put the boat up for sale this month because Eleni and I wanted to do some traveling. On the 23rd I showed the boat to someone and then went to mom's for her 90th birthday with a large cake. The next four days I taught a class in Fort Lauderdale. When I got back we had to move the terrace furniture back into the apartment because the painters were coming to do the terrace ceiling, walls, and rails.

Debbie was trying to get a restraining order against Mark because he would constantly call her yelling, screaming, and cursing at her and even in front of the girls when he came to pick them up. We decided to take a trip to go to Tampa.

August 2001 – Nick, My Nephew

On Friday, August 5th Eleni and I went to the Hyatt Regency to see my nephew Nick. We had a beautiful suite with two bathrooms which was why we always took a suite. That night we all had dinner at Armein's. The next night, even though we got hit with a tropical wave, Nick took us to a great Cuban place for lunch called

Columbia's. That night we took Nick to the Windham Hotel for dinner at Shula's Steakhouse. Nick was a great guy and we had a good time. We left the next day for home because Hurricane Alberta was in the Caribbean. We ordered our Christmas cards as we did every year at this time. We always had them ready to be mailed on December 1st. We also made our reservations for Greece. I went to the boat for a few days to wash and clean it. Saturday the 11th we went to dinner at Ambrioso's. Sunday morning at 5am I went to Debbie's to baby sit and I made dinner there that night.

On the 14th the broker for the boat came with a contract and a $35,000.00 deposit. I called Petee and he said don't sell the boat, it keeps you busy, and Eleni said the same. I began to wonder so I gave back the deposit and cancelled the sale. The men were painting all the rails and the terrace looked great, thank God that was over. I bought a new outdoor electric grill for the terrace. Sunday the 19th we went to church and I cooked dinner on the terrace. I spent the next week cleaning the condo. Petee called and he thought he might buy the boat. He always worked very hard and I told him if he wanted the boat he could just take over the payments. Petee said he would be down on August 31st. On Friday the 24th Hurricane Debbie hit Florida but we were okay. The next week I had a couple of bad bleeding days but it went away after two days. I was just thinking that now I had everything, money, a big condo in Palm Beach, a yacht, and now it seemed my health was giving me a problem.

CHAPTER–THIRTY SIX
911

Chapter–Thirty Six – 911

September 2001 – Gloria and Petee

Gloria and Petee arrived Saturday night and we all had dinner at Café L'Europe. Sunday I made dinner at the condo. Debbie and the girls came over after dinner and Debbie was very upset. Mark was harassing her as usual. The court wouldn't do anything about it so she would call the police. Labor Day we all went to Debbie's for a barbeque. "Ozzie" Eleni's ex-husband was there, too with his wife Jackie. Ozzie and I always got along so we never had a problem. Everything was good and we all had a good time. September 5th, Petee and Gloria returned to NJ and on the 7th Eleni and I drove to Ocean Reef and stayed in the presidential suite. I didn't think it was so great.

Eleni and I drove back on Sunday because I had a class for IENGA on the 11th through the 14th. On Tuesday the 11th I was driving to Fort Lauderdale to IENGA when I stopped at my cousin Lorraine's. Just as I was leaving her house over my radio came a Fox News Alert about the World Trade buildings being hit by a plane. I arrived at IENGA headquarters 15 minutes later and everyone was watching TV. I stayed until the buildings collapsed. I was very upset thinking about my firefighter brothers being killed. The classes were cancelled because those flying in couldn't make it because the air spaces were closed by the government. All planes were grounded. I went home and was glued to the TV for the next two days.

Zelda, my cousin Lorraine's mother in law died on the 12th. I flew to NJ so I could go to NY and help my brother firefighters. I worked one day and couldn't handle it.

I flew back to Florida the next day. Hurricane Helene and Isaac were out there and we were watching them closely. I had to have my Rolex watch serviced and it cost $500.00. That wasn't bad since I had it since 1985. A new hurricane was born "Joyce". None of these hit us other than with wind and rain. Sunday the 23rd we baby sat and made dinner as we did almost every Sunday. I had a lot of fun with Jordan and Hayley. They were great kids. Saturday the 29th we had dinner at Trevini's on Worth Avenue in Palm Beach. My friend Gianni Minervini opened in the Esplanade after Café L'Europe moved. The food was great; totally first class.

I enjoyed working at the American Legion and helping Palm Beach Post 12. The girls who worked there Karan Larvan and Victoria "Tori" Kramer were great. They worked their hearts out for all the Vets, and we had a lot of laughs together.

October 2001 – Hurricane Iris

October 2nd through the 5th, I taught an IENGA class in Fort Lauderdale.

Hurricane Iris was out there but did not affect us other than high winds 25-30 knots. On the 9th a large barge was blown onto the surf next to our building. I was bleeding a lot lately so I made an appointment with my cancer doctor, Dr. Shetty. On the 15th the grounded barge was pulled out by tugs. I had been working on publishing a cookbook and was slowly getting there. October 26th I sent it to the publisher and it was copyrighted. Then I went to Dr. Shetty because of the bleeding and he examined me again. He said it was from being over radiated and my being on Coumadin. I was still leery but all three of my doctors said the same thing. The rest of the week the winds were very high. Sunday the 28th I made dinner for Lorraine, Danny, Jim and Eileen, Philip, Debbie, and the girls. I was still busy with the American Legion and I got 12 turkeys from Publix for their Thanksgiving drawing.

November 2001 – Hurricane Michelle

November began with Hurricane Michelle. Sunday the 4th Eleni and I baby sat the girls and I went to the boat to put extra lines and fenders on it. That night the storm hit the Bahamas' and we had 50-55 mph winds. I was at the American Legion to cook dinner for a meeting on Tuesday the 6th. I cooked for about 40 people. I made ½ roast chicken, carrots, and roasted potatoes. Everything was good. Saturday the 10th I made dinner for Geralynn and Nichole who were Lorraine and Danny's grandchildren and their mother Donna, Debbie, and the girls. The next day Eleni and I ate at Café L'Europe. Monday the 12th we went for our flu shots and heard American Airlines flight 587 had crashed in NY.

Tuesday the 13th I had a meeting with the assistant chief Rhett Turnquest at the West Palm Beach fire department. I arrived for the meeting at 10:30am. Chief Turnquest said he had a copy of my resume and was very impressed. He also said he was interested in having me give classes for the Fire Prevention Bureau for fire investigations. After our discussion, the chief introduced me to Chief Carter of the department. We then went downstairs and he introduced me to the fire marshal, Robert Prusiecki. We looked at each other and I remembered him from years ago. We did several fires together particularly the Comeau Bldg. fire on Clematis St. We discussed old times and he was happy to have me work with them. Within a few days Chief Turnquest had me take a two day class given by FEMA and Homeland Security for Emergency Management. I ordered my uniform, shirts, polo shirts, and ties. I did not want to work for money because I made too much and I would only be giving it back to the government. I agreed to work pro bono on my time when available. I had just gotten the feeling back in my foot about a month ago so I was very happy to be back in the fire department. My rank would be captain of the "SIU" special investigation unit.

Sunday the 18th we went to church then to mom's then home. That night we went to Cellini's for dinner. Thanksgiving we had dinner at Debbie's and of course Eleni made the turkey. She made the best turkey. Thanksgiving was the only time I let her cook. She was a good cook but I always liked to cook so I did. Even when I went away I always made food and she kept it in the freezer. How much our lives had changed since we were married. We were on top of the world, having everything we always wanted, money, yachts, cars, condos, etc. The best was my son following in my footsteps, and now back on the fire department the fire within was there.

Friday the 23rd Eleni and I put up our Christmas tree and decorations at the condo. I also would decorate the boat with lights and a tree. The last week of November I was teaching in Fort Lauderdale for IENGA. When I returned on Friday I prepared to leave for Jacksonville the next day for the Mayo Clinic. I was having dizzy spells for a few weeks. One of my local doctors had told me it was because I didn't drink enough water and had hypoglycemia. I was a great believer of the Mayo Clinic. They saved my life when they detected my heart and stroke problem, so when I wasn't happy with the results from the local doctors, I went to the Mayo Clinic because they were the world's best.

December 2001 – My Physical Issues

Monday, December 3rd, I fasted then began with an MRI and brain scan. Within a few hours I met with the doctors and they said they didn't find anything wrong and the blood clot in my brain stem was gone. That was good but the next day they addressed my dizzy spells. I met with Dr. Roland and he did several tests on my hearing. They found I had some crystals that dissolved in my ear and they repaired it. That was causing my problem. I returned home Friday and Eleni and I had dinner. I felt much better. On December 9th Philip had a Christmas party at his girlfriend, Martha's house with some of his friends. It was a nice party. The next week I stayed home working around the house. Monday the 17th we were putting all the presents under the tree. The next few days I was busy baking for the holidays. Linda's birthday was the 21st. My niece Stephanie, Linda, and Tom came to the condo to celebrate. I cooked and we had a great time. They were staying at the Gulf Stream Hotel in Lake Worth. The next evening we all went to Trevini's for dinner. Sunday we all went to dinner again in Palm Beach. I might mention that living in the Town of Palm Beach, which was voted the best place in the US to live was wonderful and had the best restaurants.

Christmas Eve I had a big party. Linda and Tom, Stephanie, my godchild, Debbie Cahill, Debbie, the girls, Lorraine and Danny, and Eleni's friends, Loraine Beckenstein, and her friend Bernie were all there. Eleni's cousins Flo and Sid, Sheila, Jim and Eileen, Philip, Eleni's ex-husband Ozzie and wife Jackie all attended the party too. I had a bartender and a server, Jessica, to help me. It was a great party.

Christmas Day we all went to Lorraine and Danny's for dinner. The 26th Linda and Tom, Eleni and I went to look at new homes, then to Chuck and Harold's for cocktails and I made dinner at home. The 27th Stephanie flew home and we went to dinner at Stressa's. Friday, Linda and Tom continued looking at houses. We all went to see mom then to dinner at Ya Sou. The next day Linda and Tom went house hunting again and that night we had dinner at Café Cellini.

January 2002 - The Holidays

I had a New Year's Eve party and had Linda, Tom, Petee and Gloria, and Paul and Sandy. We had a beautiful dinner but Eleni had too much to drink and I put her to bed after she got sick. She missed 12 o'clock midnight that night. She was a little person, 98 pounds so she couldn't drink more than two drinks. The next day Paul and Sandy left and that night we went to Trevini's for dinner. On the 2nd Linda and Tom went house hunting and that night we all went to dinner at Esclair's at the Breakers. After dinner we went to the lounge to listen to a great jazz band. My sister Linda returned to Syracuse on Thursday, January 3rd. After meetings with Petee and Philip on Friday, we all went to dinner at Cuchina's. The next night we all had dinner at L'Escalier at the Breakers. Petee returned to NJ on Sunday. Monday January 7th I received a call from my publisher that they were ready to ship my cookbook. I had been working on a cookbook for a year and now they were ready. I named it, "Recipes and Remembrances" and dedicated it to my father. It would sell for $10.50. I was preparing to go in the hospital on Tuesday the 15th for a colonoscopy. Because I was on Coumadin, I had to have it done in the hospital and put on Heparin IV.

Monday the 14th the cookbooks arrived; 300 of them. They were beautiful and I already had many orders to send out. I went in the hospital and they removed five polyps. The problem was they couldn't get my blood count back so I ended up staying in the hospital until Saturday the 19th. I still had to give myself two shots a day in my stomach for seven days. Father Andrew came and blessed the house. We went to church on Sunday. Debbie and the girls came to dinner. The next week I spent time on the boat and Saturday night we went to L'Escalier at the Breakers. Tuesday the 29th I went to Fort Lauderdale to teach for IENGA until February 1st.

February 2002 – Teaching in Canada

Saturday the 2nd we went to St. Catherine's church to a dinner dance. Sunday the 3rd Eleni and I drove to Naples and had a suite at the Ritz Carlton. That night we had dinner and cocktails with friends. We met Helen and Nick Gamrillos on a ship while cruising the Islands of Greece. We had a good time. Eleni and I stayed a few days and Aunt Dolores and Debbie, her daughter, came over Tuesday. Wednesday we drove home. Friday I left for the NY office by car. I was teaching a class in Toronto,

Canada on the 12th so I decided to visit my office and see my sister in Syracuse. I arrived at the Marriott Residence Inn on the 8th and met with my staff. I stayed one night then went to Syracuse on the 10th. Eleni was sleeping over at Debbie's to baby sit on Sundays so Debbie could go to work. I stayed at the Sheridan in Syracuse and went to Linda's both days. Then I left for Toronto. It was very cold. I was teaching a class for IENGA at a large engineering company. I arrived at the hotel near their offices and it was 0 degrees. I ran from my car to the entrance of the hotel and my lips were frozen. It was an Embassy Suite and it was very large and beautiful. The next three days I taught classes. Friday the 15th I left for Syracuse and stayed over at my sister's.

Saturday I drove to NJ to the Marriott in Park Ridge. On the way, a car rolled over on Route 81. I stopped and ran over to the car which was smoking. I reached in and turned off the key. It was still smoking so I smashed the window and opened the door. The driver was unconscious and I had to pull him out and away from the car. He was bleeding from the head so I got my medical kit, which I always kept in the car and stopped the bleeding. He began to regain consciousness and I told him not to move. A trooper came and he called for rescue. He thanked me and I left. I always stopped at accidents. Now I had saved 42 lives so far in my lifetime, and I was the most decorated firefighter in the US.

March 2002 – Petee Decides to Buy the Eleni II

Petee decided to buy my yacht, the Eleni, and we looked at a marina in Haverstraw, NY. I stayed the rest of the week and left for Florida at 3am Saturday and drove straight through. I arrived home in 18 hours in Palm Beach. I spent the next week on the boat and it was cold; in the 30's. I think I brought some of the Canada cold air with me.

I was called Thursday the 7th by the nursing home and they said mom was in a fight and she had some scratches on her. I drove over and spoke to the nurse. She told me some lady in a wheel chair ran into her. She and the women were fighting each other and both had scratches. Mom wasn't bad; just a few scratches on her arm but the other lady had scratches on her face. I couldn't believe it at 93 years old she was still a fighter. All these old ladies had long nails because no one cut them. The next day I was at fire headquarters to give a class to the Fire Prevention Bureau. I now had uniforms and was becoming acquainted with the men. I also had a fire radio so I could monitor the calls in case I was needed. I started to respond to fires and was teaching the inspectors at the scenes. It felt good to be back in the fire department and it felt good not to be using a cane anymore since the feeling returned in my foot. I had several meetings at the American Legion and worked on cleaning the boat out.

I was going to leave a lot of tools and things for Petee since he decided to take the boat.

On the 21st Petee went to the Cayman Islands for R&R. Petee had started a new business called Forensic Evidence Property Storage of N.A. He would store evidence for insurance companies, attorneys, and other experts. We kept on growing and we were doing great. I made dinner for Easter Sunday, which we also celebrated, and Jim and Eileen came over.

April 2002 – My Annual Trip To Greece

April arrived and I took the boat out for a test with Philip. Everything was great. On the 9th to the 12th I was teaching in Fort Lauderdale. Eleni and I were leaving for Greece on Saturday the 17th. The 13th, Eleni and I drove to NJ. We stopped in Colonial Heights overnight then arrived in NJ at the Park Ridge Marriott on Sunday the 14th. That night we were at Petee's and Gloria's and I had a meeting with Dave Redsicker and Serge who worked with us. Monday I went to the office and that night we all had dinner at Esty Street; a great restaurant in Woodcliff Lake.

Tuesday Eleni and I met my cousin Diane at her house in NY with Aunt Dolores and went to lunch with them. I stopped at the Haverstraw Marina to see where Petee was going to put the "Eleni" when he took it from Florida to NJ. I didn't like the docks at all but he didn't have a choice.

The next day Sergei, one of my investigators, drove Eleni and me to JFK. I left the Navigator at Petee's. We left on Delta nonstop first class to Athens and arrived the next day at 10:05am. My cousin Felitsa and Alex met us and we drove to the Ledra Marriott in Athens to our usual suite. That night we ate at the hotel. The next day we went to Felitsa's house with cousin Velissairo and Katie. As always, all we did was eat, drink, and dance. We always had to visit all our cousins for dinner. They were wonderful and we were very close. Saturday Eleni and I went to the Plaka to shop. We always ate lunch at Hermion's Restaurant. It was our favorite place. After we returned to the Marriott we rested and that evening Eleni and I ate at the Kona Kai Polynesian Restaurant with cousins, Felitsa, Alex, Angeliki, Sotiris, and Theoni. The food in Greece was just wonderful. The tomatoes and lemons were to me, the best.

Monday, Eleni and I drove to Glyfada to shop and that night we ate at the top of the Inter-Continental Hotel. It was a beautiful hotel overlooking the Acropolis. Tuesday we had lunch at Velissairo's house. Katie was a great cook and made the best mousaka and keftedes. Wednesday we went to the Plaka again and had lunch outside as always at the Hermion. That night we ate at Kona Kai again. Friday I met with Anna, a real estate representative in regards to buying property in Greece. She was very informative. Sunday we drove to Voula for lunch near Sounion with Velissairo,

Katie, and Sotiris. It was a lovely day with beautiful views of the Mediterranean Sea. The 30th was Eleni's birthday and we had dinner at Velissairo's house.

May 2002 - Greece

May 1st we walked to the Plaka because of the May Day demonstration at Syntagma Square. You had to be careful because they would riot sometimes, but I knew how to get away from the area through the Plaka. I bought Eleni her birthday present; more gold. Over the years we bought a lot of gold probably in the range of $150,000.00 which we kept in the bank. The value of the gold had doubled since we began buying it. I paid $600.00 for a gold key bracelet several years ago and when I had it appraised recently for the insurance company it was appraised at $3,500.00.

Petee called me and said that Gloria and he were flying in on Saturday the 4th to celebrate Greek Easter at Porto Heli. Porto Heli was about three hours from Athens by car and 1-1/2 hours by Catamoran Hydra Foil. The family would drive there and stay at my Cousin Antonio's house. I had reservations at the Henistra Beach Hotel and made one for Petee and Gloria. On Saturday the 4th I had our taxi drive them through the mountains to Porto Heli. Eleni and I took the Hydro Foil to Porto Heli early. Felitsa picked us up and we checked in.

Petee and Gloria arrived and we all went to the Island of Spetses by boat for lunch. There were no cars on the island, only donkeys. We had a great lunch of octopus and fish. We then returned to Porto Heli to the hotel. Later we went to Antonio's house and at 9pm we all walked up the mountain to church when at midnight Easter would begin and everyone would have a candle; thousands of them would walk down the mountain to the house where we all ate dinner and cracked red eggs for good luck.

Easter Sunday we went to Antonio's and we took turns cooking the lamb on the spigot over the coals. This was the largest holiday in Greece, more so than Christmas. Remember Greece was a church state country and very religious. The Greek traditions were wonderful. Food was a major event every Greek Easter with plenty of ouzo, wine, and dancing. We later went back to the hotel and drank some more then went to bed. Monday Petee, Gloria, Eleni, and I took the Hydro Foil back to Athens and on to the hotel. We always had our own driver, "George" who had a Mercedes so he was there to meet us. The four of us went to the roof pool for cocktails then we went to the Plaka for dinner. Tuesday we all went to the pool and had lunch there. That night we all ate at Kona Kai. Petee and Gloria left for the US. The rest of the week we spent with all the family and on Sunday night the 12th Eleni and I took the entire family to Kona Kai for our final dinner as we always did every year at the end of our trip.

The next morning I returned my car and George, my driver took us to the airport. When we arrived at JFK, Serge picked us up with my Navigator and we headed to the Park Ridge Marriott. There was plenty of traffic and it took two hours. We met Petee and Gloria at Esty Street for dinner. The next day I went to the office and that night we ate at Gloria and Petee's. Wednesday the 15th we left the Marriott at 4am for Florida. We stopped at the Marriott Residence Inn in Savannah, Ga. overnight. We left at 4am the next morning and arrived home in Palm Beach at 10am.

Saturday I went to the boat and that night we went to dinner at Trevini's. We also stopped at mom's and she was fine. She told me I needed a haircut, which I didn't but she always said that. Sunday I went to Debbie's at 5am to baby sit the girls. Jordan usually was up waiting for me to play with her. Hayley was the sleeper. Then I would make them pancakes. Eleni came at about 8am and then I went to the boat. When I returned we took the girls shopping, then went to dinner and of course Papou would buy them toys.

I cooked all week because I was having Petee and Gloria, Debbie, and the girls the next Sunday the 26th. Thursday the 23rd, Gloria, Petee, and her dad, John, Eleni, and I went for drinks at the Breakers, then dinner at Café L'Europe. Friday the 24th we all went to dinner at L'Escalier's at the Breakers. Saturday we went to Trevini's for dinner, then Chesterfield's. Monday the 27th Sergei and Ray Blake, our mechanic and captain arrived, to take the boat. They would leave for NJ the next day at 6:15am. The motor yacht, Eleni was now Petee's and it was on its way to Haverstraw, NY. I had a class to teach until Friday the 31st in Fort Lauderdale.

June 2002 – NJ Office and The Eleni's New Home in Haverstraw, NY

Saturday the 1st I left at 3am for NJ by car and I arrived in NJ at 2pm Sunday. Thursday the 6th the "Eleni" arrived at Haverstraw, NY at 6:30pm. There was a leak in the nine foot strut so we had to have it repaired. I stayed on the boat all week and went to the office. I stayed on the boat again during the next week and on Tuesday the 18th my cousins Jennifer, Dominique, and Danielle paid me a visit. The next day Petee and I had dinner with my cousin Diane and Richie. Saturday I left at 2:30am for Florida and drove to Jacksonville. I stayed over at the Marriott because of severe storms. I arrived home the next day at 11am. Debbie and the girls came over and we all had dinner.

The next week I went to the fire station for a meeting with the assistant chief, Rhett Turnquest. The 24th I also had two fire investigations and I had two more fire investigations on the 25th. Thursday the 27th Linda and Tom came and stayed at the Marriott. They came to dinner and discussed looking at homes again. The next day my friend Philip Vias took Linda and Tom house hunting and when they returned they came to our house for dinner. Saturday we all went to dinner at Trevini's. Linda and Tom went to John G's where Debbie worked for breakfast then went to see mom. We went to see Frenchman's Reserve and then returned. The next day Eleni and I, and, Linda and Tom left by car for Ocean Reef. I rented a beautiful two bedroom suite for us and we loved it. We ate dinner at the Islander and had drinks at the bar.

The next day we went to the pool to relax. That night we ate at the Islander again and had a great time. The next day we went shopping at the Fishing Village then lunch at the raw bar. We went to the pool and had dinner at the Islander.

July 2002 – The Fireworks

Friday the 5th was fireworks on the island and they were great. We had drinks at the Palm Bar then dinner at the Islander. Saturday the 6th the four of us drove to Key West. It rained very hard and the streets were flooded. We were going to have dinner at "Louie's Backyard" but cancelled because of the rain. We returned to Ocean Reef and had dinner at the Islander. Sunday, Linda and Tom left for Nick's in Palm Harbor and I cooked dinner at home. We had a good time together despite the rainy day in Key West. I was called to investigate two fires in West Palm Beach as the fire within kept burning. Sunday I had Jim and Eileen, Deb and the girls for dinner.

On Tuesday the 6th I was sworn in as first vice commander of Post 12 of the American Legion. Eleni was present and it was held at the Hilton. Since I didn't have my yacht,"Eleni" anymore I was spending more time at the Fire Station and the American Legion. Saturday the 20th we went to Trevini's for dinner. Sunday I baby sat for the girls and made dinner. We also took them to see yia yia, their great grandmother, Sophia at the nursing home.

Wednesday our terrace and window cleaner came. We had the cleaning done each month because of the salt from the ocean. We faced the Atlantic Ocean and it was a beautiful view even during a storm. At night we could even hear the waves. Mom's 91st birthday was Tuesday the 23rd and I bought a large sheet cake for about 50 people. Publix made her cake every year and did a great job.

Friday the 26th I left for NJ and stopped in Alexandria, Virginia. I left very early the next morning and arrived at the Park Ridge Marriott at 10am. Petee, Gloria, and I went to dinner that night at Esty Street. Sunday Gloria and Petee had dinner at home. Gloria had a beautiful home in Woodcliff Lake where she lived with Petee. It was about eight blocks from the Marriott. The rest of the week I was in the office working. I also left the Marriott and was staying on the boat in Haverstraw, NY. Friday, Petee and Gloria went to her father's in Rumson because there was a barbeque the next day. The next day I drove to Rumson and left early after we ate to go back to the boat. The next week I worked at the office and Wednesday I met with my accountant Michael Mongelli for lunch. Saturday I left the boat at 2am and arrived in Palm Beach at 9:45pm driving straight through. Monday the 12th I bought a new Lincoln Cartier, which was very comfortable.

August 2002 – Business Meetings, Cases, and FEPS

Wednesday I had a meeting with Paul Getty and we went to John G's for lunch. Saturday Eleni and I went to dinner at Trevini's. Sunday I made lamb shanks for Jacques and his wife Denise. Jacques was our building manager; a very nice guy. Without the "Eleni" I was cooking more at home. Monday the 19th Debbie and the girls left for Los Angeles to visit her brother, Michael. The rest of the week I went to a couple of fires. I now had a fire radio so I could monitor the calls and a red light on my dashboard so I could get by the fire lines. The fire marshal, Bob Prusiecki and I got along fine. I was giving classes and training fire investigators and I loved it. I cooked dinner all week and Saturday we went to dinner with Murdock and Shiona at Tervini's.

Sunday Petee and Gloria flew down and were staying at the Breakers. The four of us ate dinner at the Four Seasons. Monday Debbie returned from Los Angeles. Philip, Petee, and I met at the Breakers because we were hiring Philip to be our representative for our other company FEPS. That night we all had dinner at Trevini's. Petee and Gloria left Tuesday the 27th for NJ.

Wednesday the 28th I left at 12:30am to drive to NJ. I got to Alexandria, Va. and stopped overnight. I left early and was in the office at 9am. I went to the boat, which I stayed on while I was in NJ. That night I ate at a great Italian Restaurant and I stopped at the ShopRite Supermarket for some items. I weighed myself and saw I was 225 pounds. That is when I decided when I go back to Florida I would go on a diet. The past few years of making a lot of money, made cost no object, so as you can see we always ate at the finest restaurants and I kept getting heavier. Eleni never gained weight and she was still 98 pounds. That night Aunt Dolores and Diane took me to dinner in Nyack, NY. Friday I drove to my office in Endicott, NY to meet with my vice president of the NY region, David Redsicker. I stayed overnight and my sister Linda and Tom came down from Syracuse and we all went to dinner at the "Number 5". It was a great restaurant, which was in an old firehouse Station "5". I had been eating there for years and it was the best place in Binghamton.

September 2002 – Eleni II in Haverstraw NY and Debbie's Girls

The next morning I left for the boat in Haverstraw. I went to the office every day. On September 11th I went to NYC for the Ground Zero Service. Saturday Karmer of the Port Authority Police provided me transport through the tunnel to Ground Zero. I proceeded down the ramp where the families were, and everyone was holding flowers to be laid at Ground Zero as a memoriam.

The ceremony began and they started to read the names of the victims. I was lined up with other NYFD firefighters but I became so emotional since we lost so many firefighters I couldn't stop crying. We all consoled each other and finally went up the ramp and walked to the Port Authority police car, which drove us back through the tunnel to my car. What an experience; I just couldn't handle it. I went back to the boat and had a drink. Friday the 13th I left early for home and stopped in Savannah, Ga. at the Marriott overnight. The next morning I arrived home at 9am. That night Eleni and I went to Trevini's for dinner. The rest of the week I gave a class at the fire department in fire investigations. I also went to a couple of fires. Saturday Eleni and I went to Café L'Europe. Sunday I made Osso Buca for Lorraine and Danny, and Murdock and Shiona. On the 26th Eleni and I drove to Ocean Reef. Debbie and the girls came for the weekend. I picked up the girls with my golf cart named "Papou's Toy" and they were so excited. We all went to dinner at the Islander then back to our suite. The next day we put the girls in the Reef Kids Club for the day. They were fed, swam, played games, and we picked them up at 8pm. Eleni, Debbie, and I had a lobster feast at the Islander. We picked up the girls and took them for a ride in the Papou's Toy.

Saturday the girls went back to the Reef Kids Club for the day. Debbie, Eleni, and I went to the raw bar for lunch. Sunday the kids went to the Reef Kids Club and Debbie left for home because she had to work. Eleni and I kept the kids for the first time. We had a good time with them and on Sunday we brought them home and I grilled lamb chops.

October 2002 – Dinners at Favorite Restaurants

The first couple of weeks in October I had a meeting and a cookout at the American Legion. I gave a Fire Prevention speech at the American Legion on the 7th. The 13th, I cooked dinner for Philip, Marcia, Harry, and Jocelyn and we had a good time.

Wednesday the 16th I left for NJ and stopped in Savannah overnight at the Marriott. Thursday I arrived in NJ and went directly to my office, then to the boat in Haverstraw, NY. The rest of the week I worked at night. I had dinner at all my favorite restaurants. The 24th I left for Florida and stopped in North Carolina. The next day I arrived home at 10am. Saturday evening we went to Trevini's for dinner, and Sunday as usual we baby sat for the girls and made dinner.

CHAPTER–THIRTY SEVEN
Retired At Age 50

Chapter–Thirty Seven – Retired At Age 50

November 2002 – Retired at 50, and Left Petee, My Son in Charge

November 9th marked 23 years in business. I was doing very well, and Petee, too. It goes to show you, that anyone can make it big in this country if you work hard and give it 100 percent. I retired when I was 50 in 1992 but played an active role to this day. My son has been running the company since then.

Veteran's Day, November 11th I was in the parade, and that evening Eleni and I had dinner at home. Saturday the 16th Eleni and I went to dinner at the Ritz Carlton, and Sunday Debbie and the girls came over and we had dinner home. The 21st Eleni and I went to Ocean Reef. We had cocktails at the Ocean Room Lounge then dinner at the Islander. The one thing I missed was coming here by boat. I started to miss my boating.

The next night we ate at the Country Club. We loved driving around in our golf cart on the reef. It was very relaxing. Saturday night we had dinner at "Carysfort" the best of them all. The next day we went home and it was cold in the 60s. To Floridians, this was freezing. I made dinner at home that night. The rest of the week I shopped because we were having Thanksgiving dinner at Debbie's and of course Eleni was making the turkey.

Thanksgiving we went to Debbie's. Debbie's ex-husband's sister Sophie who was a lovely person came along with Murdock, Shiona, and some of Debbie's friends. It was great as usual. Saturday the 30th Eleni and I ate at Lorraine's. My sister Linda called and on Tuesday the 3rd they bought a new home on the west coast of Florida in Spring Hill. I was disappointed because I wished she would be closer to me but at least they found what they wanted. Linda still seemed to be in remission with her breast cancer and we hoped for the best.

December 2002 – Birthday and the Holidays

I was teaching again from Tuesday the 3rd to Friday the 6th at IENGA. Saturday night Eleni and I dined at the Ritz Carlton. Sunday the 8th we baby sat for the girls and I made dinner. When Debbie came home from work we celebrated my birthday, which was the 5th but I was teaching. All week I was preparing for the American Legion Christmas Party on the 14th. I cooked for approximately 50 people including hors d'oeuvres. The party went well and Eleni and I went to the Breakers for dinner at L'Escalier. That week I also bought new flat plasma TVs for the house. We had four TVs now and we liked the flat screens. Thursday we decided to drive to Ocean Reef to our usual suite. We had cocktails at the Ocean Room and dinner at the country club. Friday we had cocktails at the reef bar and dinner at the Ocean Room.

Saturday we did the same because they had the seafood buffet. We returned home Saturday the 21st.

I had been on a diet for the past few months and was down to 185 pounds from 225 pounds. It cost me $800.00 for Guido, my tailor, to refit my 35 sports jackets, pants, and 12 suits, but I was happy. Christmas Eve I had a party, which as always, I cooked up a storm. We had Debbie and the girls, Lorraine and Danny, Lorraine and Bernie, Denise and Jacques, Arthur Wise, my neighbor, and Murray Cohen another neighbor, and several others from our building over for Christmas dinner.

January 2003 – My Trip to Las Vegas and California

I went to a couple of fires and on New Year's Eve Eleni and I, and Debbie went the Four Seasons for an early dinner then home. Debbie and the girls came over later and we had champagne. I never liked New Year's Eve. I always preferred to stay home and have my own party. Arthur Wise, my neighbor who was 93 years old stopped in for a drink, too. Arthur and I, for the past nine months would swim at 5am every morning. This helped me lose some of my weight.

New Year's Day we ate at Trevini's. I had started to get my tax records ready and I couldn't believe what I was spending a month on restaurants. I remember back when I was married to Rose my ex-wife we ate out twice a month. Thursday the 2nd I was packing for a trip to Los Angeles by car. I was leaving the next day. Eleni was to fly to Los Angeles on the 6th and I would meet her. I left Friday and drove to Baton Rouge, Louisiana to the Marriott. Saturday I drove to San Antonio Marriott. Sunday I went to the El Paso Marriott, and Monday I went to the Residence Inn in Beverly Hills, California.

Eleni arrived at 1:30pm and we went to dinner at the La Dolce Vita in Beverley Hills. The next day we went to Michael and Shelley's house and I took the whole family to a Greek restaurant for dinner. It was great and our grandchild Sarah was dancing. Aunt Dot, Ruth and Myles, and Roz and Lauren were also there.

We left the next day for Las Vegas and stayed at the J.W. Marriott. This Marriott was about nine miles north of the strip. It was a beautiful place next to the Rampart Casino. Friday the 10th we went to the hotel at Mandalay Bay on the strip. We had a 2,100 square foot suite, which was magnificent. My cousin Chickie was in town. We ate at our friend Charlie Palmer's restaurant who owned the Oreole Restaurant in New York and here. They had a wine cellar which was about three stories high and the wine girls would go up on a cable to get the wines. Joe Romano and his wife Megan worked there. Joe was the executive chief, and Megan was the pastry chef. They bought us drinks and we had dinner. At night I gambled, played the slots, and won $1,100.00. Saturday night we ate at a great Chinese restaurant after I won $900.00.

Sunday the 12th we met my cousin Chickie for lunch. It was great seeing her again. Chickie was a firefighter in the forestry division of the State of California. That made two of us in the family who were firefighters. We had a nice time. That night I won another $1,250.00 on the slots for a total of $3,250.00. I was very happy about that. The next day, the 13th Eleni and I drove to Scottsdale to the Marriott. We had dinner with Paul and Olivia Getty who now lived in Arizona. We ate at Michael's in Cave Creek, a great place. The next day we drove to our old house in Fountain Hills and that evening had dinner at Palm Court. Everyone was glad to see us back for dinner. Wednesday we went to Old Town and also stopped at the Mayo Clinic to see our friends there. The next day Eleni left by plane from Phoenix. I left with my car to the San Antonio Marriott. The next day I left at midnight and did a marathon run all the way to Tallahassee, Florida. Saturday morning I left for home arriving at 10am.

Sunday the 19th we took down our Christmas tree, and decorations, and took them to our storage facility. Monday, Tuesday, Wednesday was catch up time, shopping, paying bills, etc. I had a meeting at the fire headquarters and then we went to dinner at Trevini's. It was getting cold and Friday morning it was in the low 30s. Saturday it was in the 40s and 50s. We had the heat on for the first time.

Sunday we baby sat for the girls and I made dinner. I received a fire department radio this week so I could answer calls. I had my helmet and other gear from the old days. I went to a couple of fires that week. Eleni and I ate out as usual.

February 2003 – Petee's Birthday

Saturday the 1st there was the Columbia disaster. We went to Trevini's for dinner and that was all everyone was talking about. Eleni and I had watched the shuttles many times here in Florida. Petee's birthday was on the 3rd. He was 39 years old and was in Detroit on a fire. On the 6th I made dinner for Eleni's cousin Sidney and Flo. I always liked them. He was a lieutenant colonel in Vietnam. February 7th the country was on high alert (orange). All of us first responders were notified at the fire department. Chief Carter and I got along fine, and I got along with the fire marshal, Bob Prusiecki great.

I was training many of the new investigators not only at fire scenes, but in classes. As you can see the fire within was burning at a high peak. Saturday night we went to the Ritz Carlton for dinner and Sunday I cooked home. My friend Joe Bustin from Massachusetts and his wife Marcia came down and stayed at the Fairfield Inn in Palm Beach. We all went to dinner at Trevini's that night. The 13th the four of us went to Ocean Reef to our usual suite. That night we ate at Carysfort and it was great as usual. The next evening we ate at the country club. During the day we would go to the pool and have cocktails. They always had live music at the pool. Saturday night we ate at the Ocean Room. Sunday Joe and Marcia left and we went home. On the 23rd I baby sat the girls and I made dinner. The next day my chief fire investigator in NJ, Arthur Jackson, came to visit us. We all went to Trevini's for dinner.

Friday the 28th Eleni and I left at 7am to go to my sister Linda's for a visit. When we got off the Turnpike we had a blow out at 10:30am. I called AAA and they put on the donut. I found a Goodyear and they said it would be two hours before they could look at it. I drove to a Ford dealer and he said the tire couldn't be fixed. They made a call and located a new tire but because of a bad accident on the Turnpike it would be four hours to get it. I left on the donut and drove to the Hampton Inn in Spring Hill. Next door was a Midas Tire store and they located a tire in Tampa. The problem was I had oversized tires and no one had that size. It would be delivered in the morning. We drove over to Linda's and her new house was beautiful. We drove around the area then we went to Tarpon Springs for dinner. We had a great time. The next morning I had the new tire put on then we went back to Linda's and had dinner there. Sunday at 7am we left for home. It took four hours.

March 2003 – Petee and Gloria Come for a Visit

On the 4th Gloria flew to PBI and we picked her up and took her to the Breakers. I then took my FEMA test at the police academy. Wednesday we ate dinner at the Flagler Steakhouse with Gloria. On Friday Petee flew in and I had Petee, Gloria, and friends, Mary Ellen and Chris for dinner, and I made osso buco. Saturday night we all went to dinner at Trevini's. Trevini had the best food and Gianni Minervini ran a great operation. I knew him now about 13 years. Sunday Petee and Gloria left for NJ. From the 11th through the 14th I had to teach a class in Fort Lauderdale for IENGA. Saturday we ate at Trevini's. Sunday I cooked at home. Monday the 17th the war in Iraq began.

Friday evening Eleni and I ate diner at the Flagler Steakhouse. Saturday our friends Shiona and Murdock joined us for dinner at Trevini's. Sunday I baby sat and cooked dinner for everyone. Philip came for dinner too. Wednesday the 26th I left at 11:45pm for NJ and drove straight through to the Marriott in Park Ridge at 6:30pm. I had an itch and pain on the left side of my back and I stopped at a drug store. The pharmacist said it was "shingles". He gave me some salve to use. That evening Gloria, Petee, and I ate at Esty Street. I worked at the office the next few days. Saturday I went to Aunt Dolores' for dinner. Sunday Petee made dinner at Gloria's and had some other guests.

April 2003 – Greek Easter

Monday and Tuesday I worked. Wednesday the 2nd I drove to Williamsburg, Virginia to do a fatal fire for one of the engineering firms. I stayed at the Marriott and did the fire investigation on Thursday the 3rd. Friday, I drove home, straight through, arriving at 2pm. Saturday Eleni and I went to the "Tavern" for dinner. Sunday I made dinner for Lorraine and Bernie and some friends. Monday I was on the phone with the Greek consulate still working on my Greek citizenship. Thursday I drove to Hollywood to the Greek store for supplies. Saturday evening Eleni and I had dinner at the Flagler Steakhouse. Sunday the 13th Jim and Eileen came over to dinner. The 16th Eleni and I had dinner at the Flagler Steakhouse and Saturday night Eleni and I went to Trevini's. Monday the 21st I received my complete computer package from Dell. Finally I decided to get one. Wednesday I had a meeting at fire headquarters with assistant chief Turnquest. Saturday evening we had dinner at Trevini's. Saturday I also picked up my lamb for Greek Easter which was the next day. All week I cooked spinach, pies, grape leaves, keftedes (Greek meatballs), and pistachio macaroni. I also made baklava. Linda, Tom, and my friends, Sandy and Paul arrived at the Fairfield Inn. That night we all went to dinner at Trevini's. The next day was Greek Easter. We invited Philip and friends and a couple from the building to join us. We had 18 people in all. This was another great day at the Vallas residence.

Monday I received three cases of my wine from California under my own label. I had been doing business with Windsor Wines for about 10 years. Wednesday was Eleni's birthday and we went to the Flagler Steakhouse.

May 2003 – Dinners, Training, Classes and Family

On the 1st, Eleni and I drove to Ocean Reef for a couple of days and we returned on Saturday. Sunday I received a call that my Aunt Viola passed away. I felt very bad because we always had a lot of fun with her. Monday morning I had to go to a fire and returned after two hours. Everyone on the fire department was getting to know me. The rest of the week I went to the fire department in the morning early and we stayed home and each evening I cooked. Saturday, Eleni and I went to dinner at Trevini's. Sunday I had Shiona and Murdock, Lorraine and Danny, and Debbie and the girls for dinner. Monday the 12th, I drove to Atlanta to the Greek Embassy for an interview. I stayed at the Marriott overnight and returned the next day.

Saturday the 17th I had a training session at Riverwalk for Homeland Security and FEMA and dinner that night at Trevini's. Sunday I had Aunt Dolores and Debbie (my cousin) for dinner. Debbie and the girls came up too. The rest of the week I did a couple of fires and on Friday, I went for eye laser surgery. The next morning I read the newspaper and could see like I was a kid. It was great; no more glasses.

Saturday Eleni and I went to the Flagler Steakhouse for dinner. Sunday, Eleni and I drove to Fort Lauderdale to meet Shiona and Murdock for dinner at the "Greek Isles". Wednesday the 28th I went to a CPR class. Saturday the 31st we had dinner at Trevini's.

June 2003 – Trip to the NJ Office

Sunday the 1st, I baby sat for the girls and made dinner for everyone that night. Tuesday the 3rd, Eleni and I went to Ocean 11 in Boca Raton for dinner. It was very nice. Wednesday, Eleni brought her Mercedes for detailing and new brake pads, while I went to a meeting in Fort Lauderdale for IENGA. I went to a structure fire that week too. Philip was at the fire also. Sunday Debbie and the girls came up for dinner. On the 8th I had lunch at the fire department. That evening Eleni and I went back to Oceans 11 again for dinner. Thursday I made a large pot of Conch Chowder. It was great. Saturday the 14th Debbie, Eleni, and I had dinner at Trevini's. Sunday was Father's Day and I cooked dinner for Debbie and the girls. Ozzie, Eleni's ex-husband and my neighbor, Arthur Wise came too.

Monday the 16th I had a meeting at the American Legion. Tuesday the 17th I took Arthur Wise to the doctor. He was 93 years old. The rest of the week, I went to a few fires and on Saturday Eleni and I went to dinner at the Four Seasons. Sunday Debbie and the girls were to come to dinner, but her ex-husband Mark kept the girls very late so we didn't see them. Mark continued to bother Debbie. He was terrible and his mouth was worse than ever. Monday I had a house fire in the morning. I left for NJ and stopped in Jacksonville. I left Jacksonville and arrived in NJ 14 hours later to the Marriott in Park Ridge. I worked at the office and Friday evening Petee and I ate at Solari's Restaurant; our favorite. I stayed on Petee's boat Saturday night and ate at the marina. Nick, my nephew, came in on Sunday. On Monday we ate at Esty Street.

July 2003 – The Boat

Tuesday the 1st Petee and Gloria left with the boat for Newport, Rhode Island. I returned to the Marriott. Saturday the 5th I went to visit Eleni's cousin Flo and Sid in South Jersey. Sunday I went to the Greek Church in Teaneck. I worked at the office the rest of the week and Wednesday I had dinner with my CPA, Mike Mongelli. Eleni had her eye exam because she was going to have cataract surgery. Friday Petee returned from Newport, Rhode Island and we had dinner at the Marriott. Sunday the 12th at 12:15am I left NJ and arrived home at 7:30pm. The 16th I gave a bomb class at fire headquarters.

Thursday the 17th, Eleni and I drove to Ocean Reef for four days and ate at all our favorite places. It was very relaxing. We then returned home, stopped at Publix, and I cooked dinner. Wednesday, Eleni had surgery on her right eye, and I made dinner at home. Saturday we went to dinner with Lorraine and Danny at Oceans 11, and Sunday I baby sat for the girls and made dinner. Tuesday I had a staff meting at the fire department headquarters and an American Legion meeting at 10am. On Wednesday the 30th I taught a fire investigative class at Station 2 for about 25 men.

August 2003 – My Sister

On the 2nd Linda and Tom came to Palm Beach and stayed at the Fairfield Inn. We went to Trevini's that night for dinner. On Monday the 4th I had to teach an IENGA class at the Embassy Suites in Fort Lauderdale. Thursday there was a tornado at 5:12pm. It was a bit nerve racking, but just outside damage. Friday we had another tornado but escaped any damage. Eleni and I had dinner at Café Boulud in the Brazilian Court in Palm Beach. It was great. Saturday night we had dinner at Trevini's with Debbie.

The following week I did a fire investigation and I made dinner home each day. Thursday there was a blackout on the east coast, NY, NJ, CT, and Canada. Saturday we ate dinner at Café Boulud again. It was a wonderful place. The owner Daniel had a place in New York called Daniel's. I met him and he sent me a cookbook. The clientele here consisted of all the famous people like Rush Limbaugh, Rod Stuart, Vic Damone, and others. Dinner for two averaged $200.00 and up. The rest of the week we had doctor's appointments. This is what happens when you get over 50, many things go wrong. Saturday we went to Café Boulud again. Sunday I baby sat until Debbie came home then I went home and made dinner. Wednesday the 27th Eleni had surgery on her left eye.

Friday the 29th Eleni, Debbie and I went to a new Greek place on Clematis Street; the Taverna. I knew the owner Angelo and it was good. Saturday evening we went to Café Boulud again and we were becoming part of the scene. The next day Murdock came for dinner. Shiona was in the U.K. Saturday we went to Café Boulud and when we went home we watched "My Big Fat Greek Wedding" which was very funny. Sunday we relaxed at home and I made dinner.

September 2003 – IENGA and the Fire Department

Wednesday the 10th Eleni and I went to the Taverna. Angelo had hung my movie picture on the wall just like it was hanging in Trevini's. Thursday the 11th I went to 9-11 services with the fire department. Eleni and I went to Spotos on Clematis Street for dinner then there was a fire department service there and we were on TV. Saturday we ate at Café Boulud's as usual. Sunday I baby sat and then cooked dinner.

Monday I had a meeting at the fire department and then went home. Tuesday I had a 10am meeting in Fort Lauderdale with IENGA. Wednesday I did a class on search and rescue at the fire department. Thursday the 18th Eleni and I drove to Orlando to the J.W. Marriott which was connected to the Ritz Carlton. I took a large two bedroom suite for four days. It was beautiful. That night we ate at Prinio's which was just okay. Friday we ate at the Ritz Carlton at Norman's. It was great. We met Norman and he sat with us for a while. Daniel and he were friends.

Saturday we ate lunch at the Golf Clubhouse which was very good. I went to the pool in the afternoon then we had cocktails at Norman's Bar then we had dinner. Wednesday and Thursday I taught a class at the fire department. Saturday we went to Café Boulud for dinner. On Sunday the 28th I made dinner for Claude, the bartender at Trevini's, and his girlfriend Jessica. The fire within was now blazing again. It felt great going to fires again and teaching at the fire department.

October 2003 - Mom

I had noticed that mom was starting to get worse. I went there almost every day and I felt bad. Friday the 10th we went to dinner at Angelo and Maxies and it was just okay. Saturday I had made baklava and brought it to Café Boulud at dinner time. All the employees loved it. Monday the 13th I left for Lakeland, Florida to teach an IENGA class. Linda and Tom drove over and they had supper with me at the hotel. I returned home on Friday and Philip met Eleni and I at Trevini's. Saturday Eleni and I ate at Café Boulud. Wednesday the 22nd Eleni and I drove to Hilton Head, South Carolina to meet with Linda and Tom. We stayed at the Marriott. We had dinner at the Old Fort.

The next day we had lunch at Harbor Town then drinks at the Marriott. We had dinner at Antonio's and Eleni discovered she was missing her bracelet. It was a very expensive Indian made bracelet, which I had bought for her anniversary in Arizona. We went back the next day, but no one turned it in or found it. Sunday I drove to NJ and Eleni flew back to Palm Beach. I stayed at the Marriott in Park Ridge. I met with Petee and he left on the 29th with his yacht to Atlantic City.

November 2003 - The Holidays

I stayed at the NJ office and left on November 1st and stopped at the Savannah Georgia Marriott overnight. Eleni's ex-husband, Ozzie had an accident on the way to Debbie's so Eleni had to go and baby sit. I arrived home on Sunday morning. Eleni and I went to dinner at Café Boulud. The boat arrived in Norfolk, Virginia on day eight. Petee's captain was my friend, Ray Blake who always worked on the boat when I had it. Friday, the 7th the boat made it to Cape Canaveral. On Saturday I bought a new Lincoln Navigator with the works. Eleni and I went to dinner that night at Café Boulud.

I found out that the "Eleni" arrived at the Palm Harbor Marina. Sunday Petee, Gloria, Chris and Mary Ellen, Eleni and I had dinner at Trevini's. Monday Petee went back to NJ. Tuesday we met Gloria on the boat then went to Trevini's for dinner. Wednesday the 12th I went to Ocean Reef and found my golf cart stolen. I was very angry. After filling out a police report I stayed overnight and returned home the next day. Thursday the 13th Petee returned to Florida. On Friday we went to dinner at the Breakers to L'Escalier. Saturday we all went to dinner at Café Boulud. Sunday I made dinner for everyone including Debbie and the girls. I made a large leg of lamb. Monday Gloria and Petee returned to NJ. I would take care of the boat for him. Wednesday I attended a meeting for an emergency management plan. As usual Eleni had all the Christmas cards addressed and stamped for December 1st. On Friday I took Eleni to Worth Avenue to Ferragamo's and bought her a Ferragamo bag for Christmas. She was thrilled. That night we had dinner at Trevini's with Paul Getty. When we got home we found out our neighbor Matthew Stein died. Saturday Eleni and I went to Café Boulud for dinner. Sunday I baked two pumpkin pies for Thanksgiving.

The 24th and 25th I went to a couple of fires. It was funny when I arrived at the fire scene with my red lights on and a couple of West Palm Beach police offices saw me. They wanted to know how I rated a new black Navigator. I told them I was in the special investigative unit and the car was given to me by the mayor. They looked at me and I started laughing and they realized it was my personal car. After that they would refer to me as the "Black Stallion". Wednesday I washed the boat for Petee because Gloria and he were coming down on Wednesday the 26th for Thanksgiving. The next day Eleni made the turkey and we all went to Ozzie's sister's house in Boynton Beach. His sister Sophie was a scream. We always celebrated the girls' birthdays on Thanksgiving. Friday, the 28th we put up the Christmas tree and decorations. Petee flew to NJ and back the next day, that's business. I was very lucky to have a great son to take over the business.

December 2003 – The Holidays with Family and Friends

Wednesday December 3rd, Gloria, Petee, Eleni, and I booked two suites at Turnberry Island. We drove down and checked in. That night we ate at LaForge Restaurant in Miami. Thursday, Petee and I went to Adventure Mall to shop. That night we had drinks at the bar then dinner at the hotel. After dinner Petee hired a stretch limo and Petee and Gloria went to South Beach. Eleni and I didn't want to go because it would be an all night affair.

The next day we returned to Palm Beach, and that night we had dinner at Trevini's for my birthday. Saturday we all went to the L'Escalier for dinner. Sunday the 7th we all went to Flagler Steakhouse. Monday Petee went back to NJ.

The next week we rested and did chores. I was at the fire department each morning with donuts for the guys. Friday night we went to Trevini's. Saturday we went to Café Broulud and the valets made a big fuss over my new navigator. Sunday Shiona and Murdock came to dinner. Friday the 19th I took Eleni to the fire department where I was awarded the Volunteer of the Year Award. When we left the luncheon we drove to Tampa to the Marriott. Nick and his friend Laura took us to dinner then we returned to the Marriott for cocktails. The next day we went to Linda's for dinner. Sunday we returned home to Palm Beach. Monday was "doctors" day then we went to Café Boulud for dinner. Tuesday Petee and Gloria came down. We had Christmas Eve at our house, which was another wonderful time. Christmas Day we all went to L'Escalier for dinner. Friday Petee and Gloria went to visit someone in Boca. Saturday Eleni and I went to the boat for cocktails with Gloria and Petee, then to the Taverna for dinner. Petee flew back that night. On the 30th Shelley, Michael, and Sarah flew in from Los Angeles.

CHAPTER–THIRTY EIGHT
Year 2004

Chapter–Thirty Eight – Year 2004

January 2004 – The Holidays with Family and Friends

On New Year's Eve, I had a big party for everyone even Linda, Tom, Paul, and Sandy came. There were a total of about 20 people. On January 1st I had a noon brunch at the house and served omelets, pancakes, bagels, bacon, ham, and salads… just about everything. Everyone had a great time. Friday the 2nd Eleni and I took down the Christmas decorations and everyone else went home. Saturday I bought a new ice machine for the bar. That evening we went to Café Boulud. Tuesday, I had a meeting at the fire headquarters. I did two vehicle fire investigations that week, checked on the boat, and had my blood work, which I had to do every month. I went to mom's and she was about the same. Saturday we went to Café Boulud as usual and had our drinks at the bar then had dinner. We spoke to Daniel because he was in that night from NY. Petee and Gloria flew in on Wednesday the 14th. Friday night we went to Trevini's for dinner. Saturday night Eleni and I went to Café Boulud. Petee and Gloria returned on the 19th. Wednesday, January, 21st I had incident command training. The weekend got cold in the 40s and Saturday evening we went to Café Boulud.

February 2004 – Petee's Birthday

For Petee's birthday we all celebrated at L'Escalier at the Breakers. Wednesday the 4th I taught a class at the fire headquarters from 8am – 12pm. Friday, Eleni's cousins Flo, Sid, and Sheila came to dinner, and the next day I left for NJ. I stopped in Arlington, Virginia that night and I left early at 3am and arrived at the Marriott at 8am. I worked in the office all week and had dinner each night at Esty Street and one night at Solari's.

On Sunday the 15th Petee was having a 40th birthday celebration at Solari's Restaurant. He rented the entire place for the party because normally Solari's is closed on Sunday. Marco Solari was a good friend of Petee's and me. Marco was setting up a large buffet with all kinds of foods. Petee had ordered live music, slide presentations, dancing, and speeches. He invited about 100 friends and family. Sunday arrived and the party was great. Serge installed all the sound effects and photographs. Marco had a beautiful display of hors d'oeuvres; shrimp, lobster, crabs and many others. The bar was open for all and on the house. The girls that normally work at Solari's, worked the party. It was the most fantastic party I had ever been at. It probably cost him at least $50,000.00.

The next day I left for Florida and stayed in Florence, South Carolina overnight. Tuesday I left early and arrived home at 11am. Ironically, my ex-wife Rose passed away but I didn't find out until a month later. We had no contact for over 25 years so obviously, no one contacted me. Believe it or not my first wife sent me the obituary. I spent the week catching up at the fire department and at home. Eleni and I went to Trevini's Saturday night for dinner. Sunday I baby sat at Debbie's and made dinner. I loved it because the girls would wake up early because they knew I would be sleeping on the couch. I would hear them sneaking down the stairs so I would pretend I was sleeping. When they both walked up to the couch, I would jump up and scare them. Then I would make them pancakes, which they loved. On the 23rd my sister, Linda called me and said her cancer returned and was in her liver. She would now receive chemotherapy again. I got off the phone and cried. I loved my sister and I felt so helpless. She was a very sweet person and like an energizer bunny. I had a hard time adjusting to this.

Thursday the 26th Eleni and I went to Orlando to the J.W. Marriott. Linda and Tom met us there. I had my usual suite and they had a nice room. Eleni and I always took a large suite because we liked to entertain and also we liked two bathrooms. That night we ate at the Marriott Restaurant "Primo", which was just okay. After dinner we walked to the Ritz Carlton next door for drinks at the lobby bar. Friday we all had lunch at the Club House, which was great. Eleni and I always ate lunch there when we stayed here. That night we ate at Norman's in the Ritz and it was absolutely wonderful. Saturday we had lunch at the Club House and dinner again at Norman's. Sunday we all went home after breakfast.

March 2004 – Petee and Gloria Come for a Visit

The first week of March we had some heavy winds. On the 4th Petee and Gloria flew in with their friends, Jeff and Sharon. They took the boat to Boca Raton for the weekend. Saturday, Eleni and I went to Café Boulud for dinner. Sunday, Eleni, Gloria, Petee, Jeff, Sharon, Chris, Petee's other friend, and I went to Trevini's for dinner. Monday Petee went home and Gloria stayed on the boat. I had a meeting at the fire headquarters on the 10th. Gloria left on the 11th to go home. Saturday we went to dinner at Café Boulud. Sunday we had dinner home. I was called to a fire and assisted in the investigation. We ate home all week and I had a vehicle fire to investigate for my company, PVA. Saturday we went to Café Boulud for dinner as usual. Sunday our friends, Murdock and Shiona came to dinner and I made lamb. I went to a couple of fires during the next week and again we had high winds. Petee flew in on Friday. Saturday the 27th we had a big drill at Fire Station 2 for about four hours and that night we ate at Café Boulud. We also got a call from California and Shelley had a baby girl which they named Kaela. Eleni and I now had four girls for grandchildren. I knew Petee would never get married or have children because he liked his lifestyle. On Sunday we had Petee and Gloria for dinner. Monday I received a call that my godmother, Hazel Stathakis passed away.

On March 31st I investigated a fire in a Boutique Shop for West Palm Beach.

April 2004 – Mom has a Falling Accident

Saturday, April 3rd, Eleni and I went to Café Boulud for dinner. Sunday I baby sat, but had to go to a car fire then I made dinner at Debbie's. Tuesday, I did a house fire at 1am and then I got a call from the nursing home that mom fell and she was at Good Samaritan Hospital. I immediately went there and she was on a gurney in the hall. She had a lump on her head but she was okay. The nurse wanted to take her for an x-ray and brought her back to me. It was okay, but then they insisted on taking her blood. They couldn't find a vein and mom was now yelling so I told the nurse to leave her alone and I had her transported back to the nursing home.

On the 10th, Linda and Tom came and stayed at the Fairfield Inn. That night I took them to dinner at Café Boulud. They loved it. On Sunday I made dinner and had Debbie and the girls, Lorraine, and Danny for dinner, which was Greek Easter. On the 13th I had two-one hour treatments to whiten my teeth. Wednesday the 14th I left to drive to Las Vegas. I stopped in Tallahassee because I left late in the day. The next day I drove to Houston, Texas. I stayed overnight and left 1:15am and arrived in Flagstaff, Arizona at 8:45am. There was a great place called Black Bart's, which had a bar and restaurant. It was unique because all the girls and boys that worked there would sing and perform during dinner. It was great. The next morning I left for Las Vegas. Eleni flew in and met me at the J.W. Marriott. I had a limo pick her up. The next three days we ate at our favorite places and I gambled each day. I won $800.00 and on Thursday the 22nd Eleni and I drove to Phoenix to the J.W. Marriott Desert Resort. When we arrived we had room service in our suite. The next day we drove to Fountain Hills to see our old house then we went to Old Town in Scottsdale to shop and had lunch at the Quilted Bear. That night, we ate in Scottsdale at the Mexican place. Saturday evening we ate at our favorite place the Palm Court. We saw our friends there and had a good time. Sunday we had breakfast from room service, and that night we had dinner at the Marriott Steakhouse. Monday the 26th Eleni flew out to Florida and I drove to the San Antonio Marriott. I left the next morning and drove to Pensacola, Florida arriving at 12:30pm. The next morning I drove home arriving at 9:30am. It was a great trip all the way around. April 30th Eleni and I went to Trevini's for dinner for Eleni's birthday.

May 2004 – My Sister, Linda and Her Husband Come to Visit

Saturday, May 1st we went to Café Boulud with Petee and Gloria. Sunday we all went to the Flagler Steakhouse. Petee and Gloria returned to NJ on Tuesday. I was walking in our garage and fell down and bruised my knee and leg.

Friday the 7th I left for NJ and stopped at Rocky Mount, North Carolina. The next day I arrived at the Park Ridge Marriott at 9:30am. Petee, Gloria, and I had dinner at Esty Street. The next day was Mother's Day and we ate at Gloria's and Petee cooked. My ex-wife Irene was also there and Gloria's father. The next three days I worked at the office and ate at Esty Street at night. The 13th I drove to Providence, Rhode Island and to the Marriott. Eleni flew in to meet me.

The next day my friend Joe Bustin was retiring and his wife Marcia was giving him a surprise party at a large restaurant with about 100 people. Friday was his last day at work so she told him when he comes home she was taking him to dinner. I rented a stretch limo and Eleni and I were dropped off at Joe's house. I told the limo driver to park around the corner so Joe wouldn't see it. After 3:30pm we saw Joe drive up and Eleni and I hid in the kitchen. Joe came in and he kissed Marcia and I thought he was about to cry. I stepped out and when he saw Eleni and me, he got so excited. We told him we came to go to dinner for his retirement. I called my limo and we all got in to go to the restaurant. It was a catering hall and very nice. When we arrived we went to the back door and I went in first so Joe wouldn't see anyone. Then they all yelled "Surprise" and a surprise it was. It was a great night. Eleni and I left with our limo and left Joe and Marcia with their family.

Saturday we ate lunch at the Marriott and dinner at a great place, "The Gate House". Sunday I left early and drove to Florence, South Carolina. Eleni flew home from PVD. I arrived home the next day at 9am. I loved driving and I always drove at night because there was no traffic. I actually enjoyed these long trips. I never got tired. The rest of the week was catch up, and I had a fire on the 21st. Saturday we went to Café Boulud for dinner. I received a call from the nursing home that mom fell again. I went over and told them to leave her alone. I could see she was failing quickly so I told them to make her comfortable, and left. We went to Café Boulud for dinner then stopped back to check on my mother.

My friend, Bob who was the fire marshal, and his wife Kay came to dinner on Sunday. Monday the 24th there was a fire at the Winn Dixie and I went to it. Thursday the 27th I did two vehicle fire investigations. On the 28th I got a call from the nursing home that mom fell again. I went over and yelled at them. I told them to put her in a wheel chair from now on. I checked her out myself and she was okay. Saturday we went to Café Boulud for dinner. Sunday I took the girls to the swimming pool and Debbie picked them up at our house.

June 2004 – Visits from Family

Wednesday the 2nd Eleni and I went to dinner at Trevini's with Linda and Tom. I told Linda I didn't think mom was going to be with us much longer. When we went to see her she was in bed but didn't recognize anyone.

Thursday Linda and Tom, Eleni and I went to the Cobot House to look for a dining room table, which Linda bought. That night we had dinner at Trevini's. Friday, Linda and Tom returned to Spring Hill. I went to the nursing home and that is when I called Hospice. They came and they were wonderful. I knew mom was in her last days. I asked for oxygen so she could breathe more easily. Saturday I spent a few hours with mom and I learned that former President Reagan died. They were both the same age. That night Eleni and I went to Café Boulud for dinner. Sunday I went to the nursing home then I cooked dinner for our friends, Kelly and Tom Manos. Then Eleni and I went to bed.

At 12:15am the nursing home called and said mom died. I went over there and I kissed her. She looked just like my grandmother Francis did when she died. Monday she was one month short of 94 years old. I called the funeral home and they picked her up. I already had paid for her funeral two years ago because the funeral director was a friend from the American Legion. I went home and called Linda. Mom wanted to be cremated so I had all the arrangements made.

The next day I stayed home because of all the phone calls I had to make including calls to Greece. There would be no viewing and I went to the funeral home. Friday the 11th I gave the funeral director a bouquet of fresh daisies to put in her hands before they did the cremation. I told them I would pick up the ashes when I got back from a trip I had to make.

The next day I left for Baton Rouge, Louisiana to the Marriott for a week long 40 hour course on advanced terrorism and formal training. I stopped at the Tallahassee Courtyard. I checked in and the girl was a large black woman whom I saw once before there. She was very sweet. I told her I wanted to eat at a different restaurant than the Outback next door. I also told her that my mom's funeral was this morning. She went to a file drawer and started to walk over with a menu. I started to tell her that mom was cremated that morning. She stopped in her tracks and said, "I think I better send you to a different place." I said, "What's the matter with the one in your hands?" She seemed a little nervous but gave me the menu. I looked at it and the name of the place was "Smoking Bones". Well, I couldn't help laughing and neither could she.

The next day I went to Baton Rouge, and checked in. After four days of training I left the hotel Thursday on the 17th at 4am and arrived home at 5:30pm. Saturday night. We went to Lorraine's for dinner. Sunday Eleni and I went to Café Boulud for Father's Day. I had picked up mom's ashes and opened them up. I made two small containers, one for Linda and one for me. I held the rest to bury in NJ next to my father's grave. Tuesday I had to go to Fort Lauderdale to teach for IENGA all week.

Saturday the 26th Eleni and I went to Café Boulud for dinner. Saturday Eleni and I ordered our Christmas cards as we do every year at this time.

Monday I made our reservations for Greece. We always did this way ahead of time because we flew first class and always on Delta. Tuesday, we took our neighbor, Arthur to Trevini's for dinner.

July 2004 – Petee and Gloria

Petee and Gloria flew in. I had a chemical fire and then we all went to Trevini's. I left for NJ the next day and stopped in Jacksonville. The next day I went to Rocky Mountain, North Carolina. I arrived at the Park Ridge Marriott on July 4th. Petee was going to the Bahamas with the boat the next day. I met with Mike Mongelli, my CPA on Wednesday. Thursday I had to go to Newark for fingerprinting for the State Police to renew my private detective license for NJ. On Friday the 9th I drove straight to Florida because Petee was sailing back from the Bahamas. Saturday night Petee, Gloria, Debbie and the girls, and Eleni and I went to the Flagler Steakhouse. The next day Petee and Gloria went back to NJ. I had a building fire that day too. Thursday I had an arson case in a truck yard. Saturday we went to Café Boulud for dinner. Sunday I was painting in the house and we ate at home. Tuesday the 27th I did six fire investigations on vehicles. The next day I had a house fire investigation. Saturday night the 31st we ate dinner at Trevini's.

August 2004 - Babysitting

Sunday, I baby sat and made dinner at Debbie's. I had to leave in the afternoon for a large fire at a night club. On Friday the 6th I had a vehicle fire to inspect. Saturday we ate dinner at Café Boulud. Sunday I went to Petee's boat to check on it. Shortly after I got there, there was a fire over my radio in a structure on 50th Street. I responded then went home. The weather got cold the next two days and I responded to a fire at Good Samaritan Hospital on the 9th and 10th of August.

Hurricane Bonnie and Charlie were making their way to the Caribbean. On the 12th there was another fire at the Good Samaritan Hospital and I was investigating both as suspicious. Hurricane Charlie came ashore in Punta Gorda. That night Eleni and I ate at Trevini's. The next night we ate at Café Boulud. Sunday the 15th I had a fire on 3rd Street. Tuesday I had a fire on Georgia Avenue. Michael, Shelley, and the girls flew in from Los Angeles on Thursday. Friday I had two major fires, one on Congress Avenue and one on Pinewood. I spent a total of six hours investigating and training other investigators. That night we had dinner at Debbie's with all the family. Saturday, Linda and Tom came to the Fairfield Inn. I had a car fire and accident on Australian Avenue. That night we ate at Trevini's. Sunday I made a brunch for everyone, Michael, Shelly, Debbie and all four girls, Linda and Tom, Ozzie, Jackie, and Sophie. That afternoon Linda, Tom, Eleni and I had lunch late at the Gulf Stream Hotel. Wednesday the 25th Eleni and I went to Ozzie's sister, Sophie's house for dinner with Michael, Shelley, and the family.

The next day they went back to Los Angeles. Saturday Eleni and I went to Café Boulud. Sunday. I had a fire in Gramacy Park and that evening we ate at Charlie's Crab with Murdock and Shiona. Tuesday the 31st Eleni finished the Christmas cards and they were ready to go December 1st. I was now watching Hurricane Frances. Petee flew down with Gloria and we secured the boat as best we could. We also took two suites at the Hampton Inn out West on Okeechobee Blvd, one suite for Petee and Gloria, and another suite for Debbie, the girls and me. Eleni refused to leave the condo. We all had dinner at Bradley's and then went to the Hampton Inn. The storm hit us that night and the power was off all over even at the condo. That morning I left the Hampton Inn and put my red lights on and went to the boat. There were wires and trees all over the streets. I checked the boat and saw the rear port side was damaged because the dock partially collapsed.

I spent the next three days at the fire headquarters. I did go home to change and was able to go on the island to the condo because I had my emergency flashing lights on and everyone, the police and fire department on the island knew me. Eleni was fine and the building generator was working. The few people who did not evacuate including Eleni were in the party room, which was on generator power so they had lights, stoves, refrigerators, and freezers all working. Personally, I think people were better off staying home than trying to evacuate. The evacuation routes were clogged and many people were stuck in their cars.

September 2004 – Another Visit with Petee and Gloria

Monday Petee and Gloria decided to go to the Marriott Harbor Beach in Fort Lauderdale. I got a suite at the Radisson because they had power. Eleni was fine at the condo although they still had no power. The elevators, hall lights, and the large party room and kitchen were on generator and were okay, but the apartments were not.

All power was restored on Thursday the 9th at night. I went home on the 10th and we had a fire in a structure on Eddie Place. Petee returned home on Saturday morning. Eleni and I had dinner at Maxie's that night. Sunday I made dinner at home. This week I took down the inside shutters. Petee came down on the 16th to his boat. The next day, I had a tar pot fire and that night Petee, Eleni, and I had dinner at Trevini's. Saturday we were watching another hurricane "Jeannie". Petee came over and we had dinner at home. Sunday Petee left for NJ.

The next two days it was windy and rainy. I went to the store to stock up because Hurricane Jeannie was going to hit Saturday into Sunday. Saturday Flanagan's

Grill had a small fire. That night I stayed at the Radisson again because the storm was moving in. The Radisson was on the same electric grid as the hospital so they didn't lose power very often. The Radisson let me park my navigator under the front entrance in case I had to leave for a fire.

Sometime before midnight a structure fire came in and I monitored the radio. I heard a call from Captain Smoke that a man was down. I got dressed and heard another fire on Lytle Street; heavy smoke and fire. I got in my car, put on my lights, and headed to Lytle Street. I couldn't see very well because the winds were blowing at 75mph to 100mph gusts. All of the street lights and power in the homes were out. I had trouble getting there but I did. I saw that the crew were having a hard time so I suited up and strapped on my helmet. When I got to the house we were being blown all over. They had a line stretched to the rear, but the fire was advancing towards the 2nd floor of the house. I entered the rear and someone said, "Captain, you've been doing this longer than us, how can we stop the fire?" I sent for an attic ladder and told them to open the ceiling and put the 1 ½" line down the inside of the walls. This did the trick and the fire in about 15 minutes, was under control. The storm was bad and I never fought a fire in the middle of a hurricane before. I left the scene and went back to the hotel soaking wet.

The next morning I went to headquarters and then went back to the house to see what caused the fire. It was an electrical fire caused when the power lines fell. There were quite a few fires that month, more than normal. Power at the condo was restored on Monday at 11:30am. Wednesday we had a large propane explosion and fire at the Crown Plaza Hotel, which was not occupied at that time due to storm damage.

October 2004 – My Neighbor

October 1st I was at a fire in a structure and after I left I went into a Wal-Mart to have my digital photo chip developed from the fire. I walked by a large display of batteries and the belt which holds my fire radio caught on the rack and the whole rack fell over dumping batteries all over the floor. I felt like a jerk, but everyone was laughing except the girl who had to pick it up.

Saturday night Eleni and I went to the Café Boulud for dinner. Sunday I made dinner at home. Monday I did a van fire investigation. Tuesday I was teaching at Fire Station 2 when Eleni called on my cell phone. She said Arthur our neighbor was on his knees by his bed and didn't move. I told her to check his neck pulse and then use a mirror to see if he was breathing. She did, and I told her he was dead and to call 911.

Thursday and Friday I did two house fires. Petee flew to San Francisco. Saturday night Eleni and I went to Trevini's for dinner. Sunday we relaxed at home and I cooked dinner. Monday I was at fire headquarters and we had a fire on North Flagler Drive. Tuesday through Friday, I was teaching in Fort Lauderdale for IENGA. Saturday we went to Café Boulud for dinner. Sunday I did an auto fire on Pine Terrace then made dinner home. The next morning at 2am I was called to a fire in a restaurant. Later that day I responded to an explosion at the Palm Beach Yacht Club. A worker there was critically burned. Wednesday my sister called me and said the cancer in her liver had gone away. I was so happy. Anytime I spoke to her I would cry but I couldn't let her know that. I didn't' want anything to happen to my sister. Saturday I had a fire at Darcy Hall where mom used to be. It was in one room.

That night Eleni and I went to dinner at Trevini's. Monday I had a structure fire on Embassy Drive at 10am. Wednesday I had another structure fire. Friday the 29th I left for NJ at 12:28am and stopped at 12pm in Rocky Mountain, North Carolina. The next morning I left for NJ at 2am and arrived at the Park Ridge Marriott at 2pm.

November 2004 – Our Vacation in New Hampshire

I worked at the office until Thursday the 4th then drove to Providence, Rhode Island to the Marriott. Eleni flew in the next day. We ate dinner at the Capital Grill. Sunday the 7th we drove to Mount Washington in Brentonwood, New Hampshire where we were going to spend five days. The brochures were beautiful and Eleni and I were going to go horseback riding, and Eleni wanted to go ice skating. We arrived and the mountains were beautiful and the hotel was gigantic. The hotel looked beautiful, but when we moved into our suite (it was large, with two baths, fireplace, and a large living room), it was all shabby. There was a brass plate on the door indicating what famous person stayed there, some general from the early 1900s. You could actually see through cracks in the door into our living room. The whole place was falling apart. We ate lunch and it was just okay. When we walked in the halls, the floors would squeak. I think Grandma Moses lived there at one time. We had cocktails at the small wooden bar and dinner in the so called dining room. I asked about the horseback riding and they said all the horses were moved to Virginia for the winter, and the ice skating didn't start until January. We decided that for $800.00 a night it was the pits. I should have worn my George Washington coat because I would have fit in better.

The next morning we checked out and drove to Portsmouth, New Hampshire to the Marriott Wentworth by the Sea. It was beautiful. We had a two story suite with two bathrooms. It was a lovely hotel. We had lunch and dinner at the hotel and it was great. Tuesday we drove into Maine to shop in the town of Portsmouth. That afternoon we walked around the beautiful lake there. That evening we ate dinner at the hotel. Thursday we left for Providence, Rhode Island to the Marriott and had dinner at the Capitol Grill. Friday Eleni flew home. I left at 11pm and drove all the way to the Jacksonville Marriott. I left the next morning early and arrived home at 8:45am. Sunday there was a special service for Arthur, by his family in his apartment. The rest of the week we wrapped Christmas presents and on Friday I did two structure fires and one vehicle fire. Saturday Petee and Gloria were down and we went to dinner at L'Escalier at the Breakers. Sunday we had dinner home and I did two structure fires. Monday I taught a class at Fire Station 2.

Thanksgiving we went to Debbie's. Friday we went to Fire Marshal, Mike Carsillo's wedding. He married a police officer, Kelly a lovely girl. Saturday the 27th Eleni and I put all of our Christmas decorations up and the tree, then we went to dinner at Trevini's. I also had a structure fire on Gordon Street. Linda and Tom had gone on a cruise for a week.

December 2004 – Petee and Gloria Come for another Visit

On December 2nd Petee and Gloria came down and we went to the Breakers. The next day Petee and Gloria met with Chris and Mel on their boat. Saturday the 4th we all had dinner at the Flagler Steakhouse. The 5th was my birthday and we celebrated it at Trevini's. Petee and Gloria returned on the 7th. On Saturday Eleni and I had dinner at Café Boulud and Sunday we had dinner at home. We spent the next few days getting ready to leave for Tampa on Thursday the 23rd. We drove to Tampa to the Grand Hyatt to a beautiful suite. I had drinks and dinner reserved on the top of the Hyatt at Armani's. I took everyone there for dinner. Ramzi and Stephanie were celebrating their engagement. My family Nick, Linda, Tom, Stephanie, and Ramzi had a wonderful time. Christmas we all had dinner at Linda's. Linda was a great cook and we loved eating there. She was a great entertainer. We exchanged presents and then we went back to the hotel. The next morning we went home. Monday I had Petee, Debbie, and the girls for dinner. Friday New Year's Eve Eleni and I had an early dinner at Trevini's and went home. New Year's Day Eleni and I went to dinner at Café Boulud.

CHAPTER–THIRTY NINE
Year 2005

Chapter–Thirty Nine – Year 2005

January 2005 – The Holidays & Fire Investigations

January 2nd I had a fire on 33rd Street. Tuesday the 4th we took down our Christmas decorations. I also had a structure fire on Haverhill. On the 5th I had a fire at the mall and on Saturday I had a fire at Darcy Hall. Eleni and I went to dinner at Café Boulud. Sunday the 9th I went to a fatal car crash where the driver burned to death. Monday I did a car fire and a fire at the art school. Both fires were set.

Petee came down on the 12th. Friday we all ate at Trevini's. Saturday we went to dinner at Café Boulud. I was at a very bad accident involving about 11 cars. It was an MCI-1. Monday I did a fire at 5500 Flagler. Friday the 14th we ate at Trevini's and Saturday we ate at Café Boulud. Sunday I had two fires, one on Rosemary Avenue and one on Evernia Street. Wednesday we had a radiation leak, which shut down most of downtown. On the 28th Linda and Tom came for lunch. Saturday evening we went to Café Boulud. On Monday we hired a new fire chief, Robert Ridgeway. He was from North Carolina. We had been without a chief several months because Chief Carter retired. He was a good guy and I knew him from NFPA and from many other fire organizations.

February 2005 – Petee's Birthday

Thursday the 3rd Petee was 41 years old. Saturday at 1:15am, I had a restaurant fire on 15th Street. That night Eleni and I ate at Trevini's. Sunday I had three fires and a fatal accident. We ate at home that night. Fires were on the upside lately and Monday and Tuesday, I did two car fires. Tuesday I also taught a leadership class at Station 2. Thursday the 10th, I finally received a call from the Greek Consulate to come to Atlanta, Georgia and receive my citizenship. I drove to Atlanta and stayed at the Marriott in Buckhead. Friday the 11th, I took the Greek Oath and was sworn in. Now I had both US and Greek citizenships.

The next day I drove to Mobile, Alabama to visit a fire boat manufacturer for the chief then I drove to the Beau Rivage in Biloxi. I had the beautiful Cyprus suite and Eleni flew in to Gulfport, Massachusetts and I had a stretch limo pick her up. The place was lovely and we had dinner at La Cocina. I gambled that night and won $950.00. The next day we shopped in the stores and had lunch. That night we ate at the Port House, which was very good. That night I won $1,600.00 on the slots. The next day we walked around and we ate at the Port House again. That night I won another $1,100.00. I always seemed to be lucky on the $1.00 and $5.00 slots. On the 16th Eleni flew home and I drove home in 11 hours. On the 17th I had a fire on 4th Street, and Petee and Gloria came in for the weekend. Saturday I had a fire on

7th Street then we went to Café Boulud for dinner. Sunday Petee and Gloria flew back to NJ. I had a fire on Pinewood and had dinner at home. Tuesday the 22nd I made dinner for Eleni's cousin Flo and Sid, and Debbie and the girls. Wednesday, Thursday, and Friday I cooked at home. That week I had done seven fires at all hours of the day. Teaching the new investigators proved very helpful being on the scene.

Wednesday the 23rd I received my Black American Express Centurion card with a million dollar limit. Saturday we went to dinner at the Flagler Steakhouse. I did a gas leak at the high school that day too. The next day I had a structure fire at Parker & Forest Hill. Friday I had a car fire on 45th Street. As you can see I was getting enough fires lately and it was good training for the new inspectors. Saturday evening I took Eleni, Debbie, and the girls to dinner at the Flagler Steakhouse. It was Debbie's 50th birthday. The next day I baby sat the girls and cooked dinner.

March 2005 – Dinners and Meeting Famous People

The first week I had two fires and the rest of the week, a staff meeting and a fire at Wright's Trailer Park. I had lunch with the chief at Trevini's. Saturday Petee came down for the weekend. Both Friday and Saturday we ate at Trevini's. Petee and I met over business and he returned to NJ on Monday. Sunday Eleni and I ate at Café L'Europe. The next week we stayed home and I cooked. Friday we ate at Trevini's and Saturday at Café Boulud. Petee and I always ate in expensive restaurants, went to exclusive nightclubs, and had parties for many friends and lived high. I met many famous people, Rod Stuart, Donald and Ivanna Trump, and in Los Angeles I met Goldie Hawn, Stevie Wonder, Cher, Sonny Bono, Milton Berle, Tony Curtis, Elizabeth Taylor, Sidney Portier, and many others. My life had changed so much since I became so successful. I wished my dad was alive today to see me. I had a great son and a wonderful wife, and the fire within was still burning. I was a published author, twice, a movie actor; the most decorated firefighter in the US, and decorated by presidents; Jimmy Carter, and Ronald Reagan.

When I look back to 1979, all my hard work paid off. To think I was the son of a Greek immigrant who worked day and night for his family in the restaurant business, and now I made it to the top. It was a great feeling, life was a constant adventure.

The week of the 13th Bob Prusiecki, the fire marshal retired and Mike Carsillo took over. I also did two fires. Petee was down for the weekend and we had Chief Ridgeway on the yacht for drinks. Saturday night we ate at Café Boulud. Sunday we stayed home and I worked. Tuesday Eleni's cousin, Flo and Sid visited and we went to Trevini's for dinner. I had two fires on Wednesday and one on Friday. Saturday I went to a rollover accident on I-95. That evening we had dinner at Café Boulud. Easter we had Debbie and the girls for dinner. Wednesday the 30th I had a code 10 fire in an auto with a death.

April 2005 – My New Yacht – A Bigger Boat

April 1ˢᵗ, I went to Fort Lauderdale to look at another yacht. I couldn't stand being without one. This was a 70 foot Hattaras Motor Yacht with a cockpit. It was beautiful. It had a large master cabin with a king size bed, make-up table, and walk in cedar closets. There were three more state rooms; one was a VIP room with a queen size bed. All rooms had a full bath and shower and all walls were mirrored. It had a laundry room with a washer and dryer. The second deck had a large pilot house with duplicate controls, radar, GPS, chart master, auto pilot, engine synchronizers, and stabilizers. It also had the same on the fly bridge. The galley had a two-door refrigerator and freezer, microwave, convection oven, Magic Chef Stove and oven, dishwasher, compactor, and a Newton food center. The main salon had a custom wet bar, full entertainment center, three bar stools, two barrel chairs, end tables, L-shaped leather sofa, which sat eight people, and a custom glass dining room table with six chairs. The salon was finished with white ash and one wall was mirrored. There was tan and white carpeting throughout the yacht, with a central vacuum system. The salon bar also had a Scotsman high capacity ice maker, and plenty of storage and glass holders. The outside cockpit had a large refrigerator and freezer. In the salon there was a circular stairway, which led to the master cabin. All rooms had televisions, and access to the entertainment system with 16 speakers throughout the yacht. There was a stainless steel circular stairway from the wheel house to the upper fly bridge. The fly bridge was enclosed with a rear exterior deck. It had seating for 15 people, and a bar and grill, refrigerator and ice maker. There were two engine rooms below with twin diesel engines, and a complete water maker system. There were two 20k generators, 2,000 gallon (4) tanks for fuel, a 345 gallon water tank, and 40 gallon hot water heater. Replacement cost for this yacht was over 2 million dollars. When I got home I was dazzled by this beauty. Saturday Petee and Gloria came down and we also heard the pope died. Monday Petee and Gloria came to diner and I made buffalo steaks. I had a couple of structure fires too.

Petee and Gloria left on Tuesday. One of my employees, Sergei, and Ray Blake left with Petee's yacht the "Eleni" for NJ for the summer on the 8ᵗʰ. Saturday I was at a fatal car accident then Eleni and I went to dinner at Café Boulud. Sunday I baby sat, but the girls were now older, 8 years old and they were a lot of fun. Tuesday I took Eleni to see the yacht. She fell in love with it too. On the 14ᵗʰ I went to see the boat again and decided to buy it. I went home and transferred $100,000.00 to set up my finances. I paid my Lincoln Navigator off and paid $80,000.00 for the down payment on the yacht. On the 19ᵗʰ I got a call from Petee that the yacht "Eleni" hit a submerged object and was partially sunk. It was being towed to Cape May, NJ. I felt terrible since I had a similar experience once before.

Saturday night, Eleni and I ate dinner at Trevini's. The next week I prepared for the closing on my yacht. Eleni and I decided to name it "Sophia" after my mom. Petee didn't want to give up the name "Eleni" on his yacht. Saturday night we went to dinner at Café Boulud.

May 2005 – Greek Easter

May 1st was Greek Easter and Eleni and I ate home. We were busy all week getting ready for our trip to Greece on May 21st. Thursday the 5th we closed on my yacht and I decided to leave it where it was behind a house off the intra-coastal, until I got back from Greece. Saturday the 7th we went to Trevini's to eat dinner. Tuesday the 13th I went to Citibank to pick up $2,000.00 in Euros' for my Greece trip.

Thursday I left for NJ because I had meetings with Petee. We were also going to leave for Greece from JFK so Eleni was going to fly in Friday the 20th. I arrived in NJ at the Park Ridge Marriott Saturday the 14th and spent the week in the office. Eleni flew in and I had Sergei pick her up and bring her to the Marriott. The next day I left my Navigator at Petee's house and Serge took Eleni and me to the airport. We went to the first class lounge to wait for our flight. We left at 5:30pm and arrived in Athens at the new airport on Sunday the 22nd. My driver, George picked us up and took us to the Ledra Marriott. All the employees met us at the door. We were like family to them. We went to our suite to unpack and because of the jet lag, we went to bed.

The next day I picked up my rental car and we went to my cousin Velissairo's house for lunch. Sotiris, Angeliki, Costa, Katie, and Kristine were there to meet us. After the crying and kissing we ate lunch. What a family they were, so wonderful. My cousin Velissairo was not that good because of his stroke but he still had a great attitude. Tuesday, Eleni and I went to the Plaka and had lunch at our favorite "Hermion Restaurant". That night we went to Felitsa's house for dinner. Wednesday the 25th Eleni and I went to the Plaka again. We went for drinks at the Crystal Room at Ledra Marriott, and dinner at the hotel. The next day we shopped and that night went to dinner at Angeliki's house in Peristeri. She had just moved into a new condo which they purchased overlooking the Acropolis. We had a great dinner. Her two boys, Nick and Velissairo, were just great. The next day we shopped again in the Plaka and had dinner at the Ledra Marriott on the rooftop. Saturday the 28th the entire family went to the Islands of Salamina to Cousin Marikas's house. She had passed away and her son Takis met me at the cemetery where we had a service for her. Then Takis took the entire family to lunch at a lovely restaurant. Later we left on the ferry back to Athens. You see, in Greece you can drive your car onto the ferry so you can drive where ever you go. On the 29th my friend, Joe Bustin and Marcia arrived from the US. We met them at the Hotel Divani for drinks and dinner. The next day I picked them up and drove them along the seaside to Sounion. We came back and had dinner at Daphane's. The next day I took my whole family including Joe and Marcia to the Kona Kai as I always did when I left Greece. I returned the car and Eleni and I ate dinner at the hotel.

June 2005 – The Marina

June 2nd my driver took us to the airport. We left at 12:15pm and arrived back in JFK at 3:50pm the same day, because we were going back seven hours. We stayed at the Marriott and Eleni flew back to West Palm Beach on Saturday the 4th. I left at 12:30am to drive back to Florida and I arrived home on Sunday. We stayed home the next couple of days to unpack and get settled. On Friday I moved the boat to Bahia Mar Marina and took a year's lease. The marina had floating docks which were great. Eleni met me late and we went to dinner at Bimini Boat Yard. Eleni and I spent Saturday doing the bedding and getting used to the boat. I shopped for groceries. That night we ate at our wonderful Rainbow Palace. Sunday I cooked on the boat. I had decided to stay on the boat during the week and Eleni would come down on Fridays and stay until Monday.

The rest of the week I was busy shopping and buying new things for the boat. Eleni and I would customize the interior our way. Eleni came back on Friday the 17th and that night we ate at the Greek Isles. Saturday morning I got up at 4:30am, my usual time to get up. I made my breakfast then went up on the fly bridge with my coffee. My yacht was only a block from the ocean and I could clearly see the waves and the sun rising. It was beautiful and I was happy to be back on a boat. I had the "sign person" there Saturday to change the name of the boat to Sophia.

That night Eleni and I ate dinner at Jackson's, another one of our favorite restaurants. The next day was Father's Day and I cooked on the boat. Eleni returned to Palm Beach Monday morning. Wednesday Petee flew to Dublin, Ireland with Gloria and little Ray for the Bono Concert. Petee was a big fan of his. Eleni arrived at the yacht on Friday and, as usual I had my diver clean the bottom of the boat. I did this every month. That night Eleni and I, and my friend Philip had dinner at the Seasons 52. Sunday we worked on the boat and that night we ate at Capitol Grill. Sunday Lorraine and Danny came to dinner on the boat. Eleni went home Monday morning. Tuesday I had my sound system upgraded. Wednesday and Thursday, I cleaned the outside of the yacht and cleaned all my A/C filters. This yacht had seven A/C units on it.

July 2005 – 4th of July Celebration

July 1st, Linda and Tom came to spend the 4th of July with us. Eleni came down earlier to the yacht. We all went to dinner at Seasons 52. They loved the new yacht and stayed in the VIP room. The next day they went to the pool and that night we ate at the Rainbow Palace. Sunday we had breakfast and went to the pool again. That night we ate dinner at the Greek Isles. July 4th I prepared plenty of food. We had a bird's eye view of the ocean where all the fireworks would be. Thousands of people would come to A1A and the beach to watch. Debbie and the girls, and Philip came too. It was a great night and the fireworks were spectacular. The next day Linda and Tom left and Eleni went home. Wednesday I went home to the doctor's and I returned on Thursday. Eleni returned on Friday and we went to dinner at the Greek Isles. Saturday night Eleni and I ate dinner at the French Quarter, another one of my favorite restaurants. Sunday the 17th my friends Howie and Shelly came to the boat for dinner.

Eleni went home on Monday and I spent the week working on the boat. Friday Eleni came and I grilled steaks on the fly bridge. Eleni went home and I stayed all week to work on the boat. Friday Eleni came to the boat and I cooked dinner. Saturday evening Eleni and I went to a Brazilian restaurant called, "Chima" on Las Olas Blvd. While we were at the bar we met a couple we knew from Café Boulud in Palm Beach. The food was good and you could eat all night. They came around with large skewers of all kinds of meat and they had a large salad bar with all kinds of food. It was good but too much for us to eat. Sunday I made dinner on the boat and Monday Eleni drove back to Palm Beach. I worked all week on the boat cleaning, waxing, and washing. It took me about four hours to wash this large yacht, but I loved it. Eleni arrived on Friday and we went to the Greek Isles for dinner. Saturday we went to the French Quarter for dinner.

August 2005 – My Yacht

On the 3rd of August, I went home from the yacht in Fort Lauderdale to my dentist and doctor then returned to the yacht later. Eleni came on Friday and I made dinner on the boat. Saturday night we went to the French Quarter. Sunday we invited the bartender from Trevini's, Claude and his girlfriend Jessica to dinner and I made Cornish hens. On August 11th Thursday, Irene's son Ray came in and stayed on the boat. Ray and I went to the Greek Isles for dinner. Eleni came down the next day and that night we all went to dinner at Capitol Grill. Saturday Ray went swimming and later we went to dinner at the Rainbow Palace. Ray returned to NJ on Sunday, and Eleni and I had our friends Bob and Kay for dinner. The next week I cleaned and washed the boat. Eleni came on Friday and I made dinner on the boat. Cooking on the boat was great because you could look out of the galley windows and see the water. Saturday night Eleni and I went to dinner at the Greek Isles. Sunday I had Jacques, our building manager, and his wife Denise for dinner.

Monday I was watching for Hurricane Katrina. It was approaching the Caribbean Islands and heading our way. By Wednesday I knew it was going to hit us and it was a category 1 storm. I put extra lines on the boat and secured everything. I put on my canvas window covers and waited. Thursday the storm hit with 90 to 100mph winds. I stayed in my lounge all night with quite a few scotches. The noise from the wind was bad but when it passed through I hadn't any damage.

Friday, I worked on the boat and everything returned to normal, but Katrina was heading into the Gulf of Mexico. Eleni came and we went to the Marriott Harbor Beach for dinner. There were trees down and power outages but the Marriott was okay. My yacht of course had two 20K generators so we had A/C and power all the time. Saturday we went to the Greek Isles for dinner. Sunday I cooked, as usual, and Monday Eleni returned to Palm Beach.

September 2005 – Petee and Gloria Come for a Visit

September 1st Petee and Gloria flew down and we went to dinner at the Seasons 52. The next day we discussed business and that night Eleni, Petee, Gloria, and I went to Capitol Grill for dinner. Sunday night we went to the Brazilian Restaurant, Chima. Petee didn't care for it and I really didn't like it either. Monday Petee and Gloria returned to NJ. Eleni went home and I spent the week working on the boat. Saturday we went to the French Quarter for dinner. Sunday I worked on the boat and Philip came to dinner. Wednesday I installed a new white tile floor in the crews' quarter's head bathroom. It came out great so I decided to do all my bathrooms. Thursday I waxed my Navigator and it looked brand new. Friday, Eleni came and I made dinner. We always went up on the bridge for cocktails before dinner to look at the ocean. What a life, I never would have believed what I had accomplished. Everyday I wrote some pages in my autobiography. I never realized how hard this was, but at least I had my journals. Saturday, Debbie and the girls came to the boat to stay over. They were so excited. They had their own room with twin beds.

Now that they were older we took them to the Rainbow Palace for dinner. My two little ladies Jordan and Hayley were dressed lovely and they looked beautiful. Debbie left them because she had to go to work. Sunday, I took the girls to the pool at the marina and later Eleni took them home. On Monday, I installed the new floor in the mid ship bath. Tuesday I installed a new floor in the VIP bath, and Wednesday I installed a new floor in the master bath. Friday Eleni came to the boat and I received a call that my cousin Bernice died. She battled cancer as my sister was and I felt so bad. She was a real honey. I made dinner and we went to sleep early. Saturday, we went to dinner at a new place Grill 66 which we didn't like at all. Sunday I made dinner on the boat. The only time I went to a fire now was when they called me on the cell. I was too far away for my radio to work. The rest of the week I did my usual cleaning and on Friday Eleni arrived. I made dinner on the boat. Saturday we went to Capitol Grill for dinner, and Sunday we ate on the boat. I had been waiting for a slip at the Bluff's Marina in Jupiter for some time and I finally got a call from Jackie at the Bluffs that a slip would be available. I gave her a deposit on September 11th and was waiting. It was a great place. I was there for three years with the "Eleni" before Petee bought it. I decided to move to the Town of Palm Beach Marina because the boat show was coming and I had to get out as we did every year.

October 2005 – Moved My Yacht to Another Dock

On October 7th, I moved my car to Palm Beach and got a ride back from Philip to the boat. On Sunday the 9th I moved the boat to Palm Beach with Philip and Ray Blake. Tuesday night Eleni and I ate at Trevini's. Wednesday I washed the boat since we came up in the ocean and I had to get the salt off. Friday I had a party for the officers in the fire department. It was very nice. I had a fire on Flagler the same day. Saturday I had a fire in a church. That night Eleni and I had dinner on the boat. Sunday there was a fire in a senior citizen home. That night I made dinner for some friends from the building, Marty, Sandy, Ilse, and Eric.

I was watching Hurricane Wilma in the Gulf because the storm track had it heading to the west coast of Florida. On Friday the Town of Palm Beach marina told everyone we had to leave because of the storm. I called Jackie at the dock master's office at the Bluff's and she said she had one slip left. I moved the boat up Saturday, and Sunday I prepared it for the storm, which was going to hit us. They said it may be just under a category one. Eleni went home and we shuttered up the terrace. I went to the fire house to help during the storm. The storm hit but it came in as a category two, which wasn't supposed to happen. All of us at the fire headquarters were up all night including Chief Ridgeway. About 5am it was so bad it blew out the windows and buckled the engine room doors. One of the guys called me and said the rear windows of my Navigator blew in. Finally the storm let up and we had 35 calls backed up. Once the wind went below 35 mph our rescuers were able to get out. It was bad; trees, wires, power; everything was out in the county.

As soon as I could, I went to the Bluff's to check on my boat. When I got there I found the top of the bridge had been blown to bits. Everything else was okay. I spent the day removing all the debris and cleaning up. I then went to Palm Beach to check on Eleni. When I got to the bridge I put on my flashing red lights and drove over to Palm Beach. All the bridges were closed by the police, only open to emergency vehicles. I knew most of the police in Palm Beach and I stopped to chat with them. Then I went to my building and found our landscaping destroyed. The Pool Pavilion was torn off and several apartments, which did not have shutters had their windows blown in. Eleni was fine, but there was no power anywhere. The building generator was working, but Eleni wouldn't come to the boat to stay. I had generators so I had A/C and lights, etc. Eleni had no power in the apartment, but I had about eight emergency lights in the apartment for her. I returned to the boat and called for my painter to repair the fiberglass. None of the gas stations had gas. Because I was with the fire department, I was able to get gas. Eleni had filled up the Mercedes before the storm. Power was returned to our building on the 28th.

November 2005 – Canvas on the Bridge of the Boat was Damaged from the Storm

On the 1st, I brought the car to the Lincoln dealer to get repaired. Friday, Eleni came to the boat and we had dinner at Carmine's Restaurant. Saturday night we had dinner at Santorini's the Greek restaurant near us. Sunday I made dinner on the boat. Saturday the 12th I had to bring the car to Bahia Mar Marina in Fort Lauderdale because I had to bring the boat back on the 13th. Jackie still didn' have a permanent space for me. Sunday, Ray Blake, Philip, and I brought the boat down the inside of the intra-coastal waterway because the ocean was very windy and rough. It took nine hours to get back to Bahia Mar Marina.

I spent the rest of the week cleaning the boat and called a canvas company to replace the top of the bridge. Eleni came to the boat on Friday and we ate dinner on the boat. Saturday night we ate at the Rainbow Palace. Eleni returned on Monday and I stayed on the boat until Wednesday then went home because the next day was Thanksgiving. Eleni made the turkey, stuffing, and sweet potatoes and we went to her ex-husband, Ozzie's sister Sophie's as we did every year. Friday Eleni came to the boat and we went to the Greek Isles for dinner. Saturday night Eleni and I ate at the French Quarter. Sunday we went Christmas shopping and I made dinner on the boat. Eleni returned home on Monday and I stayed on the boat. I had the canvas people coming because I redesigned the top and I had to be around all the time.

December 2005 – My 65th Surprise Birthday Party

Friday, Eleni and I, Linda and Tom (who had come to the boat for the weekend) went to Bravo's, an Italian place for dinner. It was okay, but not great. Saturday we all had dinner at the French Quarter. Sunday Eleni was acting strange and I didn't know why. We were all going to go to dinner at the Rainbow Palace. About 4pm we were all getting ready to leave for cocktails and dinner when I saw Philip on the dock with two large trays. I thought, "What is he doing here?" That is when Eleni and Linda said they were having a surprise birthday party on the boat for my 65th birthday. I almost died. Eleni had planned this and had ordered everything for Philip to bring. Eleni had more food than anyone could eat. She invited about 25 people. It was a great party. When Petee walked in I was so happy.

The next day Petee and Gloria, Linda and Tom left. Eleni and I had dinner on the boat. Eleni came back to the boat on Friday and I had dinner on the boat.

Saturday Eleni and I ate at Jackson's on Las Olas Blvd. Sunday I made dinner on the boat. I went home when Eleni did and stayed over because I had work to do, so I returned to the boat on Tuesday. Eleni returned to the boat on Friday and we went to the Rainbow Palace. Saturday was the boat parade and Eleni and I watched it go by on the fly bridge. Sunday I made dinner on the boat and grilled steaks on the fly bridge. Eleni went home Monday morning and I stayed until Thursday when I went home for my dental appointment.

Eleni and I left home for the Grand Hyatt in Tampa on Friday to spend Christmas at Linda's. We had a nice suite with two baths. That night we had dinner at Armani's with Linda and Tom. Christmas Eve we went to Linda's and had a great time as always. Linda cooked up a storm as usual. Christmas Day we had dinner at Linda's and we went home Monday morning and I returned to the boat in Fort Lauderdale.

I spent the next few days working on the boat and writing my autobiography. Friday, Eleni came and we had dinner on the boat.

CHAPTER–FORTY
Year 2006

Chapter–Forty – Year 2006

January 2006 - The Holidays

On New Year's Eve Eleni and I went to "Tara's" another fine restaurant for early dinner and dancing. We then went home to bed. At 12:00 midnight Eleni woke me up, we kissed and said Happy New Year then went back to bed. New Year's Day I made dinner for Debbie and the girls and her friends, Lauren and Rob. Eleni returned home on Monday and I worked on the boat all week. I didn't realize how much there was to do when you have a 70 foot yacht. It kept me busy and it was very peaceful working on my autobiography. Friday Eleni came and we went to dinner at the Rainbow Palace. Saturday night we went to "Tara's" again. Sunday I made dinner on the boat. Monday I went home when Eleni did and had dinner at home. I returned to the boat the next day. Eleni came down Friday and I had a meeting with Paul Getty. We all went to dinner at Bravo's. Saturday we had high winds and it got cold. Saturday we went to Tara's for dinner. Sunday I barbequed lamb chops on the bridge. Eleni went home Monday and I had the new top being installed. He worked on it Monday through Thursday then finished on Friday. It was a beautiful job and I loved my design. It cost me $12,000.00 but it came out very well and I didn't give it to the insurance company because my deductible was $17,000.00. Eleni loved it too. That night we went to Capitol Grill.

Saturday evening we ate at the Rainbow Palace. Sunday I grilled on the bridge and it was lovely. It was cold but the new top protected us. Monday I had someone wax the hull and it came out great. Tuesday the 23rd I went home and Eleni and I went to Trevini's for dinner. Wednesday, I went to two fires and then returned to the boat. Eleni came to the boat Friday and I made dinner. Saturday we went to dinner at Tara's. Sunday I made dinner on the boat and Monday Eleni returned home. This week I installed new up-to-date radar, GPS, and charts. It was the new Furuno Radar System and I had it put on the bridge and the pilot house at a cost of $12,000.00. The ones I had were old and one was not working. Saturday we went to Tara's for dinner. As usual I made dinner on the boat on Sunday. Eleni returned home on Monday.

Wednesday through Friday, I taught a class at IENGA. Eleni came back on Friday. Saturday Eleni and I went to the Rainbow Palace for dinner. Sunday my diver cleaned the bottom of the boat as he did every month. It prevented growth and barnacles from accumulating. I made dinner on the boat. Eleni returned home Monday and on Tuesday I stopped home to go to the doctor then returned to the boat. Tuesday I painted things on the boat, and had the water maker system checked and changed the filters. Wednesday my cousin Michael called and said Uncle Mike died. This was a blessing for Michael because he was taking care of him as I did my mother, but the difference was he did it at home.

Friday Eleni came and we went to dinner at the Greek Isles. Saturday we shopped and had dinner at a new place called "Fish". It was owned by Jackson who was a partner with Burt Reynolds. We didn't like the food that much. Sunday I made dinner on the boat. All the years Eleni and I were married I always cooked. Eleni was a good cook also, but I loved to do the cooking. Thanksgiving was the only time she made dinner because she made the best turkey.

February 2006 – Cold Weather in Florida

New York had a big snowstorm and this weekend it was in the 40 degree area in Florida. Eleni went home on Monday and I came home Tuesday, Valentine's Day, and we went to dinner at Trevini's. Wednesday I returned to the boat. Friday Eleni came and we went to Bravo's. Saturday we went to the Rainbow Palace for dinner. Sunday I made dinner on the boat. The next week I spent waxing the bridge and cleaning. Eleni arrived on Friday and I made dinner. Saturday we went to Capitol Grill for dinner. Sunday Debbie and the girls came to the boat for dinner. Eleni went home Monday and I worked on the boat.

Wednesday I was ready to take a shower after I got undressed Eleni called me. I spoke to her and got in the shower. After I washed my hair I looked down and I had my socks on. I guess this is the after 65 syndrome. It is funny and I laughed quite a bit. Friday, Eleni arrived and later we met Philip at the Greek Isles. Saturday Eleni and I went to dinner at the Rainbow Palace. As I said before, this was the best Chinese restaurant in the country. The owner Eddie and his partner Kenny ran a top operation. The French service was excellent. The waiters wore tuxedos, and there were flowers at each table. The best ever is all I can say. I went home on Sunday because I had to prepare for my colonoscopy on Monday. On Tuesday, I had the test. Monday I lived on the toilet bowl and I was very sore. Between the prostate cancer examination and the colon tests, I couldn't keep track of how many fingers I had up my rear for the past few years.

March 2006 – Friends Came to Visit

Tuesday I had three polyps removed and I went home and ate like a pig. I went back to the boat on Wednesday. Friday Eleni came to the boat and that evening we tried a new place for dinner, Café Arugula. It was so noisy and the food was average. Saturday we returned to Capitol Grill. Sunday I grilled on the bridge. Eleni went home Monday and I worked on the boat. Tuesday I had dinner with Philip. Friday Eleni came to the boat and we went to Bravo's for dinner. Saturday we went to the Rainbow Palace for dinner. Sunday I had my old friend Howie Olshan and Shelly for dinner. The rest of the week I had people coming for repairs and Friday Eleni came to the boat. We went to dinner at Bravo's that night. Saturday Eleni and I went to a special dinner at Arturo's in Boca Raton. It was Paul Getty's 10th anniversary party. It was lovely and we had a great time. Sunday Paul, Olivia, and their friend Susan stopped at the boat for cocktails. After I made dinner for Eleni and I, Eleni returned home Monday and I spent the week doing some upgrades on the boat. Eleni came back on Friday and we went to dinner at Bravo's. Saturday we went to Capitol Grill. Sunday I grilled on the bridge again. The weather was cold and perfect. Monday Eleni went home and I stayed to work on the boat.

April 2006 – Upgrading the Yacht

During the week I always went to Seasons 52 Restaurant and Lounge adjacent to the Galleria Mall. This was a great place. I would go there almost every night for a drink and flat bread. Friday Eleni came down and I made dinner on the boat. Saturday we went to the Rainbow Palace for dinner. We both went home to Palm Beach and I had Debbie and the girls for dinner. Monday I had two doctor's appointments then went back to the boat. Tuesday I had the water maker people service the unit and Wednesday I had the sound system updated. Friday Eleni came to the boat and we went to Bravo's for dinner. Saturday we went to Capitol Grill for dinner. Sunday I had my friends, Jim and Eileen for dinner. This was our wedding anniversary.

The next week my producer Jon Stathakis and his family came to visit for a couple of hours. On Friday I went home because I was going to NJ on Saturday. Saturday I left to go to NJ. My niece, Stephanie was getting married the next weekend in Connecticut. I arrived at the Marriott Park Ridge after 16 hours of driving straight through. I spent the week in the office working. Friday, Eleni flew in and we went to dinner at Solari's. Saturday we drove to the wedding in Connecticut. The wedding was great and Stephanie looked beautiful. Her new husband Ramzi was a great guy. After the wedding we drove to NJ to the Marriott. The next day, Eleni flew home to Palm Beach and I drove home. I arrived home at 9pm; another straight drive through. Monday, early in the morning I was called to a structure fire.

May 2006 – My Sister, Linda

After I returned I went to the boat. Linda and Tom were coming to the boat because this weekend the air show was on Saturday and Sunday. Eleni came on Friday and Linda and Tom arrived the same day. We all went to Bravo's for dinner. Saturday the air show started and it was great except for the noise. They had paratroopers, landing crafts, the Blue Angels, Stealth bombers, and many other events. Late afternoon was cocktails on the bridge and I grilled lamb chops and vegetables Greek style. We had the best view of the air show from the bridge. You could see the ocean beautifully. I loved the bridge because I had the grill and wet bar and I didn't have to go up and down to the galley. Sunday afternoon was with the family and it was great. After cocktails, I barbequed buffalo steaks on the grill and we all had a great time. Monday everyone left and I stayed on the yacht for the rest of the week. It takes a lot of work to maintain and clean a yacht this size and I kept it in top shape.

One morning I had a call to assist in a fire investigation and as I left the boat my gun slipped out and slid across the dock into the water. When I returned I called my diver and after 45 minutes he found it. I cleaned it in fresh water and oiled it and it was fine. It was my fault because I hadn't pushed it completely into the holster. Eleni came on Friday and we went to Bravo's. Saturday we relaxed and went to the stores. That night we went to the Rainbow Palace. Sunday we had Cathy and Hal from our building to dinner and cocktails. We had a nice time. Eleni went home and I worked on the boat. Monday night we got hit with a bad storm. The winds were 60mph and we had hail too. Tuesday at 12:30pm we got hit with another storm.   Sometimes in Florida the severe storms were just as bad as hurricanes. Friday Philip met us and we went to Bravo's for dinner. Saturday after shopping, we went to Capitol Grill for dinner. Sunday we had our usual dinner on the boat. There is nothing better than grilling on the bridge, and having cocktails, while looking at the ocean and intra-coastal.

Wednesday I went to my old fire department in Lauderhill. They had built a new headquarters and it was beautiful. It certainly wasn't like this when I was on the department. It was great to visit. On the way back to the boat there was a woman who fell on the sidewalk. I pulled over to help her and saw she was bleeding from a large scalp wound. I got my emergency bag from the car and stopped the bleeding. The problem was I ran out of rubber gloves and I had blood all over my hands. I always bit my nails and worried about getting HIV. She was older so I didn't worry very much. I always had that risk as all emergency workers are subjected to.

Friday I received a call from Petee telling me Gloria's sister Nancy's husband Tommy "TJ" suddenly died at home. I knew them well. Tommy was a firefighter in Saddlebrook, NJ. He was only in his 30s and had two children. I felt terrible but it goes to show you anything can happen to anyone. That is why I live for today and enjoy life. For sure Eleni and I are doing this.

When Eleni arrived on Friday we went to Bravo's. Saturday Debbie and the girls came to the boat. Jordan and Hayley loved being on the boat. Their "birdbrain" father told Debbie he didn't want the girls on the boat, but we didn't pay any attention to him. That night, I took them all to dinner at the Rainbow Palace. Sunday I made dinner on the boat. Eleni went home to Palm Beach on Monday. I worked all week polishing the brass on the boat. Friday when Eleni came we tried a new, Greek restaurant called, "My Big Fat Greek Restaurant". We didn't like it very much. Eleni and I were fussy about where we ate. We liked tablecloths especially on Saturday night dinners. During the week I always stopped for a drink at the Capitol Grill then went next door to Seasons 52 and had my flatbread and wine for dinner.

Tuesday, June 3rd Capitol Grill didn't have my Glenlivet 12 scotch. Wednesday they didn't have it and I told the Maitre D' I was coming for dinner Saturday and to make sure he had it. Saturday Eleni and I went to Capitol Grill and they didn't have it. I went to the Maitre D' and he said, "Well, what do you want me to do?" I told him to cancel my reservation and we left. I was spending about $150-$200.00 a week there and we never went back again. We went next door to Seasons 52 for cocktails then to the Rainbow Palace for dinner. I knew the restaurant business very well and I could see service in many places was not satisfactory. Things were changing in many places including the department stores, and other retail places. The problem is the employees are not trained properly.

I remember one day I went to Office Max and it opened at 8am. I was standing outside the door for five to eight minutes and on the inside there were five employees just standing inside watching the few people and me outside the store. They were all standing there and waited until it was exactly 8am then opened the door. I walked away and went to another store. I recall another time Eleni and I went to the Bonefish Grill in Palm Beach Gardens. They opened at 4pm. One of the guys was standing by the door, which was opened and it was five minutes to four. I saw the bartender who I knew and waved. This stupid guy said please go back out until four o'clock, you have three minutes more. I told him to stick the place up his ass and we left. He didn't care that we always sat at the bar before dinner for a drink.

I remember dad at his restaurant. If someone was standing outside he would always let them in even if he wasn't ready. Now, Capitol Grill would lose about $500.00 or more a month and I even brought company sometimes and the bill for four people and drinks would be over $400.00. We were year round customers and not off season when the snowbirds went back north and they needed the business all the more. I blame all this on business management. We used to go to "Tara's" on 17th Street and the owner who knew us gave our table away so we never went back again. We also stopped going to Bravo's where we spent plenty of money every Friday because I asked for extra bread and she said it would be an extra $1.75. I couldn't believe it. I spent $150.00 every Friday so we walked out and never returned.

June 2006 - Hurricane Alberto

On June 9th Eleni and I went to Bimini Boat Yard for dinner. It was not our kind of place, but for quick dinner it was okay. Saturday we went to the Rainbow Palace, our favorite.

Hurricane Alberto was nearing Florida, but it was going to miss us. When Eleni returned to the boat on Friday the 16th I had made dinner. Saturday we went shopping and we went to the Grill, a new place. It was just okay. The next day was Father's Day and I invited Philip to the boat for dinner. During the next week I did some calking on the boat and corrected some minor repairs. Friday came and Philip took us to an Italian restaurant for dinner. Saturday Eleni and I went the Rainbow Palace for dinner. Sunday I made dinner on the boat and Eleni returned home on Monday. I washed the boat and waxed all week because Linda and Tom were coming in on Saturday. Eleni didn't arrive until Saturday and so did Linda and Tom. We always enjoyed having them and they liked coming to the boat. That night we went to the Riverside Hotel for dinner at the Grill room. Sunday Linda and Tom went walking on the beach then we went to the Brazilian restaurant, Chima's on Las Olas Blvd. This was quite an experience for them and Tom ate his heart out. We returned to the boat and had drinks on the bridge. Monday we walked and went to the pool again. That night we went to the Bimini Boat Yard.

July 2006 – The Fireworks and Having the Boat Varnished by "Jay"

The next day was July 4th and I had Debbie and the girls, Philip, and the rest of us for dinner and at 9pm the great fireworks display began. We had a bird's eye view from the yacht. We had a great time. The next day Eleni, Linda and Tom left for home and I stayed to clean the boat. I was also getting the boat ready to have it pulled to paint the bottom and have the running gear serviced. Eleni came on Friday and we went to dinner at the Greek Isles Restaurant. Saturday we went to the Rainbow Palace and Sunday I made dinner on the boat and invited Philip. Monday I took the boat to the boatyard and had it pulled out of the water. I drove home to Palm Beach and made dinner at the condo. Tuesday Eleni and I went to dinner at Trevini's.

Wednesday I received my first social security check for $1845.00. I was all excited. The boatyard called and said I could pick the boat up tomorrow. Thursday I drove to Fort Lauderdale and Philip dropped me off at the boatyard. Six thousand dollars later I brought the boat back to Bahia Mar Marina to my dock. Friday I washed the boat and Eleni came on Saturday and we had dinner at the Grill. Sunday I made dinner on the boat. When Eleni went home Monday, I started my varnish job. I hired a guy to do the job and I supervised. He gave me a price and I said okay, $600.00. Wednesday I taught a class at the fire department from 9am to 1pm and returned to the boat later. Friday Eleni came to the boat and we went to the Greek Isles for dinner. Saturday we went to the Rainbow Palace for dinner. Sunday I made dinner and Monday Eleni returned home. The guy who was doing the varnish came and I told him the varnish was bubbling on one side. He said he would re-sand it. I paid him the $600.00 cash and he started to sand again. Then he stopped and said he wanted more money. I told him he didn't do the job right so I wouldn't give him anymore. He got off the boat and started yelling and screaming. He said he would kill me so I went after him and he ran. I went down below and got my gun just in case he came back. A few minutes later he returned and I warned him to stay away. I called the police to make a report in case he came back again. I also told the dock master because this guy was trouble and I knew he worked on other boats. The crew at Bahia Mar Marina was great. I loved them. The dock master Chris Lowe and assistant Rob Cate were the greatest. I must mention the others, Tom Hardaway, Conrad Vanderlely, and Vincent on the fuel dock. The office girls were the best, Lucia Terrell, Leslie Monesanto, Paula Dominguez, and the funniest Terry Newby. I must mention Leroy Lloyd who brought me my newspaper every day. When I told them what happened they said they would keep him from the docks. Thursday Eleni came to the boat and we went to dinner at the Bimini Boat Yard. Friday I was still repairing the varnish job and then we went to Jackson's. Saturday, it was Rainbow Palace and Sunday as usual, I cooked.

August 2006 – Looking for New Restaurants

August 1st was doctor day so I went home and returned to the boat later. During the week when I went out for cocktails at Seasons 52, someone told me about a restaurant called "Casa Bella" on US-1 south of the airport in Dania. He said it was a great place. Friday Eleni came and that night we went there. It was a large house converted to a restaurant, very quaint and lovely. The owners were Teddy and Larry. The small bar was lovely and the bartender was Craig. The dinner was great and we loved it. Eleni and I were a hit with them and when they found out I was in the movies I had to sign a picture, which they put on the wall. Saturday night we went to the Rainbow Palace for dinner and Sunday I made dinner on the boat.

Tuesday I had a bad compressor in the pilot house. I called for service and it was replaced the next day. I went to a fire on Wednesday and I also had my computer man come because I had a problem with my laptop. Friday Eleni returned and we saw that guy Jay on the dock. Eleni was worried he would start trouble again. I always carried my gun so I wasn't that worried, but I wanted to know why he was still around. That night we went to Casa Bella. It was a great place. Saturday I asked security about that guy Jay (the varnish guy) and they said they told him to stay away from us. I wasn't happy about that at all. Saturday night I went to Jackson's on Las Olas. Sunday I grilled lamb chops. Monday Eleni went home and I had to replace an A/C pump.

Friday the 18th my cousin Lorraine, Danny, Jennifer and my godchild Debbie paid a visit to us on the boat. Eleni arrived later and we went to dinner at the Casa Bella after they left. Saturday we went to Jackson's again and Sunday I made dinner on the boat. Eleni returned home Monday and I shampooed the carpets on the boat.

The rest of the week I changed oil and cleaned all the A/C filters. Friday Eleni came to the boat. I always wanted to have all my work done so Friday, Saturday, and Sunday we were together. I was also well into my autobiography. We went to the Casa Bella and as usual it was great. Saturday we went shopping in Las Olas then had dinner at Jackson's and Sunday I made chicken and grilled vegetables. Monday Eleni went home and I was following Hurricane Ernesto, which did not affect us. One night when I was going to Seasons 52 one of the waiters from Capitol Grill stopped me and wanted to know why I wasn't coming in. I told him what happened and he said, "No excuse." They get deliveries every two days. Friday, when Eleni returned to the boat we went to dinner at the Casa Bella. We really enjoyed this place very much. The next night we went to Jackson's. Sunday I made chicken on the grill. I was now watching Hurricane Ernesto as it neared Florida. The winds were blowing 55 to 65 knots. I just stayed on the boat and watched TV.

September 2006 – Moved the Yacht from Bahia Mar Marina to Bluffs

Friday, Eleni and I went to Casa Bella for dinner and Saturday we went to Jackson's. I began talks with Jackie at the Bluffs about moving there. She said that she would let me know when. We still saw that guy Jay around the docks so we decided to move if we could. Besides, it was getting to be too much for Eleni to drive back and forth. During September we continued our normal weekends and on the 11th Jackie called from the Bluffs and said she had a place for me. I drove up and the dock was great. I was at the end on the T. I gave her a deposit and went back to Fort Lauderdale. The electric hook up was 100 amps so I had to buy a 100 amp box and a 100 amp splitter. That was $990.00. Our last night in the Bahia Mar Marina was Friday the 29th and Eleni and I went to Casa Bella. Saturday Eleni left and Philip met me at the Bluffs and I left my car. He then drove me back to the Bahia Mar Marina. All the people in the marina office gave me a party and it was great. Sunday I left at 7:30am and we arrived at the Bluffs at 11:30am. The ocean was flat and it was a good trip. After I tied up the boat, adjusted my lines, and put out my fenders, I went home. I felt much better now being back at the Bluffs Marina.

October 2006 – Dining Out

I stayed on the boat that week adjusting everything to its new dock. Eleni only had to drive about ½ hour to the boat. Friday we ate at Nick's Tomato Pie. We used to eat there on Fridays when we kept the "Eleni" at the Bluffs. We had a new restaurant open near the boat called Santarini's. It was a Greek restaurant and we knew the owner from his old restaurant in West Palm Beach called OPA. Angelo was the owner and his food was great. It was located in a shopping area next to a

Publix supermarket, which was a ten minute walk from the boat. The weather in Florida started to get cooler in October and we loved it. I decided to live on the boat while I was writing my book and Eleni would come up on Fridays and go home on Mondays as she did before. I continued to cook on the boat on Sundays. I had to teach an IENGA class on the 10th through the 13th in Fort Lauderdale. When I returned on Friday, Eleni met me at the boat. We went to Nick's Tomato Pie and as usual we sat at the bar and had our cocktails. When we sat down to eat, we ordered and I said I didn't want ziti as the extra, I wanted string beans instead. The waitress said she had to ask the manager and came back and told us it would be $1.75 extra. I couldn't believe it. We spent $125.00 every Friday and they were going to charge $1.75 more? I told her to check again and she did and told us the same. Eleni and I left and never returned again. Can you imagine how stupid the manager is, giving up $125.00 or more every Friday for $1.75?

Saturday we ate at Santarini's and Sunday I cooked on the boat. During the next week I went to several fires and taught a class at headquarters. Friday we decided to eat at the Bone Fish Grill. I was stopping there during the week when they opened at 4pm for a drink before I went to my favorite place, Seasons 52. The food was okay but nothing special although I would go back again. Saturday we went to Santarini's which was always good. Angelo was hurting for business and I told him to advertise more because he couldn't just wait until people walked in. Another problem he had with was his daughter was working as a waitress. She dressed like a pig, jeans with holes in the knees and sloppy blouses. The waiters also wore jeans and dirty shoes. This was a beautiful place. You needed to show some class.

Sunday we had our friends Tom and Kelly Manos for dinner on the boat. Monday I was at the fire department for a meeting and the temperature was cold. It was 55 degrees. When I returned to the boat, I put the heat on and everything worked. The next day was the same 55 degrees. Friday I went home for a few days. Saturday I heard from Petee they had a bad storm in NJ and a tree fell on Gloria's house. Eleni and I went to Trevini's for dinner for a change. Sunday we went to Coco Palm Beach, which we enjoyed very much. Monday I went back to the boat.

November 2006 – Thanksgiving, Dinners, and Fires

November 1st and 2nd, I had meetings at the fire headquarters then went to the boat. We had high winds over the next few days. Eleni arrived Friday and we went to Santarini's for dinner. Saturday we went to Seasons 52. Sunday, Eleni went home because we were to have our Mercedes painted on Monday. The car was ten years old and only had 55,000 miles on it. I told Eleni to go buy a new Mercedes, but the salesman told her the car was like new and that she should keep it, so she did. Monday she dropped the car off and rented a car until it was done. I was busy sanding the rails on the boat and getting it ready for varnishing. Thursday the 9th was PVA's anniversary, 27 years in business. I couldn't believe it. Things couldn't be better. I was very lucky to have Petee running the company. Friday, Eleni came to the boat and we ate at Santarini's. Saturday we went to Coco, Palm Beach.

Sunday I grilled buffalo steaks on the bridge and they were great. The next week I did all the varnishing. Wednesday I had a dead battery so I put a new one in. In Florida batteries only last about three years because of the heat. Friday I went back on the boat. Eleni and I went to a different restaurant "Porto Bello's". We sat at the bar and waited while the kid bartenders were clowning around and talking. We finally got their attention and we had our cocktails. We sat down for dinner and we waited at least 12 minutes, and finally I yelled across the dining room to the five employees who were talking and joking around. One of them came over and we ordered our dinner. Another place we will never again go back.

Saturday night we had dinner at Santarini's. The weather was good but the temperature dropped into the 40s. Tuesday Eleni picked up her Mercedes and it looked great. Wednesday I had a fire to investigate and then went to the boat. Eleni was getting the turkey ready because we were going to her ex-husband's sister-in-law, Sophie's for Thanksgiving as we always did. I stayed home that night and in the middle of the night I was called to a mutual aid fire in a commercial building on Dixie Highway in the Town of Lake Worth. After a couple of hours I worked with the state fire marshal and we found that the building had a security camera in the rear of the store. We removed it and the Lake Worth Police took us to their headquarters and we were able to play it back. We actually saw the fire start at the front of the store, which was where we had suspected. When we dug out the area, we found a shorted extension cord. That night Eleni and I went to the boat and Santarini's for dinner. The place was dead as usual. Saturday we went to a new restaurant called "Chef John's". John Jones had been a chef around Palm Beach for years and was said to be very good. Saturday night we tried it and the food was great. Prices were high and the servings were small. It was a nice place and our waitress was Judy. We met Chef John and spoke a while. His wife who was a nurse was the maitre d'. She dressed very sloppy and did not make a good presentation. The rest of the week I worked on the boat and on Friday the 30th, I had two fires to investigate.

December 2006 –The Holidays and Eleni's Recovery

December 1st Eleni fell while getting off her bicycle. She was hurting all over. Linda and Tom were over for my birthday and Petee and Gloria were down also. We all went to Coco Palm Beach for dinner, but Eleni was in a lot of pain. After dinner we took Eleni to the hospital with Linda and Tom. We waited about four hours in the emergency room and they found that Eleni broke her knee cap. Saturday Debbie got Eleni a wheel chair and brought it to the boat. That night Eleni couldn't go out so we went to Santorini's for take out and we ate on the boat. Sunday Linda and Tom left for home and Sunday night we went to Seasons 52 for dinner. We had a private room for my birthday party with Debbie and the girls, Philip, Chris and Mel, and Petee, Gloria, and Eleni. Everything was great even the Seasons gave me a large cake with a boat on it, and a Season's shirt from management.

Monday I had to take Eleni to the doctor for her injuries. They put a brace on her knee and I took her home. I felt so bad for her; she was such a sweetheart. I made dinner at home and returned to the boat on Tuesday night the 6th. I stopped home early each morning to check on Eleni who was wrapping Christmas presents. We planned to go to Linda's for Christmas. Saturday I took Eleni to Coco Palm Beach for dinner and Sunday to Trevini's. She was still uncomfortable and hurting, but a bit better.

I stayed home on Sunday and Monday. We had a big fire on Dixie Highway. Tuesday the 12th through Friday the 15th I taught a class in Fort Lauderdale for IENGA. I came home and went to the boat to check on it. Saturday I returned, and took Eleni to Coco Palm Beach for dinner. We enjoyed that place and R.J. the bartender was a scream. His wife Judy was our waitress at Chef John's. I stayed home the next two days and took Eleni to the doctor's.

Tuesday the 19th I was called in the chief's office because some fire officers complained I was getting to the fires before them and giving orders over the radio. I couldn't imagine them saying this; after all, I was doing this for years. They were all kids and I've been doing fires for 47 years to be exact. The chief said I should wait until they get there first. The last house fire I went to was around the corner from the house when the call came in. I got there and took a woman and five kids out and across the street away from the fire. I think it was jealousy and one chief said it was the union causing trouble. I just left and was amazed that the chief would even mention it. Saturday I went home and took Eleni to Trevini's.

Sunday we drove to Linda's for Christmas. Christmas Eve was wonderful and Linda, with all her trouble with cancer and chemo put on a beautiful spread. Christmas Day she made another wonderful dinner. Nick and his girlfriend Becky were there, too.

CHAPTER–FORTY ONE
My Final Chapter–For Now

Chapter–Forty One – My Final Chapter–For Now

January 2007 – New Year's Celebration and News about Eleni

The next day we went home and I returned to the boat. I felt bad for Eleni because she couldn't use the bike. The weather was cold; about 45 degrees New Years Eve. We had an early dinner at "Porto Bella's" and went home to bed. Our alarm went off at midnight and we kissed and said Happy New Year and went to sleep.

New Year's Day we went to Chef John's for dinner. Eleni kept having terrible pains in her head lately to the point that she couldn't stand it anymore. Tuesday the 2nd Eleni went to Dr. Brodner a neurosurgeon and after her MRI he told her, her spinal cord was pinched under the neck vertebrae and she needed an operation as soon as possible or she could be paralyzed for life. We immediately set the date for February 7th because she had to have other tests. We were both upset but we had no choice. The doctor said he had to rebuild her neck bones with cadaver bones and hoped he could move the spinal cord without damaging it. February 5th Eleni and I went to Santarini's for dinner. Saturday we went to Chef John's for dinner after a visit from our friends, Lucy and Bob from Long Island. Sunday I went home with Eleni and we ate at Coco Palm Beach. Eleni planned to leave Friday the 19th to fly to Los Angeles to see Michael and the kids before her operation. I couldn't go because I was in the middle of varnishing the yacht. Eleni left on time. Saturday night I went to Season's and on Sunday I made my dinner on the boat. Eleni returned on Monday and the visit was great. Tuesday through Friday I taught an IENGA class in Fort Lauderdale.

February 2007 – Eleni's Operation

Saturday and Sunday Eleni and I went to the boat. The temperature dropped to 45 degrees again so I put the heat on. It made the boat very cozy. Saturday the 3rd I went home to stay with Eleni until after her operation which was on the 7th of February. We went to Trevini's for dinner and I cooked a lamb on Sunday. Petee was working a big case in Key West where someone died.

Wednesday Debbie and I went with Eleni to Good Samaritan Hospital. She had a beautiful room; they even had a piano player in the hall and had a buffet for the families. Eleni was in surgery for three hours. Finally, the doctor came out and said the operation was successful and she was in recovery. He had cut her throat and to support the bones, inserted a titanium plate with four screws. It is amazing what can be done today. When she was brought in, she was happy and she only had to stay overnight. I took her home the next day and stayed home until she was able to do things for herself. I cooked each night and went to the boat on Tuesday the 13th. I returned home on Saturday. Sunday cousin Flo and Sid came to visit Eleni. She had to wear a neck collar for a while. Tuesday I did a fire investigation and went to the boat.

Wednesday my sciatic nerve went out and I could hardly walk. I ended up in bed for eight days at home and finally went to the doctor on the 28th of February. He gave me a cortisone shot in the back and it was awful. I will never do that again. Petee came down Saturday and I hobbled to dinner at Coco Palm Beach. The pain was terrible. Eleni was doing well, but I couldn't stay in the restaurant so I went to the car to lie across the seat. The next night we went to Flagler Steakhouse and I suffered more.

March 2007 – A Waiter has a Seizure

I had to teach a class for IENGA in Fort Lauderdale on the 6th through the 9th. I did it in a wheel chair which was horrible, but I did it. I went home on Friday and rested. Saturday we went to Coco Palm Beach. I started to move a little better and was walking again. I went to the boat on Monday to catch up on my chores. Slowly I washed the boat, which took five hours. Tuesday I received a call that my ex-wife Irene's husband had died. It was expected; he was ill for some time.

I went to the fire department a couple of days for meetings and investigated a fire. Saturday Eleni and I went to Chef John's for dinner. While having dinner one of the waiters fell to the floor with a seizure. I ran to him and then got my paramedic bag from my car. I was able to put a plastic tube between his teeth to open an airway. He was foaming at the mouth and he was turning blue. I finally got him breathing. I couldn't believe the owner's wife who was an RN just stood there. No one called 911 either, but I now had him up and his brother took him to the hospital. I started to wonder why she didn't help.

The next week I had to do go to the dental surgeon to have a tooth pulled. On Saturday we went to Chef John's. Judy was pouring my Glenlivet when a roach ran across the bar. She killed it and I thought, "I hope they weren't any roaches in our food." I'm sure every restaurant will have a roach or two so I didn't let it bother me too much.

April 2007 – Working on the Boat

Sunday the 1st, I stopped taking all the pills for my back. I worked on the boat and Friday Eleni and I went to Bianca's, an Italian restaurant with entertainment every night. I had been stopping there for a drink during the week and got friendly with Melissa, the owner. The food was good too. We found out that Santorini's had been closed and Angelo went out of business. Saturday we went to Chef John's for dinner. The next day was Greek Easter and I worked on the boat. I had to teach a class in Fort Lauderdale, April 10th through the 13th. Friday when I returned, Eleni and I went to Café Boulud and Saturday we went to Trevini's. Sunday I left early to go to my sister Linda's overnight on my way to bomb school in Destin, Florida. Every year I would attend the training because I was a member of the International Association of Bomb Technicians and Investigators.

I left Linda's for Destin on my 27th anniversary. I also heard on the radio about the Virginia Tech massacre. On the way I had a terrible pain in my left side and I almost passed out. I pulled over to the shoulder of the highway and stepped out. I had to relieve myself so I took my famous plastic jar and when I started to go, I had a terrible pain in my penis. After that I was fine. School was great. We had a live bombing at Englin Air Force Base with the US Navy Ordinance. It was a great course. On Friday we received our certificates. I had made arrangements to meet Eleni at the Beau Rivage Casino in Biloxi. The last time we were there we had a beautiful suite and the restaurants were great. I had reserved a suite again and had a limo pick Eleni up at the Gulf Port Airport. She flew in on a small plane. I arrived at the Beau Rivage early and when I checked in they didn't have my suite. I had a big argument and they said to take a regular room or nothing. I got loud and they threatened to call security. Eleni was already in transit so I was stuck. I took the room and the limo brought her to the hotel. She was also disappointed about the room, but we made the best of it. I did get even because I won $2,900.00. Eleni cancelled her flight for Monday. Monday I drove home and she came with me. I went to the doctor about the kidney pain and he said I probably passed a small stone. I went back to the boat and Friday we went to Bianca's for dinner. Saturday we went to Chef John's. Sunday I grilled lamb chops on the boat. We both returned home and that night we went to Café Boulud for dinner.

May 2007 – Running for 2nd Vice Commander

The first week of May I ordered $1,000.00 in Euros for our upcoming trip to Greece. Friday we went to Bianca's for dinner. Saturday I had a meeting at the American Legion and they expected me to be the 2nd vice commander. Karen Larven, and Victoria Kramer; our girls in the office wanted me to run. They both were great girls and always very helpful to me. I agreed to run and the election was next month. Saturday night Eleni and I went to Chef John's.

Wednesday the 9th I taught a fire department class at headquarters on fire prevention. The following week I taught a class for IENGA in Fort Lauderdale and came home on Friday the 25th. Saturday my friends Howie and Shelly invited us to a barbeque at their house. The rest of the week we prepared for our trip.

June 2007 – Our Trip to Greece

I closed up the boat and Saturday June 2nd, we flew to Atlanta then nonstop to Athens. Linda and Tom also flew to Atlanta and then nonstop to Athens. We arrived in Athens and were met by my driver, George. We went to the Ledra Marriott and as usual everyone was waiting for us. I knew all the employees there and always took care of them. We went to our suite and unpacked. That night Sotiris picked us up and we went to Velissairo's house. Velissairo was still paralyzed on his left side from his stroke. Linda and Tom stayed at the Ledra Marriott, too. Monday the 4th I picked up my rental car and we all drove to Angeliki's for dinner. All my family members were great cooks and we ate our hearts out. Tuesday the four of us went to the Plaka to shop. We had lunch at my favorite place, "Hermion's". That night we ate dinner at Koni Kai at the Marriott.

Thursday morning I drove to Velissairo's house and we took two cars and drove to Delphi. The country was beautiful and this was the first time Linda and Tom came to Delphi. We ate at a lovely village resting on the waterbed and had a great time. Delphi is in central Greece and has one of Greece's most varied landscapes. Part of the shore runs along the Gulf of Coranth and high above is Mount Parnassus. There are beautiful cliffs and when you look down you see beautiful olive trees. We went to the Temple of Apollo, which was above the museum. What a wonderful place to see.

We got back to the hotel and the four of us had cocktails at the roof bar. Friday we went to the Plaka to shop and lunch at Hermion's. We had dinner at the hotel that night because we were leaving for Santorini the next day. My driver, George picked us up and drove us to the airport. I didn't want to drive with my car and park it there. We landed at Santorini in one hour. The problem was getting a taxi. We had to split up but finally met at the Dana Villas. We had to walk down the cliff to our villa 240 steps. Eleni and I had a hard time and Linda had trouble breathing. Our villas were beautiful and the view of the ocean outstanding. The villas had a large bedroom and living room and they had an outside terrace. The only thing I didn't like was the toilet because it would flush but you had to place the toilet tissue in a special pail. The maids would come in twice a day to empty it. We settled in and we ate dinner at the little restaurant another 30 steps down next to the pool. Everything was built on the side of the mountain cliffs. The chef was wonderful and he served tons of food. Tom drank his ouzo and I had my scotch and ouzo. We decided t eat there every night so he kept the best table for us.

Sunday we had breakfast, which was great too. Somehow we managed to climb the 240 steps up to the top so we could walk into the town. It took about 45 minutes to get to the top. We walked around and did some shopping. It was lovely. We stopped for lunch at a Tavern and Tom and I drank some ouzo. We ordered lunch and what a lunch it was. The owner was from NY and he kept bringing more food then we could eat. He didn't even charge for some of it. We went back to the Dana Villas and walked down the 240 steps. It was easier to walk down but Eleni had to do one step at a time. Tom and Linda went for a swim and I sat there having ouzo. I don't go in the sun if I can help it so I sat nearby under an awning. We ate dinner again at the Villa and it was great as usual. Monday we flew back to Athens and George picked us up and took us to the hotel. We ate on the roof top that evening.

The next day we went to the Plaka and had lunch at Hermion's. Tom and Linda went on to tour some of the areas and Eleni and I went back to the hotel. That night we ate at Koni Kai's in the hotel. Thursday we were taking the whole family to dinner in the north mountain area to a family restaurant. There were 15 of us. We had grilled lamb chops, fish, shrimp, and all the Greek mezzes. We ordered plenty of wine, beer, and ouzo and we had a wonderful time. Going to the bathroom was funny because the bathroom only had a hole in the floor with two indentations for each foot. This is how it is in the villages. This was our last family get-together. It was interesting that the complete dinner bill was 230 Euros. Friday I returned my car and we went to the Plaka for final shopping. Saturday George picked us all up with both Mercedes and took us to the airport. We arrived in Atlanta at 5:30pm and Tom and Linda left to fly to Tampa. Eleni and I had to wait until 7:30pm because our plane was late. When we boarded we had to sit on the plane 1 ½ hours because they had to make a repair. Finally we taxied out and the plane went dead. They fixed that in ½ hour and we left for West Palm Beach. Our driver, Ron picked us up. We were late by five hours. The next day we were "dead", but we managed to unpack. I made a chicken for dinner. I also stayed home on Monday the 25th.

Linda had her PET scan and she called to let me know the cancer was now in her lungs. They had to take a quart of liquid from her lung. I was devastated but hoped they could get it under control. Friday night, on the 29th Eleni and I tried a new place called the Limoncello. The food was good. Saturday we went to Chef John's and Sunday I cooked on the boat.

July 2007 – The Fire Department and Different Restaurants

Monday, July 2nd I did three car fire investigations for the fire department. Eleni and I stayed home on July 4th and I grilled. Thursday, Eleni and I took Debbie to dinner at Trevini's. Friday we went to dinner at the Limoncello. The food was good and Saturday we went to Chef John's. Eleni and I went home on Sunday. During the summer months, it was too hot to grill on the bridge so we started to go home on Sundays.

When I went to fire headquarters I was in my office and I saw Assistant Chief Rhett Turnquest. He said he was retiring the next week. I was shocked because he never told me he was and I was close to him. Something happened to cause him to leave. I did know there was some racial tension in the department, but I never got involved with the fire department politics.

I received a call from my Hollywood agent Mike Greenfield who said there might be a chance for a new movie. I told him I was going to Las Vegas in November so I would go to Los Angeles first to see him. I planned on driving out on the 21st of October. Eleni would fly out a week later and meet me at the Peninsula Hotel in Beverly Hills. I spent the rest of the week working on the boat. Friday Eleni came and we went to the Limoncello for dinner. After we ordered, Eleni got her food and I got nothing. Eleni finished and the waiter was embarrassed, but I cancelled my order. Saturday we went to Chef John's for dinner. I began to notice that the portions were getting smaller lately. Jan was still dressing very sloppy and it was a Saturday night and Eleni and I were at the bar and Judy was making drinks. Jan was taking inventory and getting in the way. It was pretty obvious to me that John and Jan didn't know how to run the business. John was always a chef and a good one at that, but not a great business man.

I had my back go out a few days before and I couldn't walk too well. Eleni found out her foot was bothering her and had it x-rayed. It was fractured so we had to cancel our trip to the family reunion in NJ. Sunday Judy and R.J. came to the boat for dinner.

The next week I still couldn't walk so I hired the son of my battalion chief to wax the boat. Friday we went to the Limoncello for dinner and the fish smelled. This was the last time we went there. Saturday we went to Chef John's. Sunday we went home and I grilled chicken sausage stuffed with spinach and feta cheese. I had bought them at Whole Foods. They were great. The next week I had a class for IENGA and taught from the 24th to the 27th. When I returned home on Friday, we went to Café Boulud. Saturday we went to Trevini's for dinner. Gianni, the owner of Trevini's had another place in Sapphire, N.C. called Osteria Del Monte. During the summer he was up there, but Trevini's was always open and I was hoping to go to Osteria one weekend. It was close to Ashville, N.C. Sunday we had dinner with Debbie and the girls.

August 2007 – Health Issues

August 1st I had my bone density test, which said I had arthritis of the spine. Friday Eleni came to the boat then we went to Bianca's for dinner. Saturday we cleaned the boat interior then went to Chef John's for dinner. We went home on Sunday and I worked. Monday we went to Coco Palm Beach. Tuesday I went to the staff meeting at fire headquarters. Usually I stopped at the fire headquarters every morning for coffee.

The next few days I cleaned the engine room on the boat, which was spotless. Eleni came on Friday and that night we went to Bianca's. They always had a band so we could dance once in a while when either of us could walk properly. Saturday evening as usual we went to Chef John's. I was starting to dislike the place because Jan was always dressed so badly and there were a lot of arguments. We went home Sunday and I made osso buco. Monday morning I was called to a structure fire where two people died. I spent a few hours there working with the fire marshal, Mike Carsillo. After the bodies were removed we finished our investigation.

Friday, Eleni came to the boat and we found out that my Aunt Dolores's sister Ethel passed away. Saturday we did go back to Chef John's. Sunday the fire chief and assistant chief were to come for dinner at 4:30pm. I made a complete Greek dinner and at 3:30pm the chief called and cancelled. I was disappointed, but I froze most of the food. The next week I had three fires all structures. Friday when Eleni came we went to Spotos. They had a Spotos in Palm Beach and they were good. It wasn't a fancy place but always had fresh oysters and clams. It reminded me of the Clam House in Hoboken, NJ. Saturday we went to Chef John's. Wednesday the 29th my cousin Alfi died, and he had been at the family reunion. I couldn't believe it.

September 2007 – A New Restaurant

September 1st, Eleni and I went to Chef John's. We sat at the bar and Judy was making our drinks. There were five employees and the phone was ringing. No one picked up the phone and John yelled out in the restaurant to Judy. He shouted, "Why didn't you answer the phone? When Jan comes back you go home." I was pissed that he spoke like that in front of customers. Judy resigned and Eleni and I never went back. He lost our $150.00 a week, which was very stupid. I had just heard about a new place called the III Forks on PGA Blvd so on Sunday Eleni and I went there. It was exclusive and beautiful and the lounge was all wood and glass. I met the owner Dana Borders. One of the girls from Seasons 52 was working there, too. Everyone was wearing white shirts and bow ties, and white jackets. This was my kind of place. The food was excellent and there was plenty of it. This became our new Saturday night place. I had invited my cousin Lorraine and Danny for dinner on the boat because we hadn't seen them for about eight months. The first week of September I worked on the boat.

Friday, Eleni came and we went to Bianca's for dinner. Saturday we went to the III Forks and everything was great. They also had a piano player. We went home Sunday because I had to teach next week in Fort Lauderdale for IENGA. I returned Friday and Eleni met me at the boat. Saturday we went to III Forks and again it was wonderful. Sunday we grilled on the boat and went home Monday. On Thursday the 20th my nephew Nick and his girlfriend Becky came to the boat. We took them to dinner at Seasons 52 and they stayed over on the boat in the VIP room. We had a great time together and they left the next day. That night Eleni and I went to Bianca's. Saturday we went to the III Forks. Sunday we went home and we went to dinner at the Flagler Steakhouse. We found that the place was not as good as it used to be. Eleni had to prepare for her colonoscopy on Tuesday. She wasn't a happy camper, but everything was okay. Friday the 28th Eleni and I went to visit my sister Linda. She made a beautiful dinner and Nick and Becky were there too. Eleni and I went to our hotel and we went shopping the next day. Tom picked us up at the hotel and we went to dinner at a very nice place. We returned home on Monday.

October 2007 – The Boat

I was very busy this week with doctors, phone calls, flu shots, etc. Friday we tried a new Italian restaurant called Romeo's in Jupiter. It was a very nice casual restaurant, which also had entertainment twice a week with singers and music. Saturday we went to the III Forks and had a good time. Sunday I went home and made dinner. Monday I went to the boat because I had people working on the boat; varnishing and painting my black strips. All week they came each day to work. Friday Eleni came and we went to Romeo's for dinner. The food was very good. Saturday evening we went to III Forks and the food was great. We went home Sunday and I cooked while packing for my class in Fort Lauderdale for IENGA.

Friday I came home and prepared to leave for Los Angeles. I left Saturday morning about 4am and made it to the Marriott in Baton Rouge. The next morning I drove to San Antonio to the Marriott. I always liked San Antonio. Every time I stayed there, I would always go to the Alamo. I ate dinner in different places too, and the food was good. I left at 2am and drove to the El Paso Marriott. El Paso was a busy place but the Mexican food was the best. Tuesday the 23rd I left for Scottsdale and I heard about the fire in California in Malibu. When I arrived in Scottsdale I went to dinner in Old Town and bought two dolls for Michael and Shelley's girls, Sarah and Kaela, my grandchildren. I got up at 2am and drove directly to the Peninsula Hotel in Beverly Hills. I arrived at the Peninsula at 8am and checked in. The Peninsula in Beverly Hills was one of the best hotels in the country with the best service and the most wonderful staff. I always stayed there over the years, and they had the best suites.

After I checked in I drove to Malibu and stopped at a road block on the Pacific Coast Highway. I told the CHP officer I was going to Station 70 to assist. He let me through after seeing the red lights on my windshield and my fire department license plate. The smoke was very bad and the winds were about 70-80 mph. I approached the street and saw a bunch of firefighters getting ready to move up Canyon Road. I stopped and asked if they needed another hand and they said sure. I grabbed my gear and went with them to Canyon Road. When we got to the house we dropped a line and attempted to get a hold of the fire, but the wind was so bad, it changed direction and it was like a blow torch coming at us. We put water on it but we had to retreat and fast. I helped for about six hours but I realized I am a little old for this. They said thanks and I returned to my Navigator and went a little further north on the Pacific Coast Hwy. and saw the remains of the castle on the hill. This was the Landmark Malibu Kashan Castle. What a tragedy; this place was magnificent. I also saw the Malibu Presbyterian church which was completely burned out.

I left Malibu Canyon Road and continued on to Pepperdine University which survived the fire. On the way back I stopped for coffee at a place called Spruzzo's Pizzeria & Café on the Pacific Coast Highway and many of the locals were there discussing the loss of the church. I also stopped at Los Angeles Fire Station 70 and met assistant fire chief, Regwald Lee of the L.A. county F.D., and battalion chief, Michael Flocks. They thanked me for my help and we took some pictures together. I then went to the Peninsula because I had a meeting with my movie agent, Mike Greenfield at 2:30. The meeting went well and we were to meet again in New York City with my book deal. That evening I ate dinner at the famous La Doce Vita where all the stars ate. When I walked in I was met by the Maitre'D, Ruben. I knew him before from the many times I ate there, and once when I said hello to Sidney Portier. I made a reservation for the next night because Eleni was flying in. I returned to the Peninsula to the lounge and saw all my friends. The head valet told me he had my navigator detailed and I was happy. It was filthy because of the fires. The next morning, I slept until 8am because I was tired from the fires.

The next day, Friday the 26th the hotel sent a limo to pick Eleni up. That night we went to Mr. Chow's for dinner. I had a limo and driver anytime we went to dinner. It was Hollywood as usual. Saturday we took Michael, Shelley, Shelley's parents, and the girls to lunch in Beverly Hills to the Cheesecake Factory and had a great time. That night we ate a La Doce Vita, another great meal.

The next day Eleni and I went shopping on Rodeo Drive and we had a nice day. We ate dinner at the Peninsula that night and as usual it was wonderful. Monday the 29th Eleni and I left for Las Vegas for a few days of gambling. We drove north to the Marriott off Route 98. We didn't like crowds on the Las Vegas strip so we always got a beautiful large suite at the Marriott. They had very nice restaurants and stores just like the hotels on the strip, and then the Rampart Casino was attached to the Marriott. Our suite was 3,000 square feet with a large bar, dining room, four baths, master suite, and a spare bedroom. The next three days we ate, drank, and we gambled. I won $2,700.00 on the slots, which was good.

November 2007 – The Emergency and the Rehabilitation Center

November 1st Eleni flew back to Palm Beach and I drove to Flagstaff. I liked Flagstaff because I would eat at a place called Black Bart's. All the employees would put on a continuous show of singing and music. It was great; most of them were students at the college for the professional arts. My next stop was Amarillo, Little Rock, Pensacola and then to the Marriott in Orlando on the 7th. I arrived on the 7th because I had to do a seminar with Petee for IENGA on the 8th and 9th. The 9th was our 28th anniversary of our business. I had just finished the seminar and I got a call from Eleni. She had fallen and was on the floor. It took her an hour to pull herself to the door of the condo so she could scream for help. Someone heard her and called fire rescue. They gave her the phone to call me and I immediately left for the hospital.

It took me only two hours to get to Good Samaritan Hospital from Orlando. When I arrived she was in the emergency room and Debbie and the girls were with her. She was in a lot of pain and I felt so bad I was shaking. I knew a few nurses and they showed me her x-rays and I could see that her hip was shattered. They took Eleni up to a private room and they were going to operate tomorrow. The next day, Debbie and the girls, and I went to Coco Palm Beach to get something to eat and we all returned home. I was devastated, my poor little wife suffering like that. The next morning I went into the operating prep room with her. She ran into some difficulty and the operation was called off until Sunday the 11th. Sunday, Dr. Sandall, the orthopedic surgeon, who took care of her knee operated and inserted a titanium rod from her knee to her hip with a large screw. After surgery she was in a lot of pain and they gave her pain killers in her IV. They decided to move her on the 15th to a rehab place called Manor Care. The ambulance came for her after Debbie and I had visited Manor Care the day before. It didn't look bad when we visited it, but after she was admitted it was horrible.

That night Eleni had to wait 45 minutes for someone to empty her bed pan after pushing her alarm button many times. She also saw a brown spider on the curtain. When they brought her dinner it sat in the hall for over a half hour. The food was lousy and cold when it came. In the next bed was a woman who had a CD player continuously playing Italian operas. The CD player was on all day and into the night. We complained but it did no good. The next morning I was at Manor and it was 9am and Eleni still didn't get her breakfast. All the meals were in the hall while all the help were having their coffee. I went out and yelled at them and finally they served the cold breakfast and cold coffee. Eleni is not a complainer but looking into her sad eyes told me something. Every day I was at her side. At Good Samaritan Hospital it was wonderful. The nurses and aides were the greatest, but at Manor Care, the service and the care were terrible. I spoke to Debbie and she said she would take care of Eleni that night so I could stay on the boat since I hadn't been there for a few weeks. I stopped at Seasons 52 for dinner and while sitting there I kept thinking of Eleni. I got up and returned to Manor Care. I walked in and again Eleni didn't get her dinner. The woman in the next bed had some company and they kept going to the only bathroom in the room. It was filthy. Debbie arrived and said, "When I saw your navigator I knew something was wrong." I told Debbie I wanted her out now so she called a surgical supply place and ordered a wheel chair, a raised toilet, a walker, and a shower walker. They were to deliver them to the condo within an hour. I went out and told the nurse I wanted her out immediately and she said, "You can't do that." I told her to call the police and I would file a kidnapping charge. She called her supervisor at home and was told to make up the discharge papers. I left for home. Debbie and the girls stayed with her until the ambulance came. Eleni signed the release and she was taken home and I was waiting with my doorman when the truck came with all her medical needs. I took everything up to our condo and when I returned back downstairs, Eleni had arrived. They took her on the stretcher to our bedroom and left. Debbie ordered pizza for us.

The next day I made her breakfast and called Dr. Sandall and told him what happened. He set up the arrangements for a nurse to come to the house two days a week, and a therapist to come three days a week. The week of November 19th, I did laundry, cooked and helped Eleni move so her leg and hip muscles wouldn't get stiff. They sent a physical therapist and he went in the bedroom to work with Eleni to get her to try and walk. I was in the kitchen cooking and he came in and said he was broke and needed $25.00 for gas until he got paid on Friday. I thought this was strange but I gave him $25.00. After he left Eleni told me he wanted her to wear a nightgown when he comes again. I almost flipped and called the service and told them to keep him away. They said they would replace him, which they did. The new guy was great and helped her a great deal over the next couple of weeks.

Thanksgiving Day I made a small turkey for Eleni and we spent a quiet day. In between the next few weeks I would run up to the boat to clean and wash it. Eleni was walking with a walker now and slowly getting better. I had to teach a class for IENGA December 4th through the 7th. Debbie was to watch over Eleni while I was gone. When I returned Eleni was using a cane and making breakfast and lunch for herself. I was very happy.

December 2007 – Eleni is Starting to Recover

On December 18th she started to walk again but very slowly. We decided to go to my sister Linda's for Christmas. We stayed at the Holiday Inn Express a couple of miles from Linda's house. Eleni and I never stayed at anyone's house. We always liked our privacy. We had a great time and my niece Stephanie and her husband

Ramzi were there as well as my nephew Nick and his girlfriend Becky. Even though my sister was fighting cancer she cooked and had so much food. It was wonderful.

January 2008 – Happy New Year!

New Year's Eve Eleni and I went to dinner at Trevini's for an early dinner then returned home. So far our lives were wonderful and we were happy. We are beginning a new year 2008 and hope this life continues on for all the good things it brings. The fire within continues.

The End For Now

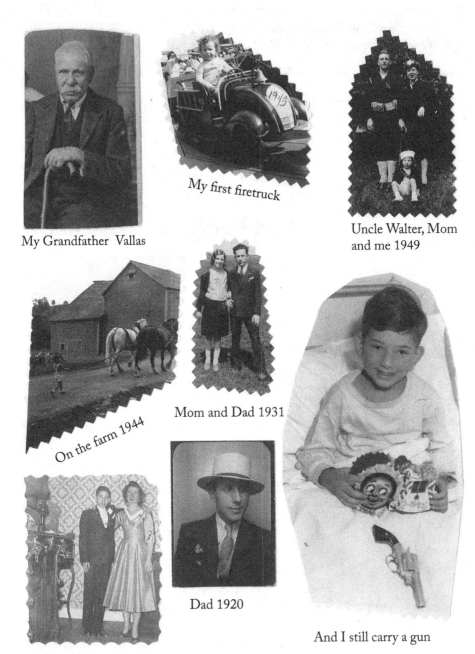

My Grandfather Vallas

My first firetruck

Uncle Walter, Mom and me 1949

On the farm 1944

Mom and Dad 1931

Aunt Ann and Me 1954

Dad 1920

And I still carry a gun

High school 1957

1957

My 1956 mercury

1958 US navy

New year 1955

Day of my wedding
Joe Bustin & I 4-16-61

Joe Burell and I 1961
Palisades Amusement Park

Cliffside Park Fire Dept.
1961

Irene Rimer and Peter
Vallas Jr. who became en-
gaged on St. Valentine's
Day.

2-14-60

Bergen Country Sheriff's Dep't
1962

President Ford and Jackey Gleason

Doreen
1970

Rose
1977

Pete the Greek

Back to New Jersey
1979

Petee 1977

Petee at his 1st fire
investigation
age 16

1959

1959

1967

1974

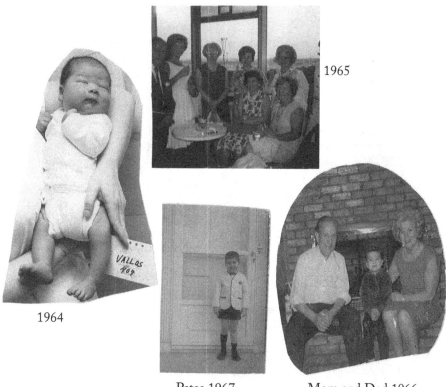

1965

1964

Petee 1967

Mom and Dad 1966

Mom and Dad 1966 1st home

I met Rhoda "Eleni"
1979

Daughter Debbie

Our first wedding May 12, 1980

at the pent house

Our second yacht "Eleni II" Behind the Florida compound

Our third yacht "Eleni"

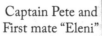

Captain Pete and
First mate "Eleni"

Our florida compound 1989

Our first yacht "The Eleni"

Pete 's Toys

Ocean Reef with cousin Lorraine, Danny and Eleni with
our new golf cart Pa Pau's toy

Eleni and I 1988 Ocean Reef

My mother Sophia, her friend Monroe and Eleni at Ocean Reef

Eleni's Baptized Greek Orthodox 1987

My son Peter who gave Eleni
away 4-16-88

The church St. Catherins where
my Dad was baptized and we were married

All my greek cousins
and Mother Sophia
in the presidential
suite

On the way to church

The wedding and Fathe Nick on left

American charactor Award
Washington D.C.
Sept. 1982
Russell Senate Office Building
Senate Caucus Room
Left Dr. Norman Vincent Reale receiving letter from President Reagan, myself, Rand Arascoe President and CEO ITT, and Senator Strom Thormond, and my nephew Nick D'Jimas

Myself, Senator Strom Thormond and Nick D'Jimas

Our new yacht "Sophia"

Arizona Compound

Dinner on the Sophia

Santorini, Greece 2004

House in Palm Beach, FL 2004

Our Grandchildren